Jesus and the Church

Theological Foundations of the Christian Church

Volume 1

Jesus and the Church

The Foundation of the Church in the New Testament and Modern Theology

Paul Avis

t&tclark

LONDON • NEW YORK • OXFORD • NEW DELHI • SYDNEY

T&T CLARK
Bloomsbury Publishing Plc
50 Bedford Square, London, WC1B 3DP, UK
1385 Broadway, New York, NY 10018, USA

BLOOMSBURY, T&T CLARK and the T&T Clark logo are trademarks of Bloomsbury
Publishing Plc

First published in Great Britain 2021

Cover design: Terry Woodley
Cover image: *There is a river 2008* © Roger Wagner / www.rogerwagner.co.uk

A catalogue record for this book is available from the British Library.

A catalog record for this book is available from the Library of Congress.

ISBN: HB: 978-0-8264-4166-9
PB: 978-0-5676-9749-3
ePDF: 978-0-5676-9619-9
eBook: 978-0-5676-9620-5

Series: Theological Foundations of the Christian Church

Typeset by Deanta Global Publishing Services, Chennai, India
Printed and bound in Great Britain

To find out more about our authors and books visit www.bloomsbury.com and sign up for
our newsletters.

Contents

Abbreviations and references

Abbreviations

ARCIC   Anglican – Roman Catholic International Commission

CD   Karl Barth, *Church Dogmatics*, ed. G. W. Bromiley and T. F. Torrance (Edinburgh/London: T&T Clark, 1975-)

ICC   International Critical Commentary

JTS   *Journal of Theological Studies*

KJB/AV   King James Bible/Authorized Version

LXX   Septuagint (Greek translation mainly of Hebrew Bible)

NICNT   New International Commentary on the New Testament

NIGTC   New International Greek Testament Commentary

NRSV   New Revised Standard Version

NTS   *New Testament Studies*

ODNB   *Oxford Dictionary of National Biography*, ed. H. C. G. Matthew and Brian Harrison, 61 vols (Oxford: Oxford University Press, 2004)

REB   Revised English Bible

RSV   Revised Standard Version

SJT   *Scottish Journal of Theology*

SNTS   Society for New Testament Studies

TDNT   G. Kittel (ed.), *Theological Dictionary of the New Testament*, trans. G. W. Bromiley (Grand Rapids, MI: Eerdmans, 1965)

TI   Karl Rahner, *Theological Investigations*, 23 vols (London: Darton, Longman and Todd, 1965–)

VT   *Vetus Testamentum*

References and acknowledgements

When a title is mentioned for the first time in any chapter, full bibliographical information is given. If the same title occurs again in the same chapter, it is referenced by the author's surname and a short title. Full bibliographical details of all books and articles that are referenced in the footnotes (and only those so referenced) are provided in the bibliography at the end of the work.

Unless indicated otherwise, Scripture quotations are from the New Revised Standard Version Bible, copyright © 1989 National Council of the Churches of Christ in the United States of America. Used by permission. All rights reserved worldwide.

Scripture quotations taken from the Revised English Bible, copyright © Cambridge University Press and Oxford University Press 1989. All rights reserved.

Preface

In this book we are setting out to examine two of the most fundamental building blocks of the Christian faith and the connection between them: Jesus and the church. We will investigate the relationship between Jesus and the church, the church and Jesus, as that is presented to us in the New Testament and in modern theology. Apart from belief in God, it is hard to think of anything that is more fundamental in Christianity than the connection between Jesus and the church. Our enquiry constitutes a quest for the true foundation of the Christian church, that is the church as an empirical reality, as we see it in history and as we experience it (or at least observe it) today. The foundation of the church, if it can be reliably identified, will necessarily be also the foundation of the *faith* of the church, what it believes, including what it believes about itself. So what we discover will affect Christian beliefs and the Christian life. Other ways of posing the same basic question are to ask, 'Where does the church come from? What is its provenance? On what fact or facts does the existence of the church rest?' The methods that we will employ in addressing these questions are biblical exegesis and interpretation, historical research, ecclesiological analysis and theological reconstruction.

The phrase 'the foundation of the church' immediately resonates in our minds with the first lines of the well-known hymn, 'The Church's one foundation is Jesus Christ her Lord.' Those lines are clearly a paraphrase of St Paul's statement in 1 Cor. 3:11, 'No-one can lay any foundation other than the one that has been laid [by God]; that foundation is Jesus Christ' (NRSV). I will look more closely at that text and at the hymn in Chapter 1 ('Rock of Ages and Living Waters'). The church's one foundation is the reality on which everything in the life and faith of the church rests – or should rest. It is the reality on which, like the Apostle Paul, we seek to build – and on no other. It is the reality to which we continually return in the repentant reform and renewal of the church's teaching, worship and mission. 'Look to the rock from which you were hewn!' (Isa. 51:1, NRSV).

My first stab at the theme of this book was an article in *Theology* in 1986 ('The Church's One Foundation') when I was in my tenth year as a parish priest. Further work proceeded at a very slow pace, being interrupted by a dozen years as a full-time ecumenical theologian and church executive for the Church of England, though my work there in ecumenical dialogue and theological conferencing no doubt improved my grasp of the central questions of ecclesiology – it certainly also enriched my appreciation of the manifold riches of the Christian tradition. So the process of study and reflection that lies behind this book includes forty-five years in parish ministry, half of that time as a full-time parish priest; the rest part-time and honorary, with cathedral and academic involvements, together with international ecumenical and theological work for the Anglican Communion. So I have to confess that I have been chipping away at this project for more than three decades. Work on it has chugged along while many other books, articles, reviews and editorial work (especially the journal *Ecclesiology*, *The Oxford Handbook of Ecclesiology* and the series that I edit for Brill *Anglican-Episcopal Theology and History*) have filled the mental and temporal space. There is no end to the books and articles that could be read and chewed over on these, the two grandest of all theological themes: 'Jesus' and 'the church'. They are being published faster than any one person can read them. But after all this time, I think I really need to draw a line as far as this book is concerned! Further volumes of this current project are already in hand and will be completed more swiftly – they had better be, or I won't be around to write them!

Before I introduce this present book, I would like to sketch in very briefly how I see the project of which it forms the first volume: *Theological Foundations of the Christian Church*. I hope to write at greater length about theological methodology in a future volume of the proposed series, when I will place ecclesiology and its various departments (including ministry, sacraments, liturgy, authority, conciliarity and polity) in a reasoned relationship to the overall theological enterprise; and I will do this by incorporating relevant biblical, historical, philosophical, systematic and ethical aspects of the project. The problematic of *Jesus-church* – the connection and tension between these two awe-inspiring realities – continues to form the subtext of the whole project and thus for all that is to come (God willing) in terms of the theology of revelation and the word of God, liturgy and sacrament, ministry and authority, the essence of Christianity and so on. But for the present I will simply comment on the basic concept or vision that lies behind *Theological Foundations of the Christian Church*.

- First, the intention is to provide *foundational* resources, to start from the beginning of things, to ask what there is to build upon. In that sense, there could hardly be any ecclesiological topic more basic, more far-reaching in its implications, and therefore more suitable to begin a series of investigations, than the relationship between Jesus and the church, the church and Jesus. My overall project looks rather like an expanded form of 'fundamental theology' or perhaps 'fundamental ecclesiology', though what I mean by that must be deferred to the fuller treatment that I have in mind for the future.
- Secondly, these foundations are theological in a specific way: not purely ecclesiological in any restrictive sense, though ecclesiological through and through. While ecclesiology is the golden thread linking all together, the approach also impinges on systematic theology, though not systematic theology only, but also philosophical and historical theology. And not only systematic, philosophical and historical theology, but also practical theology, because the whole enterprise is being carried out with a pastoral – indeed a missiological – intention.
- Thirdly, the focus of the method and approach concerns the Christian church. I say 'Christian church' to avoid any ambiguity about which church, or which aspect of the church, is in view here. It is the church as we know it, the church as we see it in history and today, the empirical church, the church with problems and challenges. Those who have dipped into some of my other work might reasonably

expect a focus on the Anglican theological tradition, the Anglican Communion or the Church of England – or at least an Anglican bias or slant. Of course, such a slant may well be detectable, but it is not part of my intention. Every theologian has a standpoint – historical, social and ecclesial (even if he or she is standing on the periphery of the church or perhaps outside it altogether). But as an ecumenical theologian (a consumer and producer of ecumenical theology), I am aiming to produce ecumenical theology on a large scale. To that end I engage with Roman Catholic and Protestant, as well as Anglican, theology. In future planned volumes on the liturgy and the sacraments, I will also draw significantly on Orthodox theology.

- Finally (for the moment), all that I write here is intended as a theology *of* the church, *from* the church and *for* the church. That is to say: a theology that concerns the church; a theology produced from within the church; and a theology intended for the use and benefit of the church. In this respect, I aspire to stand in good company: with the mighty throng of priest-theologians throughout the ages, together with the equally valued lay theologians among the faithful, of past and present, and particularly with the greatest modern ecclesial theologians, among whom I mention merely four: Schleiermacher, Barth, Bonhoeffer and Rahner. In his *Brief Outline on the Study of Theology*, Friedrich Schleiermacher insisted that theology was properly pursued to serve the church, particularly its pastors and preachers, that is the church 'leadership' (*Kirchenleitung*) and that any valid systematic theology must take the form of *church* dogmatics.[1] Karl Barth famously switched from *Christian Dogmatics* to *Church Dogmatics*.[2] In the first lines of the first section of the first volume of the *Church Dogmatics*, Barth announced (actually, it seems, echoing Bonhoeffer): 'Dogmatics is a theological discipline. But theology is a function of the Church.'[3] Although I have no pretensions to rival Barth in the number of volumes he produced, his total word count, his polemical register or his dizzying theological gymnastics, I aim to write, just as he did, from the church for the church. I also identify with Karl Rahner's insistence that 'Theology is a science of faith in the bosom of the church.'[4] I seek no other standing ground for theological enquiry than the life of grace in the church of Christ. But, as I trust this book shows, that ecclesial *locus* for theological enquiry need not and should not inhibit the asking of difficult questions and the probing of traditional assumptions.

---

[1] Friedrich Schleiermacher, *Brief Outline on the Study of Theology*, trans. Terence N. Tice (Richmond, VA: John Knox Press, 1966), §6.

[2] Karl Barth, *The Göttingen Dogmatics: Instruction in the Christian Religion*, ed. Hannelotte Reiffen (Grand Rapids, MI: Eerdmans, 1991; Edinburgh: T&T Clark, 1993), vol. 1; id., *Church Dogmatics*, ed. G. W. Bromiley and T. F. Torrance (Edinburgh and London: T&T Clark, 1975), hereinafter *CD*, by volume, part and page.

[3] Barth, *CD*, I/1, p. 3. Bonhoeffer had written the same thing in 1931, the year before the appearance of Barth's first volume of *CD*: Dietrich Bonhoeffer, *Act and Being: Transcendental Philosophy and Ontology in Systematic Theology*, trans. H. Martin Rumscheidt [*Dietrich Bonhoeffer's Works*, vol. 2] (Minneapolis, MN: Fortress Press, 1996), p. 130: 'Theology is a function of the Church.'

[4] Karl Rahner, S. J., *TI*, trans. Hugh M. Riley (London: Darton, Longman and Todd, 1988), vol. XXI, p. 101.

Now let me briefly mention the main questions and themes that I cover in this book. The whole book tackles two big questions: (a) The *historical* question: 'Did Jesus of Nazareth found, foresee or intend the church, as was taken for granted for the first eighteen centuries of Christian history and is still reflected in the official teaching of some churches?' 'If not, what did Jesus *do* about preparing his community of disciples to face the future, the imminent revealing of the reign of God? and (b) The *theological* question: 'How do the New Testament writers and modern historical-critical scholars of various Christian traditions understand the theological foundation of the church and the place of the Christ event in that? How do they make sense of the originating connection between Jesus and the church?' The argument of the book falls into two parts. The first four chapters first focus our two big questions and then proceed to look at the New Testament evidence, submitting it to theological exposition and interpretation. After a short linking chapter (5), Chapters 6 to 8 set out some of the most important ways in which modern theologians, committed as a matter of intellectual and academic integrity to 'historical-critical' methods of research, have responded to our questions. The final chapter (9) draws on the provisional findings of the whole account in order to sketch a constructive response to the challenges to ecclesial faith that are posed by the overall argument; the focus of the faith-filled theology of this concluding chapter is on the Paschal Mystery of the death and resurrection of Jesus Christ as the foundation of the church and the connecting link of the Eucharist.

Other, related, areas of investigation that arise along the way include the following:

- The implications of the foreshortened eschatological horizon of the New Testament: the clear expectation, of Jesus and the New Testament writers, of the imminent arrival of the reign of God, the *parousia*, the revelation of the new age. How should we understand this aspect of the New Testament world view and how should we respond to it? My working assumption, which I share with almost all modern doctrinal theologians, is that we cannot allow the gospel of Christ and his definitive significance for divine revelation and redemption, to remain trapped within a superseded biblical world view, including its cosmology, psychology and anthropology.
- The quest for the historical Jesus: What can we know with any assurance about what he said and did, especially with regard to his future intentions (if any) for the community that he had gathered around himself? Given that we do not have direct access to the historical events of Jesus' life, but glimpse them dimly through the mediation of the New Testament witnesses and the faith of the apostolic church, how should we assess the tension between 'the Jesus of history' and 'the Christ of faith'?
- How do we respond to the early institutionalization of the Christian church, as it acquired set forms and structures, long before the Constantinian establishment of Christianity in the early fourth century? Our discussion impinges on the perennial debate about the church as a political institution *versus* the church as a dynamic community led by the Spirit, without a legal structure of authority and organization.

- The question of when a distinctive Christ-centred community, not yet separate from the Jewish church, came into being. Was it when Jesus first called the fishermen and others to follow him? Was it at the commissioning of the apostles? Perhaps the Last Supper was the critical moment, when Jesus inaugurated the 'New Covenant'; or the Ascension or Pentecost (though with these we are moving away from events that are historically verifiable in principle, to highly symbolic, stereotyped portrayals of spiritual experiences). But perhaps we cannot identify a church separate from Judaism until after the destruction of the Jerusalem Temple and exclusion of Christians from the synagogue.
- Hoary issues of scholarly and academic freedom *versus* ecclesiastical authority within the historic churches arise within the narrative. Was scholarly research and enquiry – were the findings (or theories) of biblical scholarship – to be subject to the control of the ecclesiastical hierarchy (particularly that of the Roman Catholic Church), invoking *a priori* dogmatic principles?
- Collateral to the question of whether Jesus 'founded' the church is the question of whether (as the Christian tradition has historically maintained) he instituted a particular form of church polity, particularly of ministry, to serve the community that he formed around him and intended to continue his work in either the short or the long term.
- A question that runs through the discussions of modern theologians on our topics is that of the development of doctrine and practice in the church. How should we evaluate the phenomenon of change in the Christian apprehension of the faith that has been wrought by the ceaseless movement of the historical process. Is development a proper function of the church, alongside and in tension with its mandate to preserve 'the faith that was once for all entrusted to the saints' (Jude 1:3, NRSV)?

Finally, I wish to thank Anna Turton of T&T Clark, her former assistant Sarah Blake and her present assistant Veerle Van Steenhuyse, together with all the various production personnel, for all their friendly support and encouragement. But how can I thank Susan, my bride of fifty years, for her unfailing and uncomplaining support in making it possible for me to devote large tracts of time to this particular project and to many similar, related, scholarly enterprises?

Paul Avis
Durham University and the University of Exeter, UK
Epiphany 2020

1

Rock of ages and living waters

'The Church's one foundation/Is Jesus Christ her Lord.' S. J. Stone's familiar hymn is a paraphrase of the Apostle Paul's insistence in 1 Cor. 3:11 that God has laid the foundation of the church once for all in Jesus Christ: 'Other foundation can no-one lay than that which is laid, which is Jesus Christ.' This text is the guiding motto of this book (and of its proposed successors). Stone's hymnal paraphrase is densely packed with good biblical theology. It begins: 'The Church's one foundation Is Jesus Christ her Lord; She is his new creation By water and the word. From heaven he came and sought her To be his holy bride, With his own blood he bought her, And for her life he died.'[1] Stone's words, together with the tune 'Aurelia' which was written, two years before the composition of the hymn, by Samuel Sebastian Wesley, the grandson of Charles Wesley, make a powerful combination. Many of Stone's hymns are marked by a robust faith and hope. The juxtaposition of 'one' and 'foundation' in this hymn, that is to say the powerful metaphors of unity and solidity, has a strong appeal; it stirs our emotions and evokes our commitment. This is what the church of Christ should be, we feel – united and standing firm against every onslaught!

This hymn is sung by many English-speaking Christians all the year round, but especially at festivals commemorating the original dedication of the parish church. The text and the hymn have a special relevance at times of change and transition, at moments of uncertainty and confusion in the life of the church. The third verse – 'By schisms rent asunder, By heresies distrest [sic]' – points to the fact that the hymn was intended as a counterblast to the what Stone regarded as the heretical views of John William Colenso (1814–83), Bishop of Natal. Colenso's accommodating approach to African indigenous practices, including polygamy, and his radical (for those times) biblical criticism in his studies of Romans and the Pentateuch, provoked his

---

[1] Samuel John Stone, a clergyman of the Church of England, the son of the Reverend William Stone, was born at Whitmore, Staffordshire, 25 April 1839. He was educated at the Charterhouse and Pembroke College, Oxford, where he graduated BA in 1862. He took Holy Orders and served in various parishes. In 1874 Stone succeeded his father at the new church of St Paul, Haggerstown, East London (now Haggerston; the church was demolished and replaced in 1960 and the parish amalgamated). He was the author of many original hymns and translations, which were collected and published in 1886. He published several volumes of verse. He died of cancer on 19 November 1900. 'Lord of our Soul's salvation' was composed by command of Queen Victoria to be sung at the Service of Thanksgiving for the recovery from illness of H.R.H. The Prince of Wales (later King Edward VII) on 27 February 1872. Cf. Percy Dearmer, *Songs of Praise Discussed: A Handbook to the Best-Known Hymns and to Others Recently Introduced with Notes on the Music by Archibald Jacob* (London: Oxford University Press, 1933), pp. 147–8. See also *ODNB*.

excommunication by his metropolitan, Bishop Gray of Cape Town. First published in 1866, when Stone was the twenty-six-year-old assistant curate of New Windsor, 'The Church's one foundation' was sung at all three main services of the 1888 Lambeth Conference. Archbishop Frederick Temple (father of Archbishop William Temple) became thoroughly fed up with it, complaining that he found it sung wherever he went!

The first verse of the hymn achieves this effect by piling up powerful biblical images, one upon another. It echoes the New Testament texts that speak of Christ's Lordship and Headship over the Church (1 Cor. 12:3: 'Jesus is Lord'; Eph. 1:22: 'the head over all things for the Church'; Col. 1:18: 'he is the head of the body, the Church'). It also weaves together the metaphors of new creation and new birth (2 Cor. 5:17: 'there is a new creation, everything old has passed away'; Jn 3:3-8: 'born from above . . . born of the Spirit'). Finally, the phrase 'by water and the word' is equally a biblical paraphrase and joins together the word and the sacraments. 'By water and the word' refers to baptism (Jn 3:5: 'of water and Spirit'; Heb. 10:22: 'our hearts sprinkled clean from an evil conscience and our bodies washed with pure water') and the proclamation of the word of God in the gospel (1 Pet. 1:23: 'born anew . . . of imperishable seed, through the living and enduring word of God'). The Epistle to the Ephesians (Eph. 5:26) links the ideas of water and the word together: 'cleansing her [the Church] by the washing of water by the word'. In other words, this first verse of Stone's hymn is a brilliant pastiche of biblical allusions.

Theological pluralism

'No other foundation but Jesus Christ!' All Christians can gather round this slogan. As ecumenical dialogue shows, all churches agree on it. Of course they do, though some Christians think that other Christians deny Christ and lack the 'one foundation'. Some Christians assume that their way of being the church is closer to the will of Jesus Christ than the way of others. Our church is founded on Scripture, they insist, while yours is corrupted by tradition – as though all churches, as they have emerged through the historical process, were not the result of partial and contextual interpretations of Scripture, resulting in various distinctive forms of tradition. As an ecumenist on behalf of my church and my communion, as well as an ecclesiologist, I do not know of any church that does not intend to be faithful to Scripture. For us, but not for you, other Christians say, Christ is the only head of the church, and only he is the head of our church – as though all Christians and all churches did not recognize Christ as the church's only head and therefore prayerfully seek, through their various structures of discernment, consultation and debate (i.e. conciliarity), his will for their church. I do not know of any church that has a head other than Christ, certainly not the Church of England: since the reign of Queen Elizabeth I in the second half of the sixteenth century, the monarch has been entitled the 'Supreme Governor'. According to their lights, all churches seek to obey and follow Christ as head and build on the one foundation that God has laid in him.

Cardinal Walter Kasper, the president (until 2010) of the Pontifical Council for Promoting Christian Unity, in *Harvesting the Fruits: Aspects of Christian Faith in*

Ecumenical Dialogue, quotes a statement from Lutheran–Roman Catholic dialogue: "'The one and only foundation of the church is the saving work of God in Jesus Christ which has taken place once for all.' Everything that is to be said on the origin, nature and purpose of the church must be understood as an explanation of this principle.'[2] Here Lutherans and Roman Catholics are of one mind. Cardinal Kasper himself endorses this affirmation: 'The Gospel of Jesus Christ, preached by the apostles, is the source of all saving truth and the basis of all ecumenical dialogue.'[3]

However, to spell out what exactly it means, in today's intellectual climate, to ground the Christian church on Jesus Christ alone is by no means straightforward. In fact it is shot through with paradox and tension. Above all, the pluralism of modern Christianity – a pluralism that is proliferating at breakneck speed, especially in the developing world and in the Far East – makes easy talk of unity in faith naive. Centrifugal forces within the church are stronger than ever. The existence of more than 30,000 separate Christian denominations, spread throughout the world, gives words like 'unity' and 'schism' an air of unreality. Can they all be facets of the one church, even when, in some cases, they deny that status to each other? Do we have to accept a diversity that amounts to an ultimate incompatibility, so that we have to ask, 'Which Christianity are we talking about?' Influential liberal thinkers like Isaiah Berlin have argued that we have to accept a radical incommensurability of fundamental values in the modern world: we cannot expect to see eye to eye with other cultures or communities about what is important, and even about what is right and good.[4]

Some of the greatest Christian theologians of the twentieth century believed that we have to come to terms with an incommensurability of understanding – a cognitive incommensurability – within the Church itself. In his hugely subversive essay 'Pluralism in Theology and the Unity of the Creed in the Church',[5] Karl Rahner took an extremely pessimistic view of the possibility of meaningful communication even within the confines of his own Roman Catholic Church. Previously, Rahner observed, it was possible to assume that one could know the position of one's opponents. One could understand their view and could explain to them why one could not share it. Both parties had in common a set of terms and a philosophical framework that made communication possible. Now, however, Rahner claimed, the situation is that 'the representatives of the different schools cannot achieve, even indirectly, a position in which they can explain to one another consciously and unambiguously in what precisely the difference between their respective intellectual outlooks consists.' Rahner was saying these things in the early 1960s and was describing the problem within the

---

[2] Walter Kasper, *Harvesting the Fruits: Aspects of Christian Faith in Ecumenical Dialogue* (London and New York: Continuum, 2009), p. 55: extract from Lutheran-Catholic dialogue report *Church and Justification* (1993), p. 10, citing the German Lutheran-Catholic dialogue *Kirchengemeinschaft im Wort und Sakrament* (1984).

[3] Kasper, *Harvesting the Fruits*, p. 12; cf. p. 6: 'In the end, Jesus Christ himself is the basis and the goal of all our dialogue.'

[4] Isaiah Berlin, [e.g.], *Four Essays on Liberty* (Oxford: Oxford University Press, 1969); Michael Ignatieff, *Isaiah Berlin: A Life* (London: Chatto & Windus, 1998); John Gray, *Isaiah Berlin: An Interpretation of His Thought* (Princeton, NJ: Princeton University Press, 2013).

[5] Karl Rahner, *Theological Investigations* (London: Darton, Longman & Todd; Baltimore: Helicon Press, 1974 [1965–]), vol. 11, pp. 3–23.

Roman Catholic Church. How much more must this be true half a century later and in a total global Christian community that is twice the size of that Church? A similar point was made by Edward Schillebeeckx, with regard to increasing specialization in theology.[6] A theologian or even a group of theologians working together can have 'no more than a limited and one-sided view of the totality of the reality of faith'. This should be a recipe for theological humility, Schillebeeckx proposes – 'no theologian can say that what he does not see is theologically irrelevant or even less important than what he has himself discovered' – but in practice it makes for a failure of communication. Each of us comes to the task of theological reflection from a very limited perspective; ours is a crampingly narrow angle on the faith.

One foundation?

The metaphor of foundations is unfashionable today. It is widely assumed in theology that nothing so redolent of solidity is available to us. When the critique of 'foundationalism' in philosophy (epistemology) is imported into theology, it is often used in a derisory sense, such that to look for 'foundations' in theology, as in philosophy, is derided as a pitiful delusion. The metaphor of 'foundations' is caricatured to mean a kind of methodological straitjacket, whereby a logical argument is supposedly built on unassailable premises. It is seen as the great epistemological faux pas of modernity. It is a problem mainly, I suspect, for conservative Roman Catholics and conservative evangelicals, both of whom hanker for a scholastic methodology, one that appeals to authoritative texts.[7]

Notwithstanding the prevailing scepticism about the idea of foundations, the imagery of the city of God, with foundations that cannot be shaken, has too much invested in it, in Scripture, the theological tradition and hymnody, for us to write it off to suit current philosophical and theological scruples.[8] Such fashionable scruples are often infected with an epistemological relativism that doubts whether we can know the truth or have a clue about the nature of ultimate reality. With regard to 'the things of God', the Christian tradition has a place for the *via negativa*, which holds that we can know only what God is *not*, and for *apophatic* theology, which emphasizes the darkness

---

[6]   Edward Schillebeeckx, *The Understanding of Faith* (London: Sheed and Ward, 1974), p. 51. See also Bernard Lonergan, S. J., *Doctrinal Pluralism* (Milwaukee, WI: Marquette University Press, 1971); David Tracy, *Blessed Rage for Order* (New York: Seabury Press, 1975); id., *The Analogical Imagination: Christian Theology and the Culture of Pluralism* (London: SCM Press, 1981); id. *Plurality and Ambiguity* (London: SCM Press, 1987).

[7]   See John E. Thiel, *Nonfoundationalism* (Minneapolis, MN: Fortress Press, 1994). On the evangelical discussion, see, for example Stanley J. Grenz and John R. Franke, *Beyond Foundationalism: Shaping Theology in a Postmodern Context* (Louisville, KY: Westminster John Knox Press, 2001); Stanley J. Grenz, 'Articulating the Christian Belief Mosaic: Theological Method after the Demise of Foundationalism', in John G. Stackhouse, Jr. (ed.), *Evangelical Futures: A Conversation on Theological Method* (Grand Rapids, MI: Baker Books, 2000), chapter 4.

[8]   We will consider the biblical metaphors for the church of temple and building in Chapter 4. For the moment, in addition to 1 Cor. 3:11, let us note Isa. 28:16: 'Behold, I am laying in Zion a foundation stone, a tested stone, a precious cornerstone, a sure foundation.' Augustine, *City of God*, trans. Henry Bettenson, ed. David Knowles (Harmondsworth: Penguin, 1972).

of divine mystery (especially in Pseudo-Dionysius, Thomas Aquinas and the English mystical work *The Cloud of Unknowing*).[9] Borrowing insights from the philosophy of science, theology can follow the middle way between *naive realism*, which assumes that our knowledge corresponds veridically to reality, and *non-realism*, where we make no claim that our ideas correspond to how things really are and we cannot escape from our own inventions. The middle path of *critical realism* allows at the same time for both a meaningful grasp of the truth and a recognition of the limitations and distortions of our knowledge. What we have is simply sufficient to enable us to pursue the enquiry to the next stage. That should be enough for anyone, theologian or not.[10]

Given that what we think we know about reality is merely a pebble on the beach, profound intellectual humility well becomes the theologian as well as the philosopher. For the theologian, however, the question of divine revelation comes into play, augmenting and correcting our natural knowledge and insight. But I cannot embark on the difficult subject of revelation here: it is the subject of the next (i.e. the second) volume of this series, *Theological Foundations of the Christian Church*. I will simply say that when I talk about a possible or hypothetical 'foundation' of the church, I am not looking for any kind of dogmatic edifice of faith, nor am I promoting or advocating a systematic ecclesiology. The method that I follow throughout this book is one of critical enquiry, leading to provisional conclusions, both historically and theologically speaking.

The foundation God has laid

First, I want to home in closely on the Apostle Paul's affirmation in 1 Cor. 3:11. The slightly awkward construction in the Greek, which Paul uses for emphasis ('which [*hos*] is Jesus Christ'), is difficult to translate felicitously. The King James Bible's forceful rendering now seems ungrammatical to us: 'Other foundation can no man lay than that is laid, which is Jesus Christ.'[11] The New Revised Standard Version offers a cumbersome paraphrase that loses the impact: 'No one can lay any foundation other than the one that has been laid; that foundation is Jesus Christ.' The Revised English Bible is a little free with the text: 'There can be no other foundation than the one already laid; I mean Jesus Christ himself.' C. K. Barrett renders the text: 'No one can lay a different foundation from that which already lies there, namely Jesus Christ.'[12] Anthony Thiselton translates: 'For no one can lay down any other foundation than that which has already been laid down, namely Jesus Christ.' Thiselton underlines the definitive character of the perfect tense, 'calling attention to the permanent effects of a past act'. His comment is apt: 'the one essential thing about the building is that it depends on Jesus Christ as the

---

[9] *The Cloud of Unknowing*, trans. Clifton Wolters (Harmondsworth: Penguin, 1961).

[10] I discuss these ideas, together with 'symbolic realism', in *God and the Creative Imagination: Metaphor, Symbol and Myth in Religion and Theology* (London and New York: Routledge, 1999).

[11] The KJB/AV follows William Tyndale's translation of the New Testament (1525): 'For other foundacion can no man laye then yt [that] which is layde which is Iesus Christ': http://wesley.nnu .edu/biblical_studies/tyndale/1co.txt.

[12] C. K. Barrett, *The First Epistle to the Corinthians*, 2nd edn (London: A. & C. Black, 1971), p. 87.

foundation of its existence, coherence and identity.'[13] Yves Congar takes the point about dependence even further when he comments that the building is 'nothing more than the growth of its own foundations', because 'Christ and faith in Christ as the one and only source of grace, is the foundation.'[14] The completed building in this case cannot be something other than its foundation, Jesus Christ. In the context of the verse, Paul seems to back-track. First he says, 'I laid a foundation', then he corrects himself for spiritual presumption, affirming more properly, that *God* laid the foundation in Jesus Christ and did so once for all: 'that which has been laid', that is by God's act in Jesus Christ.

The foundation is Jesus Christ – not the Bible, though we would not know him without the Scriptures; not correct doctrine about him, though doctrine is vital; not our shifting perceptions and images of him, which change through a single human life and from culture to culture, though he has to be received into the heart, mind and life; not even the message, the gospel, that tells of him and his work of salvation, though that is implied – but Jesus Christ himself, in his person and his work.[15]

Where St Paul is emphasizing the objective act of God in laying the unique and irreplaceable foundation of the church in the Christ event, John Calvin turns it back to our human responsibility to honour Christ and to build our faith and our preaching on him – this is perhaps slightly surprising in the theologian of the sovereignty of God:

> We must therefore note how the Church is properly built up on Christ; viz. If he alone is set up for righteousness, redemption, sanctification, wisdom, satisfaction, cleansing, in short for life and glory. . . . For since Christ is the foundation of the Church, because he is the one and only source of salvation and eternal life, because in him we know God the Father, because the fountain of all our blessings is in him, then if he is not acknowledged as such, he immediately ceases to be the foundation.[16]

Continuing in the Reformed tradition, but leaping over several centuries, I want to bring in the Congregationalist theologian Peter Taylor Forsyth (1848–1921). Forsyth is often credited with anticipating some of the distinctive themes of the early theology of Karl Barth: the otherness of revelation, the miracle of the gospel, the priority of grace, the crisis of judgement and the truth of divine transcendence. In his work *The Church and the Sacraments*, which was published in 1917, before Barth had made his mark on Protestant theology, Forsyth reaffirmed the fundamental principle of Christian ecclesiology, that the church is grounded on the gospel of Jesus Christ. 'The Church's

[13]   A. C. Thiselton, *The First Epistle to the Corinthians*, NIGTC (Grand Rapids, MI: Eerdmans; Carlisle: Paternoster, 2000), p. 310.

[14]   Yves M.-J. Congar, *The Mystery of the Temple: OR God's Presence to His Creatures from Genesis to the Apocalypse* (London: Burns and Oates, 1962 [1958]), p. 162.

[15]   Gordon Fee, *The First Epistle to the Corinthians*, New International Commentary on the New Testament (Grand Rapids, MI: Eerdmans, 1987), p. 139, says that the foundation is not proper doctrine about Christ, but the gospel itself, whose content is salvation through Christ. But this is still to blur the force of Paul's affirmation.

[16]   John Calvin, *The First Epistle of Paul The Apostle to the Corinthians*, trans. J. W. Fraser, Calvin's Commentaries, ed. D. W. and T. F. Torrance (Edinburgh: Saint Andrew Press, 1960), p. 74.

one foundation', Forsyth affirmed, 'and the trust of its ministry is . . . Christ crucified'. Forsyth continues:

> The Church rests on the grace of God, the judging, atoning, regenerating grace of God . . . Wherever that is heartily confessed and goes on to rule we have the true Church . . . the Church . . . is the creature of the preached gospel of God's grace, forgiving, redeeming and creating us anew by Christ's cross. The Church was created by the preaching of that solitary gospel and fortified by the sacraments of it which are, indeed, but other ways of receiving, confessing and preaching it. The Church is the social and practical response to that grace. Wherever that gospel is taken seriously . . . there is the Church.[17]

Sources as apparently varied as Martin Luther and the Second Vatican Council have also spoken of the church being created or brought into being by the preaching of the gospel – in the first instance by Christ's own preaching of the kingdom of God. 'The church owes its birth to the Word', asserted Luther. 'If it is without the Word it ceases to be a church.'[18] Vatican II's 'Dogmatic Constitution on the Church' *Lumen Gentium* stated: 'The mystery of the Church is manifested in her very foundation, for the Lord Jesus inaugurated her by preaching the good news, that is, the coming of God's Kingdom.'[19]

Luther and Vatican II, in their own ways, refute any suggestion that the church is the product of human initiative or organization. All we can do is to make the word known; the power of the gospel will do the rest. But, strictly speaking, any talk of the word, or even the gospel, bringing the church into being – least of all 'creating' it – is misconceived. The church exists because Christ exists: there is no need to bring it into being. All we can do is to embrace the church and invite others into her fellowship. What the preaching of the gospel does in fact is to gather Christians in any one place and to evoke the coming into being of a new community of believers. And even then, as Forsyth points out, it does not do that without the sacraments, where the word is embodied in sacramental acts, giving 'form' or meaning to the 'matter' or symbolic elements. The word, the gospel, does not create the church, but it vivifies, renews and reforms the church when it is allowed to do so. And, as Luther affirmed in his Ninety-five Theses of 1517, the gospel is the Church's true treasure, her most cherished possession. 'The true treasure of the Church is the most holy gospel of the glory and grace of God.'[20] Why is the gospel so precious? Because it is the 'good news' of the kingdom of God personified and embodied in Jesus Christ and continuing in his *ekklēsia* for our true well-being in this life and in the life to come. Jesus Christ

---

[17] P. T. Forsyth, *The Church and the Sacraments* (London: Longmans, Green & Co., 1917), p. 31.
[18] *Luther's Works*, gen. ed. Helmut T. Lehmann (Philadelphia, PA: Fortress Press, 1958-), vol. 40, p. 37. Cf. P. D. L. Avis, *The Church in the Theology of the Reformers* (London: Marshall, Morgan and Scott; Atlanta, GA: John Knox Press, 1981; reprinted Eugene, OR: Wipf and Stock, 2002), p. 20.
[19] LG 5: W. M. Abbott (ed.), *The Documents of Vatican II* (London and Dublin: Geoffrey Chapman, 1966), p. 17.
[20] *Luther's Works*, vol. 31, pp. 25–33, at p. 31.

– his person, teaching, healing power, death, resurrection and glorification – is the foundation of the Christian church.

Faith and history

But how are we to understand the connection – biblical, historical and theological – between Jesus and the church? And how have our perceptions changed and our interpretations developed, as a result of the revolution in the nature of biblical research that can be encapsulated in the expression 'the historical-critical method', that has progressively impacted biblical studies during the past century and a half? I am not a professional biblical scholar, but I am not under the illusion that 'the historical-critical method' is all that is involved in the understanding and interpretation of the Bible and its application to the life of the church. Several complementary methods of biblical study and interpretation have developed since the heyday of historical criticism, including those that attempt to do justice to the role and presuppositions of the reader or interpreter and their social, economic and political context, while some of the more long-standing of them, such as form criticism and redaction criticism, are aspects of – or refinements of – the historical-critical method itself.

The 'historical-critical method' also opened up for the first time the area of theological enquiry – I could say, theological perplexity – concerning the relationship between 'the Jesus of history' and 'the Christ of faith', which was classically postulated by Martin Kähler at the end of the nineteenth century.[21] Kähler wrestled with two seismic questions for modern theology: (a) How can the Bible remain a source of normative church doctrine now that it has been shown to be historically unreliable? (b) How can Jesus himself remain the basis and the content of Christian faith when we can never attain certain knowledge of his life and teaching? Underlying both of these questions is a search for a firm foundation for the church's faith, what Kähler termed 'an invulnerable area' (*ein sturmfreies Gebiet*).

Kähler believed that we could not get behind the New Testament writings to the 'historical Jesus' because those writings represent the preaching that founded the church; they are 'confessional' writings. But they would not have come about without the real, historical Jesus; they were generated and given impetus by him; we find him in them and through them. They include genuinely historical and also 'supra-historical' elements. They provide not a history of Jesus, but a 'portrait' of Jesus infused with faith in him as Messiah, as Saviour. The 'historic' (*Geschichtliche*) biblical Christ is the Christ of history (*Historie*) for us. It is this fusion of history and faith in the portrayal of 'the biblical Christ' that constitutes the 'invulnerable area' – the foundation of faith. In the biblical Christ there is a triangulation of divine revelation, historical event and human faith. Therefore, for Kähler, the foundation of the church includes the proclamation of the church, the *kerygma*. There is no foundation without proclamation. It is the

---

[21] Martin Kähler, *The So-Called Historical Jesus and the Historic Biblical Christ*, trans., ed. and intro. Carl E. Braaten, from the 2nd German edition 1896 [1892]; Foreword Paul Tillich (Philadelphia, PA: Fortress Press, 1988 [1964]).

church that proclaims the message and it is spoken from faith. So faith, church and proclamation come together in the one foundation and behind them stands the biblical representation of Jesus as the Christ.

Rudolf Bultmann and Paul Tillich, also Lutheran theologians, were working very much within the trajectory of enquiry established by Martin Kähler and both of them echo elements of his thought. We will discuss Tillich's theology of the foundation of Christianity in the chapter on modern Protestant theology. But we can note here several relevant points that Bultmann makes, some of them quite axiomatic for our project.[22] (a) It is the Christ of the church's proclamation (the *kerygma*), not the historical Jesus, that is the object of Christian faith. (b) It is not possible to 'go behind' the *kerygma* in order to bolster or legitimate it by reference to the historical Jesus. (c) There is genuine continuity between the Jesus of history and the *kerygma*, but the Christ of the *kerygma* is not a figure who can be identified with the historical Jesus. (d) We cannot appeal to the Apostle Paul for access to the historical Jesus; he shows no interest in the details of his earthly life and fate. (e) The Fourth Gospel is not a source for the historical Jesus either; for example, while it emphasizes the humanity of Jesus (he is hungry, troubled in spirit, weeps), it fails to draw on the material provided by the Synoptics for this motif (the temptations, Gethsemane, the cry of dereliction on the cross). (f) The fact that, within the New Testament, Jesus, who came preaching the gospel of the kingdom, himself became the content of the apostles' message – 'the proclaimer became the proclaimed' – has radical implications: what we have now is the proclamation (*kerygma*), not the proclaimer. (g) Nevertheless, Jesus is present and to be encountered in the *kerygma*, the proclamation of the church. (h) The saying that 'Jesus is risen in the *kerygma*' is valid in the sense that both the resurrection and the *kerygma* are eschatological events; it is eschatology – the outworking of the saving purposes of God, already experienced but yet to be fulfilled – that holds them together.

I find that I cannot gainsay these key points of Bultmann's theology – they must be taken on board and the consequences must be faced. They are valid as far as they go, but I believe there is more to be said. For Bultmann the foundation of Christian faith is the word, the proclamation (*kerygma*) of the church. Jesus and the church become connected when the message is preached. But Bultmann seems to reduce the saving work of God in the world – and in the church – to the proclaimed word. It is the word or nothing. There is no sense that the church might be – somehow – a substantive continuation of Jesus' mission. Does the church have substance *between* preaching events? Could the church, by its life of worship, sacrament and service, continuously proclaim the gospel? Is there a foundation upon which and out of which the proclamation arises? Where are all the means of grace in this picture? What of baptism and the Eucharist (there is plenty about these in Paul)? What of the pastoral work of the ministry in addition to preaching? Where, above all, is the Holy Spirit? I would say that the self-communication of God – and therefore of Jesus, the incarnate

---

[22] Rudolf Bultmann, 'The Primitive Christian Kerygma and the Historical Jesus', trans. from 3rd German edition, 1962, in Carl E. Braaten and Roy A. Harrisville (eds), *The Historical Jesus and the Kerygmatic Christ: Essays on the New Quest of the Historical Jesus* (New York and Nashville: Abingdon Press, 1964), pp. 15–42.

Word of God – in revelation and redemption, continues in and through the church (though not to the exclusion of other avenues of the *missio dei* in the world), and that it is not confined to the overt proclamation of the word, though never without the word.

The historical-critical method is now universally accepted and practised within the scholarly community as at least the indispensable first stage, the sine qua non, of any approach to the meaning of the text that has scholarly integrity. (One of its merits is that it rules out of court the kind of romantic, sometimes sentimental, psychologizing of the inner life of Jesus, based on speculation about his personality, that was favoured by the classical Liberal Protestants whom we shall meet in a later chapter.) In the light of the historical-critical revolution in the methodology of biblical research and its generally accepted results, I want to ask, 'Is it possible any more to hold that Jesus of Nazareth founded, instituted or intended the church – and if not, how should the relationship between the church and Jesus be understood theologically?' In the following three chapters of this first half of the enquiry we shall be investigating the connection between Jesus and the church as it is portrayed in the Gospels and Epistles. In the second half of the book we shall examine what modern theologians, employing historical-critical methods of research and accepting their findings, have concluded more systematically about the significance of Jesus of Nazareth for the enduring foundation of the Christian Church.

Digging for foundations

When I wrote on this theme, even using the same title as I have chosen for this introductory chapter, in the journal *Theology* a good many years ago,[23] the article provoked an amusing riposte in the correspondence pages ('Rocks of Ages or Living Waters?'), promoting an alternative theological model, one patterned on the pastime of locals and tourists in British Columbia, in the West of Canada, of hurtling down the Fraser River, rapids and all, in an inflatable rubber raft. The author, Peter Horsfield, claimed to prefer the thrill of riding the wild waters to the sober satisfaction of laying solid foundations. That is an appropriate riposte to any fearful and defensive approach to Christian theology, but it was off-beam and missed my intention then and now. I was (and am) proposing precisely that we should allow the stream of Christian experience – the living tradition of faith and conviction, worship and prayer, discipleship and mission – to carry us forward by its own momentum and to lead us to explore the depths of the Christian mystery. 'Rock of Ages or Living Waters?' the two images are not mutually exclusive; in the Bible they are complementary. It was out of the rock that water gushed forth (Exod. 17:6). The people of Israel 'drank from the spiritual rock that followed them, and the rock was Christ' (1 Cor. 10:4). Another hymn speaks of the 'Stricken Rock with streaming side', evoking the crucified Christ and the spear-wound in his side, out of which flowed blood and water, as the Fourth Gospel describes the scene (Jn 19: 23-37).[24] The Romantic poet William Wordsworth, in an image taken

---

[23]   Paul Avis, 'The Church's One Foundation', *Theology* LXXXIX, no. 730 (July 1986), pp. 257–63.
[24]   George Hugh Bourne (1840-1925), 'Lord, enthroned in heav'nly splendour'.

from the Lake District of North-West England where he and Samuel Taylor Coleridge were neighbours, spoke of his poetic soul as 'a rock with torrents roaring'.[25] So I propose to expound the imagery of the one foundation unashamedly.

I have always wanted to get to the bottom of things, especially in theology. I am a relentless prober of arguments and weigher of evidence, motivated by a restless desire to understand more deeply and get at 'the truth', as far as humanly possible. Hence the appeal to me of the metaphor of foundations and especially 'theological foundations', the phrase that gives the title to the projected multi-volume series of which this forms the first volume. (The proposed second volume will also require me to sound the depths, since its provisional or working title is *Revelation and the Word of God*.) So I see this whole project – and this first volume in particular – as an exercise in digging for foundations. One of my theological mentors, Archbishop Michael Ramsey (1904-1988), wrote of Frederick Denison Maurice (a mentor, so to speak, of mine from the past – his work spanned the second and third quarters of the nineteenth century) that he enabled others to build because he chose himself to 'dig'.[26] Maurice saw his theological vocation as that of 'a digger', not 'a builder', because the foundation had been laid once for all by the action of God in Jesus Christ; therefore, the kingdom of Christ was already 'among us, and is not to be set up at all'.[27] In consciously Mauricean vein, Ramsey wrote that the church (he was speaking of the Church of England, but the point applies universally) needs to dig down to its foundations. Ramsey listed these foundations: 'the Gospel of God, the sacramental life, and the soundest learning that its clergy and laity can possess'.[28] A moment's reflection will show that these priorities cut across the boundaries of the generally understood 'parties' or schools of thought ('churchmanship') in the church. We are particularly familiar with them in Anglicanism where they are usually named as Evangelical, Anglican Catholic and central or mainstream (historically 'Broad Church'). Like Maurice himself, who abominated the party mentality, I do not identify with any of the three main options – except insofar as I find myself identifying with aspects of each of them!

---

[25] William Wordsworth, *The Prelude: A Parallel Text*, ed. J. C. Maxwell (Harmondsworth: Penguin, 1972), pp. 524–5 (XIII: 231/251).

[26] Arthur Michael Ramsey, *The Gospel and the Catholic Church* (London: Longmans, Green and Co., 1936), p. 216. See also id., *F. D. Maurice and the Conflicts of Modern Theology* (Cambridge: Cambridge University Press, 1951), pp. 111–12. Ramsey cites William Temple, writing at the end of his life: 'We must dig the foundations deeper' than heretofore and seek to be 'more completely dominated in thought and aspiration by the redeeming acts of God in Jesus Christ' (from F. A. Iremonger, *William Temple, Archbishop of Canterbury: His Life and Letters* (London: Oxford University Press, 1948), pp. 610–11).

[27] Frederick Maurice [son], *The Life of Frederick Denison Maurice*, 2 vols (London: Macmillan, 1884), vol. 1, pp. 136–8.

[28] Ramsey, *The Gospel and the Catholic Church*, p. 216; cf. p. 225.

2

Jesus and the church

No question in ecclesiology, I would suggest, is more pivotal than the question of the connection between Jesus and the church. I am not saying, at this stage of the enquiry, 'Jesus and *his* church', because that would beg the question that I am asking, namely, 'On what grounds can we say that the church is – or deserves to be called – Christ's church?' I am using the expression 'Jesus and the church', not as a truth to be affirmed, but as a problem to be addressed. There is a huge distance, conceptually and imaginatively, between Jesus of Nazareth, as we see him in the Gospels, and the church as it emerged into history, even in the first century, let alone after several centuries more of organizational development and expansion at the heart of the Roman Empire. That imaginative and conceptual distance is vastly increased when we consider the nearly 2,000-year trajectory that takes us from the church as it is portrayed in the New Testament to the church of today. The mismatch is vertiginous. What connects the figure of Jesus Christ, as we see him in the pages of the Gospels, with the great institution, in many diverse branches, spreading out geographically and historically, that bears his name: 'the church of Christ'? That church has become many churches, and they are generally mutually exclusive as well as internally conflicted.

To some Christians, even to raise the question, to posit some epistemic distance between Jesus and the church, seems shocking. For such Christians – and I think that they are probably the majority – Jesus and the church are inseparable; therefore, to probe the nature of the connection seems to them almost sacrilegious. In one sense, such Christians are right and I stand with them to this extent: it is a profound Christian instinct that to belong to the church is to belong to Christ and to belong to Christ is to belong to the church. The church, with its prayer, praise, sacraments, fellowship and pastoral care, is where we find him and know ourselves blessed by him. That is probably fine for many busy lay Christians who have other important areas of life and work to occupy them. But I am not sure that it will do for the 'professionals', the clergy and ministers and their bishops or other leaders. I suspect that most clergy and other ministers, who are busy and active in 'the Lord's vineyard' do not have the time or the inclination to stop and ask themselves, 'Why are we doing this?' or 'Is this what Jesus wants of us?' or 'In what sense, if any, did Jesus start this whole business off?' I think their approach tends to be largely pragmatic, rather than theologically informed. But perhaps a child, looking at the church and what goes on within it, might sometimes wonder, 'How did this all begin?' The church is and always has been 'about' Jesus; though regrettably, it is and always has been also 'about' other extraneous and alien matters. But, if we are to think theologically – and honestly – about the church, we need to reconcile the central Christian instinct that the church is 'about' Jesus with an open-ended enquiry as to *whether* the church is about Jesus, and if so *how*.

A question that will not go away

The question of the connection between Jesus and the church is one that will not go away. It is unavoidable for at least two main reasons: our modern sense of historical perspective and our God-given moral conscience both raise it. As we look at the church as it has evolved and changed through twenty centuries – the emergence of its power structures, hierarchies and bureaucracies, the fact of its conflicts, divisions and bloodshed, its sins, crimes and mundane human failings – we may well exclaim, 'What has all that to do with Jesus of Nazareth?' For those with a strong sense of historical perspective, alert to temporal change, cultural diversity and ideological development, and for those with a tender moral conscience, the relationship between the church and Jesus is problematic. I believe that the question posed here lies at the heart of ecclesiology.

There are several avenues through which the connection between Jesus and the church could be explored, including the avenues of belief and doctrine, worship and sacraments, and discipleship and ministry. These are some of the practical, experiential connections between the church and Jesus. But it is the historical and ethical aspects of the relationship and connection between the church and Jesus that are particularly problematic, that pose the greatest challenge. The mental and imaginative effort required to connect the church as we know it – the church as a diverse, complex and conflicted empirical reality in history – with the central figure of the Gospels, utterly truthful, morally flawless and sacrificially self-giving, as he stands out from their pages, is acute.

A rallying cry in the early church for those who wanted to preserve the Christian message from corruption by classical philosophy was Tertullian's question, 'What has Jerusalem [biblical revelation] to do with Athens [pagan culture and philosophy]?'[1] By analogy with this slogan, we might ask, 'What has Jesus to do with the church?' The instinctive Christian response is to reply, 'The church has everything to do with Jesus. It is his church. If it were not for him, there would be no church.' That reply has the heart of the matter in it, as far as Christian faith-commitment is concerned, but it jumps too far, too fast. The intuitive answer needs to be unpacked, even de-constructed, and that process is at least part of our agenda in this chapter. Half a century ago, the Methodist theologian John Knox commented, 'No fact about the Church would appear to be so obvious, and so obviously important, as the relation in which it stands to the fact of Jesus; and yet few problems are so baffling as that of defining just what this relation

---

[1] Tertullian, *De Praescriptionibus Haereticorum* [*Against Heresies*], §7: S. L. Greenslade, trans. and ed., *Early Latin Theology* [*The Library of Christian Classics*, Vol. V] (Philadelphia, PA: Westminster Press; London: SCM Press, 1956), p. 36.

is.'[2] To bring the question home in a more personal way, we might ask, 'How are we as Christians in the church today connected to the Jesus who walked the streets of Jerusalem and the dusty paths of Galilee? Is the worship we offer, the work we do and the organization to which we belong what Jesus intended or not?' In a nutshell: Is the church what Jesus meant to happen?

One of the most searching and radical ways, within a basically historical approach, of posing the question of the connection between Jesus and the church is to ask whether Jesus of Nazareth *founded* the church in any historically meaningful sense. The great Ceylonese Methodist bishop and evangelist D. T. Niles (1908–70) wrote: 'The answer to the problems of the world is the answer that Jesus Christ provided, which is the Church.'[3] But the question that we are facing here is, 'Did Jesus Christ in fact "provide" the church that bears his name?' There is nothing particularly obvious or self-evident about the choice of the word 'church' (*ekklēsia*) to refer to the groups or communities of disciples, believers or 'brothers' whom we find in the New Testament worshipping Jesus, risen and ascended, and witnessing to his saving name. In fact, the term 'church' is misleading and almost unusable because of its acquired historical connotations. But it is the New Testament itself, even in its earliest strata, that compels us to use the word for the early Christian communities, though in a severely qualified way, as we shall see.[4]

There are ways of equivocating about this question and softening it. The English Congregationalist New Testament scholar C. H. Dodd gave his last book the outrageously misleading title *The Founder of Christianity*.[5] But to put the matter in that way – to say 'Christianity' rather than 'church' – does not at all avoid the problem. As Paula Gooder has well written, 'Jesus made no obvious attempt to "found" anything.'[6] But it is a little easier to speak about the origins of Christianity as a historical phenomenon or even as a 'movement' (as Roger Haight, for example, consistently does in his three-volume work of *Comparative Ecclesiology*),[7] than to tackle the question – the uncomfortable but unavoidable question – that goes something like this: 'Did Jesus intend there to be a Christian church at all? Did he, moreover, intend there to be a Christian church in a form remotely resembling the church as we know it? Did he in any sense anticipate the emergence of a great international institution, divided into innumerable parts large and small, each with its structures of governance, bodies of law and weight of tradition? And did he at all foresee that much of the time each part would exclude the other parts?'

A way of sharpening the question is to ask whether Jesus could have intended the existence of the church as such without intending some kind of shape, structure and organization for it. Could one intend any kind of major institutional development

---

2 John Knox, *The Church and the Reality of Christ* (London: Collins, 1963), p. 113.

3 D. T. Niles, *The Message and Its Messengers* (Nashville, TS: Abingdon, 1966), p. 50.

4 See the discussion of James D. G. Dunn, *Beginning from Jerusalem, Christianity in the Making, Volume 2* (Grand Rapids, MI: Eerdmans, 2009), pp. 4–17.

5 C. H. Dodd, *The Founder of Christianity* (New York: Macmillan, 1970; London: Collins, 1971; Fontana edition 1973).

6 Paula Gooder, 'In Search of the Early Church', in Gerard Mannion and Lewis S. Mudge (eds), *The Routledge Companion to the Christian Church* (New York and London: Routledge, 2008), p. 17.

7 Roger Haight, *Christian Community in History*, [3 vols] *Volume 1: Historical Ecclesiology* (New York and London: Continuum, 2004).

within civilization merely as a disembodied idea, without filling in the blank with a few details? Suppose you were the ruler of a country, somewhere in the world, that had never enjoyed proper democratic institutions (not difficult to imagine) and you wanted to bequeath as your legacy a functioning democratic system for the nation. Could you do so without intending and foreseeing at least the outline of how elections and representation would work, the form of debating chambers and the basic rules of debate and decision, together with the legal checks and balances that would be necessary in order to uphold the rights of minorities and to curb abuses of power by the majority? Or suppose you were asked to initiate the first university in a developing country that had none. Could you begin to do this without sketching in what purpose the new university would serve, what subjects it would teach, who would lead and govern it, how it would be resourced with plant and financial support, and how it would relate to universities elsewhere and indeed to other institutions within civil society? I think not.

If we apply these tests to the putative founding of the church, we have to reckon with the fact that modern New Testament and patristic scholarship has brought out unambiguously the huge diversity of faith and order in the apostolic and post-apostolic church. Not only was there diversity, which we tend to regard today as basically benign and unthreatening; there was also contestation and conflict, radical and chronic. Paul's battles with rival 'apostles' and their cliques in the Corinthian correspondence – particularly his allusion in 1 Cor. 3:11-12 to 'other foundations' – and his reference in Galatians to those who preach 'a different gospel' and 'another gospel' (Gal. 1:6-7) point to the fact that the questions, 'Which Christianity?' and 'Whose Christianity?' were being fought over even before the canonical Gospels were written.[8] Christianity took shape in an arena of continuous struggle, conflict and negotiation, not only in relation to external cultural, philosophical, theological and political influences, but in relation to internal tensions and contradictory impulses.

The faith of the church was hammered out over several centuries; we have fragments of confessional material in the New Testament, as well as an assortment of early creeds to prove it.[9] The canon of the New Testament was also contested for several hundred years after Christ. Ministerial order, congregational structure and patterns of worship also varied. Three-quarters of a century went by after Pentecost before the monarchical episcopate emerged with St Ignatius of Antioch, and it took another century or more before episcopacy became more or less universal in the church. The pattern of Christian initiation was varied and the shape of the liturgy was diverse. For a long time there were no universally accepted legal norms (canons). We have to conclude either that Jesus did not envisage concretely the framework for his church, or that his vision was either frustrated or lost, neither possibility seeming very plausible. What does seem quite clear is that Jesus could not have intended the church without endowing it with certain key, intrinsic, identifying features. The alternative would have been merely a

[8] Cf. Karen L. King, 'Which Early Christianity?', in Susan Ashbrook Harvey and David G. Hunter (eds), *The Oxford Handbook of Early Christian Studies* (Oxford: Oxford University Press, 2008), pp. 66–84.
[9] Oscar Cullmann, *The Earliest Christian Confessions* (London: Lutterworth Press, 1949); J. N. D. Kelly, *Early Christian Creeds* (London: A. & C. Black, 1950).

vague aspiration on his part, and Jesus did not go in for those. But there is another factor to be considered.

It is clear that Jesus' mission was to the people and nation of Israel. Through repentance and believing the good news of the kingdom, they could be restored as God's people. He chose twelve apostles to represent the twelve tribes of Israel. He was seen as the new Moses, the son of David and a greater than Solomon. Reform and renewal of Yahweh's gathered people, not its replacement, were his agenda. Even the expression 'the *new* covenant' at the Last Supper shows continuity. Jesus' mission is the outworking of God's faithfulness to God's promises. So it is clear that Jesus did not intend, expect or foresee any institutional form of the church that was separate from Israel.

Some scholars seem to execute something of a sideways shuffle in the face of this question. N. T. Wright says of the question, 'Did Jesus intend to found a church?': 'The question is hopeless. Of course he didn't; of course he did.'[10] John Knox claims that the 'whole issue is largely irrelevant', explaining, 'The important thing is not what Jesus intended or expected, but what God did.'[11] I find these evasions and equivocations less than helpful. The challenge, 'Did Jesus, historically speaking, found or even intend the church?' must be tackled fairly and squarely. The blunt, perhaps rather naive, questions, 'Where did the church come from?', 'Did the church come from Jesus?' and 'Did Jesus want the church?' need to be asked and answered. In the second half of this book, on the foundation of the church in modern theology we will look at the different ways in which Protestant, Roman Catholic and Anglican theologians have tackled this question and the various answers that they have given.

It seems to me vital for all Christians who are active in the church, and especially for all who are called to public ministry, to be able to hold that what they (I could say 'we') do is, to say the least, in basic continuity with the vision, hopes and plans that Jesus had for his followers in his (earthly) lifetime. Do we not need the assurance that our efforts and aspirations are in keeping with the spirit and intentions of Jesus and, so to speak, have his approval, so that he can own what is done in his name and work through his human agents by the power of the same Spirit that rested mightily upon him? In the face of difficult personal decisions and dilemmas, some Christians tend to ask the entirely proper but now clichéd question: 'What would Jesus do?' But we can only ask that question if we can give an answer to a prior question, 'What *did* Jesus do?', that is to say, 'What did Jesus do with regard to the church?' So the question, 'Did Jesus found the church?' is an entirely legitimate and indeed necessary question, one that expects an answer. We can begin to address it by considering a key aspect of the conceptual context and horizon of the New Testament literature, that of eschatology. Eschatology is a dimension of the New Testament literature that is not always confronted when the origins of the church are discussed. But I am convinced that we cannot hope to understand Jesus or his relation to the church unless we take eschatology seriously. If we ignore the eschatological dimension, our understanding of the origins of the church will be seriously incomplete and distorted.

---

[10] N. T. Wright, *Jesus and the Victory of God* (London: SPCK, 1996), p. 275.
[11] Knox, *The Church and the Reality of Christ*, p. 35.

The eschatological horizon of Jesus' mission

Developments in New Testament scholarship in the late nineteenth and early twentieth centuries brought to light clearly and for the first time the dominant eschatological context and content of Jesus' mission. The eschatological horizon, as future yet already impinging, was first brought out by Johannes Weiss, Alfred Loisy and Albert Schweitzer. Although the details of interpretation of the key biblical texts are still debated, the essentials are clear enough. Jesus of Nazareth subscribed to the basic eschatological world view of the Jewish people in the period between the two Testaments. He was consciously operating within a foreshortened time span. He expected a decisive divine intervention to bring about the end of the present age or world order (though not, as often colloquially suggested, 'the end of the world') and to replace it with the kingdom or reign of God. He believed that this would happen either imminently or perhaps within a short space of time, even possibly a few years. Jesus and the apostles and evangelists interpreted his own sufferings and those that he anticipated for his disciples as belonging to the great tribulation that would serve as the birth pangs of the new age (e.g. Jn 16:16; Rom. 8:18-25).[12]

Jesus had begun his public ministry by proclaiming the imminence of the coming of the reign (*basileia*) of God: 'After John [the Baptist] had been handed over, Jesus came into Galilee proclaiming the gospel (good news) of God and saying, "The time has been fulfilled and the reign of God is at hand; repent and believe in the gospel"' (Mk 1:14-15). The centrality of the proclamation of the imminence of the reign of God in the ministry of Jesus is virtually uncontested.[13] The theme of the nearness of the reign of God is pivotal for Jesus' destiny from beginning to end. At the Last Supper, Jesus explicitly linked his death with the coming of the kingdom or reign of God (Lk. 22:28; Mk 14:25). This reinterpretation and realignment of received Jewish eschatological hopes by Jesus himself charted a course for the fundamental christological reinterpretation of the reign of God that was carried out by the New Testament writers. Future hope is drawn down and located in the event of Jesus Christ. As John Ashton says, by far the most crucial revolution in humankind's relationship with God has already been achieved by Jesus Christ: 'The decisive event, the divine intervention that occupies the gap between "before" and "after" has already taken place. The point of rupture along the line of human history has been displaced, shifted back to the time occupied by the Gospel narratives.'[14] Jewish eschatological expectations are, as it were, rerouted to pass through the death and resurrection of Jesus. As Dale Allison puts it, 'Expectation and outcome were, despite the tension between the two, made out to be promise and fulfilment.'[15]

---

[12]   Dale C. Allison, *The End of the Ages Has Come: An Early Interpretation of the Passion and Resurrection of Jesus* (Edinburgh: T&T Clark, 1987), pp. 19, 22.

[13]   As Dunn says, 'The centrality of the kingdom of God (*basileia tou theou*) in Jesus' preaching is one of the least disputable, or disputed, facts about Jesus': James D. G. Dunn, *Jesus Remembered, Christianity in the Making, Volume 1* (Grand Rapids, MI: Eerdmans, 2003), p. 383.

[14]   John Ashton, *Understanding the Fourth Gospel* (Oxford: Clarendon Press, 1991), p. 225.

[15]   Allison, *The End of the Ages Has Come*, p. 148.

The basic consensus of modern New Testament interpretation seems secure: Jesus, followed by the earliest wave of New Testament writers, expected the last times and the fulfilment of the reign of God to come upon the world either immediately or after a short interval. Neither Jesus nor his apostles anticipated that human history would continue its turbulent course for thousands of years. Surely, we must conclude, the eschatological crisis proclaimed by Jesus – indeed inaugurated by him – precluded any intention to found an ongoing institutional structure for his followers. So how could Jesus have 'founded' the church in any meaningful sense? However, in order to give a more reasoned and nuanced answer to this question, we must look a little more closely at the eschatological framework of the New Testament. A century of study of this question has arrived at a number of fairly secure conclusions. These affect our assessment of the relationship between Jesus and the church.[16]

The primary orientation of Jesus' eschatology was to the future

Johannes Weiss' *Die Predigt Jesu vom Reiche Gottes* (1st edition 1892; 2nd edition 1900; ET *Jesus' Proclamation of the Kingdom of God*, 1971) established (a) that the thrust of Jesus' teaching was indelibly eschatological; and (b) that this eschatology had a future reference. Weiss' eschatological reorientation of the Gospels overturned the Liberal Protestant theological consensus, represented especially at that time by Albrecht Ritschl (1822–89), that the kingdom of God was a realm of progressive moral attainment – a spiritual movement that was gradually permeating society and determining the course of world history. Christian believers, Ritschl wrote in his great work *Justification and Reconciliation*, 'constitute the kingdom of God in so far as, forgetting distinctions of sex, rank, or nationality, they act reciprocally from love, and thus call into existence that fellowship of moral disposition and moral blessings which extends, through all possible gradations, to the limits of the human race.'[17]

On the contrary (claimed Weiss), the kingdom of God, according to Jesus, was a wholly supernatural and transcendent reality and would come only by a decisive act of divine intervention. The coming of the kingdom would be sudden, universal, destructive and transforming. The framework of Jesus' eschatology was thoroughly dualistic: 'The kingdom of God is a radically superworldly entity which stands in diametric opposition to this world.'[18] In contradiction to the Ritschlian emphasis on the subjective, ethical location of the kingdom, Weiss asserted that, for Jesus, the

---

[16] A comprehensive resource for the general study of eschatology is Jerry L. Walls (ed.), *The Oxford Handbook of Eschatology* (Oxford: Oxford University Press, 2007). We are not particularly concerned in the present work with the theological problem of the 'delay' of the *parousia*, that is, the 'Second Coming' of Christ and the decisive manifestation, within this world, of the kingdom of God. The issue is, of course, addressed in *The Oxford Handbook of Eschatology*. Another significant study of the problem is Vicki Balabanski, *Eschatology in the Making: Mark, Matthew and the Didache* (Cambridge: Cambridge University Press, 1997).

[17] Albrecht Ritschl, *The Christian Doctrine of Justification and Reconciliation*, trans. H. R. Macintosh and A. B. Macaulay (Edinburgh: T&T Clark, 1900), p. 285.

[18] Johannes Weiss, *Jesus' Proclamation of the Kingdom of God*, trans., ed. and intro. Richard H. Hiers and David L. Holland from the 1st edition of *Die Predigt Jesu vom Reiche Gottes*, 1892 (London: SCM Press; Philadelphia, PA: Fortress Press, 1971), p. 114, cf. pp. 82, 92–3.

kingdom is never something subjective, inward or purely spiritual, but is always the objective, outwardly manifested kingdom of the Messiah.[19]

But what of those sayings of Jesus in the Synoptic Gospels that appear to say that the kingdom has arrived? Weiss interpreted the allusions in the Gospels to the presence of the kingdom here and now as anticipations on the part of Jesus of what was actually imminent but had not yet taken place. To the eyes of faith, Satan's kingdom was already crumbling.[20] In the second edition of his book, Weiss implausibly attributed this discrepancy in the words of Jesus to 'nuances of mood'. He believed that the evangelists had modified Jesus' absolute futurism and that (with the exception of the anticipations and the nuances of mood that I have just mentioned) only those words of Jesus, relating to the kingdom, that were in the future tense were authentic.

Weiss did not assume that the radical future orientation that he had discovered in the Gospels was without its difficulties. He believed that, just as a consistent futurism posed a problem for the early Christians because clearly their eschatological expectations were not fulfilled, so it also posed a problem for modern theology. Julius Kaftan (1848–1926), an eminent Liberal Protestant theologian, greeted Weiss' theory with the remark, 'If the kingdom of God is an eschatological matter, then it is a useless concept as far as dogmatics is concerned' – though eventually Kaftan became convinced that Weiss was right.[21] Weiss himself frankly acknowledged that modern theology could not share the eschatological horizon of the Gospels. He de-eschatologized, so to speak, the notion of the kingdom, referring it to the heavenly realm that believers expect to experience after death. 'We do not await a kingdom of God which is to come down from heaven to earth and abolish this world, but we do hope to be gathered with the Church of Jesus Christ into the heavenly *basileia* [kingdom].'[22]

Although Weiss' absolute futurism would be somewhat modified by subsequent scholarship (as we shall see shortly), he had drawn attention to strong elements in the Gospels that are capable of sustaining only a futurist interpretation. Jesus taught his disciples to pray, 'Your kingdom come' (Mt. 6:10). He spoke of not drinking of the fruit of the vine until the kingdom of God should come (Lk. 22:18). He assured some of those listening to his words that they would not die 'until they see that the kingdom of God has come with power' (Mk 9:1).

Albert Schweitzer (1875–1965) described Weiss' *Die Predigt Jesu vom Reiche Gottes* as one of the most important works in historical theology. 'It seems to break a spell', he said. 'It closes one epoch and begins another.'[23] Schweitzer's *Vom Reimarus zu Wrede* (1906; translated as *The Quest of the Historical Jesus*, 1910) identified Hermann Samuel Reimarus (1694–1768) as the first to realize that the world of Jewish thought that Jesus inhabited was indelibly eschatological. However, this claim overlooks not only Matthew Tindal's 1730 work *Christianity as Old as the Creation* (which is surprising because Reimarus owed much to the English deists), but also Reimarus'

---

[19] Ibid., p. 133.
[20] Ibid., pp. 74ff, 102.
[21] Ibid., p. xi.
[22] Ibid., p. 136.
[23] Ibid., p. 25.

own countryman Johann Salomo Semler (1725–91).[24] Semler rejected Reimarus' political interpretation of Jesus' messianic self-understanding, but followed Reimarus to the extent of holding that Jesus expected the imminent end of the world and that the delay, or non-arrival, of this event (the *parousia*) presented the paramount critical problem for early Christianity. Reimarus believed that Jesus saw himself as a political liberator, who would usher in a glorious age of freedom from oppression and want. Reimarus further held that the fact that this perspective is almost entirely absent from the Gospels was owing to a pious fraud on the part of the evangelists, because the crucifixion had caused Jesus' disciples to turn his own understanding on its head.[25]

In a study of Jesus' Messiahship in 1901 – designed to prepare for a possible life of Jesus – Schweitzer claimed that the New Testament sources failed to make sense of Jesus' apparent determination to sacrifice his life.[26] He detected a narrative disconnection between Jesus' public ministry and his Passion. The answer to this puzzle, Schweitzer believed, was to begin with the Passion and work back to try to understand Jesus' messianic consciousness. If investigation showed that Jesus did not believe himself to be the Messiah, this would actually deal 'the death blow' to the Christian faith, for 'The Christian religion is founded upon the messianic consciousness of Jesus.'[27] Against what Reimarus had alleged, Schweitzer believed that the evangelists did not actually 'fabricate facts' about Jesus, though the factual details of his life were not what interested them.[28] Schweitzer claimed that Jesus did not disclose his messianic consciousness to the disciples, but after the death of John the Baptist he set out for Jerusalem to face the final conflict as Messiah, believing that this would usher in the kingdom of God. In the same year William Wrede (1859–1906) explored the messianic consciousness (and 'messianic secret') of Jesus against the eschatological framework in *Das Messiasgeheimnis in den Evangelien* (1901). And after Schweitzer's publication, his teacher and mentor H. J. Holtzmann (the correspondent of Friedrich von Hügel, the Roman Catholic 'modernist' whom we shall meet in a later chapter) published *Das messianische Bewusstsein Jesu* (1907).

---

[24] Matthew Tindal, *Christianity as Old as the Creation*, facsimile of 1730 edition, ed. G. Gawlick (Stuttgart-Bad Cannstatt: Freidrich Frommann Verlag, 1967), pp. 258–62. Tindal argues that the New Testament writers clearly expected the second coming of Christ imminently; if they were mistaken (as they obviously were) about that matter, how can any of their teaching be trusted?

[25] Hermann Samuel Reimarus, 'Concerning the Intention of Jesus . . ', in Charles H. Talbert (ed.), Ralph S. Fraser (trans.), *Reimarus Fragments* (Philadelphia, PA: Fortress Press, 1970; London: SCM Press, 1971) = id., *The Goal of Jesus and His Disciples*, intro. and trans. George Wesley Buchanan (Leiden: Brill, 1970); original: Gotthold Ephraim Lessing (1729–81), 'Fragment eines Ungenannten' (i.e. the 'Wolfenbüttel Fragments'), published in Lessing's *Zur Geschichte und Literatur*, supposedly from the papers of H. S. Reimarus, though it is thought that Lessing's own input into the content was significant. See Gotthold Ephraim Lessing, *Lessing's Theological Writings: Selections in Translation with an Introductory Essay*, ed. Henry Chadwick (London: A. & C. Black, 1956).

[26] Albert Schweitzer, *The Mystery of the Kingdom of God: The Secret of Jesus' Messiahship and Passion*, trans. and intro. Walter Lowrie (London: Adam and Charles Black, 1914). This is a translation of the second part (*Das Abendmahl: Das Messianitäts und Leidensgeheimnis; Eine Scizze des Lebens Jesu*) of Schweitzer's ambitious work on the Last Supper. Apparently the work was generally ignored by German scholars.

[27] Schweitzer, *The Mystery of the Kingdom of God*, pp. 5–6.

[28] Ibid., p. 8.

Schweitzer deployed the expression *Konsequente Eschatologie*, translated as 'throughgoing eschatology'. Against the eschatological backdrop, Schweitzer portrayed Jesus as a tragic, deluded figure who believed, mistakenly, that by embracing a sacrificial death he would trigger the arrival of the new age, the manifestation of the kingdom of God.[29] There was, of course, no question of Jesus instituting the church as a structured society, but that was not the end of Jesus' mission and impact. Like Schleiermacher, Troeltsch, Herrmann and Harnack (as we shall see later), Schweitzer believed that the effect of Jesus' personality or self-consciousness continued through the ages and was impervious to historical research. Thus, Schweitzer proclaimed that a stream of spiritual influence had gone forth from Jesus and had spread from age to age. It would not be affected by the results of any historical research.

Schweitzer insisted in his later work *The Mysticism of Paul the Apostle* that Jesus and Paul shared the same eschatological expectation, that it was combined with or infused with late Jewish apocalyptic ideas, including intervention in the causal nexus of the world by angels and demons, that it conditioned the entire corpus of New Testament writings (though admittedly the Fourth Gospel lacks the apocalyptic element), and that the 'Hellenization' of this theology came later, with Ignatius of Antioch and others.[30] Notwithstanding their differences of interpretation, Reimarus and Semler, Weiss and Schweitzer were agreed in believing that the concept of the kingdom of God was the key to the correct understanding of Jesus' mission. This aspect of their work has entered into the consensus of New Testament scholarship and has not been seriously questioned for the past century.[31]

These revolutionary eschatological ideas, emanating from Germany, were adopted into British New Testament scholarship in the early twentieth century, notably by William Sanday and F. C. Burkitt. In 1907 Sanday published *The Life of Christ in Recent Research* in which he enthused about Schweitzer, though not uncritically for he did not embrace Schweitzer's extreme conclusion that Jesus was deceived about the effect of his sacrifice in triggering the coming of the kingdom of God. But Sanday was converted to the basic eschatological framework of the Gospels as future-orientated, though not exclusively so.[32] The assimilation of Weiss and Schweitzer into English New Testament scholarship was slow and faltering. In 1907 Sanday stated that there was no copy of Weiss' *Die Predigt Jesu vom Reiche Gottes*, published in 1892, in the Bodleian Library

---

[29] Albert Schweitzer, *The Quest of the Historical Jesus: A Critical Study of Its Progress from Reimarus to Wrede*, trans. William Montgomery, Preface by F. C. Burkitt (London: Adam and Charles Black, 1910). See also *The Quest of the Historical Jesus: First Complete Edition*, ed. John Bowden, Foreword Dennis Nineham, trans. W. Montgomery, J. R. Coates, Susan Cupitt and John Bowden (London: SCM Press, 2000) [actually a trans. of *Geschichte der Leben-Jesu-Forschung* (Tübingen: J. C. B. Mohr, 1913)].

[30] Albert Schweitzer, *The Mysticism of Paul the Apostle*, trans. William Montgomery, Prefatory Note by F. C. Burkitt, 3rd edn (London: A. & C. Black, 1933), pp. ix, 32, 55–6.

[31] Cf. Albert Schweitzer's last work, published posthumously: *Reich Gottes und Christentum*, ed. and intro. Ulrich Neuenschwander, trans. as *The Kingdom of God and Primitive Christianity* by L. A. Garrard (London: A. & C. Black, 1968). A convenient summary of Schweitzer's views is *My Life and Thought: An Autobiography* (London: George Allen and Unwin, 1933).

[32] William Sanday, *The Life of Christ in Recent Research* (Oxford: Clarendon Press, 1907).

or anywhere in Oxford University; he had had to turn to Cambridge, from where F. C. Burkitt had provided him with a copy.[33]

In 1909 Burkitt himself contributed the chapter 'The Eschatological Idea in the Gospel' to a symposium on current biblical research,[34] and the following year he provided a preface to Albert Schweitzer's epochal work when it was translated as *The Quest of the Historical Jesus*. Burkitt grasped that 'the central idea of the Gospel, that for which the Gospel may be said to exist, [is] the idea of the Kingdom of God.'[35] Unless we understand the idea of the kingdom in the Synoptic Gospels, he claimed, we will not understand the gospel of Jesus of Nazareth. While the Jewish idea of the kingdom was political and nationalistic – and the current, colloquial notion of the kingdom among English church people was merely of 'a good time coming', as he put it – Jesus transformed the idea of the kingdom in his time to demand repentance in the face of imminent judgement. From Weiss and Schweitzer, Burkitt advised, we may learn that apocalyptic, eschatological ideas pervade the Synoptic Gospels. The original gospel message was addressed to an unstable, turbulent age and therefore retains its validity, Burkitt interestingly implied, for the early twentieth century.

Jesus' eschatology included a crucial element of present realization

An audacious reversal of Weiss' theory was attempted by C. H. Dodd (1884–1973) with his theory of 'realised eschatology'. In *The Parables of the Kingdom* (1935; revised edition 1961), Dodd argued that the central text concerning Jesus' proclamation of the kingdom, Mk 1:14-15, should be translated, 'The kingdom of God has come.'[36] Dodd claimed that 'Jesus intended to proclaim the kingdom of God not as something to come in the near future, but as a matter of present experience.'[37] The kingdom was not merely imminent, but had actually arrived. Dodd even denied the apparently obvious future reference of Mk 9:1: 'Truly I tell you, there are some standing here who will not taste death until they see that the kingdom of God has come with power.'[38] In this provocative work, Dodd insisted that in the life and death of Jesus the kingdom of God had come and had come without remainder. There was no outstanding eschatological agenda remaining to be fulfilled. Christ would not 'come again'.[39]

Dodd's theory of 'realized eschatology' had in fact been anticipated by T. W. Manson (1893–1958) who attempted in *The Teaching of Jesus* (1931; second edition 1935) to thoroughly dehistoricize the notion of the kingdom of God. According to Manson, it

---

[33] Ibid., esp. pp. 44–61, 59.
[34] F. C. Burkitt, 'The Eschatological Idea in the Gospel', in H. B. Swete (ed.), *Essays on Some Biblical Questions of the Day* (London: Macmillan, 1909), pp. 193–213.
[35] Ibid., p. 201.
[36] C. H. Dodd, *The Parables of the Kingdom* (London: Nisbet, 1961), p. 29.
[37] Ibid., p. 31.
[38] Ibid., pp. 37ff.
[39] Dodd later came to regard the term 'realized eschatology' as 'not altogether felicitous' and as merely a useful label. He mentioned favourably the more nuanced expressions 'inaugurated eschatology' (ascribing it to Georges Florovsky) and Joachim Jeremias' 'sich realisierende Eschatologie', adding that he could not translate it into English (the usual translation is 'eschatology in the process of realization'): C. H. Dodd, *The Interpretation of the Fourth Gospel* (Cambridge: Cambridge University Press, 1953), p. 447, n. 1.

was misguided to ask whether the kingdom was present or future. It was essentially 'a personal relation between God and the individual'. The coming of the kingdom was a function of the spiritual relation adopted by individuals to 'the eternal sovereignty of God'. In his selfless dedication to God's cause, even unto death, Jesus could be seen as 'the incarnation of the kingdom of God on earth'.[40]

While Manson slightly anticipated the main thrust of Dodd's realized eschatology, Dodd was vigorously seconded by T. F. Glasson in *The Second Advent* (1945) who argued by remorseless special pleading that Jesus did not teach a futurist eschatology in any sense, though the evangelists, influenced by Pauline ideas (e.g. in 1 Thessalonians), interpreted him as so doing.[41] As far as Glasson was concerned, we had to discount both Paul and the evangelists in order to arrive at the original and authentic eschatology of the New Testament. When we did so we would find it to be an entirely realized eschatology.

Dodd had corrected a serious imbalance in the trajectory of eschatological interpretation initiated by Weiss and Schweitzer, but he had overstated his case. However, such sayings as Mt. 12:28 ('But if it is by the spirit of God that I cast out demons, then the kingdom of God has come to you') and Lk. 17:20f ('the kingdom of God is among you'), reinforced by the generally agreed realized nature of Johannine eschatology in the Fourth Gospel, secure the place of Dodd's contribution to our understanding of the overall pattern of the eschatology of the Gospels: it does contain a crucial 'realized' element.

The future and present aspects in Jesus' eschatology are dialectically related

W. G. Kümmel (1905–95), among others, attempted a position that mediated between the future (Weiss) and present (Dodd) aspects of the kingdom in the teaching of Jesus.[42] Kümmel noted that both aspects of the coming of the kingdom – future and present – were securely attested in the Gospels. He saw the two as held together in the idea that the arrival of the kingdom was neither remotely future nor wholly present, but imminent – and this too was solidly attested, he believed. For Kümmel, Jesus expected the kingdom soon, say within a lifetime, but not immediately. Kümmel ruled out both exclusively futurist and exclusively presentist interpretations. Unlike Dodd, Kümmel did not reinterpret the eschatological predictions of Jesus in the Gospels as referring to his resurrection and ascension, but frankly admitted that Jesus was mistaken about the imminence of the kingdom, pointing out that the New Testament writers appear not to have been troubled by this, happily including predictions that had been falsified by the passing of time. When he attempted to reinterpret the eschatology of Jesus and the Gospels for today, Kümmel effected what we might call a christological concentration

---

[40] T. W. Manson, *The Teaching of Jesus* (Cambridge: Cambridge University Press, 1935 [1931]), pp. 135, 140, 235.
[41] T. F. Glasson, *The Second Advent*, 3rd edn (London: Epworth Press, 1963 [1945]).
[42] W. G. Kümmel, *Promise and Fulfilment: The Eschatological Message of Jesus*, 2nd edn (London: SCM Press, 1961), p. 149.

of the kingdom. He discarded all other eschatological scenery and collapsed the kingdom into the person of Jesus. 'In Jesus the kingdom of God came into being and in him it will be consummated . . . the true meaning of Jesus' eschatological message is to be found in its reference to God's action in Jesus himself.'[43] This was to do significantly more than to affirm, as many would wish to do in company with Origen and Karl Barth, that Jesus was the kingdom in person – Origen's term *autobasilea*. It was in fact to say that Jesus was the embodiment of a kingdom with no further eschatological agenda. But that gambit, like Rudolf Bultmann's purely existentialist interpretation of the kingdom, set to one side a massive stratum of New Testament material. Kümmel's christological concentration of the kingdom, without any eschatological entailment, turns out to be a form of christological reductionism. A christological shape to the kingdom is absolutely imperative, but salvation history did not end in AD 33. Kümmel's interpretation of the New Testament was compromise, a half-way house. He attempted a mediating position between future-orientated and presently realized interpretations. He split the difference, locating the meeting point between present and future entirely in the earthly Jesus. The result was that the present and future aspects of the coming of the kingdom were not connected internally, dynamically and dialectically. That outcome was probably unavoidable given that the whole ecclesiological dimension – the church, the sacraments and the Holy Spirit – were not factored into the equation, as they certainly are in the Pauline epistles (as Kümmel hints in passing).[44]

A similar prevarication with regard to eschatology is found in E. P. Sanders' restorationist eschatology. Sanders believes that 'Jesus looked for the imminent direct intervention of God in history, the elimination of evil and evildoers, the building of a new and glorious temple, and the re-assembly of Israel with himself and his disciples as leading figures in it.'[45] He finds evidence in the Gospels of both present and future references, and if forced to choose, would put the emphasis on the kingdom as immediately future.[46] Sanders admits only that 'It is possible – no more – that Jesus saw the kingdom as "breaking in" with his own words and deeds.'[47] He does not believe that the present and future references to the kingdom refer to the same reality.[48] That is as far as Sanders believes the evidence allows him to go.

A more dialectical and theologically constructive understanding of New Testament eschatology was developed by Joachim Jeremias (1900–79). Jeremias affirmed that there was a determinative eschatological horizon of the whole New Testament. In this

---

[43] Ibid., p. 155. See also Kümmel, *The Theology of the New Testament*, trans. John E. Steely (London: SCM Press, 1974), pp. 32–9: 'one cannot deny, without doing violence to the texts, that Jesus anticipated a temporally very *near approach of the kingdom of God*' (p. 33, italics original). In 'Eschatological Expectation in the Proclamation of Jesus', in James M. Robinson (ed.), *The Future of our Religious Past: Essays in Honour of Rudolf Bultmann* (London: SCM Press, 1971 [1964]), chapter 2, Kümmel makes a close analysis of the relevant Gospel texts, in dialogue with a comprehensive range of recent scholarship. He concludes that Jesus expected the coming of the kingdom in a public and manifest way after a short temporal interlude and within the lifetime of his generation; that he was mistaken in this expectation and that the evangelists knew this and were untroubled by it.

[44] Kümmel, 'Eschatological Expectation in the Proclamation of Jesus', p. 48.

[45] E. P. Sanders, *Jesus and Judaism* (London: SCM Press, 1985), p. 153.

[46] Ibid., p. 152.

[47] Ibid., p. 140.

[48] Ibid., p. 155.

respect there was no difference between Jesus and the early church.[49] At the end of his study of the parables Jeremias mentions the expression: 'an eschatology in process of realisation [*sich realisierenden Eschatologie*]'.[50] This phrase points to the dynamic notion of an eschatology on its way, already impinging, beginning to unfold now, but with a future agenda still to be revealed in its fullness.

A further robust, comprehensive contribution to the debate, along the lines of *inaugurated eschatology*, was made by the Baptist scholar George Eldon Ladd (1911–82) in *The Presence of the Future* (1974).[51] Ladd's premise is the extremely risky one that, if Jesus had been deluded (let us say, less sensationally, 'mistaken') about the imminent arrival of the kingdom, his whole mission and authority would be discredited. But Ladd held that, if we rightly understand what 'the kingdom of God' (*basileia tou theou*) means, we will have no reason to attribute such delusion to Jesus. The kingdom is not a place or a state, he insists, but essentially the rule or reign of God. The concept of the kingdom includes both the active presence of God's reign here and now and the fuller manifestation of God's inherent universal kingship in the future. Hope for the present should not be divorced from hope for the future and vice versa: they go hand in hand in the prophetic writings – a single but complex hope. Eschatology and apocalyptic should be distinguished. Jesus repudiated the sort of apocalyptic speculation about times and seasons – the apocalyptic stage scenery – that was rife in first-century Palestine, so he would not have been interested in trying to fix a date for the *eschaton*. But his teaching and actions were essentially and thoroughly eschatological, that is to say that they had to do with the final, definitive manifestation of God's reign. The demand that Jesus made of those who heard him, like the message of the Hebrew prophets before him, was essentially ethical. It was a demand for obedient conformity to God's way and God's will in order to meet the coming hour – 'the ethical impact of the future upon the present'.[52] The *basileia* that Jesus announced was breaking in right now, in advance of the final consummation. Ladd's answer to the question, 'Did Jesus found the church?', is that those who responded to God's call in Jesus of Nazareth 'constituted neither a new Israel nor a separate synagogue nor a closed fellowship nor an organized church, but the believing remnant'.[53]

---

[49] Joachim Jeremias, *The Parables of Jesus*, trans. S. H. Hooke, rev. edn (London: SCM Press, 1963), pp. 51, 169 and *passim*. See also id., *New Testament Theology*, [2 vols] *Volume 1: The Proclamation of Jesus*, trans. John Bowden (London: SCM Press, 1971), pp. 96–100, 108, 131, 139 and *passim*.

[50] Jeremias, *The Parables of Jesus*, p. 229. Jeremias attributes the expression to a suggestion by Ernst Haenchen and notes rather archly that 'to my great joy' Dodd accepted it (p. 229, n. 3)

[51] George Eldon Ladd, *The Presence of the Future* (London: SPCK, 1974); this is a revised version of *Jesus and the Kingdom: The Eschatology of Biblical Realism* (London: SPCK, 1966 [1964]), which itself contains valuable material. John A. T. Robinson adopted the idea of *inauguration* in his 1957 work *Jesus and His Coming*, 2nd edn (London: SCM Press, 1979), p. 185. Rudolf Schnackenburg, *God's Rule and Kingdom*, trans. John Murray, 2nd edn (New York: Herder and Herder; London: Burns and Oates, 1968), also argued that the kingdom in the preaching of Jesus was neither entirely future, nor fully realized, but *inaugurated* (p. 350).

[52] Ladd, *The Presence of the Future*, p. 75.

[53] Ibid., p. 258.

Conclusion

To sum up this initial exploration of what modern critical scholarship has to say about the question of whether Jesus intended there to be a church to continue his ministry indefinitely, we may point with Rudolf Bultmann to two pivotal facts: (a) the core of Jesus' preaching was the kingdom or reign of God; (b) the reign of God is a thoroughly eschatological concept. The two ideas are combined in Mark's summary of Jesus' proclamation: 'The time is fulfilled; the reign of God is at hand' (Mk 1:15).[54] To simply say that, however, leaves open the question of whether the coming of the kingdom, in the New Testament, is to be understood as mainly future or as already present. I am persuaded that the most satisfactory interpretation of the evidence is along the lines sketched out by Jeremias, Ladd, Schnackenburg and Robinson, among others; that the coming of the kingdom has been inaugurated in the words and works of Jesus; and that, in him, it is in the process of being realized in history. It is probably not necessary to interject at this point that, of course, it is not the kingdom itself that is being inaugurated, but the *coming* of the kingdom. The kingdom or reign or sovereignty of God is an eternal and necessary, not a temporal and contingent, reality, though it is a reality that is waiting to be more fully manifested or realized in the creation through the carrying out in history of God's salvific purpose. It is also a thoroughly Old Testament concept, permeating the Hebrew Bible. Jesus and the apostles worked with what was a 'given' of the Jewish faith. They would not have been true prophets or messengers of God if they had not orientated their message to the kingdom of God but had somehow devised a new and strange language to describe God's interaction with the world.

So to those two basic points, drawn from Bultmann – the core of Jesus' preaching is the kingdom or reign of God and the reign of God is a thoroughly eschatological concept – we may add a third, crucial point. While the kingdom of God was made present in the person and the words and deeds of Jesus and filled his life and mission to overflowing, it was not restricted to Jesus' person and work there and then, nor exhausted by it. What is inaugurated continues in its trajectory; if a process of realization is begun, that process continues. How it might manifest itself and what form it might take is a question that we must postpone until we examine, in the second half of this study, how some major theologians from the principal Christians traditions, have attempted to answer that question. But for the moment we may reliably conclude that the eschatological horizon of the New Testament, as modern biblical scholarship understands it, prevents us from ascribing any overt intention on the part of the historical Jesus to found the Christian church as a coherent organization, institution or structured society that was set to continue indefinitely through time. This conclusion represents the full consensus of modern Gospel scholarship. I do not know of a single reputable academic New Testament specialist or systematic theologian in recent decades who has expressed a contrary view.

---

[54] Rudolf Bultmann, *Theology of the New Testament*, trans. Kendrick Grobel, 2 vols (London: SCM Press, 1952), vol. 1, pp. 4–5.

But that is not all that can be or should be said. The eschatological horizon of the Gospels does not preclude our attributing to Jesus what we might call a minimal ecclesial purpose for his followers after his death. Texts such as Lk. 12:35 ('Be dressed for action and have your lamps lit') and Mark 10:39 (where Jesus foretells that James and John will come to share his sufferings) suggest that (as Christopher Rowland puts it) at the very least 'Jesus did see a role for a community of his followers after his departure.'[55] The most that can be claimed, on the basis of the evidence, for Jesus' ecclesial intentions is stated by Rowland like this: 'He may have prepared for the existence of a sect within Judaism as a temporary measure during the short period before the kingdom of God came, by delegating his authority to preach and act on God's behalf to his followers.'[56] In short, 'Jesus' proclamation of the kingdom did not exclude a community.'[57] This sparse conclusion, stated negatively as it is, cannot in itself provide a basis for the developed ecclesiology of the Christian church, which as we shall see, must be constructed on other, more oblique and sophisticated grounds than a direct appeal to the overt intentions of the historical Jesus, as far as they can be inferred from the documents. However, although it does not place a decisive veto against all forms of developed ecclesiology, our conclusion at this point certainly rules out some of the bolder traditional claims of the churches for their particular forms of ecclesiastical polity, whether papal, episcopal, Presbyterian or congregational.

In particular, the eschatological framework and foreshortened time span of the New Testament, as it has been brought to light during the past century and more, completely undermines the traditional forms of Roman Catholic apologetic that traced the monarchical papacy and the hierarchical structures of church government back to direct institution by Christ. The decree *Lamentabili*, published by the Holy Office in 1907, condemned certain views which it attributed to the 'modernists' within the Roman Catholic Church. Among the views that were explicitly condemned were that Jesus expected the imminent arrival of the kingdom and that he did not intend to establish a church with 'dogmas, sacraments and hierarchy'. The decree also condemned the view that 'It was far from the mind of Christ to establish the Church as a society that would last on earth for a long succession of centuries; in fact, in the mind of Christ the kingdom of heaven together with the end of the world was imminent.'[58] It is still the official teaching of the Roman Catholic Church that Jesus appointed an apostolic college with Peter at its head and intended him to hand on the power of the keys to his successors, the popes.[59] As Avery Dulles points out, 'The Catholic Church repeatedly

---

[55] Christopher Rowland, *Christian Origins: An Account of the Setting and Character of the Most Important Messianic Sect of Judaism* (London: SPCK, 1985), p. 152; see also id., *The Open Heaven: A Study of Apocalyptic in Judaism and Early Christianity* (London: SPCK, 1982).

[56] Rowland, *Christian Origins*, p. 153.

[57] Ibid.

[58] J. Neuner, S. J. and J. Dupuis, S. J. (eds), *The Christian Faith in the Doctrinal Documents of the Catholic Church*, rev. edn (London: Collins, 1983), p. 236; cf. H. Denzinger and A. Schönmetzer, S. J. (eds), *Enchiridion Symbolorum: Definitionum et Declarationum de Rebus Fidei et Morum*, 22nd edn (Freiburg im Breisgau: Herder, 1963), p. 672 (§2052/3452).

[59] See, e.g. *Catechism of the Catholic Church* (London: Geoffrey Chapman, 1994), nos 765, 880.

affirms that its doctrinal, sacramental and governmental structures are founded in divine revelation.'[60]

The eschatological horizon also has adverse implications for some other forms of appeal to direct dominical institution in support of specific structures of the church. The classical Catholic notion of apostolic succession which postulates an uninterrupted sequence of manual ordinations going back to the apostles, who were (on this view) intended by Jesus to be the first bishops and to endow all their successors with apostolic authority, is a case in point. We can affirm that, while the eschatological horizon of Jesus' ministry certainly did not preclude his appointing leaders of the eschatological community, it does seem to rule out any explicit intention, on his part, of initiating a sacramental line of continuity through the ages. The principle of the orderly transmission of authority is vital for the continuity and consistency of the church and can be amply supported from practice and precept in the New Testament. But the notion that the visible succession of ordinations is the only dominically approved form of transmitted authority is undermined by the eschatological context of the mission of Jesus and of the apostles, which presupposed a foreshortening of history, an impending, transforming, interruption of the historical process.

A more dynamic understanding of apostolicity is called for in response to the eschatological ecclesiology of the New Testament. The World Council of Churches' Faith and Order Commission's Lima Statement *Baptism, Eucharist and Ministry* provides such an understanding when it defines apostolicity in a holistic way as 'continuity in all the permanent characteristics of the Church of the apostles'. Then these 'permanent characteristics' are identified as 'witness to the apostolic faith, proclamation and fresh interpretation of the Gospel, celebration of baptism and the eucharist [*sic*], the transmission of ministerial responsibilities, communion in prayer, love, joy and suffering, service to the sick and needy, unity among the local churches and sharing the gifts which the Lord has given to each'.[61] What is striking about this definition is that the marks of the eschatological community in the New Testament are seen to be the abiding characteristics of the Christian church at all times. They properly belong to the essential apostolicity of the church, as it is confessed in the creed, because the ecclesiological concept of apostolicity holds together the church's original apostolic foundation and its ongoing mission, infused with the message and spirit of the apostles.

If some aspects of the traditional Roman Catholic (and Anglo-Catholic) ecclesiology are called into question by the eschatological thrust of the New Testament, other more sophisticated justifications, falling short of claiming divine right (*ius divinum*) for the Roman primacy and the historic episcopate, are not affected to the same extent. One such *apologia* is that advanced in the *Final Report* of the Anglican – Roman Catholic International Commission (ARCIC 1), which deploys John Henry Newman's principle of the development of doctrine. ARCIC's approach sees the traditional structures of Catholicism, especially the episcopate and the primacy of the Bishop of Rome, as emerging under the guiding hand of providence from their implicit origins in the New

---

[60]   Avery Dulles, *Models of the Church* (New York: Doubleday, 1974), p. 39.
[61]   *Baptism, Eucharist and Ministry* (Geneva: World Council of Churches, 1982), M34.

Testament church.[62] Another approach, one that is not as vulnerable to the eschatological veto, can be gleaned from the Protestant Reformers and Karl Barth, on the one hand, and the Russian Orthodox theologians in exile and some Roman Catholic theologians of the Vatican II era, especially Henri de Lubac, on the other. In their different ways, these sources have much to offer in terms of a more pneumatological and kerygmatic ecclesiology, because they see the church constituted dynamically through word and sacrament in every Eucharistic community.

A viable response to the blanket eschatological veto on some inherited claims and counterclaims is to recognize that the eschatological horizon of the New Testament, far from inhibiting all intimations of ecclesiology deriving from Jesus himself, actually demands it, or at least demands a particular form of it. Biblical eschatology (taking the inter-testamental period into account also) included a concept of the church as the messianic community of the last days: the gathered elect, the faithful remnant. As Schnackenburg insists, the kingship or reign of God in Scripture always presupposes a community, for it is God's purpose to fashion a people for himself.[63] The gathered community, however small and weak, stands as a testimony and a witness to God's unchanging purpose in history, God's reign.

Jesus did not attempt to organize any kind of institutional church. Clearly, that was of no interest or concern to him. The form of the community called into existence by God was already given in the nation of Israel to which Jesus belonged. He consecrated himself to a cause, to a divine purpose that already existed – that of the kingdom or reign of God.[64] The kingship of God was the driving power behind Israel's destiny and would generate the continuing community of the true Israel. The forms that did emerge in the New Testament church were crystallizations of what the early Christian communities believed that Jesus himself had said, done or commanded, namely, proclaiming the good news and teaching the word of God; administering baptism and the laying on of hands; celebrating the Lord's Supper; and caring for the community's vulnerable members, the widows, the poor and the sick.

While Jeremias, needless to say, accepts the eschatological framework of the Synoptic Gospels and acknowledges that Jesus in no way envisaged the church in the form that emerged in history, he warns that we should not be misled about Jesus' intentions by the dearth of technical terms, such as *ekklēsia*, in the Gospels. He stresses Jesus' clear intention to form a body of disciples and to gather 'the community of salvation', just as, immediately before him, the mysterious Teacher of Righteousness had gathered the Essene community at Qumran – a community of religious and moral perfection – and John the Baptist had summoned the people to the River Jordan and urged them to repentance and a changed life, to be signified by baptism.[65] Jesus constantly speaks, in a variety of pictures, images and parables, of a community of his followers, notably of the flock and the shepherd or of the gathering of the people of God. Jeremias does not believe that the expectation of the imminent end of the age calls this intention of

[62] Anglican – Roman Catholic International Commission [ARCIC], *The Final Report* (London: CTS & SPCK, 1982).
[63] Schnackenburg, *God's Rule and Kingdom*, p. 351.
[64] Paul D. Hanson, *The People Called: The Growth of Community in the Bible*, with new intro. (Louisville, KY and London: Westminster John Knox Press, 2001 [1986]), p. 428.
[65] Jeremias, *New Testament Theology*, vol. 1, pp. 167–78.

Jesus into question at all. It was precisely because Jesus believed the end to be near that he purposed to gather God's people for salvation. Indeed, according to Jeremias, 'the *only* significance of the whole of Jesus' activity is to gather the eschatological people of God.'[66] The great difference between the purpose of Jesus and the purposes of the Pharisees and the Essenes is that, while theirs were exclusive communities of initiates, of devotees, of those who had proved themselves worthy to belong, Jesus called and gathered 'sinners' into God's fold, manifestly imperfect, compromised and marginalized people. The theme of the Lord stepping in to gather together once again his scattered flock runs through much of the Hebrew Bible and the inter-testamental literature and is a marked feature of Jesus' ministry. It seems clear that he saw himself as fulfilling the prophetic promises that refer to the gathering of God's people in the end time. 'How often would I have gathered your children together . . . and you would not' (Lk. 13:34).[67] The only conditions for entry into his fellowship were repentance before God and faith in him, leading to discipleship. Critically, Jesus did not require his followers to separate from unworthy outsiders – quite the reverse: he entered their homes and shared their meals. His rejection of the type of community rationale that marked the Pharisees and the Essenes was, again and again, found 'offensive, provocative and disturbing.'[68]

In surveying the New Testament material, I am haunted by Alfred Loisy's dictum that Jesus announced the kingdom, and it was the church that came. While Jesus looked for the reign of God in a new age, where human beings would be as the angels in heaven, loosed from carnal and earthly ties, the movement that emerged after his death and resurrection consisted of a miscellaneous collection of men and women who were patently mortal, sinful, and implicated in the ways and means of the world, whose common life was significantly determined by social and political factors and developed in a bewildering diversity of ways, often in contradiction and conflict one with another. As we have already noted, this observation is incompatible with any simplistic appeal to a God-given pattern and polity for the church and its structures, whether papal, Presbyterian, congregational or episcopalian. It should elicit some theological humility and caution, some epistemological uncertainty in the claims we make for our own brand of the church. But ecclesiastical polity is merely the tip of the iceberg of the uncertainties that historical-critical study of the Bible throws up with regard to the church. Later in this study we will effect a transition from a mainly historical to a mainly theological approach, as we review some of the ways in which some significant modern theologians of the major Christian traditions have responded to the questions and dilemmas raised for ecclesiology by the scholarly study of the New Testament, including its eschatological framework. But first we must look at some of the ways in which the relationship between Jesus and the church – which lies at the heart of our enquiry – is presented in the New Testament documents. While these are unquestionably 'historical' sources, they are in truth no less 'theological', no less expressions of creative theological interpretation, than the writings of modern theologians that we will be examining in the second half of the book.

---

[66] Ibid., p. 170.
[67] See also Pss. 106:47; 147:2 (The Lord . . . gathers the outcasts of Israel'); Isa. 27:12; 52:12 (LXX) ('he who gathers you'); 56:7; 60:4-9 ('gather your children'); Jer. 31:8ff (cf. 25.4ff); Zech. 2:6ff (LXX); 2 Macc. 1:27; 2:18.
[68] Jeremias, *New Testament Theology*, vol. 1, p. 177.

3

Biblical speech about the church

The subject of this chapter and of the next one is the various ways in which the Bible speaks about the church, with a special focus on the language of the New Testament. Our enquiry is accompanied by an ongoing interest in asking whether – and if so how – this biblical language, these canonical concepts, go back to Jesus himself and how they might relate to him as the possible founder or foundation of the church. In the present chapter we look at three key biblical terms for the Christian community: *ekklēsia* (assembly) and *koinōnía* (fellowship, communion) and their relation to the kingdom (*basileia*) of God. Finally, we will consider what I call 'the subtle grammar' that the New Testament writers employ when speaking of this community somewhat obliquely. These are the terms and constructions – even tiny prepositions – that do not shout 'church', but which on closer inspection turn out to be ecclesiologically extremely rich, even pivotal.

In these enquiries we are on the trail of the corporate identity of the Christian community as the New Testament depicts it and its connection – weak or strong as the case may be – with Jesus of Nazareth who is called the Christ. We will explore the theology behind the phenomenon of the community of disciples in the Gospels, the Epistles and the Acts of the Apostles. But we will draw on the Old Testament (Hebrew Bible) background as we do so. For there is a church in the Old Testament, as well as a church in the New Testament; a church of the nation of Israel (for Israel was an ecclesial nation, a nation-church, a theocracy), as well as a church of Christ. I think it is important to put down a major marker about this straight away, or we may seriously misunderstand biblical salvation history.

The church before the church

The church – the community of God's people – did not begin with Jesus because *salvation history* did not begin with Jesus. Paul Minear writes: 'The early Christians did not date the beginning of God's people from Jesus' birth or ministry, from his Eucharistic feast or resurrection, or even from the descent of the Spirit at Pentecost, but from the covenant-making activity of God in the times of Abraham and Moses.'[1]

---

[1] Paul S. Minear, *Images of the Church in the New Testament* (London: Lutterworth Press, 1960), pp. 70–1.

And although both the Old Testament and the New Testament sometimes speak of a 'new covenant' (Jer. 31:31; 1 Cor. 11:25; Heb. 8:13; 9.1), in truth it is a *renewed* covenant that is meant. There is but one biblical covenant – one essential, critical relationship based on divine promise, between God and God's people – though it receives several expressions, instantiations or (one might guardedly say) dispensations. By the same token there is one Israel of God, not an old Israel and a new Israel. Israel is renewed, reformed and restored in the church of Jesus Christ (Gal. 6:15-16; Eph. 2:20; Heb. 11:25-26). Christians are the children and descendants of the Abraham with whom Yahweh made a covenant (Rom. 4:16; Gal. 3:29). As Minear points out, 'The analogy between the church and Israel . . . became a method of coordinating two stories, not two entities.'[2] In order to understand the church we must reckon with, so to speak, *the church before the church*. This step is impossible to avoid, because, as we shall see repeatedly, the Bible uses the same language of Israel as it does of the church. To put it another way, the New Testament applies the language of the Hebrew Bible about the nation of Israel to the Christian community. In the next chapter, we will turn to some of these key biblical images, drawn initially from the Old Testament, but fulfilled and elaborated in the light of the Christ event in the New. These images tend to reappear in later periods of church history and ecclesiological renewal. Two salient examples are Martin Luther's deployment of the priestly language of the Bible to refer to the whole Christian body, 'the general priesthood', and the Second Vatican Council's use of the images of 'people of God' and 'body of Christ' and the subsequent – and ongoing – fierce debates within the Roman Catholic Church about the relative priority of these two images. So it is important to register their methodological significance and to take them fully on board now. They are packed with import about how St Paul and other New Testament writers understood the connection between Jesus and the church. But first, in the present chapter, we begin to consider some key aspects of the biblical language of 'church', beginning with our most used or 'default' term for the Christian community: church (*ekklēsia*).

Ekklēsia: The default language of church

If we look for explicit mentions of 'church' (Greek *ekklēsia*) in the four canonical Gospels, we will find very few. But what we do find in abundance are various other ways of speaking about or portraying the community of disciples that Jesus of Nazareth gathered around him; the historical nucleus of the church that bears the name of Jesus Christ; and the church that would come into being as a result of the passion, death and resurrection of Jesus, followed by the outpouring of the Holy Spirit at Pentecost. When we come to the Epistles, there is no shortage of mentions of 'church' (*ekklēsia*), but that term by no means exhausts the ecclesiology of the Pauline or other letters, as we shall see. In the Acts of the Apostles we have not so much a theology of the church as the

---

[2]   Ibid., p. 77.

language of church revealed in action.[3] Both the sparse mentions in one Gospel and the numerous instances in the Epistles are all too often understood anachronistically, by assimilation to later concepts and expressions of the Christian church.

'Church' is our normal, default, everyday word for the company of Christian believers or worshippers, gathered in community. We tend to use the word 'church' unreflectingly and indiscriminately in different senses, as when we say: 'I'm going to church'; 'I enjoyed church this morning'; 'We are church!'; 'I believe in one holy, catholic and apostolic church'; perhaps even, sometimes, 'The church makes me sick!' In the light of our English language common usage, it is significant that 'church' (Greek ἐκκλησία, *ekklēsia*) is also the Apostle Paul's most favoured word for the Christian community. As J. D. G. Dunn puts it, '"church" is the term with which Paul most regularly conceptualized the corporate identity of those converted in the Gentile mission.'[4] But we should be wary of filling Paul's term *ekklēsia* with modern content.

There are in fact two separate tributaries to the English-language use of the word 'church'. The English-language word for the local church building comes from the Greek *kyriake*, belonging to the Lord (*kyrios*), the Lord's possession; so coming to refer to the Lord's house, the church building (cf. the Scots, 'kirk', which can refer to the building or the institution). But the more theological term, beginning with the stem 'eccles-', that we have in more technical words – 'ecclesiastical', 'ecclesiological', 'ecclesial', and so on – comes from the Greek *ekklēsia*, via the Latin *ecclesia*, and this has a Hebrew background.[5]

The Greek *ekklēsia* is a secular term for an assembly of people and goes back to the city state of ancient Athens. It is not, in origin, a religious word. It is derived from the verb to call. *Ekklēsia* was used by the translators of the Hebrew Bible (Christian Old Testament) into Greek (the Septuagint, LXX) to translate the Hebrew *qāhāl*, assembly, which in turn derives from the Hebrew for voice (*qol*). *Qāhāl* is used for the gathering of the Israelites at Sinai and on subsequent occasions (Deut. 4:10; 31:30ff; Josh. 24:1-28). The LXX does not always use *ekklēsia* to translate *qāhāl*; sometimes it uses συναγωγή, *synagōgē*. These two Greek translations of the Hebrew *qāhāl* are sometimes used interchangeably. In each of the two main biblical languages, then, the community is understood as the assembly of those who are called.

In the Old Testament the emphasis falls on being called by God to come together as God's people and to worship and serve him. The 'assembly of Yahweh' is called together

---

[3]   General studies of New Testament ecclesiology (in English) include Hans Küng, *The Church*, trans. Ray and Rosaleen Ockenden (London: Search Press, 1971 [1968]); Robert Banks, *Paul's Idea of Community*, rev. edn (Peabody, MA: Hendrikson, 1994 [1979]); the relevant chapters of Richard N. Longnecker (ed.), *Community Formation in the Early Church and Today* (Grand Rapids, MI: Baker Academic, 2002).

[4]   James D. G. Dunn, *The Theology of Paul the Apostle* (London and New York: T&T Clark, 1998), p. 537.

[5]   See K. L. Schmidt, in *TDNT*, vol. 3, pp. 501–36; J. Y. Campbell, *Three New Testament Studies* (Leiden: Brill, 1965), chapter 3 (Campbell disputes the scholarly consensus that Paul's use of *ekklēsia* is based on the LXX; in origin, according to Campbell, the term simply referred to a Christian meeting); M. Bockmuehl and M. B. Thompson (eds), *A Vision for the Church: Studies in Early Christian Ecclesiology in Honour of J. P. M. Sweet* (Edinburgh: T&T Clark, 1997), esp. chapter 4, 'Luke's Vision for the Church'; Longnecker (ed.), *Community Formation in the Early Church and Today*, chapter 5 (by Longnecker).

by God into covenant, so that God's presence may dwell in the midst of the assembly and that the people may hear and receive God's word, spoken through Moses or other prophets. The assembly's proceedings conclude with sacrifice, sealing the communion of the people with God and their obedient covenantal devotion to him.

Some interpreters – mainly preachers, I suspect – suggest that *ekklēsia* in the New Testament has the sense of being 'called out', that is, out of the world. But the consensus of modern scholarship casts doubt on this emphasis; it suggests in fact that there is no real justification for interpreting *ekklēsia* in the New Testament in that sense. Rather – and this is certainly a major theme of both Testaments – God's people are called together into God's presence to worship God and in order that they might be empowered and equipped to be sent out to witness to God's truth in the world. This thought is encapsulated in the words of Mk (3:13-15): 'He [Jesus] went up the mountain and called to him those whom he wanted, and they came to him. And he appointed twelve, whom he also named apostles, to be with him, and to be sent out to proclaim the message, and to have authority to cast out demons.'

Paul uses *ekklēsia* (church) and *ekklētois* (the called ones) almost synonymously and in the same breath: 'Paul . . . to the church of God that is in Corinth . . . called to be saints' (*klētoi hagioi*, 1 Cor. 1:1-2; cf. v. 24, *tois klētois*). 'The called' (*hē klēsis*), as a collective noun, is a common early designation for the church. As Gregory Dix comments, to call the church 'the called', 'places the whole emphasis on the Divine constitution, not the human aggregation, of the Christian Society'.[6]

In the New Testament, the thought underlying the use of *ekklēsia*, post-resurrection and post-Pentecost, is perhaps on being called together into the presence of the risen Christ to rehearse what God had done through him and to break bread and share of the cup of new covenant and then to be sent out into the world in discipleship and witness. So the Christian concept of *ekklēsia* distinctly echoes and fulfils the Old Testament motif of the covenantal gathering of Israel. The church is made up of those who have heard the call of Christ in the gospel and have responded to it through the grace of the Holy Spirit. The church, wrote de Lubac, 'is a *convocatio* before being a *congregatio*'.[7]

However, *ekklēsia* is not, in its origin, a technical theological term. It was borrowed from civic use in the Greek-speaking world, usage which was normally structured and orderly, and Paul adapted it to apply to his Gentile congregations. It was, as Park stresses, a serious and honourable institution in the minds of Paul's contemporaries.[8] They now become 'the *ekklēsia* of God', meaning not of some other power (1 Cor. 1:1;

---

[6] Gregory Dix, *Jurisdiction in the Early Church, Episcopal and Papal*, intro. T. M. Parker (London: Church Literature Association, 1975 [1938]), p. 11, n. 2.

[7] Henri de Lubac, *Catholicism: A Study of Dogma in Relation to the Corporate Destiny of Mankind*, trans. Lancelot C. Sheppard (London: Burns, Oates & Washbourne, 1950), p. 24.

[8] Young-Ho Park, *Paul's Ekklesia as a Civic Assembly* (Tübingen: Mohr Siebeck, 2015); David G. Horrell, *Solidarity and Difference: A Contemporary Reading of Paul's Ethics* (London: T&T Clark, 2005); id., *Becoming Christian: Essays on 1 Peter and the Making of Christian Identity* (London and New York: Bloomsbury T&T Clark, 2015); Bruce Hansen, *All of You Are One: The Social Vision of Galatians 3.28, 1 Corinthians 12.13 and Colossians 3.11* (London and New York: T&T Clark, 2010); Paul Trebilco, 'Why did the Early Christians Call themselves ἡ ἐκκλησία?', *NTS* 57, no. 3 (2011), pp. 440–60; George H. van Kooten, 'Ἐκκλησία τοῦ θεοῦ: The "Church of God" and the Civic Assemblies (ἐκκλησίαι) of the Greek Cities in the Roman Empire: A Response to Paul Trebilco and Richard A. Horsley', *NTS* 58, no. 4 (2012), pp. 522–48; Ralph J. Korner, *The Origin and Meaning of* Ekklēsia in

15:9; 2 Cor. 1:1; Gal. 1:1, 13; etc.), though (contrary to some suggestions) its application was not intended to be politically subversive. *Ekklēsia* in the New Testament retains basic functional connotations, but acquires ontological significance in the process of theological development, particularly on account of the need for the early Christian communities to undergo an urgent process of identity formation, to be formed and shaped as distinctive social entities in the polyglot Roman Empire, to assume a unique social profile and to distinguish themselves from the hostile synagogue (*synagōgē*) in the Jewish diaspora. The secular Greek and the LXX meanings came together, and this conjunction of meanings suited early Christian writers because they wanted to avoid any possible pagan, cultic overtones when they spoke of their meeting together. It is interesting that 1 Peter, which contains one of the richest ecclesiological passages in the New Testament (1 Pet. 2:1-12), does not use *ekklēsia*. Here the church is a temple, a race, a priesthood, a nation, a people, but it is not designated as an assembly. Is this perhaps because the author of 1 Peter wanted to play up the continuities between the Christian community and Israel's role in salvation history (as the imagery certainly suggests), but also to play down the continuities or similarities, the common ground, with 'secular', or rather civil life in the Roman Empire with its constituent assemblies, lifting up the Christian community as a distinctive, alternative, counter-institution, to the institutions of the world?[9]

The transition in the meaning of *ekklēsia* from 'assembly of citizens' to 'church' in the theological sense clearly occurs within the New Testament. Surprisingly, the word *ekklēsia* is found in only one of the Four Gospels – Matthew, where it is used three times in two passages. Matthew did not invent the usage; as Gundry points out, *ekklēsia* 'had long been in use among Christians by the time Matthew wrote'.[10] *Ekklēsia* occurs twice in one verse where it clearly means simply 'assembly', that is, of Christians (Mt. 18:17). But the other instance (Mt. 16:18) has a wider, more expansive, sense: 'You are Peter (*petros*) and on this rock (*petra*) I will build my church (*ekklēsia*).' Most scholars (not only Protestant ones) do not believe that the equivalent of this saying in the original Aramaic (where the two words for rock would have been the same) can be attributed directly to Jesus. The concept 'church' (*ekklēsia*) seems to be too advanced in terms of ecclesiological development, to be found on the lips of Jesus. For such scholars, the saying therefore invites the suspicion that it is a retrospective legitimation for the leading role of Peter in at least part of the apostolic church. In 1991 the doyen of Matthean studies, Ulrich Luz, noted that an ecumenical scholarly consensus existed that regarded Jesus' designation of Peter as the rock as belonging to the post-Easter period.[11] On the other hand, Gundry believes that the whole saying (vv. 18–19)

the Early Jesus Movement (Leiden: Brill, 2017): a comprehensive analysis of Greek, Jewish, Imperial and epigraphical sources.
[9] Cf. Reinhard Feldmeier, *The First Letter of Peter: A Commentary on the Greek Text*, trans. Peter H. Davids (Waco, TX: Baylor University Press, 2008), p. 140, n. 4.
[10] Robert H. Gundry, *Matthew: A Commentary on His Handbook for a Mixed Church under Persecution*, 2nd edn (Grand Rapids, MI: Eerdmans, 1994 [1982]), p. 332.
[11] Raymond E. Brown, Karl P. Donfried and John Reumann (eds), *Peter in the New Testament: A Collaborative Assessment by Protestant and Roman Catholic Scholars* (Minneapolis, MN: Augsburg Publishing House and Paramus, NJ: Paulist Press, 1973; London and Dublin: Geoffrey Chapman, 1974); Ulrich Luz, 'The Primacy Saying of Matthew 16.17-19 from the Perspective of Its Effective

originated, in Greek, with Matthew and is a blend of editorial creation and borrowing from elsewhere in his Gospel. So, according to Gundry, there is no need either to delve for possible Aramaic originals or to ask whether Jesus spoke about the church at this point. Gundry also holds that Jesus is not referring to Peter, but to his own teaching or law, when he invokes the 'rock'.[12] However, I am tentatively persuaded by (a) Oscar Cullmann's demonstration of the Old Testament and Aramaic semantic background to this saying and (b) W. D. Davies' and Dale C. Allison's argument from partial parallels in the New Testament (including Mk 3:16 and Jn 1:42; 20:23) to Jesus' designation of Peter as the rock, that there is a scope to hold tentatively that the saying is based on a genuine dominical pronouncement (in Aramaic, of course).[13]

If, with all four of the evangelists, we attribute to Jesus the possession of a messianic consciousness in some form, the calling and gathering by him of a messianic community automatically follows because this task was intrinsic to the role and work of the Messiah as understood in Jewish thought of the time. The way that the *ekklēsia* is introduced into the narrative at Mt. 16:18-19 shows the connection being made by the evangelist between Messiah and community. The whole passage in question (Mt. 16:13-20) is framed by Peter's confession of Jesus as Messiah at one end and Jesus' stern injunction to the disciples not to tell anyone that he is the Messiah, at the other end, with *ekklēsia* in the middle. The Messiah and his community are inseparable: no community, no Messiah.

Whether spoken by Jesus or not, the original meaning of this verse in Matthew must have been something like, 'on this rock [Peter as confessor of Jesus' Messiahship] I will gather and secure my community of disciples'. The sense of Jesus' original saying might have been along the lines of the 'little flock' of Lk. 12:32, taken against the background of all the shepherd and flock imagery of both Testaments with its motifs of calling and gathering, which has then undergone development via the Hebrew *quāhāl* (again calling and gathering) in the early tradition into something that sounds to our ears rather more solidly institutional, the *ekklēsia*. However, we should not read back modern perceptions and experiences of the institutional church into the biblical context where *ekklēsia* still means those called together into an assembly or congregation. There are no grounds here for deducing that, when Jesus stated that he would build his *ekklēsia*, he intended to construct any kind of enduring institutional edifice. So, particularly in view of the pronounced eschatological horizon of the Synoptic Gospels in particular and of the New Testament in general, this Matthean text should not be taken to mean (as Barrett puts it) that 'the church will stand unharmed while age after

---

History', in id., *Studies in Matthew*, trans. Rosemary Selle (Grand Rapids, MI: Eerdmans, 1991), chapter 9, pp. 165–82, at p. 165. So too Eduard Schweizer, *A Theological Introduction to the New Testament*, trans. O. C. Dean, Jr. (London: SPCK, 1992), p. 18: Matthew 18.17 is 'almost certainly projected back from the time after Easter'. In the present work, I am not interested in discussing the possible papal connotations of this text, either exegetically or historically.
[12] Gundry, *Matthew*, pp. 328–37.
[13] Oscar Cullmann, *Peter: Disciple, Apostle, Martyr*, trans. Floyd V. Filson, 2nd edn (London: SCM Press, 1962), pp. 164–217, esp. 192–204; W. D. Davies and D. C. Allison, *Matthew 8-18*, ICC (London and New York: T&T Clark, 1991), pp. 602–30, at pp. 603, 605.

age of secular history is unrolled', but rather that 'the eschatological community will weather the storms of the last days, the last desperate attacks of evil before the End.'[14]

Moreover, the leading role of Peter in the early Christian community's understanding of salvation history is well established on the basis of many other references in the Gospels and would not be affected even if Mt. 16:18 had never been written. In the Synoptics, Peter is the first to be called and first to be (re-)named of the disciples. Matthew's ecclesiology in particular among the Gospels is grounded in Christology and salvation history, within which Peter has a key role. The church that Christ will build on this rock is a messianic (christological) community that will inevitably contain some institutional features.[15] Similarly, Barnabas Lindars concludes, in the light of a close analysis of the Old and New Testament sources that lie behind this saying in Matthew, that the rock symbolism here is 'not so much a matter of belief or unbelief in Jesus the Messiah [as elsewhere] as of adherence or opposition to the true congregation of the people of Israel'. The text has to do with 'the formulation of the doctrine of the Church' and of 'developing ecclesiastical institutions' in Matthew's day.[16]

The Anglican scholar Alan Richardson, interpreting Mt. 16:18 and influenced by Cullmann, sees no reason to doubt the authenticity of Jesus designating Peter as the rock on which he would build his *ekklēsia*, mainly on the grounds of the role given to Peter elsewhere in the Gospels. Richardson states: 'We must conclude that Jesus intended to "found" the Church', but he immediately adds that, in modern terms, the expression 'founder' is inadequate because of its connotations of 'founding' a charitable organization or a religious society. He therefore explains that Christ 'is not so much the "Founder" of the Church as he *is* himself the Church, since the Church is . . . the body of those who have been incorporated into the *persona* of Christ, *totus Christus . . .*' The church came into being, Richardson believes, with the outpouring of the Holy Spirit upon the disciples by the risen, ascended Lord; the church is the resurrection body of Christ.[17]

In the Epistles and the Acts of the Apostles, *ekklēsia* occurs frequently. The earliest use, known to us, of *ekklēsia*, to stand for the Christian community, occurs in Paul's First Epistle to the Thessalonians (1:1), which is in fact the earliest extant Christian document: 'Paul, Silvanus, and Timothy, to the church (*ekklēsia*) of the Thessalonians in God the Father and the Lord Jesus Christ: grace to you and peace.' We may note three significant facts about this statement. First, it seems that Paul applies the term 'church' to the Christians of Thessalonika in a rather routine way; he avoids the risk of shocking them by throwing a theological bombshell in his first sentence. No doubt they were familiar with this theological construction from Paul's teaching on his missionary visit, which had taken place sometime beforehand (2:1). It appears that the application

---

[14] C. K. Barrett, *Church, Ministry and Sacraments in the New Testament* (Exeter: Paternoster Press, 1985), p. 17. Davies and Allison, *Matthew 8-18*, pp. 630–34, support this view.

[15] Charles E. Carlston and Craig A. Evans, *From Synagogue to Ecclesia: Matthew's Community at the Crossroads* (Tübingen: Mohr Siebeck, 2014), pp. 315–25.

[16] Barnabas Lindars, *New Testament Apologetic: The Doctrinal Significance of Old Testament Quotations* (London: SCM Press, 1961), pp. 175–86, at pp. 182–3.

[17] Alan Richardson, *An Introduction to the Theology of the New Testament* (London: SCM Press, 1958), pp. 307–11.

of *ekklēsia* to the Christian community was already taken for granted before AD 50, the probable date of the epistle. Secondly, we may notice that Paul slightly adapts the Old Testament (LXX) expression *ekklēsia tou kuriou* (assembly of the Lord), so that it becomes 'the assembly in God the Father', where we understand 'the Father of our Lord Jesus Christ', as well as the Father of all God's children. The Christ event is the decisive new factor in the Jewish Christians' relationship to the God of Israel. Thirdly, as already implied, a critical new dimension is added to this Old Testament concept by the words, 'and [in] the Lord Jesus Christ'. Paul uses 'Father', rather than 'Lord', partly because Jesus Christ is now 'Lord' (*kurios*). He has a theologically critical position alongside the Father. The reality of being the church for these Jewish Christians is now christologically determined.

Three major ways in which *ekklēsia* is deployed in the Epistles and the Acts can be discerned, in addition to its secular uses (e.g. Acts 19:32, 39, 41) and its application to the people of Israel in the desert (Acts 7:38, where *ekklēsia* is translated 'congregation' in the NRSV and 'assembly' in the REB).

1. First, *ekklēsia* refers to the local Christian assembly, namely a single gathering 'in church' (as Paul puts it in 1 Cor. 14:35 NRSV) or multiple gatherings: 'All the churches of Christ greet you' (Rom. 16:16). This use is clearly closest to the literal sense of the word. This local church may be in a city, such as Rome, Corinth or Philippi, or it may be in a house, such as Nympha's (Col. 4:15; cf. Rom. 16:5; 1 Cor. 16:19; Phlm. 2). Probably, a 'city church' was made up of a number of house churches (*oikoi*). Paul speaks of 'the whole church' 'coming together' for worship, which meant charismatic worship, though it probably also included the Lord's Supper or *Agape* (Love Feast) and Paul gave strict instructions for the order and structure of its celebration in Corinth (1 Cor. 11:20-34). Similarly, 'churches' (in the plural) sometimes refers to the several Christian communities in a region, such as Macedonia (2 Cor. 8:1) or Judaea (Gal. 1:22). In Acts we have again the expression 'the whole church' (Acts 5:11), which may suggest that the Jerusalem church was made up of various smaller groups. There is a broader regional reference in Acts 9:31: 'the church throughout Judaea, Galilee, and Samaria', which certainly implies a composite understanding of *ekklēsia*. The one great *ekklēsia* is not split up into many minature *ekklēsiai*; nor are the many local *ekklēsiai* added together to make the one great *ekklēsia*. Rather, the one *ekklēsia* is to be discerned and identified as present in all those places; it is concretely instantiated in the plurality of *ekklēsiai*.

2. Secondly, *ekklēsia* sometimes refers to the whole church, or as we might say, the universal church. The expression, 'the church of God', which parallels 'all the flock' in Acts 20:28 (a rather centralized concept perhaps, certainly in Park's view) is perhaps transitional to this broader sense, the church in the *oikoumene*, the inhabited world, for here at Miletus Paul gathers the elders (*episkepoi*) from more than one city, yet he speaks of the church of God as a single entity. A similar generic sense of 'church' occurs in Gal. 1:13: 'I persecuted the church of God.' Here almost certainly more than one local assembly of Christians is in view; Paul does not mean that he harassed the Christians in Damascus only.

3. Thirdly, in the later, possibly pseudo-Pauline, letters, *ekklēsia* refers to what we might call the mystical or cosmic or transcendent church: God has made Christ 'the head over all things for the church, which is his body, the fullness of him who fills all in all' (Eph. 1:22); 'He is the head of the body, the church . . .' (Col. 1:18). This trans-local reference of *ekklēsia* in the later Epistles does not entail that the term was universally adopted by Christians throughout the Roman Empire.[18] Nevertheless, this developed use of *ekklēsia* can be seen as a stage on the way to the later credal meaning, 'one, holy, catholic and apostolic church', which signifies the whole church on earth and in heaven, militant and triumphant. Even at this point in the New Testament canon, *ekklēsia* has almost, but not completely, shed its original meaning of a physical assembly and has become a communion that transcends the limitations of time and space.

Interestingly, the substantive *ekklēsia* remains unqualified and unadorned in the New Testament; no 'ornamental epithets' are applied to it. Only in the post-apostolic period do adjectival titles accrue to the church. For the apostles it was enough to say, 'the church of God' or 'the church of Christ'.[19]

Koinōnía: The common life of the body

The common life in the church, that is to say in Christ and in the Holy Spirit, that the first Christians enjoyed – fragile and vulnerable though it evidently was – is indicated in the New Testament by the Greek term *koinōnía* (Latin *communio*) in various permutations.[20] *Koinōnía* occurs eighteen times in the New Testament, twelve of them being in Paul, four in John and one each in Acts and Hebrews. It is translated in various English-language Bibles as 'communion', 'fellowship', 'sharing', 'participation' or 'partnership'. Thiselton brings out the core meaning by translating it at certain points in 1 Corinthians (particularly 1:9) as 'communal participation' which avoids the rather cosy connotations of 'fellowship' in some modern church circles.[21] So what is meant by *koinōnía*?

[18] Korner, *Origin and Meaning of* Ekklēsia.
[19] *TDNT*, vol. 3, pp. 505, 532 (K. L. Schmidt).
[20] *TDNT*, vol. 3, pp. 796–809 (F. Hauck); Stephen Benko, *The Meaning of Sanctorum Communio* (London: SCM Press, 1964), chapter VII; L. [Lionel] S. Thornton, C.R., *The Common Life in the Body of Christ*, 3rd edn (Westminster: Dacre Press, 1950); Campbell, 'Koinonia in the New Testament', in id., *Three New Testament Studies*, pp. 1–28; Anglican – Roman Catholic International Commission (ARCIC), *Church as Communion* (London: CTS/SPCK, 1990); John Reumann, 'Koinonia [sic] in Scripture: Survey of Biblical Texts', in Thomas F. Best and Günther Gassmann (eds), *On the Way to Fuller Koinonia*: Official Report of the fifth World Conference on Faith and Order (Faith and Order Paper no. 166, Geneva: World Council of Churches Publications, 1994), pp. 37–69; Wendell Willis, 'The Koinonia [sic] of Christians – and Others: I Corinthians 10: 14-22', in id. (ed.), *Eucharist and Ecclesiology: Essays in Honor of Dr. Everett Ferguson* (Eugene, OR: Pickwick Publications, 2017), chapter 12; Andrew T. Lincoln, 'Communion: Some Pauline Foundations', *Ecclesiology* 5, no. 2 (2009), pp. 135–60.
[21] Anthony C. Thiselton, *The First Epistle to the Corinthians*, NIGTC (Grand Rapids, MI: Eerdmans/ Carlisle: Paternoster Press, 2000), pp. 103–5.

Koinōnía refers to sharing together in a reality greater than ourselves, joint shareholders or participants in a common entity or enterprise. It cannot mean a voluntary association of individuals, as in a society or club. It is the shared relationship, the common participation, that gives it substance. According to the New Testament, believers have been placed by the Holy Spirit within a reality of *koinōnía*, the economy of grace, through faith and baptism. Through faith and baptism, the Holy Spirit has made Christians ontologically one in the body of Christ (1 Cor. 12:13). To be united with baptized believers in the body of Christ is to be united with Christ himself. *Koinōnía* refers to the fellowship of Christians with the Father and the Son and with each other (1 Jn 1:3), not forgetting 'sharing (*koinōnía*) in the Spirit' (Phil. 2:1). It includes communal participation in the body and blood of Christ in the Lord's Supper (1 Cor. 10:16) and participating in Christ's sufferings (Phil. 3:10). It points to fellowship and solidarity (*koinōnía*) with the apostolic community in the teaching, the breaking of bread and the prayers (Acts 2:42). It involves practical partnership and mutual support in proclaiming the gospel (Phil. 1:5). *Koinōnía* stands for joint participation in the life of grace, lived union with God, Jesus Christ and the Holy Spirit – and with all the baptized (2 Cor. 13:13). The Second Epistle of Peter even speaks of Christians as *koinōnoi* (partakers) of the divine nature (2 Pet. 1:4).

Koinōnía in the New Testament is, at one and the same time, both mystical and practical; it can refer to sharing in Christ's sufferings and to gifts of material support for the apostolic mission (Phil. 3:10; 1:5). So it is profoundly spiritual and at the same time right down to earth. In the New Testament and particularly in Paul, it transcends any rather mundane origins and associations and becomes a profoundly theological concept, rooted in the fact of a mystical unity of Christians with Christ in the Lord's Supper (Eucharist): *koinōnía* in [or of] the blood and body of Jesus Christ (1 Cor. 10:16-17).[22] As we can see from the above references, *koinōnía* is a dynamic reality, rather than a static state of affairs; it can be deepened and enlarged, as we see particularly in 1 John 1, where new possibilities of fellowship/communion/*koinōnía* with the Father and the Son and with fellow Christians are opened up. So it belongs with the pervasive biblical imperative, 'Become what you are.' *Koinōnía*, the common life, is one fundamental way in which the New Testament construes the life of the church.

The church and the kingdom

The kingdom or reign of God (*basileia tou theou*) has figured centrally in our discussion of the proclamation of Jesus in relation to the eschatology of the Gospels. Here we will note briefly the relation of the kingdom to the church. 'Kingdom' or 'reign', applied to Yahweh or Jesus in Scripture, is clearly a metaphor, but it is also something more than a metaphor. It is a metaphor worked up into a complex image, a numinous symbol of divine kingship, sovereignty and rule. Because this image or symbol has an unparalleled and theologically pivotal role in shaping biblical theology, especially New Testament

---

[22]   Benko, *The Meaning of Sanctorum Communio*, p. 79.

ecclesiology, I am going to consider it here, rather than in the next chapter which is devoted to a range of other images of the church. The Hebrew concept *malkūt* rarely stands for a royal territory, a geographical realm; it normally stands for the sovereignty, governance and authority of the king. It is a dynamic concept, denoting the reign of God in action.[23]

All scholars agree that Jesus' message centrally concerned the kingdom or reign of God; in Matthew the expression is 'the kingdom of the heavens' (*hē basileia tōn ouranōn*) – a Jewish reverential circumlocution to avoid naming God (Mt. 4:17, etc.). Jesus proclaimed, as a matter of supreme urgency, that the kingdom was 'near' or 'at hand' (*ēngiken*, Mk 1:14-15; Mt. 4:17), and that this fact was the 'good news', the gospel (εὐαγγέλιον; *euangelion*). The Markan text is evidently designed as the fulfilment of Isa. 52:7: 'How beautiful upon the mountains are the feet of the messenger who announces peace, who brings good news, who announces salvation, who says to Zion [Jerusalem], "Your God reigns!"'. The messenger or herald of the gospel of the reign of God was then the prophet and is now Jesus. Jesus proclaimed the closeness, the imminence, the immediacy and indeed the actual presence of the reign of God, so long promised, longed for and prayed for by the Jewish people. His language (the Greek equivalent, of course) is perpetuated by Paul when he acknowledges that the Corinthian Christians 'await the revelation' (*apokalypsis*, ἀπο κάλυψις) of Jesus Christ and reassures the Philippians that 'the Lord is near' (*eggus*, Phil. 4:5) and by James that the 'appearing (*parousia*, παρουσία) of the Lord is near/ is at hand' (Jas. 5:8).

It is not feasible to expound here the concept of the kingdom of God (*Yahweh*) in the Hebrew Bible or the developments that it underwent in the inter-testamental period of Jewish history and literature. Standard accounts of Old Testament theology tend not to give substantial separate attention to the concept of the kingdom, kingship or reign of God, but there are many specialized studies and the standard dictionaries of biblical theology guide us to the principal texts.[24] Against the introduction of the institution of the monarchy in Israel, it is insisted more than fifty times that only Yahweh is Israel's king.[25] But it is particularly relevant to note that, in Hebrew parallelisms, the kingdom is unambiguously equated with God's mighty acts in history. This is particularly clear in Psalm 145: 'I will extol you, my God and King. . . . One generation shall laud your works to another and shall declare your mighty acts. On the glorious splendour of your majesty and on your wondrous works I will meditate. . . . They shall speak of the glory of your kingdom, and tell of your power, to make known to all people your mighty deeds, and the glorious splendour of your kingdom.' Against that background in the Jewish Scriptures it made sense to the disciples of Jesus that his works of preaching, healing, exorcism and gathering the scattered ones were signs that the kingdom of God

[23] Joachim Jeremias, *New Testament Theology* [2 vols], *Part One: The Proclamation of Jesus*, trans. John Bowden (London: SCM Press, 1971), p. 98.

[24] See esp. art. Βασιλεία, *TDNT*, vol. 1, pp. 564–93 (K. L. Schmidt). Martin Buber, *Kingship of God*, trans. Richard Scheimann from 3rd German edition (London: George Allen and Unwin, 1967 [1956]) is a series of dense interrelated studies that engage continuously with scholarly interlocutors.

[25] Ludwig Koehler, *Old Testament Theology*, trans. A. S. Todd (London: Lutterworth Press, 1957), p. 31.

had come among them, and that an act of God was unfolding in their midst (Mt. 12:28; Lk. 11:20; cf. Mt. 11:2-11).

How does this primary message of Jesus of Nazareth, echoed elsewhere in the New Testament, relate to the possible founding of the church by him? Are we justified in thinking that the act of God that is taking place in the ministry of Jesus includes or perhaps eventuates in the church? There is no suggestion in the New Testament that the church replaces the kingdom. The powers of the kingdom are at work in the church, but the early communities maintain the hope of the coming of the kingdom of God and of Christ (e.g. Acts 8:12; 14:22; 20:25-26; 1 Cor. 15:50; Eph. 5:5; 2 Thess. 1:5; 2 Tim. 4:1, 18; 2 Pet. 1:11; Rev. 11:15). The reign of God is infinitely bigger than the church and cannot be reduced to it. We cannot place any limits on the working out of God's sovereign purpose of love and justice; we cannot contain it within our ecclesiology. Even the most visionary missiology, taking its rise from the concept of the *missio dei* (mission of God), cannot exhaust the meaning of the kingdom or reign of God. The kingdom infinitely transcends the church. Augustine was somewhat mistaken in identifying the church with the kingdom rather absolutely on the basis of his exegesis of certain Gospel parables.[26] But the church remains intimately connected to the kingdom; they are not two separate matters; we should not try to prise them apart, to play them off, one against then other, as has been the tendency in some Protestant theology. In the purposes of God, the church serves the kingdom and owes its existence to it. It spearheads the coming of the kingdom; it even mediates the kingdom. The church is, as it were, the nodal point of the reign of God, the concretization on earth of the reign of God, a human, institutional expression of it and a medium or channel for it. Augustine was not far wrong.

How can this be? It is because Jesus Christ not only proclaimed the good news of the impending and already impinging reign of God, but in his life, teaching and mighty works, he brought the reign of God into the midst of the world. Thus he is, as Origen (c. 184–254) first said, the kingdom itself (*autobasileia*; Latin *ipsum regnum*).[27] Christ is the reign of God personified, encapsulated in one person and life. And the church is Christ embodied in the world and the instantiation of the kingdom on earth. The connection between the kingdom and the church is twofold, in fact dialectical. 'On the one hand, the Kingdom of God is the Church's frontier of judgement [*sic*]; on the other hand, it is the whole substance of the Church.'[28] In one sense the church and kingdom are intimately related through the mission of Jesus Christ on behalf of the kingdom, but in another respect the church can prove to be a counter-sign of the kingdom, defying the reign of God in justice and peace. Because the church is full of sinners (who are being sanctified by word and sacrament), and because the church as an institution sometimes commits crimes (or allows them to be committed by its representatives), it remains always subject to, even subservient to, the kingdom. The church is compelled to submit to the authority of the reign of God and to allow itself

---

[26] Augustine, *City of God*, ed. David Knowles, trans. Henry Bettenson (Harmondsworth: Penguin, 1972), pp. 914–18 (XX. 9). Cf. R. A. Markus, *Saeculum: History and Society in the Theology of St Augustine* (Cambridge: Cambridge University Press, 1988 [1970]).

[27] Origen on Matthew, 14.7, *Patrologia Graeca* (Paris: J.-P. Migne, 1862), vol. 13, cols. 1197–8.

[28] K. E. Skydsgaard, 'Kingdom of God and Church', *SJT* 4, no. 4 (1951), pp. 383–97, at p. 393.

to be judged, purified and reformed in the light of the kingdom – a process of which it continually stands in need.

The subtle grammar of ecclesiology

Key ecclesiological prepositions

The social (as well as spiritual) solidarity of the Christian community is primarily expressed in the load-bearing metaphors or images of body, temple, people, bride, priesthood and new humanity that are the subject of the next chapter. At this stage, however, we need to take into account certain key prepositions, used by St Paul, which have the effect of articulating – albeit obliquely – an actual ecclesiology. Dunn points out the strange neglect of this prepositional theology in Pauline studies.[29] Moreover, because these prepositions are often used to refer to Christians collectively, as well as individually, they are also an under-explored source of New Testament ecclesiology.

The first of these pivotal prepositions is *in* (Christ). *En christo* occurs eighty-three times in the whole Pauline corpus and occasionally elsewhere, notably in 1 Peter (3:16; 5:10, 14), while Revelation has 'in Jesus' and 'in the Lord' (1:9; 14:13). If we include the pronoun equivalents ('in him', etc.) and 'in the Lord' (*en Kyriō*) the total is much higher. This is a significant New Testament way of speaking about the relation of the individual Christian and the Christian community to Christ. For Paul, the reality of being 'in Christ' is the key to the union between Christ and every baptized believer, and at the same time, between Christ and his body, the church. It equates to 'in union with Christ', which is how it was sometimes translated in the *New English Bible* and its successor *The Revised English Bible*. (The presence of the preposition in the Greek is sometimes disgracefully obscured in rather free translations, such as 'Christian' for *en christo* in 1 Peter 3:16, REB.)

But the import of *en christō* is not simply union (with Christ), but position (in Christ). The preposition 'in' is a compressed, shorthand metaphor of locality: Christ's body is where believers are placed by God through the Holy Spirit in baptism (1 Cor. 12:13). We may adapt what Paul says on Areopagus about God the Creator, and say, 'in Christ, we live and move and have our being' (cf. Acts 17.28). 'The believer "exists" within the sphere of being of the corporate Christ.'[30] The locative power of the preposition *en* can be seen in the fact that Paul uses it in 2 Cor. 5:19 to describe – certainly not to explain at this point – God's presence, person and power in the life and work of Jesus: 'God was *in* Christ, reconciling the world to himself.' The reality for which Paul employs a mere preposition, would be expressed by later generations, beginning with the author of the Fourth Gospel (Jn 1:14: 'the word was made flesh') by the word 'incarnation'.

[29] Dunn, *The Theology of Paul the Apostle*, pp. 396–408, at p. 397.
[30] Margaret E. Thrall, *The Second Epistle to the Corinthians*, [2 vols] *Volume 1*, ICC (London and New York: T&T Clark, 1994), pp. 424–9, at p. 428.

All the blessings of Christian existence are said to be given 'in Christ': redemption (Col. 1:14; Eph. 1:7), eternal life (Rom. 6:23), deliverance from condemnation by the law (Rom. 8:1), sanctification (1 Cor. 1:2), grace (Eph. 1:6), fullness of life (Col. 2:10), comfort (Phil. 2:1) and freedom (Gal. 2:14). The initiatory rite of baptism (including probably the laying on of hands and the gift of the Holy Spirit) is never far from Paul's (and Pauline writers) usage here.[31]

For Albert Schweitzer, 'Being-in-Christ' was the 'prime enigma of Pauline teaching'; 'once grasped', Schweitzer went on, 'it gives the clue to the whole.'[32] And as Bultmann points out that 'in Christ' is not only a soteriological formula, having to do with the salvation of individuals, but an ecclesiological formula too, relating to the reality, unity and solidarity of the church.[33] Whole churches and the 'saints' corporately conceived are 'in Christ' (Gal. 1:22, NRSV, where REB again has 'Christian' which weakens the force; cf. 1 Thess. 1:1, where REB has 'belong to', and 2:14, where REB makes a hash of it by trying to avoid translating the preposition literally).

'In Christ' has 'realist' force: believers are united into a single entity, even a single being, 'in Christ': 'You are all one in Christ Jesus' (Gal. 3:28) – and nothing that might go wrong in the life of the church can alter that fact. Bonhoeffer argued in *Sanctorum Communio* that to be in Christ is the same as to be in the church: *en christō = en ekklēsia*, for (as Bonhoeffer memorably put it) 'Christ exists as the church.' The image of the body, in particular, identifies Christ and the church. The church has become a person in Christ, so that Christ and the church share the same 'corporate personality' (see further in the next chapter).[34]

Alongside the prepositional phrase 'in Christ', Paul uses 'with Christ' (*syn christō*) to convey his sense of the solidarity of Christians, individually and corporately, with Christ, and once again this is understood as being effected through baptism (faith being presupposed). Baptized believers are described as 'living' (Rom. 6:8), 'suffering' (Rom. 8:17), 'crucified' (Rom. 6:6; Gal. 2:20), 'dying' (Rom. 6:8), 'buried' (Rom. 6:4; Col. 2:12), 'made alive' (Col. 2:13; Eph. 2:5), 'raised' (Col. 2:12; 3:1; Eph. 2:6), 'glorified' (Rom. 8:17) and as 'reigning in heavenly places' (Eph. 2:16; 2 Tim. 2:12) 'with Christ' in every case. So St Paul's formula 'with Christ' refers to the origin, progress and ultimate destiny of Christians, from baptism to heaven, through their solidarity with the life, death, resurrection and glorification of Jesus Christ within the unfolding drama of redemption – a solidarity that is effected and realized sacramentally in

[31] See further, in detail, Ernest Best, *One Body in Christ: A Study in the Relationship of the Church to Christ in the Epistles of the Apostle Paul* (London: SPCK, 1955). On baptism in Paul see Nicholas Taylor, *Paul on Baptism* (London: SCM Press, 2016); Oscar Cullmann, *Baptism in the New Testament*, trans. J. K. S. Reid (London: SCM Press, 1950). Also relevant are some essays in Michael J. Thate, Kevin J. Vanhoozer and Constantine R. Campbell (eds), *'In Christ' in Paul: Explorations in Paul's Theology of Union and Participation* (Grand Rapids, MI: Eerdmans, 2018 [2014]).

[32] Schweitzer, *The Mysticism of Paul the Apostle*, trans. William Montgomery, Prefatory Note by F. C. Burkitt, 3rd edn (London: A. & C. Black, 1933).

[33] Rudolf Bultmann, *Theology of the New Testament*, trans. Kendrick Grobel, 2 vols (London: SCM Press, 1952), vol. 1, p. 8.

[34] Dietrich Bonhoeffer, *Sanctorum Communio*, trans. from the 3rd German edition by Ronald Gregor Smith (London: Collins, 1963), pp. 99–100.

baptism. So 'with Christ' is an ecclesiological, as well as a soteriological formula, just as 'in Christ' is.

To complete the picture, we should mention Paul's third, and in this case, *kinetic* preposition: 'into Christ' (*eis christon*). The sense of movement, of translation, into a new location, a new environment, is evident.[35] Of the three, this is perhaps the expression that brings out most explicitly the baptismal dimension of the Christian's incorporation into Christ's body: 'As many of you as were baptized into Christ have put on Christ' (Gal. 3:27). 'All of us', writes Paul, 'who have been baptized into Christ Jesus were baptized into his death' (Rom. 6:3). The passage Rom. 6:3-11 brings together 'into Christ' and 'with Christ' in the context of baptism.

So, to sum up these brief expositions: those believers who have been baptized *into* Christ, and have therefore died and been raised *with* Christ, thereafter live their Christian existence *in* Christ. But when we take Paul's theology as a whole into account, it seems misguided to take such passages as those catalogued above in a purely individual sense. What is this body of Christ which is crucified, dead and buried, then raised again, into which we are baptized? It is, as we know full well, the church. In 1 Cor. 12:12 an extraordinary correspondence and equivalence is effected between 'body' and 'Christ': in referring to the church, Paul calls the church 'Christ'.

The saving name

We turn now briefly to another approach to the question of the relationship between Christ and the believer in the New Testament, one that is closely complementary to the 'prepositional' avenue: the 'name' of Jesus. To invoke the name of Jesus, in preaching, worship, healing, exorcism or apostolic authority was to express a confidence in the nearness, presence and power of Jesus Christ in the church. The expression 'in the name of Christ' (*eis to onoma christou*) may be taken as a circumlocutory equivalent to 'into Christ'. It could be rendered, '*into* the name of . . .' In both Testaments, the 'name' of anyone is a freighted term, carrying a weight of identity, efficacy and power. The name stands for the person and their attributes and authority.[36] To a greatly (infinitely) enhanced degree, this applies to God and to Jesus. In Hebrew parallelism to 'praise the name' of YHWH and to 'sing to his name' was simply an elaboration of 'to praise YHWH' (Ps. 135. 1,3). But to 'call upon the name of YHWH' was to call YHWH's power to one's aid in time of peril and to claim YHWH's presence and protection in a strange land (Gen. 12:8; 13:4). To 'name' a place where one has sojourned, as the Hebrew Patriarchs and Judges did, is to give it significance for one's faith and to fix its place, not only in geography, but in salvation history. The references are too abundant to begin to enumerate.

In the petition of the Lord's Prayer 'Hallowed be thy name', 'name' is used in the Hebraic idiom as a reverential circumlocution for the unutterable 'YHWH'. A 'name'

---

[35] Dunn, *The Theology of Paul the Apostle*, p. 404.

[36] Edmond Jacob, *Theology of the Old Testament*, trans. A. W. Heathcote and P. J. Allcock (London: Hodder and Stoughton, 1958 [1955]), pp. 43–8, 82–5; Walther Eichrodt, *Theology of the Old Testament*, trans. John Baker, 2 vols (London: SCM Press, 1967), vol. 2, pp. 40–5.

can also become hypostatized as the agent, so to speak, of the one who bears the name. 'Name' is synonymous with identity, power and authority (Mt. 7:22; Lk. 10:17; Acts 2:38; 4:7, 10, 30; 1 Cor. 5:3-5; see the triple usage of 'name' in Acts 9:14-16). It can also be a circumlocution by Jesus' enemies to avoid using the hated name itself (Acts 5:28; 9:21). 'Name' has a revelatory import. The 'name' and the proclamation of Jesus are sometimes equated with the kingdom in the New Testament.[37]

In the Acts of the Apostles, healings are performed and demons are driven out in the name of Jesus Christ (Acts 3:6, 16; 4:7, 10; 5:40; 16:18; 19:13-17). In Paul's use of 'the name' there is a sense of dynamic momentum, of translation from one state or reality to another. Paul asks the rhetorical question, 'Is Christ divided? . . . Were you baptized in (*or* into) the name of Paul?' (1 Cor. 1:13-15). The answer expected is, 'No, certainly not; you were baptized in (*or* into) the name of Christ', which carries the clear implication, 'He is the ground of your unity; there cannot be divisions when you are united in him.' Matthew employs a similar formula to give the church its dominical mandate to 'make disciples of all nations, baptizing them in the name [i.e. into the identity, power and authority] of the Father and of the Son and of the Holy Spirit' (Mt. 28:19). The truth implied here is that the name into which disciples are to be baptized is singular, though there is a threefold trinitarian identity within the one name in this baptismal formula. The singularity of the name underlines the unity and solidarity of the church – all are baptized in and into the single name of God. In the apostolic preaching, as depicted in the Acts, baptism into Christ's name opens the door to sharing in the gifts and powers of his kingdom: 'Repent, and be baptized, every one of you, in (*epi to onomati*) the name of Jesus Christ for (*eis*) the forgiveness of your sins, and you will receive the gift of the Holy Spirit' (Acts 2:38). There is nothing 'nominal' about 'name' as it is employed in the Scriptures. 'Name' speaks of God as revealed in Jesus. It stands for the power and authority of one named, present and effective. 'Jesus Christ' is the saving name, cherished and proclaimed in the church.

Johannine equivalents

In looking for the subtle grammar that expresses the connection between Jesus and the church in the New Testament, we should also take account of the typically Johannine way of expressing the relation of Christians to Christ and to each other. The nearest equivalent in the Johannine Gospel and Epistles to Paul's use of the three pivotal prepositions, 'in', 'with' and 'into' (Christ), is the pervasive language of 'abiding' or 'dwelling' (*manere*) in Christ. We find the language of dwelling in relation to God and to Christ in the first person and the third person, in both singular and plural forms: 'in me' (Jn 6:56; 14:20; 15:4-7; 16:33; 17:21); 'in him' (God: 1 Jn 2:6, 28; 3:6; 4:13; 5:20); 'in us' ('the truth', 1 Jn 1:8; 'his word', 1 Jn 1:10; 3:24; God, 1 Jn 4:12); 'in you' ('what you heard from the beginning', 1 Jn 2:24); 'in love' (1 Jn 4:16); 'in the Son and in the Father' (1 Jn 2:24); 'he abides in them' (1 Jn 3:24).

[37] Bultmann, *Theology of the New Testament*, vol. 1, pp. 27, 38; art. Βασιλεία, *TDNT*, vol. 1, p. 589 (K. L. Schmidt).

In the Fourth Gospel often the bare preposition 'in' points to a profound sense of communion: 'I am in my Father and you in me and I in you' (Jn 14:20); 'As you, Father, are in me and I am in you, may they also be in us' (Jn 17:21). In the Johannine Epistles the preposition 'in' does a great deal of work, in the same sense, speaking of the salvific location of Christians in Christ, in God, in the truth, and so on; indeed, it is pervasive. The language of mutual indwelling or abiding, that we find throughout the Gospel and Epistles of John, finds extended figurative expression in the parable of the vine, the branches and the grapes ('fruit') in Jn 15:1-17. As the branches are united with each other, being held together by the whole vine, so they will bear much enduring fruit. The individual branch, separate from the vine and the other branches, can bear no fruit and is doomed to perish. This is a corporate or holistic image of the church in its relation to Christ. In this particular 'I am' saying, Christ *is* the whole vine, including its branches, so becoming a parallel to the Pauline 'body' metaphor, where the body includes the head as well as the members (as we shall see in the next chapter).

Conclusion

Even when the Christian community is not explicitly named as *ekklēsia* or alluded to metaphorically by means of one of many complementary images, or indicated by one of the tiny but powerful prepositions, it is still an all-pervading presence in the New Testament. The church that remains an inescapable presence in the Gospels is, of course, the Jewish church, the congregation or assembly of Israel, with its Hebrew Scriptures and rabbinic commentaries, its synagogue worship and Temple cultus, its teachers, priesthood and leaders. The Jewish church, with its Temple in Jerusalem and its synagogues throughout the Roman Empire, remains the context for much of the Acts of the Apostles, though Christian house churches and city-wide churches also figure in the Acts, as well as in the Epistles.

Besides the Jewish church, the New Testament presupposes and takes for granted the existence, presence and activities of the nascent Christian church, in the sense of the community of disciples, formed, led and governed by apostles, apostolic delegates (Timothy and Titus) and James the brother of Jesus. The Christians are not a shapeless, random bunch of individual believers, each doing their own thing, but already an ordered community or society. The community holds together through what is held in common (*koinōnía*). In Matthew's Gospel, particularly, we see a church that already has certain rudimentary structures, which are related to the core beliefs, activities and rites that form the church. Chapters 18 and 23 of Matthew show that the church has already had to take certain steps to deal with the abuse of those structures.[38] When that order and coherence begins to become fragile, the apostles exert themselves to restore it; it matters almost more than anything. When that order, the framework of communion, is drastically disrupted, as it was at Corinth by multiple abuses, stern measures are taken to restore it, so that all should be done 'decently and in order' (1 Cor. 14:40). The

---

[38] Carlston and Evans, *From Synagogue to Ecclesia*, p. 305.

basis of the community is located not only in the proclamation (*kerygma*), but also in structured teaching (*paraenesis*) and in ethical precepts that overlap with Jewish mores and classical wisdom (*didache*).

The canonical authors, whether of the Old Testament or the New, set out to guide, shape, nurture and reform their church, its beliefs and practices. This motive is particularly prominent in Paul, who was a moralist as well as a theologian: 'As a moral teacher, Paul seeks to shape communities of character.'[39] The New Testament books were written almost entirely for existing communities of Christians, though they already possessed a treasury of oral traditions, some rather fragmentary written sources (Q) and of course certain rites, especially baptism and the Lord's Supper, which embodied and proclaimed the gospel and united the church to Christ sacramentally. The word, the sacraments, prayer and song were vehicles of the Spirit of Christ in their midst, making them a pneumatological community. It is true to say that the church preceded and gave birth to the New Testament. But having brought forth the literature now gathered together in the New Testament (as well as other works, including Gospels, now lost or deemed uncanonical) and having awarded it apostolic, normative and canonical status, the church knows that it must continually return to those fundamental documents, the trust deeds of the church, as it reflects on its origins, identity and mission – and allow itself to be judged and reformed by them.[40]

---

[39] Luke Timothy Johnson, 'Paul's Ecclesiology', in J. D. G. Dunn (ed.), *The Cambridge Companion to St Paul* (Cambridge: Cambridge University Press, 2003), chapter 14, at p. 200.

[40] Cf. Frank Matera, 'Theologies of the Church in the New Testament', in Peter C. Phan (ed.), *The Gift of the Church: A Textbook on Ecclesiology in Honor of Patrick Granfield, O.S.B.* (Collegeville, MN: Liturgical Press, 2000), chapter 1, at p. 3.

4

Images of Christ and the church
in the New Testament

The images for the church that we find in Paul's Epistles and other New Testament writings are the earliest evidence that we have for how the first generation of Christians understood theologically the connection between Jesus Christ and the church. Books have been written that describe them as 'images of the church', but they are more properly understood as 'images of Christ-and-the-church'. There are dangers in picking out individual Greek words from the New Testament, like *ekklēsia* and *koinōnía*, or phrases, such as 'the kingdom of God', from their context, isolating them from their use in the daily life, thought, worship and practice of the community. Without careful attention to the overall context, mere word-study can lead us astray.[1] There are, however, other ways in which the Christian community is depicted in the New Testament, particularly the metaphors or images for the relation between Jesus and the church. So this chapter explores some key images of the church in the New Testament – though it would probably be more true to the scriptural approach to think of 'the church in the images', rather than 'images of the church', as though the church were one thing and the images another. In the ecclesiology of the New Testament the church largely subsists in the images, but not the church in separation from Christ. Most of the images are intensely relational. They portray the relationship, the connection, between the church and Jesus Christ. It follows that to explore and unpack these ecclesiological images, in what follows, is an exercise in the theological interpretation of Scripture.

Understanding the images

Paul and the other writers of the New Testament Epistles employ a rich repertoire of metaphors or images, almost all derived from the Hebrew Bible, to open windows into the nature of the church.[2] We should not make the mistake of assuming that these images are 'mere' metaphors, somehow inferior to supposed 'literal speech'. There is, in truth,

---

[1]   James Barr, *The Semantics of Biblical Language* (Oxford: Oxford University Press, 1961).
[2]   For general surveys of images of the church see Paul S. Minear, *Images of the Church in the New Testament* (London: Lutterworth Press, 1961); Avery Dulles, *Models of the Church*, 2nd edn (New York: Doubleday, 1987; Dublin: Gill and Macmillan, 1988); Geoffrey Preston, O.P., *Faces of the Church*, ed. Aidan Nichols, O.P., Foreword Walter Kasper (Edinburgh: T&T Clark, 1997).

no such thing as 'literal' speech; every presumed 'literal' statement contains buried metaphors. And the notion of 'mere' metaphor, understood as a purely ornamental figure of speech, as surface decoration, is another common misconception. Language is constituted by metaphors and other figures of speech and they are what give it its life, energy and colour. Metaphors and images are powerful presences in thinking and language, infused with the power of creative imagination. They impart vitality to our discourse, create unlooked-for connections and open up new avenues of exploration. For this reason, Walter Kasper prefers to speak of the images of the church as 'symbols', because 'symbol' suggests, perhaps more readily than 'metaphor', that it participates in what it represents and is therefore a channel conveying the depths of reality.[3] Kasper also usefully points out that these symbols complement each other and are mutually interpreting, so that no single one of them – not even 'body of Christ' – should be allowed to dominate ecclesiological reflection and certainly not to drive the others from the field.[4]

Though prefigured in the Old Testament, the images or symbols are filled out by the New Testament authors (and subsequently elaborated by the Apostolic Fathers and the Early Fathers) in the light of the Christ event. Minear's analysis is the most thorough and detailed, though he protests – rather unconvincingly – that it is not exhaustive. Minear found more than eighty images of the church in the New Testament, of which he judged thirty to be minor images (including salt of the earth, boat/ark, fish/fish-net, vineyard/branches of the vine). Minear judged even 'bride of Christ' and 'plantation/building' to be minor images, though I take a different view, as do other scholars. Minear identified as many as fifty major images, though some even of his 'major' examples are not, strictly speaking, images but passing figures of speech. In any case, here we must be more selective.[5]

The most significant of these ecclesiological images or metaphors are body of Christ (1 Cor. 12:12-27; Eph. 4:4-16); people of God (Acts 15:14; Rom. 9:25-26; 2 Cor. 6:16; 1 Pet. 2:9-10); household, family and friends of God and Christ (Jn 15:12-15); temple or building of God and of the Holy Spirit (1 Cor. 3:10-17; Eph. 2:20; 1 Pet. 2:4-8); bride or spouse of Christ (Eph. 5:25-33; Rev. 19:7; 21.2); new humanity (1 Cor. 15:22; Col. 3:10; Eph. 4:24); city of God (Heb. 11:10, 16; 12:22; 13:14; Rev. 21:1 – 22:5); ark of salvation (1 Pet. 3:20-22); royal priesthood (1 Pet. 2:9); mother of the faithful (Gal. 4:26). While all of these images stress the corporate solidarity of the community in union with Christ, 'body' and 'bride' are deeply intimate images of the corporate union of the church and Christ. In a moment I will expand briefly on some, though not quite all, of these key images of the theological connection between the church and Christ in the New Testament.

---

[3]   Walter Kasper, *The Catholic Church: Nature, Reality and Mission*, trans. Thomas Hoebel, ed. R. David Nelson (London and New York: Bloomsbury T&T Clark, 2015), p. 119. For an exposition of the critical-realist or symbolic-realist import of metaphor, etc., see Paul Avis, *God and the Creative Imagination: Metaphor, Symbol and Myth in Religion and Theology* (London and New York: Routledge, 1999).

[4]   Kasper, *The Catholic Church*, p. 119.

[5]   Minear, *Images of the Church in the New Testament*.

I have not included *ekklēsia* in this section. In a sense, *ekklēsia* is also an image, one of gathering or assembling together. The imagery of being called is the basic metaphor here. Some treatments of the church treat it as one image among others. But because *ekklēsia* has become rather a technical term for the church or a church, I have discussed it separately in the previous chapter. However, we should not overlook its basic metaphorical structure and its status as a symbol for the Christian community. Incidentally, 'community' is another metaphor, one of being united together – but there is no end to the unravelling of metaphors within metaphors and images within images, so we are concentrating on those that are given constitutive status in the ecclesiological material of the New Testament.

It is also important to note that this repertoire of images is not an alternative version of New Testament theology to the eschatological theological framework found in the proclamation of Jesus and in most of the New Testament literature – it presupposes it. We are talking about an eschatological body, an eschatological people, an eschatological temple, bride, city, royal priesthood and so on. Albert Schweitzer concluded from a review of the evidence, and notwithstanding the fact of development in Paul's thought, that 'from his first letter to his last Paul's thought is always uniformly dominated by the expectation of the immediate return of Jesus, of the Judgement, and the Messianic glory.'[6] It is within this dominant eschatological context that the images or symbols of the church should be understood.

Finally, before examining some key images of the church, I would like us to take to heart one more fundamental point. The images that we are about to look at are not something other than the ecclesiology of the New Testament. They are not illustrations or ornamentations of an ecclesiology that can be found elsewhere in these documents. It is not that we can find and study and explicate a doctrine of the church and then use the images to elucidate it, to expatiate on it. The images *are* the doctrine. It is in these images that the ecclesiology of the New Testament is largely contained. Without them, the ecclesiological resources of the New Testament would be greatly diminished and impoverished. If we should still feel that the study of the images is in some way a second best approach to the church in the Scriptures, it may be that we have not yet understood the essentially figurative complexion of language or the power of metaphor to disclose unforeseen truths, or the power of symbols to induct us into the reality that they symbolize and to unite us with it. The poetic and the metaphorical is the royal road to truth, and truth in the biblical perspective is reality understood, followed and obeyed in the light of God.

Body of Christ

The doctrine of the church as the mystical body of Christ was, as J. N. D. Kelly points out, common to both Eastern and Western forms of ecclesiology in the patristic period and was understood in a strongly realist sense. Kelly quotes Hilary of Poitiers' (AD

---

[6]   Albert Schweitzer, *The Mysticism of Paul the Apostle*, trans. William Montgomery, Prefatory Note by F. C. Burkitt, 3rd edn (London: A. & C. Black, 1933), pp. 32–3.

310–68) teaching that through baptism we 'enter into fellowship with Christ's flesh'. For, as Hilary puts it, 'he is himself the church, comprehending it all in himself through the mystery of his body'.[7] St Paul's epistles are the primary, though not the sole, source of the body image for the church in patristic theology and in the church today, where it is probably the most popular image of all.

The image of the church as the body of Christ is found substantially only in Paul, with some passing allusions in other New Testament writers. Within Paul it is found only in 1 Corinthians 12 and Romans 12, together with Ephesians, assuming that letter to be 'Pauline' in some sense. Although it occurs sporadically, this image has been described as 'the keystone of Paul's theology'.[8] Certainly, it takes us to the heart of his ecclesiology. Within the basic image of corporeality there is a creative, flexible play on the terms body, members and head. Walter Kasper, influenced naturally by the approach of the Second Vatican Council, expounds 'people of God' first, as the base image, followed by 'body' and 'bride' taken together. But I will address the body metaphor first because I see it as pivotal and as perhaps the strongest of the images – it holds well together, like a loaf of wholemeal bread baked with 'strong' flour.

Paul's use of 'body of Christ' for the church presupposes a holistic biblical anthropology. The dualism of body and soul that has been pervasive in Western thought and culture for centuries is Hellenistic, rather than Hebraic, in origin and is alien to biblical anthropology (though that fact definitely does not in itself settle the question of the mind/body relation in human biology, psychology, philosophy or theological anthropology). In Scripture the body signifies the whole person, embodied personal existence. So when Paul exhorts the Christians in Rome to present their bodies as a living sacrifice (Rom. 12:1), he does not mean them to exclude their minds – he glosses it as their 'reasonable' or 'rational' service (*logikene latreian*). Both the body of Christ (Rom. 7:4: 'you have died to the law through the body of Christ', that is Christ's sacrifice of himself) and the body of Christians (Rom. 7:24: 'the body of this death', that is, my mortal, sinful existence) stand for the whole person. So the body stands for the whole (embodied) self – though it does not follow that *sōma* actually *means* 'whole self'.[9] When Paul says that we long for 'the redemption of our bodies' (Rom. 8:23), the eschatological liberation of the creation that is subject to decay, he means the whole created organism of our existence in the world. Thus, when Paul calls the church the body of Christ, he means that the church is the *actuality* of Christ in the world, his personal being in our midst. (This Pauline usage provides unequivocal biblical support for Bonhoeffer and Barth when they speak of the church as the 'existence' of Christ in the world – as we shall see in due course.) This strong, realist identification between Christ and the church becomes explicit in 1 Cor. 12:12: 'For just as the [human] body is one and has many members, and all the members of the body, though many, are one body, so it is with Christ.' John Calvin brings out the bold, daring, nature of this

[7]   J. N. D. Kelly, *Early Christian Doctrines*, 3rd edn (London: A. and C. Black, 1965), p. 409.
[8]   John A. T. Robinson, *The Body* (London: SCM Press, 1952), p. 9.
[9]   E. H. Gundry, *SŌMA in Biblical Theology* (Cambridge: Cambridge University Press, 1976); James D. G. Dunn, *The Theology of Paul the Apostle* (London and New York: T&T Clark, 1998), pp. 55–61, at p. 58.

assertion, when he comments, 'Paul calls the Church "Christ"'.[10] (Michael Ramsey was struck by this identification of the church and Christ in Calvin and quoted it *The Gospel and the Catholic Church*, 1936.)[11] We may compare the superficially weaker statement of Rom. 12:5, 'We, though many, are one body in Christ (*en christō*)', which is in truth just as robust as the other, when we consider, as we have done in the previous chapter, the huge theological force of *en christō*.

If Paul identifies the church with Christ by means of this physical, corporeal metaphor, he also identifies individual Christians with Christ and the church using the same metaphor.

1. He speaks of the *whole* church and its members as the body of Christ in 1 Cor. 12:28: 'Now you are the body of Christ and individually members of it. And God has appointed in the church first apostles . . .' Since the number of apostles was limited (though larger than popularly assumed), with not enough to provide one for each local congregation, this must refer to the local church within the totality of existing churches. Ephesians (though it is doubtfully by Paul) puts the same thought even more strongly: 'Christ is the head of the church, his body, and is himself its saviour' (Eph. 5:23). Then the author becomes quite carnal, so to speak: 'No man ever hates his own flesh, but nourishes and cherishes it, as Christ does the church, because we are members of his body' – flesh of his flesh, we might say (Eph. 5:29-30).

2. The local church, the assembly or congregation, is also described by Paul as the body of Christ. This image underpins his appeal to the Corinthians for unity, harmony and mutual consideration, especially in the exercise of charismatic and other spiritual gifts: 'You [plural] are the body of Christ and individually members of it' (1 Cor. 12:27).

3. But then, rather counter-intuitively, the individual Christian is also described as the body of Christ. Let us look at this aspect a little more closely. Bearing in mind that, for the biblical writers, the body signifies the whole person, we can appreciate the force of Paul saying, 'Your bodies are members of Christ' (1 Cor. 6:15). But to say that individual Christians are part of the body, members of it, is not the same as to say that Christians individually are bodies of Christ. However, Paul does go that far and his argument has three steps. First, Paul lays it down that the body belongs to Christ and is the object his care and purpose: 'the body is meant not for fornication, but for the Lord and the Lord for the body' (1 Cor. 6:13). Secondly, just as whoever 'joins himself to a prostitute becomes one body with her' (the two become one flesh), so 'anyone united to the Lord becomes one spirit with him' (vv. 16–18). Here 'spirit' (*pneuma*) is not meant in antithesis to 'body', but in antithesis to 'flesh' (*sarx*). This contrast is common in Paul's thought (cf. Rom. 1:3-4: God's Son was 'descended from David according to the flesh [*kata sarka*]), and designated Son of God in power according to the spirit [*kata*

[10]   John Calvin, *The First Epistle to the Corinthians*, trans. J. W. Fraser, *Calvin's Commentaries*, ed. David W. Torrance and Thomas F. Torrance (Edinburgh: The Saint Andrew Press, 1960), p. 264.
[11]   A. M. Ramsey, *The Gospel and the Catholic Church* (London: Longmans, Green & Co., 1936), p. 35.

pneuma] of holiness by his resurrection from the dead'). Probably by 'spirit' here Paul means a 'spiritual body' (1 Cor. 15:44), which is not at all a non-physical, immaterial, body, but a physical body that is 'imperishable'.[12] Body and spirit belong together inseparably – not as a duality, but as a polarity: 'there is one body and one spirit' (Eph. 4:4). The spirit (or Spirit) of Jesus dwells in his body. So Paul might equally well have said, 'Whoever is joined to the Lord is one body with him', and he has already said as much, even if not in those words, as we have seen. The third step is to claim the bodies of Christians as temples of the Holy Spirit, but we will consider the temple metaphor separately in a moment.

What was it in the tradition that Paul had received and passed on (1 Cor 11:2, 23) that led him to elaborate his immensely subtle theology of the church as the body of Christ? I think (though not all interpreters agree)[13] that the answer is to be found in the institution narrative that he 'received from the Lord' concerning the words and actions of Jesus at the Last Supper, culminating in the moment when he gave them the bread saying, 'This is my body that is for you. Do this in remembrance of me' (v. 24). Here there is an implied transition from, 'This is my body', to 'You are my body'; from receiving to becoming. It is possible that this identification of the church with the person (body) of Christ was first triggered in Paul's imagination by his encounter with the risen Christ on the Damascus Road: 'I am Jesus whom you are persecuting.' In persecuting the church of God (1 Cor. 15:9; Gal. 1:13), Saul was wounding Christ himself. This interpretation goes back at least as far as Augustine of Hippo and is endorsed by some modern interpreters. Jewett's view seems plausible: the Damascus experience sheds light on the unity between Christ and the church, which the formula *sōma christou* expresses, but it does not explain its origin.[14] That very probably lies in the institution of the Lord's Supper, combined with imagery of the social body that was current in ancient thought.

The thought of the Last Supper/Lord's Supper is never far away in Paul's use of the body metaphor. He can use it with several layers of intentional ambiguity. Admonishing the Corinthians for their unseemly behaviour at the Lord's Supper/*Agape*, he warns them of the danger of 'not discerning the body' (1 Cor. 11:27-29). Does this mean treating the (sacramental) elements of bread and wine without proper respect? Or does it mean behaving in an inconsiderate manner towards the gathered community? Or does it mean failing to show brotherly care and love to the humbler members, who have little to bring to the supper, but rather humiliating them (as v. 11 seems to suggest)? That last interpretation could draw support from Mt. 25:31-46, the parable of the sheep and the goats: 'As you did it (not) to one of the least of these (my brothers),

---

12 Robinson, *The Body*, p. 79.
13 Ernest Best, *One Body in Christ* (London: SPCK, 1955), p. 91. Best tends not to allow the full force of some of the more uncomfortable aspects of Paul's corporeal imagery.
14 Robert Jewett, *Paul's Anthropological Terms: A Study of their Use in Conflict Settings* (Leiden: Brill, 1971), p. 246; see his chapter 5 on *sōma*. Cf. Alan Richardson, *A Theology of the New Testament* (London: SCM Press, 1953), p. 251, n; Robinson, *The Body*, p. 58; Emile Mersch, *The Whole Christ: The Historical Development of the Doctrine of the Mystical Body in Scripture and Tradition*, trans. J. R. Kelly (London: Dobson, 1938), p. 104; Ramsey, *The Gospel and the Catholic Church*, p. 37.

you did it (not) to me'; there is the very same quasi-physical identification of Christ and Christians. Paul's use of 'body' in 1 Corinthians 11 is at one and the same time sacramental, ecclesiological and christological.

When he speaks of the church as Christ's body, Paul is not consciously elaborating an ornamental figure of speech; he is thinking realistically, almost literally. Albert Schweitzer asserted that Paul's concept of 'the Mystical Body of Christ' is no mere 'pictorial expression . . . but an actual entity'; Christians are 'physically interdependent in the same corporeity [*sic*]'.[15] As John Robinson comments,

> It is almost impossible to exaggerate the materialism and crudity of Paul's doctrine of the church as literally now the resurrection *body* of Christ. . . . The body that he has in mind is as concrete and as singular as the body of the Incarnation. His underlying conception is not of a supra-personal collective, but of a specific personal organism.[16]

Lionel Thornton put it memorably: 'We are members of that body which was nailed to the cross, laid in the tomb and raised to life on the third day.'[17] 'Body' remains a metaphor (what else could it be?), but it is meant in the strongest possible (realist) sense.

It seems likely that it was not only the tradition that prompted or perhaps demanded use of the body metaphor, but also contemporary ideological issues. Clearly, traditional themes would have had little purchase unless they resonated with current issues that were circulating in the bloodstream of the community. Use of the body image did not originate with the New Testament and is certainly not confined to it; it is generic in conceptual construals of society. In the ancient world the Stoic elaboration of the body image pervaded Graeco-Roman culture, and Paul would have absorbed this, even if he had not, as a Pharisee, formally studied the writings of Seneca, Plutarch and others. Striking parallels have been detected between Stoic cosmology and ethics, on the one hand, and Paul's use of the body metaphor in 1 Corinthians. The Stoics conceived the cosmos as a body and humanity as a body within it – in both cases a body infused with the energy and life of spirit (*pneuma*) and ordered by mind (*nous*). Paul sees the church

---

[15] Schweitzer, *The Mysticism of Paul the Apostle*, p. 127.

[16] Robinson, *The Body*, p. 51. See also E. L. Mascall, *Christ, the Christian and the Church: A Study of the Incarnation and Its Consequences* (London: Longman, Green & Co., 1946), p. 112; but cf. Gundry, *SŌMA in Biblical Theology*, chapter 17. Michelle V. Lee, *Paul, the Stoics and the Body of Christ*, SNTS (Cambridge: Cambridge University Press, 2006), pp. 1–3, sides with Gundry against Robinson's literal interpretation, but rather puzzlingly endorses Schweitzer's description in *The Mysticism of Paul the Apostle*, 'shared corporeity', and insists that the body image stands for identity and unity between Christ and the church. Jewett, *Paul's Anthropological Terms*, pp. 215–16, also approves Schweitzer's notion of 'somatic union' and endorses Robinson's central insight into the corporal concept, pp. 220–2. G. B. Caird, *New Testament Theology*, ed. L. D. Hurst (Oxford: Clarendon Press, 1994), p. 175, warns against 'the excesses of those who have concentrated on his [Paul's] figurative use of the word "body" and have mistaken vividness of imagery for "ontological realism", that is to say, a relation between Christ and the believer that is less than personal.'

[17] Lionel S. Thornton, *The Common Life in the Body of Christ*, 3rd edn (London: Dacre Press, 1950), p. 298.

as inspired by the Holy Spirit and guided by the revealed mind of Christ.[18] We can take this perspective a step further.

In *The Corinthian Body* Dale Martin attempts an ideological reading of the battles over 'body' in the Corinthian community as reflected in Paul's letters, and does so in the light of ancient culture, medicine and philosophy.[19] Martin argues that Paul was engaged in a dispute with a section of the Corinthian church about the ideological construction of the human body and consequently about the body of the church. While Paul himself and probably the majority of the Corinthian Christians saw the body as 'a dangerously permeable entity, threatened by polluting agents', an influential minority known as 'the Strong' stressed the hierarchical arrangement of the body and the proper balance of its constituent parts, without, however, being particularly concerned about bodily boundaries or threats of pollution. The rival ideological stances corresponded to different the social status of the two groups, with Paul deliberately identifying himself with the so-called 'weak'.

Martin's study reminds us of the fact that theological terms, and especially images, which are always open to ambiguity, have ideological uses. They not only lend themselves to being appropriated to defend the social status and privileged position of some over against others, but are actually shaped by such factors from the beginning – infused with ideological interests. There is no theological statement and no biblical image that is ideologically innocent. Divine revelation does not protect against that. Ideological distortion always has to be allowed for and corrective action has to be taken, partly by bringing other, complementary biblical material to bear on the issue. The ideological contamination of biblical concepts, images and terms is an uncomfortable reality that we should bear in mind as we continue now to look at the New Testament images of the church.

People of God

It has been claimed for the image of the church as the people of God that it is 'the oldest and most fundamental concept underlying the self-interpretation of Israel and of the Christian Church. In comparison with this, the various images used of Israel and the Church are secondary. The people of God is the reality underlying the images.'[20] (Though, of course, 'people' is an image too!) The Second Vatican Council made the image of the church as the people of God normative and fundamental in the document that is itself the normative and fundamental document of the Council, the 'Dogmatic Constitution on the Church': *Lumen Gentium* (LG). The image, model or symbol of the people of God is, to that extent, to be counted as the first of the first, the image of images.

---

[18] Lee, *Paul, the Stoics and the Body of Christ*.
[19] Dale Martin, *The Corinthian Body* (New Haven, CT: Yale University Press, 1995).
[20] Preston, *Faces of the Church*, pp. 13–14. See also the expositions in Hans Küng, *The Church*, trans. Ray and Rosaleen Ockenden (London: Search Press, 1971 [1968]), pp. 107–32 and Dunn, *The Theology of Paul the Apostle*, pp. 548–52.

'People' has a specific sense here: a people as an entity, a unit; not a loose collection of individuals as when we say 'a crowd of people', or 'people in general'. Minear brings out the biblical, Hebraic, understanding of this matter: 'People in general do not exist; there are only particular peoples. . . . Every person belongs to a particular people . . . and this people is not reducible to the mathematical aggregate of its members. The people defines the person.'[21] Minear continues: 'To identify a particular society as the people of God is immediately to set it over against all other peoples. This people and it alone has been constituted in a special way by this God's action, by his taking it as his own possession.'[22]

From the call of Abraham onwards, God (Yahweh) purposed to form a people and a nation for himself (Gen. 12:1-3). In the history of Israel, as reflected in its Scriptures, the lines of demarcation between the early tribal clans, the nation first formed under David, the exiled people of God in Babylon and in the *diaspora* are far from clear-cut. The relationship and connection between the land, the nation and the people is dynamic and shifting according to the vicissitudes of history. Part of the reason for this state of affairs is that the period when Israel was together as a nation and a people dwelling in a land within their own borders was brief – less than a century, under David and Solomon, immediately after which the kingdom broke into two parts. So the national dimension of being a people remained an ideal – in fact an eschatological point of reference for an understanding of what it meant to be the people of God. However, the fact that being such a people was not necessarily tied to the empirical reality of nationhood and territory meant that the concept of the elect people of God could be transferred to the Jews of the dispersion throughout the centuries (perhaps as a race, more than as a people, in the eyes of the other nations, races and peoples), and it could also be applied to the early Christians, as we will see when we look at the New Testament evidence in a moment.[23]

In the beginning this people of God, the Jews, were called out of the other nations: Abraham went out from Ur of the Chaldeans; the Israelites made the Exodus from Egypt; the exiles returned from Babylon. They were called out precisely in order to be gathered together by God in order to worship and serve God. The Exodus from slavery in Egypt is the biblical paradigm of Israel being delivered and gathered by God to serve and worship him. In retrospect it appeared to some prophets that in the wilderness the people of Israel offered pure worship (most of the time, perhaps) without the benefit of a temple and its cultus. The link with Abraham is made when Paul calls the Christians whom he is addressing 'Abraham's descendants' (Rom. 4:16; Gal. 3:29; 4:26-28). And 1 Peter makes the connection with Babylon when he depicts his addressees as 'aliens and exiles . . . among the Gentiles' (1 Pet. 2:11-12)

From the beginning, this calling to become God's worshipping people was never meant to be an end in itself but was intended to benefit all peoples and nations, to bring universal blessing (Gen. 18:18; 22:18; 26:4; 28:14). God's purposes would eventually

---

21 Minear, *Images of the Church in the New Testament*, p. 68.
22 Ibid., p. 68.
23 R. E. Clements, *Old Testament Theology: A Fresh Approach* (London: Marshall, Morgan & Scott, 1978), pp. 79–87.

embrace all the nations and they would receive the same blessing (Isa. 11:10; 60:3-5; Zech. 2:10-11). The day would come when the knowledge of the glory of God would fill the earth as the waters cover the sea (Hab. 2:14).

'People of God' is an eminently covenantal concept. In the turbulent, violent and unstable political conditions of the ancient Near East, nothing was more to be desired than to be 'a people', to enjoy the integrity and security of knowing where and to whom they belonged and to be protected and defended by their God. The heart of the covenant promise, reiterated again and again, was that God would deliver Israel from their enemies and that they would be God's people and God would be their God (Exod. 6:7; 19:6; Lev. 26:12; Deut. 7:6; Jer. 32:38; Ezek. 11:20; Ps. 95:7).[24]

God's covenant is a relationship with the whole people corporately, rather than with individuals within it, though it is made with representative persons such as Abraham and David. Yahweh relates to the people as such, not to the individuals that make it up. The notion of a separate individual personality is not known to the Hebrew Bible. 'It is an axiom of the Old Testament revelation that God deals with society . . . with the community. The individual can live before God only as a member of the community.'[25] To describe this phenomenon of Israelite collective identity the term 'corporate personality' was coined by H. Wheeler Robinson. He found it particularly in the representative identity of the 'I' of the Psalmist, the King in Israel, the Suffering Servant of Deutero-Isaiah and in Paul's Adam/Christ parallel.[26] Robinson's idea has come in for heavy criticism, especially from John Rogerson, mainly for its dependence on certain questionable anthropological theories about primitive mentality.[27] H. H. Rowley, writing before Rogerson's critique, accepts the term in his discussion of 'Individual and Community' in ancient Israel.[28] Cyril Rodd outlines the theory and the criticisms, insisting – perhaps too forcefully – that the concept of corporate personality

---

[24] Rolf Rendtorff, *The Covenant Formula*, trans. Margaret Kohl (Edinburgh: T&T Clark, 1998); G. P. Hugenberger, *Marriage as Covenant: A Study of the Biblical Law and Ethics Governing Marriage, Developed from the Perspective of Malachi*, Supplement to *Vetus Testamentum*, vol. 52 (Leiden: Brill, 1994); Scott J. Hafemann, 'The Covenant Relationship', in id. and Paul R. House (eds), *Central Themes in Biblical Theology: Mapping Unity in Diversity* (Nottingham: Apollos, 2007); Walther Eichrodt, *Theology of the Old Testament*, trans. John Baker (London: SCM Press, 1967), vol. 1, pp. 36–69; Clements, *Old Testament Theology*, pp. 96–103; see also the discussion of the covenant concept in Paul Avis, *The Vocation of Anglicanism* (London and New York: Bloomsbury T&T Clark, 2016), chapter 4, 'A Covenantal Vocation'.

[25] Ludwig Koehler, *Old Testament Theology*, trans. A. S. Todd (London: Lutterworth Press, 1957), p. 65, italics removed. See the discussion of collective and individual elements in ancient Israelite sociology in Eichrodt, *Theology of the Old Testament*, vol. 2, pp. 231–67.

[26] H. Wheeler Robinson, *Corporate Personality in Ancient Israel*, intro. by John Reumann and Cyril S. Rodd, rev. edn (Edinburgh: T&T Clark, 1981) [previous edition, without Rodd's Introduction, Fortress Press, 1964]. The two key essays collected in this volume were first published in 1936 (Göttingen) and 1937 (Oxford) respectively. But Wheeler Robinson had set out his ideas on 'corporate personality' in 1911, in *The Christian Doctrine of Man*, 3rd edn (Edinburgh: T&T Clark, 1926 [1911]), pp. 27–42.

[27] John Rogerson, 'The Hebrew Conception of Corporate Personality: A Re-Examination', *JTS* 21 (1970), pp. 1–16, reproduced with some shortening of the notes in Bernhard Lang (ed.), *Anthropological Approaches to the Old Testament* (Philadelphia, PA: Fortress Press; London: SPCK, 1985), pp. 43–59; see also J. W. Rogerson, *Anthropology and the Old Testament* (Oxford: Blackwell, 1978), especially pp. 55–65. See further J. R. Porter, 'The Legal Aspects of the Concept of "Corporate Personality" in the Old Testament', *VT* XV (1965), pp. 361–80.

[28] H. H. Rowley, *The Faith of Israel* (London: SCM Press, 1956), pp. 99–123, at p. 118.

is 'completely inapplicable' to the New Testament,[29] while James Dunn finds it 'more of a hindrance than a help' in explicating Paul's Adam/Christ parallel in Romans 5.[30] However, I think myself that though the concept of personality, whether individual or corporate, is probably an anachronism when applied to the psychology of the ancient Hebrews, the assumption of a collective, rather than essentially individual identity for the ancient Hebrews, that Robinson highlighted, remains valid for the interpretation of the Hebrew Bible and contributes to the background of the New Testament image of the people of God as a collective or corporate entity.

The covenant relationship of the people of Israel to their God became strained by Israel's disobedience and idolatry. Her persistent unfaithfulness amounted to a breach of the covenant on her side. Israel, once the people of God, were now 'Not my people' (Hos. 1:9). But through the prophets Yahweh promises to restore them to a covenant relation to himself so that they will be his people again (Hos. 2:23; cf. Jer. 7:23; 24:7; 32:38; Ezek. 11:20; 14:11). Those who had not been a people will be a people once more and belong securely to their God. To know yourselves collectively to be the people of God was of the essence of salvation history.

In the New Testament the references to the people of God in the Old Testament (*laos* in the Septuagint, LXX) are taken up, quoted and directly applied to the church (Acts 15:14; Rom. 9:25-26; 2 Cor. 6:16). There are 140 uses of *laos* in the New Testament; Luke-Acts having more than all other books put together.[31] This extension of 'people' status from Israel to the church is further underlined when we take into account the fact that, in the LXX, *laos* is only ever applied to Israel, never to the Gentiles who are called *ethnē*, nations. The covenant promises are fulfilled in the church of Christ; Christians are now 'the people of God' (*laos tou theou*). In the New Testament the theological equivalent of 'people of God' and 'people of Israel' in the Old Testament is the *ekklēsia* or *ekklēsia tou theou* ('church of God'). Perhaps the richest text in which Christians are described as the people (*laos*) of God is 1 Pet. 2:9-10, where the author immediately quotes Hos. 2:23: 'Once you were not a people, but now you are God's people.'[32] Minear comments: 'Its previous existence was one of shadowy nonexistence in darkness. The transition into being coincided with the transforming operation of God's mercy. This transition was, in turn, inseparable from the vocation of declaring God's wonderful deeds.'[33]

To be God's people is not the only privilege that the author of 1 Peter ascribes to his readers and auditors; they are also 'a chosen race, a royal priesthood, a holy nation'.

---

[29]   Rodd, introduction to Wheeler Robinson, *Corporate Personality*, p. 13.
[30]   James D. G. Dunn, *Romans 1-8, Word Biblical Commentary* (Dallas, TX: Word Books, 1988), p. 272. Similarly, Ernst Käsemann, *Commentary on Romans*, trans. from 4th German edition [1980] and ed. Geoffrey W. Bromiley (Grand Rapids, MI: Eerdmans, 1980), p. 142, judges this 'greatly overworked' idea unhelpful in explicating the Adamic Christology.
[31]   *TDNT*, vol. 4, pp. 29–57 (H. Strathmann).
[32]   The whole quotation in 1 Pet. 2:9-10 is a conflation of three texts from Hos. 1:9-10; 1:6; 2:23. In Rom. 9:25-26 Paul quotes the verses from Hosea in a slightly different form, adapting the LXX to suit his emphasis on the admission of the Gentiles to covenant mercy and status. The overall import of the quotations in 1 Peter 2 and Romans 9 is the same: the Gentiles have been incorporated into the people of God and this is the eschatological fulfilment of ancient prophecy.
[33]   Minear, *Images of the Church in the New Testament*, p. 69.

Here we have a succession, a build-up, of honorific titles that all refer to the corporate nature of the church: a race (*genos*, the only ecclesial, rather than biological, use of this term in the New Testament), a priesthood, a nation (*ethnos*, again a rare use), a people. Nothing is said about individual Christians apart from the whole. To be within the church means assuming a corporate or collective identity. We will say something about the royal priesthood shortly.

Is the image or symbol of the people of God in tension with that of the body of Christ? Joseph Ratzinger (Pope Benedict XVI) wrestled with this question. Was the image of the body more hospitable to the notions of hierarchy, law and authority that he wished to affirm and the image of a people more communitarian and democratic in its tendency? In his doctoral dissertation of 1964 he found a form of words that could point to a way of overcoming the tension: 'The church is just the people of God existing as the body of Christ.' The body image was the determining element that shaped the image of the people of God.[34] I think that Ratzinger was right to see the two metaphors as complementary; they are indeed ecclesiologically interdependent. But I would go beyond Ratzinger's 1964 formulation by saying that not only is it the case that the people of God exists as the body of Christ, but also that the body of Christ exists as the people of God. If the body metaphor emphasizes the 'holding together in solidarity' aspect of the church and the interdependence of all its parts (limbs and organs), it is no less true and important that the people metaphor underlines the identity of the church as the community that belongs to God, has been called by God and brought into being by divine election in the course of history in order to be a privileged instrument of God's purpose, the reign of God. As Walter Kasper puts it, 'The ecclesiology of the people of God places the ecclesiology of the body of Christ more clearly into an eschatological context. . . . The language of the people of God thus expresses the historical nature of the Church.'[35] The church receives its identity from God as it moves forward through time, through history. 'People of God' is a dynamic image of the church, with overtones of emergence, development and forward direction. But a people can move forward – spread out – in space as well as time, so 'people of God' has a synchronic as well as a diachronic dimension.

Against the Old Testament background, the 'people of God' image suggests two further, far-reaching thoughts. First, it is a more egalitarian image than 'body', because a body has a head and some parts of the body are more useful and more presentable than others (as Paul himself admits: 1 Cor. 12:22-24). On the other hand, to be a people is suggestive of equal status – though even a people needs a leader or leaders. While 'body of Christ' is centred on Christ and therefore on the body too, since he is its head and the body is therefore the whole Christ (*totus christus*), 'people of God' is centred on God, rather than on the people. As Kasper says, it is theocentric. While *ekklēsia* suggests, from its civic uses, a coming together to confer, to take responsibility and to decide, the connotations of *laos* (people) are 'to listen to and celebrate what God has decided and done' and in response to 'offer spiritual sacrifices' and to 'proclaim God's

---

[34] Cited Theodor Dieter, 'Joseph Ratzinger', in Paul Avis (ed.), *The Oxford Handbook of Ecclesiology* (Oxford: Oxford University Press, 2018), chapter 20, at p. 450.
[35] Kasper, *The Catholic Church*, p. 124; so also Küng, *The Church*, p. 224.

wonderful deeds' (1 Pet. 2:5, 9). This adoring attitude and these kerygmatic actions give the church as 'the people of God' a 'doxological structure' (Kasper).[36]

Royal priesthood

We have drawn on 1 Peter for the image of the people of God (which is linked to the image of 'a chosen nation'). Without using the word *ekklēsia* or adverting to Paul's metaphor of the body (which the author may have known), this epistle greatly enriches the imagery of the church in its relationship to Jesus Christ. As well as the images of race, nation, temple and flock, it is a prime source for the images of priesthood ('a holy priesthood') and kingdom ('a kingdom of priests') – the two being amalgamated in the double-barrelled designation 'royal priesthood'. If we add the fact that the purpose of this priesthood is 'in order that you may proclaim the mighty acts of him who called you out of darkness into his marvellous light' (here we have both an allusion to baptism or Christian initiation – enlightenment – and the prophetic function of proclaiming the word of God), we have the picture of a triple identity in Christ: a royal, prophetic, priesthood (1 Pet. 2:5, 9). We note, once again, that in 1 Peter this designation of the church is a continuation and eschatological fulfilment of what is said in the Jewish Scriptures about ancient Israel (Exod. 19.6; Isa. 43:20-21, both from the LXX). But now all of this spiritual drama takes place 'in Christ', a term that is used three times in 1 Peter, without being elaborated theologically as it is in the Pauline and Johannine literature.[37]

The 1 Peter passage is difficult grammatically, its interpretation is contested and the way that it makes use of Old Testament texts is an exegetical minefield.[38] Without wilfully misinterpreting it or going into exegetical detail, we may be assured that in the theology implied in this text a corporate priesthood is attributed to the church and that this image takes its place within a range of Old Testament metaphors or images that are applied to the church in the New Testament. The 1 Peter 2 reference is not alone: in the Book of Revelation the sacerdotal term for priest, *hiereus*, is used in the expression 'a kingdom of/and priests', though *hiereus* is avoided elsewhere in the New Testament, including in 1 Peter, presumably because of its pagan cultic associations (Rev. 1:6; 5:10; 20:6).

In both of his painstaking and exhaustive studies (footnoted immediately above), John H. Elliott is at pains to point out that 1 Peter 2 provides no support whatever for what he calls 'the Reformation doctrine',[39] but which is in fact the post-Reformation

---

[36] Kasper, *The Catholic Church*, p. 125. See also Tord Fornberg, 'The People of God' in Sven-Olav Back and Erkki Koskenniemi (eds), *Institutions of the Emerging Church*, Library of New Testament Studies 305 (London and New York: Bloomsbury T&T Clark, 2016), pp. 129–44.

[37] E. G. Selwyn, *The First Epistle of St. Peter: The Greek Text with Introduction, Notes and Essays*, 2nd edn (London: Macmillan, 1947), p. 83.

[38] J. N. D. Kelly, *The Epistles of Peter and Jude*, Black's New Testament Commentaries (London: A. & C. Black, 1969), pp. 95–8; Selwyn, *The First Epistle of St. Peter*, pp. 268–81; J. H. Elliott, *The Elect and the Holy: An Exegetical Examination of I Peter 2: 4-10 and the phrase Βασίλειον ἱεράτευμα* (Leiden: Brill, 1966); id., *1 Peter: A New Translation with Introduction and Commentary*, Anchor Bible (New York: Doubleday, 2000).

[39] See specially the 'Detailed Comment' on this topic, Elliott, *1 Peter: A New Translation with Introduction and Commentary*, pp. 449–55, at p. 453.

popular Protestant notion of 'the priesthood of all believers' (every Christian their own priest), at one end of the ecclesiological spectrum, or for the traditional 'Catholic' idea of a mediating, sacramental priesthood, at the other end. The emphasis in this passage, as in the LXX sources that it mainly draws upon, Elliott insists, is firmly on the divine election, ethical holiness and collective unity of the people that God has claimed as his own. Nevertheless, the image of a priesthood (*hierateuma*) is ineradicably embedded here and moreover it is anchored to the robust image of the kingdom, thus reinforcing the concept of the church as a corporate, royal, prophetic, priesthood.

If we then ask. 'What kind of priesthood is this? What is its nature?' the answer must be that the character of the priesthood is determined by the sacrifices that it offers, because sacrifice belongs to the *raison d'être* of priesthood. The spiritual sacrifices are not defined in 1 Pet. 2:5, but in Rom. 12:1 they are designated 'living', 'holy', 'acceptable' and 'reasonable'. And in Rom. 15:16, Paul's mission to the Gentiles and his consequent offering to God of their conversion is his priestly service of the gospel. So Christians offer lives – their own lives and those that they have won for Christ – to God through Christ. In living their life Christians continuously carry out works of charity and fellowship that are pleasing to God (Heb. 13:16). But because as sinful humans we are unworthy to offer any sacrifice, except though the mediation of Christ, the offering of spiritual sacrifices is properly connected, in the liturgies of most churches, with the Eucharist – the Eucharist understood as a sacrifice of prayer and praise in union with Christ's self-offering to the Father (cf. Heb. 13:15). Much of this idea is present in 1 Peter 2, as a sort of subtext. As Selwyn puts it, 'the sacrifices offered by the priestly body, the Church, are intimately connected with the atoning work of Christ, and also serve to shew [*sic*] it forth in all its rich and reconciling mercy.'[40] Selwyn adds: 'Temple – priesthood – sacrifices: we are not entitled to regard these terms as purely metaphorical. The ethics of the Apostolic Church are inseparably bound up with its worship, and the term "sacrifice" is used of the latter as freely as of the former.'[41]

Household, family and friends of Jesus and God

One interesting possibility that I will not explore in much detail is the image of the church as a family. Although Banks in *Paul's Idea of Community*[42] makes considerable play of this picture of the church, I am doubtful whether any New Testament writer explicitly calls the church a family. The image of a family may be an anachronistic way of looking at the church, reading back modern (but certainly not postmodern) social structures and ethical values regarding the 'family unit' into the biblical text. The metaphor 'family' is not explicitly used; the analogy has to be inferred from several sources. Christians are described as 'members of the household (*tous oikeious*) of faith' (Gal. 6:10, translated 'family' in NRSV) and as 'no longer aliens (*paroikoi*)' but 'members

---

[40] Selwyn, *The First Epistle of St. Peter*, pp. 295–6. See further Alan Richardson, *An Introduction to the Theology of the New Testament* (London: SCM Press, 1958), pp. 297–301.

[41] Selwyn, *The First Epistle of St. Peter*, p. 296.

[42] Robert Banks, *Paul's Idea of Community*, rev. edn (Peabody, MA: Hendrikson, 1994 [1979]).

of the household (*oikeioi*) of God' (Eph. 2:19). In the ancient world, the household consisted of the extended family with the addition of dependent relatives, business associates, servants and slaves; everyone had their particular roles and responsibilities. The household of the classical world was a far cry from the modern, Western nuclear family. In the Old Testament and in early Judaism, the place where God and God's people meet is called the 'house' (principally the temple, of course, while it stood) and the people of God a 'household' (Hebrew *bayit*). As Longnecker points out, when the word 'household' was used, 'ideas of order, structure and functional responsibility' were implied.[43] 'House' (*oikos*) and 'church' (*ekklēsia*) are directly equated in 1 Timothy 3:15. Commonly, Christians are addressed as 'brothers' (which is interpreted in modern translations as 'brothers and sisters'). God is addressed intimately as 'Abba', Father, and Jesus called his disciples his mother and brothers.[44] Paul says that believers are adopted sons of God, and Peter that they have been 'born anew'. So we can say that there is at least the making of an image of the church as the 'family of God' in the New Testament.

In *Community of the New Age: Studies in Mark's Gospel*, Howard Clark Kee points to the image of 'the redefined family' in support of his assertion that 'in every case the images employed in Mark to represent Christian existence are corporate' (the other corporate images in Mark that he expounds are kingdom, flock, Exodus, vineyard/ building and covenant people).[45] Kee's reading of such passages in Mark as 3:20-21, 31-35; 10:28-31 leads him to conclude that 'all genetic, familial, and sex distinctions are eradicated in this new concept of the true family. The corollary of the new family identity is rupture with the actual family'.[46] This reading serves well in bringing out the radical, subversive implications and consequences of the eschatological thrust of Jesus' message in Mark, the earliest of the canonical Gospels.

Modern Bible translations make 'brothers' (*adelphoi*) into 'brothers and sisters', which is fine and probably necessary for public reading and liturgical purposes. But such a paraphrase is misleading for study and research purposes when we need to get as close to the original context, notwithstanding the blatant sexism, androcentrism and patriarchy of the culture of the time, which recognized only men as typical and representative human beings. We gain nothing by trying to pretend that the biblical literature is 'inclusive' when it plainly is not – inclusivity is a late-modern virtue. However, the seeds of a radical inclusivity are definitely present in Jesus' own attitude and practice with regard to women, social outcasts such as lepers, and others who did not fit the current canons of social and ritual acceptability. Jesus rejected no one and treated everyone alike, with love, compassion, truthfulness and respect, except for the

---

[43] Richard N. Longnecker (ed.), *Community Formation in the Early Church and Today* (Grand Rapids, MI: Baker Academic, 2002), p. 77 (by Longnecker).

[44] *The Household of God* is the title of a work of ecclesiology by Lesslie Newbigin (London: SCM Press, 1957), which though now dated, was remarkable in its day for its serious biblical and ecumenical ecclesiology. The family motif is brought out by Banks, *Paul's Idea of Community*, chapter 5.

[45] Howard Clark Kee, *Community of the New Age: Studies in Mark's Gospel* (London: SCM Press, 1977), p. 107.

[46] Ibid., p. 107.

Pharisees whom he condemned as a bunch of legalistic hypocrites (though this group characterization has been challenged as prejudiced stereotyping by early Christians).[47]

The church as a company of Jesus' friends is perhaps a more theologically promising image than 'family' and has a firmer biblical basis. Abraham was called 'the friend of God', and no higher accolade was conceivable (2 Chron. 20:7; Isa. 41:8; James 2:23). The Apocryphal book *The Wisdom of Solomon* says that 'in every generation [wisdom] passes into holy souls and makes them friends of God and prophets' (Wisdom 7:27). In the Synoptics Jesus is called the 'friend (*philos*) of tax collectors and sinners', a derisory, abusive term that has gratefully been taken to the hearts of generations of Christians, as in the gospel hymn 'What a friend we have in Jesus/All our sins and griefs to bear' (Mt. 11:19; Lk. 7:34-35, both statements explicitly making the connection with Wisdom 7:27). Jesus even greets Judas as 'friend' (*hetairos*) when Judas comes to the Garden of Gethsemane to betray him (Mt. 26:50).

These biblical instances remain at some distance from the idea of the church as the Christian community. However, in the Fourth Gospel, on the eve of the crucifixion, Jesus calls his disciples 'friends'. Why? Because he has shared with them his deepest thoughts, fears and prayers; so they are no longer 'slaves', but 'friends'. The word *doulos/douloi* (slave/slaves), is softened to 'servants' in some modern translations, perhaps because the translators thought that most readers would not understand that in some households in the ancient world slaves were treated almost as part of the extended family and were well looked after. But that is not the issue in the Johannine text with regard to the metaphor of slavery. The point is, as Jesus points out, that 'the slave does not know what the master is doing'. The slave has no rights, no independence and no responsibility that is not derived, lent for the time being and indeed imposed. But here Jesus gathers the disciples around him in an intimate way as the company of his friends, for whom he will lay down his life (Jn 15:12-15; cf. Lk. 12:4). There is a parallel with the Good Shepherd who lays down his life for the sheep (Jn 10:11, 15). Jesus, the personification of holy Wisdom, has entered into their very being – they will never be the same again – making them (as Wisdom puts it) 'friends of God and prophets', even apostles. As such, they are the pioneers and the nucleus of the church.

The idea of friendship with God and with (as well as through) Jesus, as an image of the church, has a particular appeal today. There is no mystification in it; it is immediately understandable and resonates with human experience. It meets an evident need and longing for fellowship and mutual support in an impersonal, anonymous society. The theme of friendship is a virtuous theme, concerned with the character, integrity and authenticity of the church, rather than with its structure, organization or claims of authority. It can help the church to rediscover its true nature as a welcoming, hospitable, relational and nurturing community.[48] The church as the company of friends of Jesus, and therefore of each other, is perhaps the most *affective* of the ecclesiological images: it touches our hearts and registers on our emotions. This approach is not special pleading

---

[47]   On the 'inclusivism' question see Richard A. Burridge, *Imitating Jesus: An Inclusivist Approach to New Testament Ethics* (Grand Rapids, MI: Eerdmans, 2007). For Jesus and the Pharisees see E. P. Sanders, *Jesus and Judaism* (London: SCM Press, 1985).

[48]   Further on the notion of friendship in ecclesiology see Steve Summers, *Friendship: Exploring Its Implications for the Church in Postmodernity* (London and New York: T&T Clark, 2009).

or stretching biblical terms to suit our modern sensibilities or political correctness. It is firmly grounded in the Scriptures, particularly the Gospels, but with significant precedents in the Hebrew Bible and the Wisdom books of the Apocrypha. The fact that Christ stretched out the hand of friendship, solidarity and unconditional acceptance to all whom he encountered belongs to the quintessence of his ministry. One aspect of his method in founding his continuing community was that he invited his disciples into an especially intimate relationship as his friends. The outstretched arms of Jesus on the cross have rightly been seen, in Christian devotion and liturgy, as a symbol of his universal, loving embrace.

Temple not built with hands

When the people of Israel journeyed from bondage in Egypt to the land that God had promised to the patriarchs, God's presence was symbolized for them by the pillar of cloud by day and of fire by night (Exod. 13:21-22). God's presence was also located concretely for them in the travelling tabernacle (Exod. 25–27) and later at certain shrines, such as the one at Shiloh where the infant Samuel heard the call of God (1 Sam. 3). The Jerusalem temple, the primary site of God's awesome presence in the midst of his people (2 Chron. 5:13-14; 6:1; 7:1-3), was the destination in view when people 'went up' to seek the presence of the Lord (Ps. 5:7; 27:4; 42:2-4; 43:3-4). In times of disaster and of exile, the temple – whether still standing or simply present to the imagination – was the focus of Jewish hopes and longings. The vision of the prophets, as Ezekiel shows at great length and in extraordinary detail (Ezek. 40–46), was that when the people returned safely to their homeland, the temple would be rebuilt. The temple represented the integrity of the Jewish nation as the people chosen by God. The future temple is symbolic of the future of God's people. 'The restoration of Israel means the restoration of the temple, and the restoration of the temple means the ingathering and reunion of Israel.'[49]

But not the ingathering of Israel only: in Deutero-Isaiah the vision of restoration includes the universal gathering in of the Gentiles (Isa. 56:7; 60:3-7). The nations will flock to Jerusalem, which is regarded as the centre of the earth. The new temple is now seen as the symbol, not only of Israel's unity but also of the unity of all humanity. The criteria for admission to the temple are ethical and spiritual. Its purpose is one of prayer for all. The sacrifices offered in it – it is repeatedly emphasized – will be 'acceptable'. The thought of Peter's 'spiritual house' and 'spiritual sacrifices' is present in the temple motif. Haggai, Zechariah and Malachi (3:1-4) explicitly connect the temple with the coming of the Messiah. In the inter-testamental period, when Jewish monotheism reigned unchallenged, the theme of the temple as a symbol of unity became intensified: one God, one temple.[50] Jewish apocalyptic envisioned an eschatological temple descending from heaven or being miraculously constructed upon earth. In a rather

[49] R. J. McKelvey, *The New Temple: The Church in the New Testament* (Oxford: Oxford University Press, 1969), p. 14.
[50] Ibid., p. 19.

Platonic way, it would be a copy of the heavenly temple. In response to failed hopes and successive national disasters, the temple idea became allegorized or spiritualized: this development paved the way for the appropriation of the temple theme by Jesus himself and the writers of the New Testament.

Paul makes the temple a key metaphor of the work of the Holy Spirit in the church and of the church as the dwelling place of the Holy Spirit. Most of the images or metaphors that we are considering in this chapter have their Spirit dimension: the body of Christ is a Spirit-bearing body; the members are baptized into it by the Holy Spirit (1 Cor. 12:13); the people of God is a people led by the Spirit (Rom. 8:14; Gal. 5:18) and given spiritual gifts (*charismata*) (1 Cor. 12–14); the new humanity is a humanity endued with the Spirit, conforming it to the image of God (1 Cor. 15:45); the royal priesthood is a prophetic priesthood because, like the prophets, it is inspired by the Spirit to 'proclaim the mighty acts of him who called you out of darkness into his marvellous light' (1 Pet. 2:9). The ecclesiology of the Gospels and Epistles is an 'epicletic' ecclesiology, emphasizing the Spirit descending and resting upon the church, in answer to prayer and intercession (Latin: *invocatio*), as it rested upon Christ at his baptism (Mt. 3:16; Mk 1:10; Lk. 3:21-22; cf. Acts 2:1-4; 4:31). But it is the temple image above all that lifts up the pneumatological dimension of the church in the New Testament.[51]

Obviously, Paul did not invent the image of the temple as the *locus* of God's saving presence with God's people. We have already glanced at the background in the Hebrew scriptures. Its use in the New Testament reliably goes back, in both word and deed, to Jesus himself. In Mark we have the parable of the vineyard, which – intriguingly – concludes with the image of a building: 'The stone that the builders rejected has become the cornerstone [etc.]', a stock proof text of early Christian apologetic, designed to show that though the Messiah had been rejected and crucified, he was indeed God's chosen foundation for the redeemed community (cf. Acts 4:11; Eph. 2:19-22; 1 Pet. 2:4, 7). The community in Mark is portrayed as a community in the process of construction, of upbuilding, with Jesus the Messiah as its foundation.[52] In John 15 we have the thought-provoking image of Christians 'indwelling' the vine (Jesus), as though the vine were a temple. Garden, vineyard, vine, building, temple and body merge into one another in the repertoire of New Testament images. Karl Barth, whose extended exposition of 'the upbuilding of the community' is an unrivalled commentary on this image, points out that 'it is not for nothing that in the New Testament the picture of building is often confusingly intermingled with that of the divine planting'. The simple reason is that humans can no more build the church themselves than they can make the plants grow – both of these phenomena of growth are the unique, sovereign work of God.[53]

False witnesses at Christ's trial accused him of claiming that he would destroy the Temple made with hands and in three days erect another – and this is the eschatological bombshell – 'not made with hands' (Mk 14:58). Even if the specific mention of the

---

[51]   Kasper, *The Catholic Church*, pp. 135–45.
[52]   Kee, *Community of the New Age*, p. 113.
[53]   Karl Barth, *Church Dogmatics*, ed. G. W. Bromiley and T. F. Torrance, trans. G. W. Bromiley (Edinburgh: T&T Clark, 1975-), IV/2, pp. 626–41, at p. 631.

three days should be regarded as a secondary addition, and even if Jesus predicted the destruction of the temple, rather than threatened to destroy it himself ('destroy' should probably be attributed to hostile testimony), it was certainly believed that Jesus had foretold both the destruction of the temple (Mk 13:1-2) and its replacement with a spiritual temple. What is commonly referred to as 'the cleansing of the temple' should more correctly be understood as a prophetic sign of the its impending destruction and eschatological restoration, or rather replacement. In current Jewish hopes and expectations this scenario regarding the temple was seen as the critical moment and central event in the restoration of Israel as the covenant people of God.[54] Jesus' entry into Jerusalem and his so-called cleansing of the temple were prophetic, proleptic signs of the coming of the kingdom, grounded in his personal authority (*exousia*) and in his words and deeds, so that God's saving presence with God's people was now invested in him, as the agent of the coming reign of God.[55] This interpretation, that is securely anchored in the vocation, mission and self-understanding of Jesus himself, as far as we can access it, was elaborated and made explicit by New Testament writers.

The Fourth Gospel places together, at an early and determinative point in the narrative, two sayings of Jesus at the cleansing of the temple that in the Synoptics belong, with that episode, to the close and climax of his ministry: first, the words, 'My Father's house'; secondly, 'Destroy this temple and in three days I will raise it up.' John makes it clear that the significance of these words and deeds eluded the disciples at the time, but that they made the connection between temple, resurrection and the church after Christ had risen. John states it in the cryptic aside, 'He spoke of the temple of his body' (Jn 2:16-22). This is a truly explosive connection – indeed it is more than a connection: it is a radical transposition from the temple and Israel to the resurrection body and the church. It is the same Gospel that provides the theological elucidation when Jesus explains to the woman at Jacob's well in Samaria, 'The hour is coming when neither on this mountain nor in Jerusalem will you worship the Father . . . the true worshippers will worship the Father in spirit and truth' through the mission of the Messiah (Jn 4:21, 26). Kasper comments on this christological interpretation of the temple: 'Jesus himself is God's temple in his person. He is the place where God has irrevocably and totally made his dwelling, where God's glory has finally appeared (Jn. 1:14). In him God wanted to dwell in his whole fullness (Col. 1.19).'[56] The temple is the site of God's glory. In the incarnation that glory dwelt (*eskēnōsen*) in Jesus Christ (Jn 1:14). Now it is the church that is the intended site of God's glory (2 Cor. 3:18; Eph 3:21). The images of temple and body are closely aligned in the sources.[57]

On this dominical foundation Pauline theology portrays the Christian church at every level of its existence – universally, locally and in its individual members – as the temple of the Holy Spirit. There is still only one temple. McKelvey points out that

---

[54]   Sanders, *Jesus and Judaism*, esp. chapters 1 and 2; N. T. Wright, *Jesus and the Victory of God* (London: SPCK, 1996), pp. 405–37, 615.

[55]   Cf. Wright, *Jesus and the Victory of God*, pp. 426, 436, 615.

[56]   Sanders, *Jesus and Judaism*, p. 106.

[57]   They may have been brought together in Qumran or other Essene communities: Bertil Gärtner, *The Temple and the Community in Qumran and the New Testament* (Cambridge: Cambridge University Press, 1965).

Paul, formed in the Jewish faith, could not and did not think in terms of many temples, but only of one.[58] The temple image speaks of the unity of the church in all its various instantiations.

- The *whole church*, the universal church, or as we might say, the church catholic, is a temple: 'the household of God, built upon the foundation of the apostles and prophets, Christ Jesus himself being the chief cornerstone, in whom the whole structure is joined together and grows into a holy temple in the Lord, in whom you also are built together in the Spirit into a dwelling place for God' (Eph. 2:19-22). 1 Peter also suggests that the whole church ('a chosen race, a royal priesthood, a holy nation') is a temple ('a spiritual house') where spiritual sacrifices are offered (1 Pet. 2:4-5).
- The *local* church is a temple: 'Do you [plural] not know that you are God's temple and that God's Spirit dwells in you?' (1 Cor. 3:16); 'We [collectively] are the temple of the living God' (2 Cor. 6:16; cf. Eph. 2:19-22).
- The individual Christian is also the temple of God: 'Do you not know that your body is a temple of the Holy Spirit within you?' (1 Cor. 6:19). At baptism Christians receive the indwelling Spirit, a foretaste or down-payment of the eschatological, heavenly body temple that God has in store for them (1 Cor. 12:13; Rom. 8:11; cf. 2 Cor. 5:1-5). 'Not made with hands' is a kind of code for the eschatological temple. The image of the temple, a metaphor of indwelling, connects both with the Johannine language of abiding or indwelling and Paul's use of *en christō*: the indwelling is mutual, he in us and we in him.

In all these manifestations, universal, local and personal, there is only one temple.

In the last book of the New Testament and of the Christian Bible, the temple motif reappears – the temple as city and as garden.[59] In Revelation 21 the city/garden/temple stands for nothing less than the redeemed and regenerated cosmos. (In Isa. 65:17-18 the 'new heavens and new earth' is parallel to the city of Jerusalem.) When John the Seer beholds 'a new heaven and a new earth', what he actually sees is a 'holy city, new Jerusalem', coming down from heaven. He sees 'no [physical] temple in the city, for its temple is the Lord God, the Almighty, and the Lamb'. In other words, the divine presence (*shekinah*) fills the city, just as the glory of the Lord filled Solomon's temple (2 Chron. 5:14; 7:1-2), bestowing on the city the character of a vast temple, the dwelling place of God. This vision builds on the vision of Ezekiel (40–48) who had foreseen the enlargement of the Temple to fill Jerusalem and even the whole land of Israel; as these chapters of Ezekiel unfold, temple, city and land become coterminous.[60]

Within the dwelling place of God in revelation, there is a garden and in it stands the tree of life, just as in Eden. The Garden of Eden had been understood in Jewish

---

[58]   McKelvey, *The New Temple*, p. 106.
[59]   G. K. Beale, *The Temple and the Church's Mission: A Biblical Theology of the Dwelling Place of God* (Downers Grove, IL: IVP, 2004).
[60]   I have not been able to include the theme of 'the land', with its connections to the people, the temple and the mission of Jesus. See especially W. D. Davies, *The Gospel and the Land: Early Christian and Jewish Territorial Doctrine* (Berkeley, CA: University of California Press, 1974).

thought as the first temple (as we see in the deliberate correspondences between Eden, the temple and the heavenly city in, for example, Ezekiel 28:13-19). Solomon's temple had trees and fruits. In Psalm 92 the righteous flourish like palm trees and cedars planted on rock in the 'the house of the LORD . . . the courts of our God' (vv. 12–15). The first Psalm has the same thought and the temple may be implied in the phrase 'the congregation of the righteous' (v. 5). In Revelation, Eden is also the last temple, or rather the last temple is construed as Eden, the Garden of God. Temple and garden are interchangeable here.

There are many other correspondences, such that between the Holy of Holies, lined with gold, and the gold of the city/temple in Revelation. Particularly, significant is the fact that the Jewish tabernacle had been designed to represent the cosmos; now John the Divine can say, 'Behold, the tabernacle (*skēnē*) of God is with men [NRSV mortals] and he will tabernacle (*skēnosei*) among them' (Rev. 21:3). Here is an echo of Jn 1:14: 'And the Word became flesh and tabernacled (*eskēnosen*) among us.' All this is a Johannine way of invoking the same truth as we have seen Paul affirming: the church is the dwelling place of God and the Garden of God (cf. 1 Cor. 3:6-10). What are John the Evangelist and John the Divine and the Apostle Paul doing, but speaking about the church under the almost interchangeable metaphors and images of garden, temple and city? Put together, they suggest that the church is indeed a gift of God and God's dwelling place, but also that it needs human effort and responsible stewardship: the church as city-temple comes down out of heaven from God (Rev. 21:2), but the garden needs to be planted and watered (1 Cor. 3:6-10), though even there 'only God gives the growth' (v. 6).[61] What holds it all together, creating a bridge – a bridge with several arches – between the physical temple, the Christian community as the body of Christ, and the new Jerusalem as the seat of heavenly worship, is the person and work of Jesus Christ. In him 'all the fullness of God was pleased to dwell' (Col. 2:9); and in coming to know the infinite love of Christ we too may be 'filled with all the fullness of God' (Eph. 3:19).[62]

Bride and spouse of Christ

Like the images of body and temple, the image of the church as the bride or spouse of Christ speaks not only of the union of Christ and his people collectively, but also

---

[61] I note the remarkable and prolific studies of Margaret Barker on the significance of the (First) Jerusalem Temple for Jesus and the early Christians. See *Temple Theology: An Introduction* (London: SPCK, 2004). Barker claims that 'the original gospel message was about the temple [of Solomon]' (p. 1) and that 'The gospel as it was first preached by Jesus, and as it was developed and lived by the early Church, concerned the restoration of the true temple' (p. 11). Many of Barker's detailed applications of her thesis are ingenious and she certainly sheds uncommon light on the temple motif in the New Testament. However, like many other of her readers, I find her wholesale recasting of early Christian theology in relation to Solomon's temple unconvincing, in fact bizarre. Possibly, she has been misled by an over-literal interpretation of New Testament language that should be recognized as metaphorical. The transposition of the physical temple idea into the 'temple of his body' (Jn 2:21) is pivotal here.

[62] See also Nicholas Perrin, *Jesus the Temple* (London: SPCK, 2000).

of the union between Christ and every baptized Christian believer. In the writings of the Hebrew prophets, Yahweh courts Israel and betroths her to him. The wilderness journey to the Promised Land was seen by some as a honeymoon period when Israel entered into a covenant union with Yahweh, her husband (Jer. 2:2). The sexual imagery becomes more explicit in Ezekiel (16:8) where Yahweh 'spreads his skirt' over the nubile Israel, just as Boaz spread his skirt over Ruth and made her his own when she needed protection (Ruth 3:9). Hosea came to see that, just as he had married a prostitute (or a woman who later became a prostitute), so Yahweh had married unfaithful Israel. But Yahweh would court her again, woo her back to himself, so that she would say, 'I will return to my first husband' (Hos. 2:7; cf. vv. 16, 19). The Isaianic school looked towards the renewal of the covenant when the land would again be married (*beulah*) to the Lord (Isa. 62:4-5).

Paul picks up this theme of the Hebrew Bible when he writes to the Corinthians, 'I betrothed you [NRSV, 'promised you in marriage'] to Christ to present you as a pure virgin (*parthenos*) to her one husband' (2 Cor. 11:2). Ephesians (5:21-33) develops a sustained analogy of Christ the husband and the church his bride. Citing Gen. 2:24, 'For this reason a man shall leave his father and mother and be joined to his wife, and the two shall become one flesh', the writer (if not Paul) adds, 'This is a great mystery and I say [it refers] to Christ and the church' (v. 32). Again we may note that Paul (or the author of Ephesians, if not Paul) did not invent the application of this image to the church – it comes from Jesus in the Gospels. Jesus compares himself to the bridegroom, in whose presence fasting would be out of place (Mk 2:19). Matthew has the parables of the marriage feast (22:1-10) and the ten virgins (25:1-13), while in Jn 3:19 John the Baptist represents himself as the friend of the bridegroom (or 'Best Man'). John chose to depict Jesus performing his first 'sign' at a marriage feast, where he 'manifested his glory' (Jn 2:1-11). Sometime after Paul and the Synoptics, the Book of Revelation speaks of the marriage supper of the Lamb (19:7-9) and of 'the holy city, new Jerusalem, coming down out of heaven from God, prepared as a bride adorned for her husband' (21:2). (It is fascinating to note that this passage fuses together the images of city, bride, temple and garden.) All of these are, we might say, corporate images, referring to the whole (the Catholic) church. But the New Testament also images the relation between the individual Christian and Christ in terms of a conjugal union.

First, Paul reminds the Corinthians that, just as sexual union with a prostitute makes a man 'one flesh' with her ('flesh' (*basar*) has sexual overtones in the Hebrew Bible anyway), so whoever is united to the Lord becomes one spirit with him. The Greek *kollao* (unite, join) is used in the LXX to translate Gen. 2:24: 'a man . . . *cleaves to* his wife and they become one flesh'. Secondly, in Rom. 7:1-14, Paul employs some subtle rabbinic exegesis to show that Christians have been freed from their obligation to keep the law – they have been widowed by being united with Christ in his death, so that they may be married to Christ. Paul's logic appears unconvincing to us, but the imagery of the conjugal union between Christ and the believer comes through clearly enough. Finally, Ephesians speaks of Christ uniting his church to himself *through baptism* as a pure, unblemished bride (Eph. 5:25-27). So here it is all the baptized who share in the nuptial union with Christ (though Paul can speak of the church corporately being baptized: 1 Cor. 10:1-4). While the motif of marriage to Christ has traditionally been applied to female religious (nuns), the New Testament depicts all baptized Christians as united to Christ as though in a marriage bond. So I do not understand why Walter Kasper claims that 'the mysticism of the bride remains restricted to Catholicism'. Surely the conjugal mysticism of the Christian's union with Christ must be acknowledged and celebrated wherever the Scriptures of the Old and New Testaments are studied, taught and meditated upon.[63]

The image of the church as the bride or spouse of Christ is somewhat out of favour at the present time, for politically correct reasons, except among conservative Catholics, Roman or Anglican. While both male and female theologians who are influenced by and sympathetic to feminism are wary of deploying this imagery lest it should seem that they are not fully committed to the equality of women, conservative Catholics favour it because it speaks to them of the submission of women to men and seems to provide a rationale for restricting holy orders to males. By a process of bizarre logic, the image suggests to them that while men can be identified in a quasi-physical way with Christ the bridegroom and can therefore represent him at the altar (*in persona christi*), women should be identified with Christ's bride or spouse, over against him, so to speak. The image also resonates with the gender stereotype that men are active and women passive; men initiate, women receive. Both groups – feminists and conservative Catholics – overlook the fact that the spouse or bride of Christ is the whole church, made up of men as well as women, clergy as well as laity. It is an abuse of the image to use it as an argument against the ordination of women to the priesthood or the episcopate. However, there is some validity in the 'over-againstness' argument: Christ and his spouse are indeed juxtaposed. If the 'body of Christ' image suggests the identity of Christ and the church, the 'bride/spouse' image juxtaposes them. It certainly speaks of their union, but it is a union of differences.[64]

New humanity

The 'new humanity' of the Pauline literature is the church by any other name. A single new human being (*anthrōpos*, man, human) has been created by the saving work of Christ, just as Adam was created by the breath of God (Gen. 2:7). The Adam-Christ motif is not unique to Paul; it is also alluded to by Paul's physician, Luke (3:21–4:13).[65] In his genealogy Luke traces Jesus' descent back to Adam, while Matthew goes no further back than Abraham (Mt. 1:1-16). The intentional significance of the Christ–Adam connection that Luke makes is reinforced for us by the fact that Luke places his genealogy, not at the start of his Gospel as Matthew does, but immediately before the narrative of Jesus' temptations. The voice from heaven at Christ's baptism, 'You are my

---

[63] Kasper, *The Catholic Church*, p. 133. Kasper undermines his claim that the mysticism of the bride is 'restricted to Catholicism' by immediately stating that the (Lutheran) composer Johann Sebastian Bach shared it, having derived it from Lutheran theology. It has been said that no one understood Martin Luther's theology better than J. S. Bach; as far as my knowledge goes, I am inclined to agree.

[64] Kasper, *The Catholic Church*, p. 132. See further the exposition in Preston, *Faces of the Church*, pp. 76–84.

[65] See art. 'Adam', *TDNT*, vol. 1, pp. 141–3 (Jeremias).

Son, the Beloved', is taken up at the end of the genealogy in the words '. . . son of Adam, son of God' and then reprised in the temptations with the refrain, 'If you are the Son of God . . .'. Luke's Jesus recapitulates the destiny of Adam: the divine inbreathing, the sonship and the temptation, without of course succumbing to the latter, but triumphing over it through the power of the scriptural word. The corporate, representative persona of Christ as the new humanity is implicit in Luke's Adam typology of divine sonship. In Paul it is elaborated into a salient image of salvation where 'sonship' – the divine sonship of Jesus (Rom. 1:4) which generates the divine 'sonship' of the children of God through the gift of the Holy Spirit (Gal. 4:4-7) – is a major theme.

There has come into being, through the salvific work of Jesus Christ, a new representative corporate person into whom Christians are incorporated by baptism. Translators have struggled with the Greek *anthrōpos*: literally 'man', more profoundly but less poetically 'generic humanity'. In the KJB/AV of 1611, 'man' was assumed to be unproblematic. The RSV and REB have 'nature' and the NRSV has 'self'. But 'new humanity' seems to me to be the best translation; it is gender-inclusive for today's sensitivities, without being untrue to the Greek usage and meaning or to the biblical Adam-imagery of 1 Corinthians 15 and Romans 12 that lies behind it. Like Adam, the baptized Christian is being (re)created in the image and likeness of God, his or her creator (Col. 3:10; Eph. 4:24; cf. Gen. 1:26). 'New' refers not merely to time (a novelty: *neon*, Col. 3:10), but to qualitative difference from the old, fallen humanity (*ton kainon anthrōpon*, Eph. 4:24). Those who have been baptized (Col. 2.12) have 'put on Christ', not as a mere outward vesture, but as a total new humanity, one that transcends worldly distinctions and abolishes the discrimination built on them: 'There is neither Jew or Greek . . . slave or free . . . male or female, for you are all one [Greek: one man; so one person, one human] in Christ Jesus' (Gal. 3:27-28).

Paul thinks of the new creation of humanity taking place and being effected through baptismal incorporation into Christ: 'If anyone is in Christ, there is a new creation (*kaine ktisis*)' (2 Cor. 5:17). Christ is the new (redeemed) corporate and representative humanity, just as Adam (= mankind, humanity) was the old sinful corporate and representative humanity (Rom. 5:6-21; 1 Cor. 15:22), for 'as in Adam all die, so in Christ shall all be made alive' (1 Cor. 15:22). Presumably, Paul takes Adam to have been a real, historical person, in the same way that Jesus was, as well as an archetypal, representative figure (as Jesus too was and – in the faith of Christians – is).[66] Just as in our fallen, mortal humanity we have borne the image of the man of dust (Adam), so in our renewed, incorruptible humanity, we shall bear the image of 'the man of heaven', the Adam of the end time, the eschatological Adam (1 Cor. 15:49, 45), who is 'the type of the one who was to come' (Rom. 5:14). The theological background is not only eschatology but also apocalyptic. Paul deliberately sets aside current apocalyptic speculation about a universal, pre-existent, mythic 'primal man'; instead anchoring his argument in history and in a sequential narrative of events. As Käsemann says, 'Typology fundamentally presupposes history.'[67] Adam is first; Christ is last; Adam is from the earth, Christ from heaven. The logic is not one of identity or continuity, but

---

[66]   Dunn, *The Theology of Paul the Apostle*, pp. 94–5, 199–204, 241–2.
[67]   Käsemann, *Commentary on Romans*, p. 142.

of contrast and actual reversal.[68] As Dunn puts it, 'The whole sweep of human history is embraced by the two epochs instituted by Adam and Christ.'[69]

Once again it is unlikely that Paul (and the writers of Colossians and Ephesians, if not Paul himself) completely originated the Adam Christology and with it the concept of Christ's corporate humanity. The New Testament shows the messianic significance of Psalm 8:4-6 ('son of man': Hebrew *ben adam;* Greek *huios anthrōpou*) and Psalm 110:1 to the early Christians.[70] The personification of Wisdom, from Proverbs 8:22-31 through *The Wisdom of Solomon* to rabbinic speculation in the early CE, particularly in 1 Enoch, also fed into the formation of Christology. Jesus himself may have indirectly suggested it in typically styling himself 'Son of Man'.[71] There is probably an intentional ambivalence about the name 'Son of Man' on the lips of Jesus. On the one hand, it suggests the humility, self-effacingness and anonymity of a man who could be despised, rejected and ultimately (apparently) eliminated. This reminds us of the title of Primo Levi's narrative of the Holocaust, *If This Is a Man,* and of King Lear's 'Is man no more than this?' when he encounters Tom o'Bedlam (actually Edgar) on the storm-swept heath.[72] On the other hand, 'Son of Man' recalls the corporate conception of Daniel 7:14, 27, where 'one like a son of man' stands for 'the people of the saints of the Most High', revealed in divine glory and triumph, and the further development and elaboration of this concept in the Similitudes of Enoch (which may or may not have influenced the New Testament uses of 'Son of Man'; that remains the subject of scholarly discussion). As Richardson says, 'Paul dispenses with the Semitism 'Son of Man' but retains the idea.'[73]

In his study *Christ and Adam,* Karl Barth emphasizes the corporate, representative nature of both Christ and Adam in the Bible.[74] Jesus Christ, says Barth, 'is an individual

---

[68] See the discussion and thorough review of the literature in Thiselton, *The First Epistle to the Corinthians,* pp. 1224–90.

[69] Dunn, *Romans 1-8,* p. 271. See his discussion of the primal man myth, pp. 277–8. Cf. James D. G. Dunn, *Christology in the Making,* 2nd edn (London: SCM Press, 1989), pp. 98–128. See also Joseph A. Fitzmyer, *Romans, Anchor Bible* (New York: Doubleday, 1992; London: Geoffrey Chapman, 1993), pp. 407–8. Morna Hooker, *From Adam to Christ: Essays on Paul* (Cambridge: Cambridge University Press, 1990), chapters 5–7, provides a broader background to the Adam-Christ theme.

[70] Dunn, *Romans 1-8,* p. 279.

[71] Käsemann, *Commentary on Romans,* p. 145, rejects the connection (against Jeremias in *TDNT,* vol. 1, p. 143), but Käsemann takes the possible connection a bit too literally. On the vexed question concerning the origins, interpretation and application to Jesus and by Jesus of the term 'Son of Man', see (in addition to specialized monographs, which we cannot deal with here): Oscar Cullmann, *The Christology of the New Testament,* trans. Shirley C. Guthrie and Charles A. M. Hall, 2nd edn (London: SCM Press, 1963), pp. 137–66 (Cullmann endorses the ambiguity of humiliation and exaltation, and of individual and collective references in the title: pp. 154–5.); Joachim Jeremias, *New Testament Theology,* vol. 1: *The Proclamation of Jesus,* trans. John Bowden (London: SCM Press, 1971), pp. 257–76; Dunn, *Christology in the Making,* pp. 65–97 (though he is mainly pursuing the question of the possible 'pre-existence' of the Son of Man in Jewish and Christian thought, Dunn provides much useful background material). A useful summary discussion and evaluation is provided by Edward Schillebeeckx, *Jesus: An Experiment in Christology,* trans. Hubert Hoskins (New York: Seabury Press; London: Collins, 1979 [1974]), pp. 459–72.

[72] Primo Levi, *If This Is a Man and The Truce,* trans. Stuart Woolf, intro. Paul Bailey (London: Abacus [Sphere Books], 1987); William Shakespeare, *King Lear,* III.4.105.

[73] Richardson, *An Introduction to the Theology of the New Testament,* p. 138.

[74] Karl Barth, *Christ and Adam: Man and Humanity in Romans 5* (published for the *SJT;* Edinburgh: Oliver and Boyd, 1956), trans. T. A. Smail from *Christus und Adam nach Römer 5* in *Theologische Studien,* 35 (Evangelische Verlag A. G. Zollikon-Zurich, 1952).

in such a way that others are not only beside Him and along with Him, but in their most critical decision about their relationship to God, they are also and first of all *in Him*.[75] For Barth's theological method, the human relationship to Adam is secondary; the relationship to Christ is primary; we start from God's act in Jesus Christ and extrapolate or work outwards from that. This is 'the primary anthropological truth and ordering principle'.[76] This inclusion, representation and mutual responsibility is, for Barth, the key to the understanding of created human nature and therefore the norm of all anthropology. So the Christ–Adam motif mirrors what is inherently true of human nature and speaks to us of that.

It is surely significant that this corporate humanity – the eschatological 'perfect man, the measure of the stature of the fullness of Christ' – is identified with 'the whole body' which builds itself up in love, in Eph. 4:13, 16. In rabbinic midrash, Adam filled the whole earth and contained all generations in himself; he was a symbol of the unity and integrity of the human race. So when Paul uses the Adam typology, the unity of the church is part of the subtext.[77] In baptism we put on a new human nature by being incorporated into the divine humanity of the risen, ascended, glorified Christ, which exists on this earth in the form of the church, deemed to be his body. Hence John Robinson's arresting remark, 'The resurrection of the body starts at baptism.'[78]

---

[75] Barth, *Christ and Adam*, p. 4.
[76] Ibid., pp. 5–6; cf. pp. 41, 44.
[77] W. D. Davies, *Paul and Rabbinic Judaism: Some Rabbinic Elements in Pauline Theology*, 2nd edn (London: SPCK, 1955 [1948]), chapter 3.
[78] Robinson, *The Body*, p. 79.

5

From 'founder' to 'foundation'

In this short linking or bridging chapter – hardly deserving the name of 'chapter' at all! – I will attempt to ease the transition from the previous chapters, which examined, from the historical and the theological angles, the connection between Jesus and the church in the New Testament, to the next three chapters which will critically investigate how modern – mainly systematic or doctrinal – theologians in three major Christian traditions have responded to the findings of historical-critical research regarding the relation between Jesus and the church. I will summarize the arguments and conclusions of the book to this point and then I will indicate what I am attempting to achieve in what now follows. The dynamic can be encapsulated in the phrase 'From "Founder" to "Foundation"'.

In the first half of this study we have investigated the connection between Jesus of Nazareth and the church, as they are presented in the New Testament Gospels and Epistles. We have examined the relationship between the church and Jesus both historically and in terms of biblical theology. We could summarize our findings in two main ways. On the one hand, we have found that the overwhelming – in fact unanimous – consensus of scholarly opinion is to the effect that Jesus had no intention of 'founding' a church of any kind. There are two compelling reasons for this conclusion. The first reason is that his mission was to 'the lost sheep of the house of Israel', God's church (*ekklēsia*, as it is designated in the LXX), the church of the covenant. The second reason is because the New Testament writings convey an overwhelming impression that Jesus and his followers expected the imminent manifestation of the kingdom or reign of God and the transformation and glorification of the world order. It follows unavoidably from these two factors that Jesus did not 'found', intend or foresee any kind of separate institutional existence for his community of disciples – or, to put it another way, any separate institutional embodiment of the mission of God that was taking place in and through him in the last times. It follows from this first major conclusion – one that will not be news to any New Testament scholar today – that Jesus could not meaningfully have instituted or ordained or required any specific form of the ministry to serve that (non-existent) institution into the future.

Before I go on to summarize the second main conclusion of Part One, we need to take note of an important qualification to the above narrative. What I have described so far (the existence of the Jewish church; the eschatology of imminent crisis) is how modern New Testament scholarship reads the evidence for the question of Jesus and the church. But these two points have not always been recognized or given their due – far from it. In the first place, a 'supercessionist' view of the relationship between Israel and the Christian church, assumed that the church of God had been transferred, so to speak, from the one to the other, so that it was no longer necessary or appropriate to think of the people of Israel, in the Old Testament, as 'the church of God'. This perspective was dominant in Christian theology and ideology until very recently and is still promulgated by right-wing, fundamentalist Christian groups. It was the Second Vatican Council's 'Declaration on the Relation of the Church with Non-Christian Religions' (*Nostra Aetate*, 1965), the shortest and arguably the most radical of the Council's documents, that was chiefly responsible for bringing about a change of theology and of attitude with regard to the Jewish people and a new respect for the integrity and perpetuity of God's covenant with them.[1] Secondly, as we have seen in Chapter 2, it was only in the late nineteenth and early twentieth centuries that the historical-critical study of the New Testament, at the hands of Johannes Weiss, Albert Schweitzer and Alfred Loisy, opened the eyes of students of the Bible to the dominant framework of imminent expectation of the reign of God and the sense of crisis and decision that Jesus and the apostles attached to the preaching of this 'good news'. The eventual combination of these two developments, from the 1960s onwards – first the revaluation of the place of the Jewish people (or church) in the purposes of God, and second the discovery of the foreshortened time-scale of New Testament eschatology – required a radical reconsideration of the traditional belief, and key tenet of the church's teaching about itself in all the major Christian traditions, concerning the founding of the church (the question of Jesus and the church), and correspondingly about the claims that could be made about the dominical institution of church structures (the question of the church and Jesus). The central ecclesiological issue inevitably emerged: Did Jesus want there to be anything like the church as it soon appeared in history?

On the other hand (and this is the second major conclusion of the first part of the book), a study of the Gospels and Epistles also clearly shows that Jesus gathered around him a band of disciples (it was normal for a notable rabbi to do that) and that he then turned some of them ('The Twelve') into his emissaries or apostles, preparing them by his fellowship, teaching and example to be sent throughout the land with his announcement that the reign of God was at hand. It belonged to the messianic, eschatological expectation that there would be a community of the last days, even a faithful remnant. At the Last Supper Jesus bound his followers together in a 'new' covenant with God through the sacrifice of himself that he was about to make. After the crucifixion, the post-Easter appearances and the experienced presence of the risen Christ and then their being filled with his Spirit at Pentecost, together with the rejection by the Jewish authorities of the messianic claims that they made on behalf of Jesus of Nazareth, formed the disciples/apostles into a coherent community in its own right. At an early date, apostles and evangelists reached out into 'Gentile' lands with the gospel concerning Jesus as the Christ and, as a result, communities of Christians were formed in many parts of the Roman Empire, beginning among the Jewish diaspora. These distinctive communities were bound together by certain crucial ecclesiological ties: core beliefs about the God of Israel's unique salvific act, in fulfilment of the

---

[1]   http://www.vatican.va/archive/hist_councils/ii_vatican_council/documents/vat-ii_decl_1965102
8_nostra-aetate_en.html

Hebrew scriptures, in Jesus the Christ; a few essential sacred rites (baptism, the laying on of hands, the Lord's Supper and *Agape* (love feast) perhaps the ritual washing of feet) and a rudimentary and flexible structure of leadership, especially the ministry of the word and of pastoral oversight and discipline. The key New Testament images for Christ and the church give theological interpretation to the experience and the faith of the early Christians and their communal life in its worship, fellowship and witness. These images speak of an intimate, loving, faithful relationship and union between the risen Christ and the community which is deeply impressive. These communities of Christians needed an identity and a name. Soon the language of 'the church' and of 'the foundation of the church' was being used, thus setting an agenda for subsequent theological exploration and elaboration of these concepts by Christian theologians.

In the following three chapters I will undertake a critical investigation of the various ways in which major modern theologians from three of the main Christian traditions – Protestant, Roman Catholic and Anglican – have handled the question whether Jesus of Nazareth 'founded' or intended the church, and if so in what sense and with what implications. (I do not include here a discussion of any scholarly work or theological reflection, on our key questions, that have taken place within the Orthodox family of churches, and this for two main reasons. (i) I lack the knowledge of Orthodox biblical and historical scholarship during the past two to three centuries. (ii) Partly at least owing to their long subjection to non-Christian or anti-Christian regimes and their ideologies, the Orthodox churches, and universities and the nations within which they were placed did not experience the Enlightenment and the subsequent rise of the historical-critical movement to the same extent and to the same degree of intensity as the countries, churches and universities of Western Europe.)

Unpacked a little, the phrase 'Jesus and the founding of the church' can stand in these modern Protestant, Roman Catholic and Anglican authors for at least two possibilities: the founding of the church *by* Jesus Christ (an historical act) or the founding of the church *on* Jesus Christ (a theological interpretation). Of course, the one does not necessarily exclude the other: an affirmative 'historical' answer also implies the 'theological' answer; but the theological answer does not ipso facto entail an affirmative historical answer. A number of theologians who concluded, on the basis of the prevailing scholarly consensus with regard to the biblical material, that Jesus could not have explicitly founded the church as an historical act, fell back on the defensive line that the church was always, and is still today, founded *on* Jesus, that it derives from the Christ event. But they also tended to hold, as a corollary, that the affirmation that Jesus Christ is the theological foundation of the church remains true, whatever view one takes of the historical and biblical evidence regarding the beginnings of the church.

As this way of putting the issue suggests, the answer that these modern theologians give to our central question may be stated in either historical or theological terms, or both. To answer our question affirmatively in strictly historical terms would amount to saying that Jesus of Nazareth consciously initiated and instituted the church by a specific historical action, or series of actions, during his earthly ministry. But it seems that he could not have done that without also intending a certain content or shape for the church that he was founding. That is to say that Jesus could not have founded the church in an institutional sense without, at the same time, providing some kind of 'blueprint' for his community that would give it identity, shape and coherence. It would have meant his instituting at the time certain structures, ordinances and protocols for that church, such as specifying the following matters: who was entitled to belong to it; whether he meant it to spread beyond the land and nation of Israel; what beliefs were to hold it together; who was to lead it and what authority they would have; how it was to come together socially; what corporate activities, including sacred rituals, would sustain it in existence through history; and what the mechanisms would be for perpetuating it to future generations. Traditional theology insisted that Jesus Christ did specify in detail the polity of the future church, as papal, episcopal, Presbyterian, congregational, or what have you. But the obvious historical fact that this traditional theology was also at loggerheads within itself about the identity and shape of the church that Jesus was said to have 'founded' and the ministry that he was said to have 'instituted', dividing along confessional lines, strongly suggests that these instructions (if that is what they were) remained opaque and ambiguous and therefore could have had little meaning.

On our side of the watershed of the emergence and progressive acceptance of historical-critical methods of study of the Bible and early church history, any claims that Jesus specified the shape of the church that he was in the process of founding would need to be supported by evidence, mainly from ancient texts, or possibly from archaeological artefacts that have survived, though the claim could hardly be refuted by lack of historical evidence – which would be arguing from the negative, which is always a weak tactic. Nevertheless, the fact is that even the early Christians, as we see abundantly in the New Testament, let alone in the bitter controversies of the first few Christian centuries, were not agreed about the identity and shape of the church and argued passionately about these questions, and theologians throughout the ages have been equally divided on such issues. If the answer that modern scholarship gives to this complex of historical questions about Jesus founding or planning the church turns out to be overwhelmingly in the negative, we will then turn to what it has to say on the theological question, 'In what sense is the church founded *on* Jesus, if not *by* him, and therefore fulfils the intentionality behind his mission and subsists in faithful continuity with it?' Following the three chapters on Roman Catholic, Protestant and Anglican theology, I will attempt in the last chapter to give my own constructive response to the whole problematic that I will have set out in this book, drawing on the arguments and insights of the scholars whom I have critically reviewed in the second half of this book and returning to some of the aspects of biblical interpretation that we engaged with in the first half.

An answer to our question in strictly theological terms, that did not feel able to claim that the historical Jesus of Nazareth explicitly, by word and/or deed, founded the church, would amount to asserting that the existence of the church in the world and in history is founded on the Christ event as a matter of theological continuity and congruity. However, it would not be theologically acceptable if this account of the origin and source of the church were to conceive of the theological continuity or congruity between the church and Jesus as a merely voluntary or wilful human action, effected retrospectively. Such an autonomous human action would struggle to connect meaningfully with the events concerning Jesus of Nazareth, which Christian theology holds to be events originating in divine initiative and driven by divine action. Moreover (as we shall shortly see Karl Rahner putting it), any such arbitrary human decision to rest the church or found the church on the Christ event would make the church self-originating and self-validating, nothing more than a purely human creation. So 'founded theologically upon' would have to be meant in the sense of the church being continuous and congruent, to a significant extent, with the rationale, the internal logic, of Jesus Christ's own mission and what it meant to belong to his earliest community and therefore true to his deepest intentions – in essence, theologically faithful to Jesus as the Christ.

By 'modern' theologians in the three chapters that follow, I do not mean merely theologians who have lived in 'modern' times, say since the dawn of the cultural, intellectual and scientific movement that we loosely call the Enlightenment, stemming from the late seventeenth century. What I mean by modern theologians in this context is those theologians who, dissatisfied with the allegedly unarguable claims of 'tradition' and of church authority, embraced, to one extent or another, the historical-critical method of biblical and historical research that developed during and after the Enlightenment, from the mid-seventeenth century onwards, reaching its peak in the second half of the twentieth century. Although vigorous debate about specifics continues, this overall 'scientific' method of biblical research – historical, empirical and critical – is now the unchallenged norm (though it is not all there is to the full and faithful interpretation of the Scriptures).[2] So our enquiry will involve some sketching out of the attitude taken by these 'modern' theologians to the results of modern biblical research and, in particular, their response to the 'discovery' by Johannes Weiss, Alfred Loisy and Albert Schweitzer of the imminent eschatological time-frame of the Four Gospels and of most of the Epistles.

Beyond the issues concerning Christian origins that were generated by the historical-critical method in biblical research and exegesis lie deeper theological questions and controversies. These questions and debates largely concern what is meant by divine revelation and divine action or intervention, particularly: (a) whether revelation is exclusively or primarily given in verbal or at least propositional form, as was traditionally believed in all the major streams of Christianity; (b) whether, alternatively, revelation should be located in acts of divine creativity within the historical process, accompanied by divinely guided interpretation; or perhaps (c) whether revelation is rather to be discerned in the area of religious experience, in moments that bring a sense of divine presence and disclosure, of inspired insight, informed and shaped by the tradition, which is subsequently interpreted and articulated in necessarily fallible human ways. We shall need to touch on these issues of revelation and interpretation also to some extent, while reserving a much fuller treatment to the immediate sequel to this volume, *Revelation and the Word of God*.[3]

---

[2] Selected representative works on the rise of the historical-critical method of Bible study: Henning Graf Reventlow, *The Authority of the Bible and the Rise of the Modern World*, trans. John Bowden (London: SCM Press, 1984 [1980]); Klaus Scholder, *The Birth of Modern Critical Theology: Origins and Problems of Biblical Criticism in the Seventeenth Century*, trans. John Bowden (London: SCM Press, 1990 [1966]); Stephen Neill, *The Interpretation of the New Testament, 1861-1986* (Oxford: Oxford University Press, 1988); John Rogerson, *Old Testament Criticism in the Nineteenth Century: England and Germany* (London: SPCK, 1984); John Barton, *The Nature of Biblical Criticism* (Louisville, KY: Westminster John Knox Press, 2007).

[3] See also my chapter, 'Revelation, Epistemology and Authority', in Balázs M. Mezei, Francesca Murphy and Kenneth R. Oakes (eds), *The Oxford Handbook of Divine Revelation* (Oxford: Oxford University Press, forthcoming).

6

The foundation of the church
in Protestant theology

Towards a critical revolution

The creative impulse behind the theology of the Reformation was the power of the biblical word – especially in the form of the preached gospel – to reform and renew the church. These biblical and patristic texts were approached employing the methods of Renaissance Humanism (the study of humane literature). It is perhaps not too much to claim that the Reformers were critical scholars according to their lights. From the first, Protestant scholarship was receptive to critical-historical methods in principle.[1] For Martin Luther in particular, the church was the dynamic creation of the word, *creatura verbi*, including the sacramental word.[2] However, Protestant theology lost much of its dynamism in the seventeenth century. It developed three retrograde characteristics: (a) a complacent acceptance, on the part of many, of the existing divisions in the church (between the Roman Catholic Church and the Reformation churches, on the one hand, and within Protestantism, between the Lutheran and the Reformed churches, on the other); (b) a confessionalism with regard to the identity of the church and its theology that tended to treat, for example, the Lutheran Augsburg Confession (1530) and the Formula of Concord (1577) and the Reformed Heidelberg Catechism (1563) or the articles of the Synod of Dort (1618–19) in practice as on the same level of authority as Holy Scripture; and (c) a movement towards a basically scholastic model of theological method that promoted logical analysis and systematic coherence, along with an exaggerated emphasis on doctrinal precision.

In the late seventeenth and early eighteenth centuries the movement of spiritual vitality known as pietism, led by P. J. Spener and A. H. Franke, reacted against what it regarded as the dead orthodoxy of the Lutheran Church in Germany. In its spiritual rigour and fervent devotion, it prepared the ground for a renewal of ecclesiology. That renewal came in the work of F. D. E. Schleiermacher, himself a spiritual son of pietism

---

[1] Paul Avis, *In Search of Authority: Anglican Theological Method from the Reformation to the Enlightenment* (London and New York: Bloomsbury T&T Clark, 2014), chapters 1–3.
[2] Paul Avis, *The Church in the Theology of the Reformers* (London: Marshall, Morgan & Scott; Atlanta, GA: John Knox Press 1981; reprinted Eugene, OR: Wipf and Stock, 2002), chapters 1–6; id., 'The Church and Ministry', in David M. Whitford (ed.), *T&T Clark Companion to Reformation Theology* (London and New York: T&T Clark, 2012), chapter 9.

in the form of the Moravian movement. Schleiermacher retrieved the authentic impulse of Reformation theology by approaching Christian doctrine in an existential and pastoral way. Protestant ecclesiology typically stresses the inward, spiritual reality of the church and is suspicious of the institutional, societal and hierarchical model favoured by Catholics (both Roman and Anglican). Schleiermacher was an outstanding critical scholar of the Bible, but his distinctive approach, which is typical of Protestantism, renders ecclesiology less vulnerable to a critique informed by the eschatological horizon of the New Testament.

Friedrich Schleiermacher

Friedrich Schleiermacher (1768–1834) is the father of modern theology and the founder of Liberal Protestantism within it. He is the most important Protestant theologian between Calvin and Barth – and he is as unlike each of them as it is possible to be! Schleiermacher was both an inheritor of the Enlightenment (*Aufklärung*) within German Lutheranism (as we see especially in his biblical studies) and a child of the Romantic movement in European thought, literature and general culture (as we see first in *Speeches to the Cultured Despisers of Religion* and then in all his major works).[3] As a theologian, Schleiermacher's *forte* was theological methodology and heuristics, apologetics and hermeneutics – altogether the exploration and discovery of new pathways of theological integrity in harmony with contemporary culture. Combining the Enlightenment's fearless interrogation of traditions with Romanticism's ardent sensibility and creativity, Schleiermacher devised radically fresh approaches to the question of how theology was to be conceived and practised in order for it to have intellectual, critical validity in the bracing intellectual climate of early nineteenth-century Prussia. But, as a pastor and preacher, he also strove to resource and nurture the Christ-centred spiritual experience of ordinary Christian folk and the spiritual, pastoral effectiveness of church leaders. He wrote for the sceptical intelligentsia in society; he wrote for the professorial academy; and he wrote for the church leadership. Schleiermacher proposed at least a twofold revolution in theological method in his *Kurze Darstellung des theologische Studiums* (*Brief Outline on the Study of Theology*, 1st edition 1811; 2nd edition 1830) and the *Glaubenslehre* (known in English as *The*

---

[3] F. D. E. Schleiermacher, *On Religion: Speeches to Its Cultured Despisers*, trans. John Oman, intro. Rudolf Otto (New York: Harper and Row [Harper Torchbooks], 1958); id., *On Religion: Addresses in Response to Its Cultured Critics*, trans. and ed. Terrence N. Tice (Richmond, VA: John Knox Press, 1969); id., *On Religion: Speeches to Its Cultured Despisers*, intro., trans. (of original 1799 edition) and notes Richard Crouter (Cambridge: Cambridge University Press, 1988). Jack Forstman, *A Romantic Triangle: Schleiermacher and Early German Romanticism* (Missoula, MT: Scholars Press for the American Academy of Religion, 1977); Albert L. Blackwell, *Schleiermacher's Early Philosophy of Life: Determinism, Freedom and Phantasy*, Harvard Theological Studies 33 (Chico, CA: Scholars Press, 1982); H. L. Friess, trans., *Schleiermacher's Soliloquies: An English Translation of the* Monologen*, with a Critical Introduction and Appendix* (Chicago: Open Court Publishing Co., 1926); David Jasper (ed.), *The Interpretation of Belief: Coleridge, Schleiermacher and Romanticism* (London: Macmillan, 1986); Richard Crouter, *Friedrich Schleiermacher: Between Enlightenment and Romanticism* (Cambridge: Cambridge University Press, 2005).

Christian Faith, 1st edition 1821–22; 2nd edition 1830–31; ET *The Christian Faith*).[4] Thus, Schleiermacher effected 'a complete re-orientation of the theological task'.[5]

The first step in Schleiermacher's reconstruction of Christian systematic theology ('dogmatics') was (to summarize rather crudely) to transpose Christian doctrines from one category to another: from the ontological to the existential and from thinking to feeling (in his slightly idiosyncratic sense of pre-theoretical and pre-reflective awareness). For Schleiermacher, dogmatics was the theological discipline that gave critical articulation to the living experience – the vital faith – of the church of 'today', in a way that would enhance the ministry of the preacher and pastor, the church leadership (*Kirchenleitung*). Dogmatics was re-conceived as *Glaubenslehre* – the doctrinal exposition, the 'logical ordering' of the living faith, the articulated piety, of the church.[6] It intended to facilitate the self-representation (*Selbstdarstellung*) of that faith, allowing it to reveal and present itself, the dogmatician having merely a maieutic role (as a midwife, bringing to birth).

It seems at first blatantly reductionist when, in §30.2 of *The Christian Faith*, Schleiermacher declares bluntly that 'the fundamental dogmatic form' is purely 'the description of human states' (for him, states of pious feeling).[7] Although he is clear that, in a secondary way, pious feeling is also related to what is held as true about the world and about God, he is here unmasking the spurious objectivity traditionally claimed for doctrinal theology, as a 'reading-off' from divine revelation located in the Bible and in the confessions and traditions of the church. In reality all theological claims are 'descriptions of human states', whether human states of pious feeling, as with Schleiermacher, or human states of mind and thought and verbal expression, as with most theologians. To pretend otherwise is to succumb to false consciousness. In the same vein, Schleiermacher makes some bold conjectures about the inner life and the personality of Jesus, so charting a path that Liberal Protestant theologians – notably Troeltsch, Herrmann and Harnack – would follow (though it proved to be a dead end historically).

---

[4]   F. D. E. Schleiermacher, *Brief Outline on the Study of Theology*, trans. Terence N. Tice (Richmond, VA: John Knox Press, 1966); id., *The Christian Faith*, trans. H. R. Mackintosh and J. S. Stewart (Edinburgh: T&T Clark, 1928); this is the translation referenced in this book; id., *Christian Faith: A New Translation and Critical Edition*, trans. Terrence N. Tice, Catherine L. Kelsey and Edwina Lawler, ed. Catherine L. Kelsey and Terrence N. Tice, 2 vols (Louisville, KY: Westminster John Knox Press, 2016). A useful broad introduction to Schleiermacher is Martin Redeker, *Schleiermacher: Life and Thought*, trans. John Wallhausser (Philadelphia, PA: Fortress Press, 1973 [1968]). A helpful guide to the structure of Schleiermacher's method and its eccentric terminology is B. A. Gerrish, 'Friedrich Schleiermacher', in Ninian Smart, John Clayton, Steven Katz and Patrick Sherry (eds), *Nineteenth Century Religious Thought in the West, Volume 1* (Cambridge: Cambridge University Press, 1985), chapter 4. For a concise, critical introduction to Schleiermacher's dogmatic method see Paul Avis, *The Methods of Modern Theology* (Basingstoke: Marshall Pickering, 1986), chapter 1.

[5]   Thomas H. Curran, *Doctrine and Speculation in Schleiermacher's Glaubenslehre* (Berlin: Walter de Gruyter, 1994), p. 2. I am sympathetic to Curran's strong suspicion of Schleiermacher's claims in the *Glaubenslehre* to be putting forth a purely empirical, historical and entirely non-speculative representation of the Christian self-consciousness. But here we are not concerned with the critique or deconstruction of Schleiermacher's method, so much as with the conclusions to which he believes it leads him.

[6]   Schleiermacher, *The Christian Faith*, p. 126.

[7]   Ibid.

A major consequence of Schleiermacher's revolutionary method was that dogmatics was concerned only with what was of its nature ephemeral and therefore could not claim permanent validity for its conclusions. Dogmatics was normative – but only for the present time. Its task was to describe, systematize and critique (ostensibly with reference to internal criteria) the doctrine that was prevalent in a particular church at a particular time. Description and 'logically ordered reflection' are prerequisites for the final task of 'purifying and perfecting' the doctrine accessed by that method.[8] It connected with the *present moment* of the church, so to speak. Doctrine was a critical crystallization and exposition of the corporate Christian consciousness of a specific community at a specific juncture of history.

The second step in Schleiermacher's revolutionary method was – paradoxical at first sight – to locate dogmatics, precisely as a descriptive, empirical science, within the discipline of *historical theology*. Gerrish comments that Schleiermacher 'was moving towards the notion of man's "historicity" as a description of his temporal existence, and this was a notion whose time had not quite come'.[9] It arrived in a full-blooded way with Ernst Troeltsch a century later, as we shall see. Nevertheless, Schleiermacher approached theology with an acute historical consciousness, as his ground-breaking theories of hermeneutics and his ethics reveal. History was a record of the moral and religious endeavours and of the struggles and attainments of humankind, and its study was therefore a moral and religious discipline. A human being was a moral agent within an historical process. The act of historical understanding and retrieval (hermeneutics) was a moral act, one that involved the whole person. As Richard R. Niebuhr puts it, Schleiermacher regarded the writings, the texts, of past authors as 'deeds symbolizing the moral lives of their authors and the language that spoke through them, and . . . defined the task of interpreting these lives through their deeds as . . . a moral act'.[10] In this perspective, Schleiermacher recast Christian dogmatics – paradoxical as it may seem to us – as the historical theology of the present time, focused on a specific, historically given mode of believing (*Glaubensweise*) and intended to serve the church and its ministry, As Gerrish puts it, in Schleiermacher, 'the theological task is thoroughly "historicised" – made into a function of history'.[11] The content of the given mode of believing (*Glaubensweise*) is always moving into the past and thus making room for what is contemporary, fresh and challenging. Nevertheless, Schleiermacher's designation of dogmatics as an historical discipline is idiosyncratic. Curran notes that 'not a single major German theologian of the

---

[8]   Ibid., pp. 81 (§16 'Postscript'), 92 (§19 'Postscript').
[9]   B. A. Gerrish, 'Ernst Troeltsch and the Possibility of a Historical Theology', in John Powell Clayton (ed.), *Ernst Troeltsch and the Future of Theology* (Cambridge: Cambridge University Press, 1976), chapter 4, at p. 108.
[10] Richard R. Niebuhr, *Schleiermacher on Christ and Religion* (London: SCM Press, 1965), p. 92. Schleiermacher's hermeneutical writings have been translated into English in F. D. E. Schleiermacher, *Hermeneutics: The Handwritten Manuscripts*, ed. Heinz Kimmerle, trans. James Duke and Jack Forstman (Missoula, MT: Scholars Press for the American Academy of Religion, 1977) and trans. Andrew Bowie, *Schleiermacher: Hermeneutics and Criticism and Other Writings* (Cambridge: Cambridge University Press, 1998).
[11] Gerrish, 'Ernst Troeltsch and the Possibility of a Historical Theology', p. 102.

nineteenth century followed Schleiermacher in regarding dogmatic theology as a subdivision of "historical theology".[12]

By defining the task of dogmatics (doctrinal theology) in this way, Schleiermacher retrieved the authentic impulse of Reformation theology: a living and lived faith, filled with the dynamism of the word of God. The keynote for Schleiermacher was *self-communication*. The momentum of the word in the church, according to Schleiermacher, stemmed from the proclamation of Jesus, which was his most important and typical work. As the *logos*, he conveyed not merely ideas about God but the reality of God's self-communication to humankind. But what Jesus proclaimed was not something other than himself. In his preaching he gave of himself by communicating his God consciousness in speech in a way that imparted his life with God to his disciples and created the community around him. His preaching was the expression of his identity before God, his relationship to God. The preaching of the same message and word in the church today, Schleiermacher argues, conveys the presence and power of Christ in the community. Through the church's preaching Christ continues to assume believers into his God consciousness, his unclouded blessedness of fellowship with God. The church lives in and by the *kerygma*; and the way that the *kerygma* is proclaimed in the church inevitably involves the self-communication of the Christ-shaped God consciousness of the preacher.[13]

For Schleiermacher the function and purpose of the church, its *raison d'être*, is to promote heartfelt piety, though that must then be related to knowledge and action. While in his lectures on ethics (*Sittenlehre*) Schleiermacher paid serious theological attention to Christian activity (*Handlungen*),[14] the organization or polity (*Kirchenregiment*) of the church was subservient to imperative cultivation of the religious affections (piety) and no part of *Glaubenslehre*. The church is simply (merely?) the constitution of the world in relation to the ongoing process of redemption. While the community's relation to Christ is changeless, being continually mediated through word and sacrament, its relationship to the world is changeable and varied. Inwardly it changes not; the constant outward changes are not theologically significant.[15] No single form of the church is mandatory; no particular polity is required. Schleiermacher's model of communal piety is at the opposite end of the political spectrum to the concept of the *societas perfecta* (the church conceived as a complete and self-sufficient society) of post-Tridentine Roman Catholicism. Schleiermacher was not uninterested in church history – he lectured on it first in 1821–22 – but in the *Glaubenslehre* he is not concerned with the historical, political church, so the historical question of whether Jesus of Nazareth founded the church as an intentional act cannot arise for him in this context. The experience of Christian piety is its own assurance that in the Christian community we have to do with Jesus Christ, from whom the life of the community takes its rise. However, the historical question concerning the foundation of the

---

[12] Curran, *Doctrine and Speculation in Schleiermacher's* Glaubenslehre, p. 199.
[13] Niebuhr, *Schleiermacher on Christ and Religion*, pp. 145–7.
[14] Curran, *Doctrine and Speculation in Schleiermacher's* Glaubenslehre, pp. 201–3.
[15] Schleiermacher, *The Christian Faith*, pp. 582–3.

community by or through Jesus of Nazareth is asked and answered by Schleiermacher in another academic context, as we shall see.

The ecclesiological tradition formed by the creative work of Schleiermacher – his theological legacy – typically stressed the inward, dynamic and spiritual reality of the church and tended to be suspicious of the societal, institutional and hierarchical model favoured by Catholic ecclesiology in its Roman, Orthodox and Anglican forms. This is true not only of Liberal Protestantism, in Ritschl, Harnack, Herrmann and Troeltsch, but also of the reaction to Liberal Protestantism in the 'Dialectical Theology' of Barth, Gogarten, Brunner and Bultmann. Protestant theologians tended to regard the institutional dimension of Christian faith as, at best, a concession to practicality, a decline from the authentic Christianity and as alien to the gospel. This stance made Protestant ecclesiology highly sensitive to the early intimations of ecclesial forms and structures – incipient institutionalism, *Urkatholizismus* – in the New Testament, especially in the Gospel of Matthew and the Pastoral Epistles.[16] But it also made Protestant ecclesiology less vulnerable than Roman Catholic ecclesiology to the fundamental question raised by the rediscovery in the late nineteenth and early twentieth centuries of the dominantly future orientation of the eschatological horizon of the New Testament – the question, 'Did Jesus found the church and, if not, how should we understand the connection between Jesus and the church?'

Schleiermacher located the essence of Christian faith and life not in the realm of knowledge (belief) or action (morals), but in the realm of feeling. By feeling (*Gefühl*) Schleiermacher meant not a particular emotional state, but the immediate, unreflective awareness or consciousness of the whole of one's existence as infused with a sense of absolute dependence on God.[17] For Christians the consciousness of dependence on God is mediated by the redeeming work of Christ which consists in the imparting of his own unsullied God consciousness. The distinctive, generic religious experience of knowing oneself to be absolutely dependent on God is shaped for Christians by the God consciousness of Jesus and this is imparted to believers in the fellowship of the church, so constituting a distinctive 'mode of faith' (*Glaubensweise*). This Christ-shaped God consciousness is conducive to fellowship or communion, which is sustained by the fact that believers communicate their self-consciousness, so formed, through speech –

---

[16] A striking example is Ernst Käsemann's attack on 2 Peter, which he says 'is from beginning to end a document expressing an early Catholic viewpoint and is perhaps the most dubious writing in the canon': 'An Apologia for Primitive Christian Eschatology', in id., *Essays on New Testament Themes*, trans. W. J. Montague (London: SCM Press, 1964 [1960]), chapter VIII, pp. 169–95, at p. 169.

[17] The pre-reflective immediacy of *Gefühl* (feeling) in the *Glaubenslehre* transcends the subject–object antithesis in perception; subject and object merge in an experiential identity. See John E. Thiel, *God and World in Schleiermacher's Dialektik and Glaubenslehre* (Bern: Peter Lang, 1981), p. 108. For discussion of whether the consciousness of absolute dependence is truly pre-reflective or does in fact incorporate, even in an inchoate form, philosophical, metaphysical or 'speculative' elements, see R. B. Brandt, *The Philosophy of Schleiermacher* (Westport, CT: Greenwood Press, 1968 [New York: Harper Bros., 1941]) and Curran, *Doctrine and Speculation in Schleiermacher's* Glaubenslehre, pp. 272–84. See also Robert R. Williams, *Schleiermacher the Theologian: The Construction of the Doctrine of God* (Philadelphia, PA: Fortress Press, 1978), pp. 4, 23; Gerhard Spiegler, *The Eternal Covenant: Schleiermacher's Experiment in Cultural Theology* (New York: Harper and Row, 1967); Claude Welch, *Protestant Theology in the Nineteenth Century, Volume I, 1799-1870* (New Haven and London: Yale University Press, 1972) is also helpful; see especially p. 66.

especially preaching – and so edify each other. The traditional ecclesiastical distinction between clergy and laity is, for Schleiermacher, incompatible with the Christian understanding of redemption in which Christ assumes all believers equally into the power of his God consciousness and into the fellowship of his unclouded blessedness. The sense or experience of vital unity that is possessed by this fellowship is identified in faith as the reality of the Holy Spirit. This impulse to unity will, Schleiermacher believes, eventually prevail in the church (he was writing a systematic theology or dogmatics for a politically 'United' Lutheran and Reformed territorial Church, the Prussian *Landeskirche*). It is a basic principle for Schleiermacher that the inner essence of the church, the feeling, consciousness or awareness of being related to God through Christ, which is communicated in word, accompanied by sacrament, is constant; it never varies. On the other hand, the outward form of the church is contingent, subject to variation through time and circumstance, but this fact is, theologically speaking, a matter of indifference.[18]

In returning in this way to the unchanging heart or essence of the church's existence, grounded objectively in the word derived from Scripture and subjectively in the experience that believers enjoy of communion or fellowship with God and with each other, Schleiermacher justifiably saw himself as picking up again the central ecclesiological concern of the Reformers. The Reformers insisted that Christ is present in the church through the twin manifestations of the gospel – word and sacrament – and that these are sufficient to guarantee the authentic existence of the church. For Schleiermacher, the experience of Christians in the church today is continuous with the experience of the apostles and the early Christians; it is the experience that provides continuity. The communal piety – the Christ-shaped God consciousness that makes the church – is a 'given', an historical datum, not in the sense that it can be traced back through time to a particular historical event, such as the explicit founding of the church by Jesus of Nazareth, but in the sense that it emerges into the present as a given fact of history. Just as, for Schleiermacher, dogmatics does not need to prove the existence of God, but presupposes it, so too ecclesiology has no need to establish the original foundation of the church, because the church is a given, present, reality of Christian life and faith. So for Schleiermacher, critical, post-Enlightenment theologian though he was, the historical question of whether the church was founded by Jesus of Nazareth in history remained dogmatically irrelevant.[19] So we may now ask, 'How does Schleiermacher understand the significance of the founding events of Christianity as they are presented in the Gospels?'

First, it is important to acknowledge Schleiermacher's commitment to the historical-critical study of the biblical documents, as that study was understood at the time, and to honour his prowess in the field. In the *Brief Outline on the Study of Theology*, Schleiermacher had insisted on unrestricted critical enquiry into the sources of theology. In relation to the Gospels he practised an early form of redaction criticism

---

18 Schleiermacher, *The Christian Faith*, pp. 582–5.
19 Cf. Stephen Sykes, *The Identity of Christianity: Theologians and the Essence of Christianity from Schleiermacher to Barth* (London: SPCK, 1984), p. 100, n: '[I]t is a remarkable fact that none of the disciplines preparatory to the task of Schleiermacher's dogmatics is in any simple sense history.'

(i.e. he postulated a process of oral transmission of *pericopē* and believed that Luke had compiled, edited and arranged previously existing documents); he also achieved an approach towards the form-critical method, with a discernment of the literary genres and units ('shapes') of Luke's Gospel. Schleiermacher was a prince of interpretation. His hermeneutical method was twofold: empathetic, intuitive indwelling of the world of the text was combined with acute analytical attention to the structure of the text, its language, grammar and syntax. He recognized the distinctive theological standpoint of each Gospel. But he assessed the historicity of the Gospels in ways that would soon be dismissed: he judged Mark to be the least historically reliable (followed by Matthew; the priority of Mark was not yet established), and he believed John to be the most reliable (he assumed it to have been written, except for the last chapter, by John the son of Zebedee, the brother of James). Schleiermacher lectured on the New Testament continuously between 1804 and 1834, a period that coincided with the development of his hermeneutics. He planned commentaries on all four Gospels, though he completed only his work on Luke, which was the most congenial to him theologically.[20] He has been credited with inaugurating the quest for the historical Jesus in his *Life of Jesus* (see below).[21]

Secondly, the concept of the kingdom of God plays a significant role in Schleiermacher's evaluation of the place of Christianity among the religions. He distinguishes between two fundamental types of religion: the aesthetic, which is typically passive in its interface with the world, and the teleological, which is typically orientated to the fulfilment of a moral task. Christianity is a strenuously active religion, in which 'the consciousness of God is always related to the totality of active states in the idea of a Kingdom of God'.[22] But, Schleiermacher adds, the symbol of the kingdom of God, 'which is so important and indeed all-inclusive for Christianity', gives expression to the fact that 'in Christianity all pain and joy are religious only in so far as they are related to activity in the Kingdom of God, and that every religious emotion which proceeds from a passive state ends in the consciousness of a transition to activity'.[23] The central role of the idea of the kingdom of God in Christianity points to the fact that it is a social religion and takes the form of a society. When individuals submit to the lordship or kingly rule of Christ they enter a society to which they did not previously belong. Thus, in ascribing kingship to Christ, we are acknowledging that he did indeed 'intend to found an organic community', for he himself must have

---

[20]   Friedrich Schleiermacher, trans. and intro. Connop Thirlwall, ed. Terrence N. Tice, *Luke: A Critical Study* (Lewiston, etc.: Edwin Mellen Press, 1993 [1825]). Thirlwall's introduction runs to 149 pages. See the concise but rigorous account in Christine Helmer, 'Schleiermacher's Exegetical Theology and the New Testament', in Jacqueline Mariña (ed.), *The Cambridge Companion to Friedrich Schleiermacher* (Cambridge: Cambridge University Press, 2005), chapter 12; and Verhyden's introduction to Friedrich Schleiermacher, *The Life of Jesus*, trans. S. Machean Gilmore, ed. and intro. Jack C. Verhyden (Philadelphia, PA: Fortress Press, 1975).

[21]   D. F. Strauss bitingly attacked Schleiermacher's approach to the life of Jesus, condemning it for residual supernaturalism: David Friedrich Strauss, *The Christ of Faith and the Jesus of History: A Critique of Schleiermacher's Life of Jesus*, trans., ed. and intro. Leander K. Keck (Philadelphia, PA: Fortress Press, 1977 [1865]).

[22]   Schleiermacher, *The Christian Faith*, pp. 42–3.

[23]   Ibid., p. 43.

initiated this kingdom.[24] This truth is established by the deliverances of the religious self-consciousness in the church, rather than by historical research, which is another department of theology altogether.[25] Although the kingdom of God receives outward expression in the fact of the church, in its essence it is an interior reality. Christ's saying, 'My Kingdom is not of this world' (Jn 18:36) is decisive for Schleiermacher in this respect, showing that his kingly authority is not concerned with the things of this world and that 'nothing remains as the immediate sphere of His kingship but the inner life of men individually and in their relation to each other.'[26] In accordance with the spiritual principle of the kingdom, Christ also makes no use of worldly, material or political means for the exercise of his kingly reign, but employs means or ordinances that he has himself instituted in his church.[27]

Thirdly, Schleiermacher was apparently the first person to lecture on the life of Jesus and to establish it as a formal part of academic theology. His lectures on the life of Jesus were reconstructed from notes and published thirty years after his death.[28] He believed that a connected account of the events of Jesus' life was unattainable. Instead, Schleiermacher focuses on the power of Jesus' God consciousness and the communication of this to the disciples/apostles and on their transmission of this inner power to others in the formation of the early Christian communities. Schleiermacher believes this interpretation to fall within the domain of history because it is concerned with action and effect. His work on the life of Jesus inaugurates the fatal Liberal Protestant fascination with Jesus' inner life. He distinguishes between the 'outer' and 'inner' aspects of the ministry of Jesus: the outer referring to the geographical and social setting, and the inner to the presence and power of the kingdom of God in his person, his teaching and the calling of the disciples. Jesus forms a community through proclaiming God's 'loving invitation' to enter the kingdom. Jesus' mission is empowered by his gracious self-communication to all who came within his orbit. His self-communication is itself the nearness of the kingdom. The disciples' sense of absolute dependence is, so to speak, the organ of receptivity for Christ's self-communication to them. Schleiermacher finds this theme particularly strongly represented in John. The Fourth Gospel is especially congenial to him because he cannot accept the reality of conflict and struggle, as the Synoptics portray it in the Garden of Gethsemane or on the cross, in Jesus' unclouded, blissful consciousness of God. But how did the group of disciples become the church?

Fourthly, the band of disciples could not have become formed into the church during Jesus' earthly ministry simply because his followers each had a direct relationship to him, especially through having been baptized in his name (Jn 4:1-2). Jesus called them into a privileged relationship with himself. They enjoyed table fellowship and domestic intimacy with him as he taught them privately. He gathered them into an 'inner circle' to prepare and train them. What they received in close company with Jesus was 'the consistent and more constant effect of his personality on them and the

---

[24] Ibid., pp. 42–3.
[25] Ibid., pp. 466–7.
[26] Ibid., p. 467.
[27] Ibid., pp. 467–8.
[28] Schleiermacher, *The Life of Jesus*.

quiet and unbroken understanding of his whole being.'[29] Schleiermacher asks whether this gathering together by Christ and for the sake of the kingdom can be regarded as an embryonic institution, but confesses that the sources are not sufficiently clear to enable us to answer that question. However, Schleiermacher affirms that 'the apostles were not only set apart to teach, but also to found and maintain the Christian society'.[30] There was no structured Christian society in Jesus' lifetime; it was only after the resurrection that they could have a strong relationship to each other and be bound together into a community that could be called 'the body of Christ'.[31] But did the church that eventually emerged in history correspond to what Jesus wanted for his disciples? The most that Jesus could or would have anticipated was that the temple cult would continue, though now merely as an expression of the political nation, while the new life of his community would continue alongside it, 'free from externalities, grounded on direct fellowship with God' and with devotion to Jesus placed at the centre.[32]

Fifthly, the Christian society, the church, is destined to become integrated with the wider society in which it sits and with the surrounding culture. Like leaven (fermented yeast), it will permeate the whole, until a seamless relationship pertains between them. That does not mean that the church, with its grasp of the essence of Christianity – that everything in Christian belief is related to the redemption accomplished by Jesus of Nazareth – and society culture become indistinguishable, but rather that their relationship should be seen in terms of an 'eternal covenant'. Christianity cannot tolerate the idea that cultural achievement and the advance of civilisation should go its own way, without the blessing and presence of Christ in its midst.[33] Schleiermacher, a prince of the church, was also a polymath of the humanities. He felt responsible for the progress of culture and for its leadership. Barth's snide comment is not without its element of caricature, but it nevertheless makes a valid point: 'The kingdom of God, according to Schleiermacher, is utterly and unequivocally identical with the advance of civilization.'[34]

Adolf von Harnack

Adolf von Harnack (1851–1930) was the doyen of German church historians and the prince of Liberal Protestant publicists at the turn of the nineteenth century into the twentieth. His celebrated – and much overrated – work *Das Wesens des Christentums* (ET *The Essence of Christianity*) was basically a corrected transcript of his lectures of 1899 to 1900, delivered extempore to 600 students from all faculties of the University of Berlin. The lectures more or less coincided with the publication of the second

---

[29] Ibid., p. 353.
[30] Ibid., p. 352.
[31] Ibid., pp. 356–7.
[32] Ibid., pp. 360–1.
[33] Daniel J. Pedersen, *The Eternal Covenant: Schleiermacher on God and Natural Science* (Berlin: De Gruyter, 2017).
[34] Karl Barth, *Protestant Theology in the Nineteenth Century: Its Background and History*, trans. Brian Cozens and John Bowden, new edn (London: SCM Press, 2001), p. 421.

(expanded) edition of Johannes Weiss' *Die Predigt Jesu vom Reiche Gottes* (1900). Although Harnack must have been aware of Weiss' revolutionary thesis about the imminent, supernatural eschatology of the New Testament (the first edition of *Die Predigt Jesu vom Reiche Gottes* had appeared in 1892), he showed no sign of letting it influence his argument.

Harnack claimed that the earliest form of Christianity was a purely interior matter. Primitive Christianity was intrinsically non-institutional. It resided in the heart and was basically an individual ethical response to the 'leading features of Jesus' message' and the inspiration emanating from his compelling personality. The Synoptic Gospels, Harnack insisted, presented 'a powerful, compelling, uncontrivable [*sic*] personality'. '[T]he personal life' of Jesus generates spiritual, ethical power even to the present day. As we shall see again, Liberal Protestant Christology pivoted on the supreme value accorded to the 'personality' of Jesus. The three key features of the gospel, according to Harnack, were: the kingdom of God and its coming; the Fatherhood of God and the infinite value of the human soul; and 'the higher righteousness and the commandment of love'. The gospel generated an ethical intentionality towards human fellowship (the brotherhood of man).[35] Jesus was the last and greatest in the long line of biblical prophets. His impact continues through the great personalities who have been influenced by him, particularly Martin Luther, and these are also prophetic figures. In his slender and intellectually slight work of published lectures on *Christianity and History*, Harnack stated: 'The spiritual purport of a whole life, of a personality, is also an historical fact: it has its reality in the effect which it produces; and it is here that we find the truth that binds us to Jesus Christ.' History should be understood through the categories of personality and development, with the latter being determined by the former.[36]

But where is biblical eschatology in this picture? For Harnack the eschatological context and colouring of the Synoptic Gospels should be discounted as merely the subjective passionate emotions that clothed the message of both John the Baptist and Jesus himself. Eschatological language was simply inherited conceptual baggage (as was the demonology of the Gospels: these 'absurdities', as Harnack calls them). In what may be a swipe at Weiss' ideas, Harnack claims that scholars who exaggerate the eschatological and apocalyptic elements in the Gospels stand corrected by the evidence of Q, the sayings source common to Matthew and Luke, but not known in its original, integral form, which (Harnack insists) is purely religious and ethical in content.

The historian's task was to separate the kernel from the husk. The kernel was heartfelt love of God and man – a love that was not dependent on outward religious practice, least of all ritual. Eschatology – in fact the entire biblical cosmology – was the husk. Harnack claimed that the structured, institutional elements of the historical church – rule by bishops, the ecumenical creeds and church law – were later developments, essentially alien accretions to the original, ethical and inward form of

[35] Adolf von Harnack, *What Is Christianity? Sixteen Lectures Delivered in the University of Berlin during the Winter Term, 1899-1900*, trans. Thomas Bailey Saunders, 3rd edn (London: Williams and Norgate, 1912), esp. pp. 39–76.

[36] Adolf von Harnack, *Christianity and History*, 2nd edn, trans. Thomas Bailey Saunders (London: A. & C. Black, 1900 [1896]), pp. 60–2.

Christianity, which remained the authentic Christian message. Harnack claimed that his conclusions were the result of pure 'historical science'. He staked a great deal on his prowess as an historian. Enlightenment through history was absolutely the key to his avowed theological method. The knowledge of God the Creator could not bypass knowledge of the created world; 'so far, however, as this religion teaches that God can be truly known only in Jesus Christ, it is inseparable from historical knowledge'.[37]

As Glick points out, in what is perhaps the most substantial treatment of Harnack's *Essence* book in English, thirty years of solid but brilliant historical investigation culminated in this work; it subsumed Harnack's whole purpose as scholar and churchman.[38] Glick prefers to translate *Wesen* as 'reality', rather than 'essence', but it is clear that Harnack boils down or summarizes the whole of the New Testament and subsequent Christian tradition to a few key affirmations, the essentials, the true heart of the faith, in his view. These tenets are certainly what Harnack regarded as the most 'real', that is the most relevant, the most inspiring and the most enduring elements in original Christianity; but they are so because they are the most 'essential'.[39] Harnack was engaged in a life-long quest to grasp the 'inner form of Christian truth' and to do so by purely historical methods.[40] His great history of dogma (*Dogmengeschichte*) was undertaken with the aim of bringing to the light of day the true gospel of Jesus (and, as it happens, of Luther – as interpreted, of course, by Harnack). By exposing the human sources of the origin and development of Christian doctrine, the history of dogma provides the means of liberating the church from dogmatic Christianity.[41] Harnack staked everything on objective historical investigation; but his readers, then and now, from Loisy and Troeltsch onward, have suspected that he has imported an overriding subjective criterion into his historical interpretation.[42]

For Harnack, then, the institutional, legal and hierarchical dimensions of historical Christianity were alien to its pure essence – the kingdom of God in the heart, a trusting confidence in the Fatherhood of God, and an ethical imperative to love all as 'brothers'. Moreover, the gospel concerned the individual's relationship to God: 'God and the soul, the soul and its God'.[43] In the face of the Lord's Prayer being cast in the first person plural, Harnack insists that it 'leads us to the height where the soul is alone with its God'.[44] The individual focus of the gospel, as Harnack understood it, was obviously not compatible with the institutional, legal nature of the church as it developed. So Harnack claims that it contradicted the character of the gospel and of the community

---

[37] Adolf von Harnack, *Outlines of the History of Dogma*, trans. E. K. Mitchell (Boston, MA: Starr King Press, 1957), p. 1, cited Sykes, *The Identity of Christianity*, p. 130.
[38] G. Wayne Glick, *The Reality of Christianity: A Study of Adolf von Harnack as Historian and Theologian* (New York: Harper and Row, 1967), p. 3. See also Wilhelm Pauck, *Harnack and Troeltsch: Two Historical Theologians* (New York: Oxford University Press, 1968). Pauck draws attention to Harnack's life-long admiration for and devotion to Goethe, whom he regarded as the embodiment of Western humanistic civilization, pp. 20, n. 26; 102–4.
[39] Glick, *Reality of Christianity*, p. 4.
[40] Ibid., pp. 8–11.
[41] Harnack, cited Pauck, *Harnack and Troeltsch*, p. 22, from *Grundriss der Dogmengeschichte*, 9th edn (Berlin, 1921), p. 5.
[42] Glick, *Reality of Christianity*, p. 213.
[43] Harnack, *What Is Christianity?*, p. 49.
[44] Ibid., p. 58.

founded upon it that the church developed any legal ordinances whatsoever.[45] To substantiate this thesis, Harnack needed to show that Jesus had not, as a specific historical act, founded the institutional church or intended or foreseen it. Everything in the history and current life of the church that savoured of an historical institution or a legal structure had to be shown to be a post-resurrection addition or invention by the early church – in fact a series of alien accretions from the ancient world and its culture.

Harnack argued this case substantially in *The Constitution and Law of the Church in the First Two Centuries* (ET 1910) as well as elsewhere.[46] In this powerful work, a tour de force, Harnack begins by insisting that both the (Roman) Catholic and the Protestant versions of the doctrine that Christ deliberately founded the church in an institutional sense 'have the whole historical development of the apostolic and post-apostolic age against them'. Moreover, he asserts, these claims stand or fall on the authority of a few New Testament passages, mainly in Gospel of Matthew – passages which 'by all the rules of historical criticism' we are bound to discount and set aside. Without these few texts, 'every direct external bond between Jesus and the "Church" and its developing orders is severed'. (The word 'orders' reveals Harnack's animus against every form of hierarchical and hieratic ministry, what he would regard as priest-craft and sacerdotalism.) But, for Harnack, even though Jesus neither founded nor even intended the church as we know it, 'the inner spiritual bond' with him and his teaching remains (p. 3).

Harnack also insists that Jesus could not possibly have founded the church because the church (in his sense) existed before Jesus, having been founded by the Hebrew prophets when they charted a way out of the darkness of legalism and envisioned a spiritual society in which 'God and his holy moral law reign supreme', such that 'all subsequent developments are changes of form' only (p. 4, n. 1). For Harnack, as for Schleiermacher and in fact later for Barth, the external 'form' of the church was purely incidental.

Harnack invokes in his support Rudolf Sohm's *Kirchenrecht* (1892) and particularly Sohm's Appendix I, 'Wesen und Ursprung des Katholizismus' (1909) which postulated a profound gulf, both chronological and conceptual, between primitive Christianity and the emergence of early Catholicism, the beginning of the institutional concept of the church. Harnack endorses Sohm's indictment of the Roman Catholic system as an 'apostasy' from Jesus' intentions (p. 5). However, he concedes that the legal structure of Christianity emerged by an inevitable process (Sohm also believed that legal forms were an historically necessary development). It was inevitable because Jesus' disciples saw themselves as the messianic community of the last days and because that eschatological vision required separation from the world, communal regulation of the social relations of Christians and strict moral holiness of life. Such a regime could not have been achieved without rules and regulations, sanctions and punishments, even excommunication (p. 4, n. 1). Several other factors were also conducive, in Harnack's view, to the rise of legalism: (i) the Jewish background of early Christianity (Judaism=legalism); (ii) the Apostle Paul's policing of the moral life of

---

[45] Ibid., p. 46.
[46] Adolf von Harnack, *The Constitution and Law of the Church in the First Two Centuries*, trans. F. L. Pogson, ed. H. D. A. Major (London: Williams & Norgate, 1910). Page references in my main text.

the Gentile converts; (iii) the distinction between clergy and laity; (iv) the emergence of the ministerial orders of (monarchical) bishop, presbyter and deacon which had become fixed by the end of the second century (pp. 114, 121); and (v) the interface of the Constantinian church with the state, requiring the development of structures of jurisdiction.

So, for Harnack, the whole historical process, with the exception of the reforming momentum stemming from Martin Luther, conspired to corrupt the original pure impulse of Jesus' teaching into a highly regulated, hierarchical institution, which was furthest from Jesus' intention (pp. 23, 52). According to Harnack, following Sohm, nothing could be more mistaken, misguided and contrary to the will of God than the church as we know it.

Ernst Troeltsch

In our review of the attempts, within modern Protestant theology, to establish a connection between Jesus and the church, especially in relation to the historical and theological foundation of the church, we turn now, in contrast, to the intellectually formidable yet also somehow vulnerable figure of the German theologian Ernst Troeltsch (1865–1923).[47] Troeltsch was a great deal more than a theologian: an historian of ideas and cultural-social movements, a philosopher of religion and of history, a political activist, a politician and a social researcher. Troeltsch was a close contemporary of Harnack and a latter-day disciple of Schleiermacher. '[N]o other contemporary theologian', Troeltsch claimed for himself, 'stays as close to Schleiermacher's method and approach, nor feels himself in such inner agreement with him'.[48] The content of Troeltsch's theology can be seen as a repristination of one aspect of Schleiermacher's theology, the emphasis on individual subjectivity and religious experience, but recast by Troeltsch from an empirical and phenomenological mould into an historical one.

---

[47]   Introductory: Hans-Georg Drescher, *Ernst Troeltsch: His Life and Work*, trans. John Bowden (London: SCM Press, 1992 [1991]); id. 'Ernst Troeltsch's Intellectual Development', trans. Michael Pye, in Clayton (ed.), *Ernst Troeltsch and the Future of Theology*, chapter 1; Robert Morgan, 'Introduction: Ernst Troeltsch on Theology and Religion', in Robert Morgan and Michael Pye (eds), *Ernst Troeltsch: Writings on Theology and Religion* (London: Duckworth; Atlanta, GA: John Knox Press, 1977), pp. 1–51. Sarah Coakley, *Christ without Absolutes: A Study of the Christology of Ernst Troeltsch* (Oxford: Clarendon Press, 1988) is an incisive study with applications to Troeltsch's thought in areas additional to Christology. Mark D. Chapman, *Ernst Troeltsch and Liberal Theology: Religion and Cultural Synthesis in Wilhelmine Germany* (Oxford: Oxford University Press, 2001) is especially useful on the cultural, theological and inter-disciplinary context of Troeltsch's thought. Trutz Rendtorff and Friedrich Wilhelm Graf (trans. Sarah Coakley), 'Ernst Troeltsch', in N. Smart, J. P. Clayton, S. Katz and P. Sherry (eds), *Nineteenth Century Religious Thought in the West, Volume III* (Cambridge: Cambridge University Press, 1985), chapter 9, is a clear and concise introduction to Troeltsch's philosophy of history and the implications that he perceived for Protestant theology.
[48]   Ernst Troeltsch, *The Christian Faith*, Foreword Marta Troeltsch, ed. Gertrud von le Fort, trans. Garrett E. Paul (Minneapolis: Fortress Press, 1991), p. 113.

The challenge and burden of history

In contrast to what he identifies as Schleiermacher's attraction to ontological monism and panentheism, Troeltsch is the exponent par excellence of historical consciousness, historical development and historical relativism (*Historismus*); they were his *métier*, but also his crushing burden. In his *Glaubenslehre* (literally, 'doctrine of faith' or 'faith-teaching'; posthumously edited, and published in 1925; translated – as in the case of Schleiermacher's work with an identical title – as *The Christian Faith*), Troeltsch states: 'The old understanding of history has come to an end. Human history now consists of immeasurable periods of time, of historical events that are all equally conditioned and finite. The principles of historical criticism are universally established. Now the question is how the relationship between faith and history can be maintained under these circumstances.'[49] Troeltsch critiques the influential 'Ritschlian' school, especially Herrmann, for evading the questions of objectivity with which historical study confronts us. The scope for making faith statements that are independent of historical research is, Troeltsch claims, now dwindling to vanishing point. The Ritschlian method of asserting theological judgements based on faith experience is, he alleges, a reversion to the metaphysics that both Ritschl and Herrmann actually repudiate.[50]

Troeltsch sought ultimately to break out of the constraints of history to find a solid basis for faith elsewhere. He achieved this through an idealist projection of certain selected Christian insights ('the essence of Christianity', which was ostensibly derived from the study of history) into an ahistorical ethical realm of the human spirit.[51] In doing so he came full circle back to Schleiermacher. Karl Barth called Troeltsch 'the last great Romantic in theology'.[52] The 'Romantic' concept that inspires his work is the vitality of individual forms of life as they pass in succession while we review what we know of the historical process. Troeltsch vowed that he would never surrender this life-giving vision to any rationalistic theological system that crushed the life out of them.[53] Whether or not his life's project was successful (most interpreters think not), Troeltsch showed great intellectual and spiritual courage in holding on to a vision of the wholeness of reality and of truth and in resisting the metaphysical dualisms of his

---

[49]   Ibid., p. 74.
[50]   Troeltsch, 'Half a Century of Theology: A Review' (1908), in Morgan and Pye (eds), *Ernst Troeltsch: Writings on Theology and Religion*, chapter 1, at pp. 73–5. For Ritschl himself, the study of history was a key component of theological construction. Hefner comments that Ritschl had learnt from F. C. Baur that 'the nature of Christianity is to be ascertained by subjecting it to critical-historical enquiry in its total historical development': Philip Hefner in id. (ed.), *Albrecht Ritschl: Three Essays* (Philadelphia, PA: Fortress Press, 1972), p. 24. For Ritschl, historical study was the preferred alternative to metaphysics: id., p. 28.
[51]   Troeltsch's essay 'What Does "Essence of Christianity" Mean?' (1903, 1913), in Morgan and Pye (eds), *Ernst Troeltsch: Writings on Theology and Religion*, chapter 3, covers familiar Troeltschian ground, though obviously from the point of view of the 'essence' question. Here we find Troeltsch engaging with Harnack and Loisy on that question, which is not irrelevant to our own enquiry in this book. We cannot pursue the 'essence' question here; it needs separate, substantial treatment. Meanwhile, see Sykes, *The Identity of Christianity*, chapter 7.
[52]   Barth, *Protestant Theology in the Nineteenth Century*, p. 333.
[53]   Gerrish, 'Ernst Troeltsch and the Possibility of a Historical Theology', p. 130.

predecessors, Ritschl and Herrmann (and we might add, proleptically his successors: Karl Barth and Rudolf Bultmann).[54]

According to Troeltsch, our interpretation and understanding of the historical process is governed by two principles that reflect the nature of historical reality. The principle of *individuality* refers to the particularity and uniqueness of the objects of historical research, to their organic wholeness and integrity. The principle of *development* refers to the fact that the object of historical study exists in a state of becoming, which consists in the continual unfolding of the possibilities that are latent in its inner life, as it interacts with other individual 'objects' and all that they contain. It follows, for Troeltsch, from these two principles that in history there can be no 'absolute' or definitive event or person; no finality or even radical discontinuity. Historical 'objects' must be understood by analogy with other historical objects. This criterion rules out 'supernatural' interventions and miracles, whether in the form of revelation, incarnation, redemptive acts or eschatological scenarios. The religious and moral significance of Jesus remains valid for European civilization – and Troeltsch worked heroically to protect Christ's significance in the face of the erosion by historical relativism of traditional supports – though other advanced religions may have equal validity in their own particular contexts. However, even in its European context, Christianity could one day become obsolete and be superseded by other faiths and philosophies. Christianity, like all other historical phenomena, was specific to its context and therefore relative, not absolute.[55]

Troeltsch entertains the language of 'foundations' – historical, theological and experiential. He explicitly raises the question of the 'historical foundations' of Christian faith, only to downgrade the question itself:

> This will not be accomplished through historical-critical research into questions of detail, but rather by emphasizing those historical elements that shape the personal and spiritual foundations: the details of historical research are allowed to fall into the background. Faith assimilates these historical-personal-spiritual foundations, valuing and interpreting them as the summit of divine self-communication and revelation. As a result, our historical-religious propositions are truly religious statements, not historical-critical ones.[56]

The historical work is necessary, indeed indispensable, for Troeltsch, but the redemptive impulse that originates from Jesus Christ in history continues under its own momentum. Once personal faith feels the redemptive power of the personality of Jesus in its own life, it need not bother about history; it can kick away the ladder

---

[54] Troeltsch's unyielding ethical passion for the unity of all knowledge is brought out in Chapman, *Ernst Troeltsch*, especially chapters 7 and 8.

[55] Ernst Troeltsch, *The Absoluteness of Christianity and the History of Religions*, trans. David Reid from the 3rd German edition, 1929, intro. James Luther Adams (London: SCM Press, 1972 [1902]).

[56] Troeltsch, *The Christian Faith*, p. 75.

of historical enquiry.[57] Troeltsch believes that, historically speaking, at this point it is enough to be assured that what comes from him must have been present in him.[58]

The kingdom of God and the ethical personality of Jesus

The foundational reality of Christianity for Troeltsch is the 'personality' of Jesus. Everything in Troeltsch's system is predicated on Jesus' 'personality' (though occasionally, Troeltsch uses the more robust and more ethical term 'character' as a virtual synonym).[59] Jesus is the revelation of God neither as a teacher nor as an example, but as a personality – a personality characterized by 'extraordinary sublimity, mildness, and strength'. His religious power and purity, his knowledge of God and his proclamation of redemption and forgiveness are what create faith.[60] Jesus' extraordinary personality attracted from his followers the ascription of the messianic identity and title. It generated the resurrection appearances. It gave rise to his proclamation (as far as the early tradition faithfully conveys it) concerning the kingdom of God. What does Troeltsch understand by the kingdom of God in the message of Jesus? If we strip away, as Troeltsch wants us to do, the Gospels' eschatological world view of imminent judgement and world-transformation, we find that Jesus 'does not speculate' about the nature of the kingdom; 'it simply includes all ethical and religious ideals'.[61] But whose ideals are these, we might ask: those of first-century Palestine or those of the liberal intelligentsia of late nineteenth-century German Protestantism? Where is historical relativism now?

The contents of the concept 'the kingdom of God', as proclaimed by Jesus, are the Fatherhood of God, the infinite value of the individual soul and the brotherhood of humankind (here Troeltsch is at one with Harnack).[62] It is Jesus' personality, not his incarnation and divine–human nature (which Troeltsch does not accept), not his death and resurrection, nor his message and teaching, that constitutes the foundation of Christianity (or 'Christian civilisation', as Troeltsch often puts it). The totality of Christ's personal life is the foundational, original revelation of the Christian life-world.[63] In 'The Significance of the Historical Jesus for Faith' (1911), Jesus is said to be the 'symbol' or 'picture' of the Christian reality.[64] Because the continuing historical trajectory of

---

[57] Ibid., pp. 276–7.
[58] Ibid., p. 98. On the questions of the relation of faith and history, in the shadow of Troeltsch, the following studies remain useful: Alan Richardson, *History Sacred and Profane: Bampton Lectures for 1962* (London: SCM Press, 1964); Van A. Harvey, *The Historian and the Believer: The Morality of Historical Knowledge and Christian Belief* (London: SCM Press, 1967); S. W. Sykes and J. P. Clayton (eds), *Christ, Faith and History: Cambridge Studies in Christology* (Cambridge: Cambridge University Press, 1972); A. O. Dyson, *The Immortality of the Past* [Hensley Henson Lectures, 1972–1973] (London: SCM Press, 1974).
[59] Troeltsch, *The Christian Faith*, p. 88. See also on this theme, id., 'The Significance of the Historical Jesus for Faith' (1911), in Morgan and Pye (eds), *Ernst Troeltsch: Writings on Theology and Religion*, chapter 4 (a rather rambling and repetitive essay).
[60] Troeltsch, *The Christian Faith*, p. 274.
[61] Ernst Troeltsch, *The Social Teaching of the Christian Churches*, 2 vols, trans. Olive Wyon (London: George Allen & Unwin, 1931; [1911]), vol. 1, p. 51.
[62] Troeltsch, *The Christian Faith*, p. 88.
[63] Ibid., p. 89.
[64] Troeltsch, 'The Significance of the Historical Jesus for Faith', chapter 4, at pp. 202, 205–6.

the impulse that stems from the personality of Jesus equates to the effectiveness of the original revelation and the development of it, it must be regarded as a continuing revelation in itself.[65]

What is the role of Jesus Christ in Troeltsch's theology?[66] The key proposition is that the personality of Jesus forms 'the foundation of the Christian religious life-world'. The prophetic history of Israel leads up to it and the history of Christianity flows from it as the 'further development of the revelation'.[67] The key to the religious meaning of human history, the significance of history for faith, lies in the total *Gestalt* of Jesus, provided that he is not separated from his historical context. Troeltsch alleges, not without reason, that his arch-rival for theological hegemony in German Protestantism, Wilhelm Herrmann (1846–1922), had done precisely that, treating Jesus as though he had fallen from heaven like a meteorite. And Troeltsch also finds fault with Schleiermacher for bestowing on Jesus attributes that are not derived from history, but from the theological or dogmatic tradition. The real 'picture' or 'image' (perpetuating Schleiermacher's language) of Jesus consists in his self-testimony, which was grasped by the faith of the disciples and by the faith of the whole of Christian history that followed, 'wherein his life always appears anew'. We no longer have access to his actual words, Troeltsch concedes (probably overstating the matter), but we still have access to the life which flowed from them. The foundation of the church is the spiritual impulse that stems from Jesus and lives in the faith of his followers in past history and today.[68] It is that spiritual impulse, touching our lives, that constitutes redemption – not any notion of an objective atonement, any kind of transaction. The only meaning that can be given to Christ's suffering and death is historical and psychological: 'the effect it has on believing souls'.[69] I find this a seriously inadequate account of the significance of Jesus Christ. The theological weight is all 'on us' and not 'on him'; the subjective experience is disproportionate to the objective source; the 'objective correlative' (to borrow T. S. Eliot's phrase) is deficient. 'Personality' is a flimsy basis for Christology. How was it possible for Jesus' personality to have such a dynamic effect in history unless we believe that 'God was in Christ' in a unique, unprecedented and unsurpassed way? And if that is the case, is not 'incarnational' language – which Troeltsch rejected – unavoidable in some sort? Essentially, Troeltsch postulated an effect without a sufficient cause.

Jesus and the Christian community

Troeltsch rejected, not only on historical, but also on theological and ethical grounds, the idea that Jesus of Nazareth could have founded the church as an institution: 'Jesus did not organize a Church. He simply asked for helpers who would spread the message by preaching'.[70] Again, during Christ's earthly ministry 'there was no sign of an

---

[65] Troeltsch, *The Christian Faith*, p. 102.
[66] Coakley, *Christ without Absolutes*, dispatches en route a number of crude caricatures of Troeltsch's Christology.
[67] Troeltsch, *The Christian Faith*, p. 76.
[68] Ibid., pp. 76–7.
[69] Ibid., p. 89.
[70] Troeltsch, *Social Teaching of the Christian Churches*, vol. 1, p. 58.

organized community. A visible community was only formed after his death.[71] So we should ask what theological and sociological assumptions underlie Troeltsch's position here.

The 'personal' was his guiding category; it was a personhood immersed in history and indelibly shaped by it. Personhood is understood by Troeltsch in a radically and unashamedly individualistic way. The basically ethical teaching of Jesus (according to Troeltsch), epitomized in the Sermon on the Mount, determined the form taken by the sociological character of early Christianity. The defining mark of this ethical teaching (Troeltsch blushes not to say this) was 'an unlimited, unqualified individualism' – an 'absolute religious individualism'.[72] The individual's relationship of filial love, devotion and service to God as the Father of his children, flowed from the principle of the uniquely precious value of the soul (so too Harnack and German Liberal Protestantism generally). To us, after more than half a century of writing on philosophical and theological personalism, by Martin Buber, John Macmurray, Michael Polanyi and Emmanuel Levinas, to name but a few, this seems a strange kind of 'personalistic' theology. There is little sense in Troeltsch of our personhood being mutually constituted, little awareness that there is no 'person' until there are at least two 'persons in relation'. Troeltsch puts it bluntly: 'Autonomy is not the starting point of religious development, but its high point.'[73] The individual person was at the centre of Jesus' mission and message, not any kind of collective entity.

As an early twentieth-century German scholar, Troeltsch accepted the latest theories, associated with Johannes Weiss and Albert Schweitzer, regarding the eschatological world view of the New Testament, particularly of the Synoptic Gospels. Jesus' demanding ethic was for the few, being formulated in 'the expectation of the final Judgement of the imminent End of the World'.[74] In view of the impending curtailment of all human affairs, Jesus showed no interest in practical matters of social organization or reform, nor was he concerned with the state. But at the same time his message eliminated all social distinctions by concentrating solely on the ethical character, rather than the status, of individuals. A common ethical character leads naturally to the formation of fellowship, and this is just as fundamental as the idea of individual value: 'this absolute individualism leads to just as absolute a fellowship of love among those who are united in God'.[75] Once again, it is not entirely clear whether this fellowship is mutually constitutive for the simple reason that we cannot exist as mere individuals, or whether it represents merely the gravitating together of individuals who share a common spirituality.

For Troeltsch, the biblical concept of a loving, fatherly God who calls us to perfection of character, yet forgives our sins where we fall short, is manifested not only in the Law and the Prophets, but also in Jesus' interpretation of them, in the form of a revelatory

---

[71] Ibid., p. 61.
[72] Ibid., p. 55.
[73] Troeltsch, *The Christian Faith*, p. 75.
[74] Troeltsch, *Social Teaching of the Christian Churches*, vol. 1, p. 55. The eschatological expectation was not actually of 'the end of the [physical] world' as such, but the end of the present world *order* and its regeneration and transformation.
[75] Troeltsch, *Social Teaching of the Christian Churches*, vol. 1, p. 56; cf. p. 63: 'a Communism of Love'.

impulse or (as Troeltsch puts it) 'authority and revelation'. It is in this way that the idea of authority is irrevocably introduced into the sociological structure of Christianity. In other respects, this sociological structure is 'a completely free fellowship of thought and knowledge' (so Troeltsch claims, rather inconsistently, having just introduced the notion of authority).[76] It seems, therefore, that the element of 'authority' belongs not to any kind of institutional church, but to the revelatory impact of Jesus' personality as it reverberates down the centuries.

In an unfinished fragment on 'The Christian Doctrine of Religious Community' in his *Glaubenslehre*, Troeltsch insists that 'the idea of community is *central* to Christianity' and is 'the *correlate of redemption*'.[77] Community is the 'essence' of Jesus' proclamation of the kingdom of God.[78] It is, however, a community of elevated spirits, without human structures or organization. It permeates human society and culture and has no discrete, structured existence of its own. In Jesus' lifetime the contexts of the kingdom were the temple and synagogue; only after the separation of the community from Judaism did it require a shape of its own and this was the work and achievement of Paul.[79] From Jesus to today, the true kingdom of God, partly present and yet always transcendent, is without structure and without organization. So what becomes of the sacraments, the ministry, the creeds and the authority of Scripture in the Christian community (deferring to Troeltsch's susceptibility, we do not need to say 'church' in order to pose the question)? In fact the sacraments, in Troeltsch's view, have been transformed in modern critical-historical thinking from channels of grace, created by the working of the Holy Spirit, to expressions of human religiosity, the self-presentation of the community, whether in baptism or in the Lord's Supper. Modernity has seen 'the dissolution of sacramentalism', that is to say 'belief in the efficacy of clerical miracle-working through certain visible means and institutions'.[80] Again, 'sacramentalism' stands for 'an intrinsic connection between a material procedure and a supernatural divine agency'. It belongs to an outmoded idea of the church as a 'divine instrument of salvation', the sphere of miraculous grace. The fact that Martin Luther retained a realist understanding of the sacraments was, according to Troeltsch, a function of Luther's own 'particular pathos'.[81] 'On Protestant soil', Troeltsch remarks, a sacrament is only a means of grace if it is seen as a visible word (*verbum visibile*), a picture of the Christian message. Protestantism has – or soon will have – eliminated the Catholic concept of a sacrament, where it was bound up with superannuated notions of sin and grace. Doctrinally, sacraments have a twofold character (a) as 'solemn and festive representations of the Word' and (b) as 'an act of the community's common life and confession'.[82]

Although the concept of community figures prominently in Troeltsch's presentation of the current validity of Christianity, as mediating the individual's personal

---

[76]   Troeltsch, *Social Teaching of the Christian Churches*, vol. 1, p. 58.
[77]   Troeltsch, *The Christian Faith*, p. 291.
[78]   Ibid.
[79]   Ibid., pp. 292–3.
[80]   Ibid., p. 26.
[81]   Ibid., pp. 36–7.
[82]   Ibid., pp. 297–8; id., *Social Teaching of the Christian Churches*, vol. 1, p. 388.

relationship to Jesus, he discards the concept of 'the church' as too institutional, too supernaturalistic, as hidebound and limiting: 'now the church is a free, purely spiritual, living nexus that emerges from Christ'. The religious interpretation for today of the history of Christianity no longer requires the concept of the church. Instead we have common or communal spirit/Spirit that emanates from the personality of Jesus and draws those of like mind and heart together in his name. The 'Christian life-world' replaces the church.[83] I think what is missing here is a robust doctrine of the Holy Spirit, as the active presence of God, making Christ real in the world and building up the church as his body and as the sign, instrument and foretaste of his kingdom. So not only is Troeltsch's Christology inadequate, but his pneumatology is virtually non-existent. On two of the three 'sites' of trinitarian theology, he fails. Troeltsch was a God-focused man, but the God that dominated his thought and feeling was not the God revealed in Jesus Christ, to whom the New Testament, the creeds and the worship of the church bear witness.

Eschatology eliminated

In an article on 'Eschatology' in 1910 Troeltsch begins by equating religion with 'last things', that is 'a sense . . . of ultimate realities and values that are absolute and unconditioned', though necessarily expressed poetically and mythically.[84] (This is almost a paraphrase of how Schleiermacher defines religion in his *On Religion: Speeches to its Cultured Despisers*: 'a sense and taste for the infinite').[85] For Troeltsch, religion – and only religion – is concerned with the Absolute, with last things and values. The terminology of 'the Absolute' here resonates with Troeltsch's wrestling, at the beginning of the century, with the question, given currency by Hegel, of 'the absoluteness of Christianity' in relation to the 'history of religions' school of comparative theology. Christianity may indeed be affirmed as the highest expression of religion so far attained by humankind and as normative for the present time and it may even be hypothetically unsurpassable as a religion; but historical method treats everything as related or interconnected (relative in that mild sense) and thus precludes any judgements of absoluteness.[86] It is a debasement of religion when the last things are dressed up as heaven, hell, the resurrection of the dead, the last judgement and so on. Eschatology must be understood in personalist terms, as referring to the eternal destiny of the ethical individual. The fulfilment of personhood consists in the perfection of the individual through moral struggle and by engaging with their tasks in this life until, after death, they become immersed in the divine life. As for the eschatology of Jesus (Troeltsch adds this in passing; it is not his main concern here), it did not coincide with his proclamation of the kingdom of God, but was merely the late Jewish cosmology that he inherited. In sum, eschatology today means the return of finite spirits to God

---

[83] Troeltsch, *The Christian Faith*, pp. 102–3.
[84] Ernst Troeltsch, *Religion in History*, ed. James Luther Adams, trans. James Luther Adams and Walter F. Bense (Edinburgh: T&T Clark, 1991), chapter 10, 'Eschatology', pp. 146–58 (article originally published in *Religion in Geschichte und Gegenwart*, 1910).
[85] Schleiermacher, *On Religion: Speeches to Its Cultured Despisers*, trans. John Oman, p. 39.
[86] Troeltsch, *Absoluteness of Christianity*.

through the moral effort of the exercise of freedom and the consequent transformation of natural beings into spiritual beings, that is, persons who are now capable of being absorbed back into God after death.

In the *Glaubenslehre* Troeltsch acknowledges the imminent character of the eschatological framework of the New Testament, as that had been brought to light or rediscovered by German scholars in his lifetime. But he does not allow it substantially to inform his interpretation of the kingdom of God. He discounts it, just as Harnack did, as an aspect of an archaic world view. In the dictated fragment on the place of eschatology in the theological system, he attributes all forms of eschatology, ancient or modern, to the fertile human imagination, manufacturing colourful, poetic images of what cannot be known. What Troeltsch affirms is that beyond death there is 'redemption from nature and creatureliness'; 'space and time' will be excluded and 'creaturely personality' will merge into the life of God, into 'the all-will'.[87] Several points are striking about these comments. (a) There is no mention of Jesus Christ; no thought of 'We shall be like him for we shall see him as he is', which is the one thing that the New Testament says that 'we know', about the afterlife (1 Jn 3:2). (b) The human destiny beyond death is entirely individual – the communion of saints has no place here – until the individual ceases to exist as a drop of water merges with the ocean. (b) Having earlier disparaged Schleiermacher for succumbing to the allure of monism and totality, Troeltsch now postulates immersion in the divine life as the goal of existence. (c) The great philosopher of history can envisage nothing more blessed than to be freed from history – from time and space – at last. Troeltsch's burden will fall away in the end (*eschaton*).

In discounting, as we are all bound to do, the literal meaning of the various incompatible apocalyptic scenarios of the Bible, including the Gospels and Epistles (and even more so the Book of Revelation – 'The Apocalypse'), with their drama and violence, Troeltsch has also largely abandoned – or at least transposed out of all recognition – the major biblical and theological category of eschatology. But the latter does not follow from the former: eschatology is not necessarily apocalyptic. Consequently, Troeltsch's altogether benign understanding of Jesus' proclamation and of its continuing momentum through the centuries is seriously defective and reductionist. I grant that Troeltsch's version of the *kerygma* has more life and passion than Harnack's; he has filled the same basic message with considerable existential power. But in my opinion, Troeltsch, much more than Schleiermacher, deserved the nemesis of Liberal Protestant theology that was to be delivered by Karl Barth, the greatest – though far from infallible – twentieth-century theologian.[88]

Karl Barth

Karl Barth (1886–1968) saw his work overall as precisely the antidote to Schleiermacher's approach and that of Liberal Protestantism generally – as represented most notably in

---

[87] Troeltsch, *The Christian Faith*, pp. 300–3.
[88] See the valuable discussion by Morgan, 'Ernst Troeltsch and the Dialectical Theology', chapter 2.

his day by Harnack, Herrmann and Troeltsch, each in his different way. Barth therefore typically conducted his project in critical dialogue with Schleiermacher and the legacy of Liberal Protestant theology, as we see continually throughout his massive *oeuvre*, but especially in parts of *Protestant Theology in the Nineteenth Century*.[89] In fact Barth never succeeded in escaping the gravitational field of Liberal Protestantism, especially its life-or-death struggle with the authority of historical research and its consequent desperate search for an escape route from 'history'. Barth seems to have thought that he had found such a route in the concept of salvation history, to be regarded as distinct from ordinary history and to which one was obliged to adopt an entirely different approach, one that was theologically sui generis and unaccountable to any academic criteria. But the fact is that Barth's escape route involved an intolerable and perverse methodological dualism and was, in truth, a dead end for Christian theology – though there are many shafts of insight to be gleaned by us on the way.

Barth and Liberal Protestantism

Although Schleiermacher had been dead for nearly a century, Barth sparred obsessively with his shade. Barth could not get his great predecessor out of his hair. In his theological method Barth failed to escape from the gravitational pull of Schleiermacher's method in his *Glaubenslehre*, though he professed to despise it. In the heading or thesis of the very first section of the *Church Dogmatics* Barth defines 'The Task of Dogmatics' as 'the scientific self-examination of the Christian Church with respect to the content of its distinctive talk about God'.[90] In *Dogmatics in Outline*, based on lectures given extempore in Bonn immediately after the end of the Second World War and thus well after the publication of the first volumes of the *Church Dogmatics*, Barth states that 'The subject of dogmatics is the Christian Church' – shortly expanding that definition to include the church's proclamation.[91] This is a distinct echo of Schleiermacher, the method and content of whose dogmatics Barth was ostensibly contesting. It also smacks of reductionism to those who think of Barth as a theologian who typically advocated a kind of direct reading off of dogmatic theology from divine revelation (the word of God). In fact Barth had no choice but to adopt such a Schleiermacherian description of the task of dogmatics. Theology is obviously, by definition, ultimately about God. But

---

[89]   Barth, *Protestant Theology in the Nineteenth Century*, passim; id., *The Theology of Schleiermacher*, ed. Dietrich Ritschl (Edinburgh: T&T Clark, 1982); James O. Duke and Robert F. Streetman (eds), *Barth and Schleiermacher: Beyond the Impasse* (Philadelphia, PA: Fortress Press, 1988). For a concise introduction to Barth's theological method, with criticisms, see Avis, *The Methods of Modern Theology*, chapter 3. See also Thomas F. Torrance, *Karl Barth: An Introduction to his Early Theology, 1910-1931* (London: SCM Press, 1962). Biography: Eberhard Busch, *Karl Barth: His Life from Letters and Autobiographical Texts*, trans. John Bowden from 2nd German edition (London: SCM Press, 1976); Paul Silas Peterson, *The Early Karl Barth: Historical Contexts and Intellectual Formation 1905-1935* (Tübingen: Mohr Siebeck, 2018). For discussion of Barth on Schleiermacher see S. W. Sykes (ed.), *Karl Barth: Studies of His Theological Methods* (Oxford: Oxford University Press, 1979); James E. Davison, 'Can God Speak a Word to Man? Barth's Critique of Schleiermacher's Theology', *SJT* 37 (1984), pp. 189–211 (a judicious survey).
[90]   Karl Barth, *Church Dogmatics*, ed. G. W. Bromiley and T. F. Torrance (Edinburgh: T&T Clark, 1975-) [hereinafter *CD* by volume and part], I/1, p. 3.
[91]   Karl Barth, *Dogmatics in Outline*, trans. G. T. Thomson (London: SCM Press, 1949), p. 9; cf. p. 11.

the transcendent, infinite and ineffable Creator cannot ever be the subject of human scrutiny, but remains veiled in darkness and mystery. God can be known only through the effects of God in the world: in creation, preservation, revelation, redemption and sanctification. One of the principal and privileged arenas of the divine action is the church; it is among the effects of God in the world. Although Barth has a problem (as we shall note below) with the notion of any human, institutional, mediation of divine grace, he has no option but to accept that theology studies the effects of God through the church, which is precisely where, above all, the word of God is received, believed, embodied and proclaimed.

In his early work Barth took every opportunity to snipe at Schleiermacher's reputation. Barth's informal comments in 1923 verge on the insolent and fall into the category of speaking ill of the dead. Schleiermacher elicits grudging respect, a man (Barth says) 'before whom one must lift one's hat even when one would like to take him by the throat!' In Schleiermacher's Christology 'one wades knee-deep in monstrosities and horrors'. Schleiermacher's *Glaubenslehre* is 'one gigantic swindle' and so on.[92] In 1926 Barth commented that Schleiermacher was 'a force' that one could not expect to come to terms with on the first, second or even third attempt.[93] In *Protestant Theology in the Nineteenth Century*, however, Barth adopted a more balanced approach and a more judicious tone, though some of his compliments are backhanded ones.

Barth's argument with Schleiermacher spanned a range of theological topics – theological method, epistemology, anthropology, revelation, Christology and so on – but ecclesiology was not particularly one of them. In fact their respective understandings of the relation between Jesus and the church are uncannily similar – though the theological reasons for this convergence are poles apart. On the perennial polarity in ecclesiology between spirit and structure, inwardness and institution, Schleiermacher and Barth are both exponents of ecclesial 'inwardness' and are uninterested in – even suspicious of – the externality of the church. Both of them are protagonists of the spirit and disengaged from questions of structure. They both sat lightly to the *form* that the church has taken or should take in history and in human society. To put it rather programatically, their ecclesiologies point away from *polity* and towards *proclamation*. In this respect, they reveal themselves as representatives of Protestant theology and its basic ecclesiological impulse, whether in the Reformers themselves (especially Luther), in the Liberal Protestantism whose progenitor was Schleiermacher, or in the confessional and dialectical reaction to Liberal Protestantism, led by Barth himself. Indeed, as exponents of a proclamatory ecclesiology, Schleiermacher and Barth alike bring out the strength and vitality of Protestant theology. In reality, however, to play off proclamation against polity is to succumb to a false dichotomy. Who or what is doing the proclaiming? It must be some kind of social (and that means socio-political)

---

[92]   James D. Smart, trans., *Revolutionary Theology in the Making: Barth-Thurneysen Correspondence, 1914-1925* (Richmond, VA: John Knox Press, 1964), pp. 158–9, 168.
[93]   Barth, 'Schleiermacher' (1926), in id., *Theology and Church*, intro. T. F. Torrance (London: SCM Press, 1962), p. 199. See also Barth, ed. Dietrich Ritsch, trans. G. W. Bromiley, *The Theology of Schleiermacher* (Edinburgh: T&T Clark, 1982), Barth's lectures at Göttingen, 1923–1924, together with 'Concluding Unscientific Postscript on Schleiermacher', from 'Nachwort' in H. Bolli, ed., *Schleiermacher-Auswahl* (Siebenstern Taschenbuch: Munich and Hamburg, 1968).

entity, that is to say an institution. An institution cannot exist without a structure. That structure is of a political nature because it has to do with the distribution of power, authority and resources, with the weighting of various constituent elements and consequent constraints on freedom of action. Every institution, however unpretentious, has a polity, and it is the polity that makes possible any acts of public intervention, witness and proclamation. To profess, as a theologian, to be uninterested in the polity of the church, or to relegate it to a secondary level, is irresponsible and an abdication of the full scope of the theological calling.

Barth studied under Harnack and was a fervent, dedicated student, regarding Harnack as '*the* theologian of the day'.[94] He was equally bowled over by Wilhelm Herrmann's teaching and writing, later recalling of his reading of Herrmann's *Ethics:* 'I think that my own personal interest in theology began on that day'.[95] His adherence to Herrmann involved a repudiation of Troeltsch with his historical-critical and sociological methods.[96] But in 1914 Barth reacted against Harnack, Herrmann and what they represented and symbolized: the liberal-theological-political hegemony that had betrayed its birthright by publicly supporting Prussian militarism and aggression in the First World War.[97] For Barth, this act of unquestioning fealty to Kaiser Wilhelm II's ruthless, amoral imperial policy completely discredited all that, as a student, sitting at the feet of Harnack and Herrmann, he had wholeheartedly embraced. Barth claimed that, for him, it brought the whole edifice of German Liberal Protestant theology crashing down (though there was probably as much continuity as discontinuity in his future theological relationship to Herrmann and Liberal Protestantism).[98] He began to look for another theological pathway – the trail once blazed by the biblical prophets and apostles, and by Luther and Calvin. Once Barth had sufficiently developed his ideas to produce the second edition of his *Romerbrief* (1921), Harnack came into the picture once again.

In the early 1920s, Harnack chastised Barth for making a revelation theology of the word a substitute for what Harnack called 'scientific theology', namely, critical-historical research into the life of Jesus and the formation of the early church. Harnack asked, 'If the person of Jesus Christ stands at the centre of the gospel [on which they were agreed], how else can the basis for reliable and communal knowledge of this person be gained but through critical-historical study so that an imagined Christ is not put in the place of the real one?'[99] Given that Barth was concerned above all for the effectiveness of preaching, leading to faith, Harnack asked whether faith in Christ

---

[94] Busch, *Karl Barth*, pp. 38–9.
[95] Ibid., pp. 40–1. On Barth's education within the portals of the Liberal Protestant academy and especially with regard to the theology of Wilhelm Herrmann (and behind him Albrecht Ritschl), with the lines of continuity and discontinuity to Barth, see Bruce L. McCormack, *Karl Barth's Critically Realistic Dialectical Theology: Its Genesis and Development 1909-1936* (Oxford: Clarendon Press, 1995), chapter 1.
[96] Peterson, *The Early Karl Barth*, p. 19. See also Christophe Chalamet, *Dialectical Theologians: Wilhelm Herrmann, Karl Barth and Rudolf Bultmann* (Zurich: TVZ, 2005).
[97] Busch, *Karl Barth*, pp. 81–2. Troeltsch did not sign the document.
[98] Peterson, *The Early Karl Barth*, pp. 44–51. Chapman, *Ernst Troeltsch*, is also sceptical about Barth's promotion of 1914 as the great theological watershed.
[99] H. M. Rumscheidt (ed.), *Revelation and Theology: An Analysis of the Barth-Harnack Correspondence of 1923* (Cambridge: Cambridge University Press, 1972), p. 31. Peterson, *The Early Karl Barth*, pp. 192–6.

could exist independently of belief in his historical manifestation. Barth's reply was defiant but impossibly fideistic: '[T]he reliability and communality of the knowledge of the person of Jesus Christ as the centre of the *gospel* can be none other than that of the God-awakened faith.' Invoking 1 Cor. 3:11, Barth added: 'Critical-historical study signifies the deserved and necessary end of *those* "foundations" of this knowledge which are no foundations at all since they have not been laid by God himself.'[100] Sykes describes this tactic as 'an epistemological grand-slam', adding (and putting the words into Barth's mouth), 'If the conventions of historiography lead us to despair of historical knowledge of Christ, so much the better.'[101] Sykes comments that Barth 'consistently refuses to assign to historical scholarship of Christian origins a consistent and intelligible role; his evasions on this issue make a most unpleasing impression.'[102] Harnack concluded that Barth was spinning theological creations out of his own entrails and that his abstruse theological convolutions were obscuring the simplicity of the gospel. He was shocked at Barth's studied indifference to the manifestations of the divine in the great events and personalities of the past. Barth's insistence that the gospel did not make the world a better place was, to him, scandalous and perverse.

Strangely enough, Barth's *Protestant Theology in the Nineteenth Century* has no chapter on Harnack or Herrmann; it ends with a rather slight and sour piece on Albrecht Ritschl, Herrmann's teacher. But, before the end of the century that Barth is covering, Harnack had published many notable works of theological, not simply historical, significance, including his great work on the history of dogma (*Lehrbuch der Dogmengeschichte*), the first volume of which had appeared in 1885. Indeed, if 1900 is to be reckoned the last year of the old century, Harnack's *Das Wesen des Christentums* (English translation, *What is Christianity?* 1901) appeared within the nineteenth century. Similarly, Herrmann had made his greatest contribution before the close of the century: his *The Communion of the Christian with God* appeared in 1895. It was really inexcusable of Barth to have omitted Harnack and Herrmann from this compendious work.

Apart from some snide remarks, Barth also failed to engage seriously with Troeltsch, with whom he overlapped chronologically. He made an excuse for not continuing *Protestant Theology in the Nineteenth Century* as far as Troeltsch.[103] His fullest comment in the *Church Dogmatics* comes in IV/1, pp. 383–7, on the doctrine of sin in Troeltsch's *Glaubenslehre*. Barth not unjustly accuses Troeltsch of floundering: first flirting with pantheism and notions of the kingdom of God as the progressive moral amelioration of society, and then backtracking somewhat and taking refuge in the ultimate mystery and unknowability of God (apophatic theology). Barth's verdict is scathing: with Troeltsch, 'the doctrine of faith was on the point of dissolution into endless and useless talk.'[104] Once again we find an unresolved intellectual entanglement

---

[100] Rumscheidt (ed.), *Revelation and Theology*, p. 35.
[101] Sykes, *The Identity of Christianity*, p. 185.
[102] Ibid., p. 186.
[103] Barth, *Protestant Theology in the Nineteenth Century*, p. ix.
[104] Barth, *CD*, IV/1, pp. 383–7, at p. 387. For other substantive references in the *Church Dogmatics* to Troeltsch see Morgan, 'Ernst Troeltsch and the Dialectical Theology', p. 53, n. 96.

with a great predecessor in German thought and culture.[105] But Barth had deliberately stopped his ears to Troeltsch's insistence that, as theologians, we must face up to the questions raised by historical study; Barth did not want to know.

Barth and history

Barth was frankly uninterested in the kind of detailed historical research that Harnack embraced as his life's work and vocation. Barth was equally unconcerned with the questions of the philosophy of history and the problems of historical relativism (historicism, *Historismus*) that occupied Troeltsch throughout his career, particularly in his last years. Barth deplored, in nineteenth-century Protestant theology, 'the none too dignified sight of a general flight, of those heads that were wisest, into the study of history'.[106] (Schleiermacher was excused from this Gadarene descent: he remained steadfastly loyal to the dogmatic task, though of course, according to Barth, he went widely astray therein.)[107] Barth's answer to the massive challenges that confronted him in the academic milieu of early nineteenth-century Germany – challenges that were symbolized by the achievement and stature of these two outstanding scholars – was to create an alternative conceptual superstructure. Within his theological cosmos, Barth proposed and elaborated, at enormous and inordinate length, an idiosyncratic meaning for 'history'. He proposed a concept of the 'history' of God's saving acts that was not subject to the received canons of historical enquiry, accompanied by a quixotic use of 'time' and 'the times' that was not intelligibly connected to historical time. This was a colossal strategy of evasion, not to mention self-deception. No less so than the Liberal Protestant writers whose efforts he affected to despise, Barth was looking for a way of escape from the threat of what objective historical research could do to the received faith of the believer and the church.[108]

In the Preface to the second edition of his Romans commentary, written from his pastor's study in Safenwil, Switzerland, in September 1921, Barth defends himself against the charge that he was an enemy of historical criticism of the Bible. It is both necessary and justified, he protests. But when it has done its work on establishing the best text, on the meaning of words and on the circumstances of composition, there still remains the task of theological exegesis, in the model manner of Luther or Calvin, to bring out the meaning and message of the text for the church today.[109]

---

[105] Barth's relationship with Troeltsch has been explored in T. W. Ogletree, *Christian Faith and History: A Critical Comparison of Ernst Troeltsch and Karl Barth* (New York: Abingdon Press, 1965); Wilfried Groll, *Ernst Troeltsch und Karl Barth – Kontinuität im Widerspruch* (Munich: Kaiser Verlag, 1976); Morgan, 'Ernst Troeltsch and the Dialectical Theology'; and Van Harvey, *The Historian and the Believer*.

[106] Barth, *Protestant Theology in the Nineteenth Century*, p. 416.

[107] Ibid., p. 417.

[108] See Ogletree, *Christian Faith and History*; D. F. Ford, 'Barth's Interpretation of the Bible', in Sykes (ed.), *Karl Barth: Studies of His Theological Methods*, chapter 3; David Kelsey, *the Uses of Scripture in Recent Theology* (Philadelphia, PA: Fortress Press, 1975), chapter 3.

[109] Karl Barth, *The Epistle to the Romans*, trans. from the 6th German edition by Edwyn C. Hoskyns (Oxford: Oxford University Press, 1933), pp. 6–12. See Bruce L. McCormack, 'Historical Criticism and Dogmatic Interest in Karl Barth's Theological Exegesis of the New Testament', in Mark S. Burrows and Paul Rorem (eds), *Biblical Hermeneutics in Historical Perspective* (Grand Rapids, MI:

Barth's implied comparison of himself with Calvin must surely have backfired because Calvin's commentaries are closely focused on the text, spare in comment, judicious in weighing possible interpretations, serviceable to the student and minister, whereas Barth's so-called commentary on Romans is hyper-inflated with rhetoric, bombast and hyperbole and studded with confusing esoteric, idiosyncratic and abstruse terminology.

In this Romans commentary Barth consigns not simply the study of history, but history itself to the dustbin. In the first edition (1919) Barth operated with a sophistical distinction between 'so-called history' (what we call 'history') and 'real history' (the secret work of God and God's kingdom within the empirical historical process). To refer to ordinary human history as 'so-called' is a perverse devaluation, an arrogant dismissal, of human striving, suffering and achievement. Barth's motive is plain; as McCormack puts it, 'He wanted to put the movement and action of God in history beyond the reach of historical investigation.'[110] At this point Barth is still very much the disciple of Herrmann who had tried to find a safe space for God's saving action within the human spirit, that is in religious experience, outside the uncertainties and difficulties of historical research.[111] Even in the second and subsequent editions of the *Romerbrief* (1922–) Barth speaks of the action of God in revelation and redemption, intersecting the world process from above, as not itself part of history, nor as historically discernible. Thus, the resurrection of Christ is not an event in history at all. History is meaningless, except in so far as it has a negative value in pointing to a better world.[112] If history is meaningless, the idea of a church founded in history and thereafter embedded in history will be meaningless also.

Is Barth's position on the question of the authority of historical enquiry for theology very different in the *Church Dogmatics*? Although it is customary to claim that Barth embraced a fresh theological paradigm in the *Church Dogmatics*, one that took much more seriously the reality of time and space and human life in this world, I am not so sure. It is true that, in his great treatise 'The Obedience of the Son of God' (CD § 59), Barth insists that the crucifixion and death of Christ was an 'occurrence' and 'a matter of history', that it 'happened in this way, in the space and time which are those of all men'.[113] But, while Barth affirms the historical factuality of the Passion, he resists any excursion into the historical analysis of the narratives. 'In the editing and composition' of the Gospels, he writes, 'the interest and art and rules of the historian do not matter'. So there can be no question of 'digging out and preserving' Christ and his history in order to analyse them. They are separated and secluded from us by the events of the Resurrection and Pentecost. At the coming of the Holy Spirit a new age, a new history, was inaugurated, that of the church. Though historians may protest (Barth

---

Eerdmans, 1991), chapter 19, pp. 322–38. McCormack defends the scholarly integrity of Barth's biblical interpretation, pointing out that Barth accepted critical-historical study as a necessary starting point. However, I see Barth's protestations to this effect in the Preface to his *Romans* as largely paying lip service.

[110]   McCormack, *Karl Barth's Critically Realistic Dialectical Theology*, p. 146; cf. pp. 230–5.

[111]   Ibid., pp. 61–8.

[112]   Barth, *Romans*, pp. 29–30, 77, 107. See the sceptical analysis of Barth's later account of the 'historicity' of the resurrection (in *CD*, III/2.i) in Van Harvey, *The Historian and the Believer*, pp. 153–9.

[113]   *CD*, IV/1, pp. 247–8.

comments), we have to insist that 'the voice and form of Jesus' cannot be 'distinguished with any finality' from the community that he brought into being and filled with his life at Pentecost.[114] It is as though the event(s) of Resurrection-Pentecost have brought down an opaque curtain that cannot be penetrated by historical enquiry. But Barth also seems to apply this veto retrospectively to the miracles of the Gospel narratives: he insists that the question of whether they happened in the way described does not belong to the dogmatic exposition of the Christian faith.

In this connection, the resurrection of Jesus Christ is a crux. Barth seems to say that it both is and is not part of history. On the one hand, the resurrection 'has happened in the same sense as His crucifixion and His death, in the human sphere and human time, as an actual event within the world with an objective content . . . it happened in time, as a particular history in history generally, with a concrete factuality'.[115] Barth could hardly, it seems, be more explicit about the historical actuality of the resurrection. On the other hand, in recognizing that the accounts of the resurrection appearances in the New Testament are not consistent with one another and confront us with 'obscurities and irreconcilable contradictions', Barth appeals to 'the peculiar character of this history, which bursts through all general ideas of history as it takes place . . . in space and time'. There is no scope here, he insists, for the 'historicist' (i.e. Troeltschian) concept of history (i.e. as a web of immanent and interrelated causes and effects). But if (Barth concedes) we are to conform to the ideas of modern historical science, then the resurrection, just like the creation, must be categorized as 'saga' or 'legend', though never 'myth', he insists (which makes me doubt whether Barth fully understood this repertoire of literary genres).[116] Thus, 'The death of Christ can certainly be thought of as history in the modern sense, but not the resurrection.'[117] I think that what has happened here is that Barth has impaled himself on the horns of a theological dilemma: he wants to inhibit historical scrutiny of the biblical narrative, but he does not want to lose the scandal of particularity by removing the 'events' into a realm of timeless general truths, because that would be to surrender the ground he had won at such cost in his first and great battle with Liberal Protestantism.[118]

It might appear at first sight that when, in the *Church Dogmatics*, Barth applies the language of sacramentality to salvation history – as he does apply it, though rarely, obscurely and rather tantalisingly, to Jesus Christ, Israel and the church – he is opening the door to historical enquiry into the founding events of the Christian faith.[119] The existence of the human nature of the incarnate Jesus Christ, he says, constitutes 'the basic reality and substance of the sacramental reality of [God's] revelation'. Through union with the eternal Word, 'this creature' becomes 'the supreme and outstanding work and sign of God'. It was 'a unique occurrence', a 'unique happening'. Yet, through the 'existence of the man Jesus', 'a sacramental continuity stretches backwards into the

---

[114] Ibid., p. 320.
[115] Ibid., p. 333.
[116] See Paul Avis, *God and the Creative Imagination: Metaphor, Symbol and Myth in Religion and Theology* (London and New York: Routledge, 1999).
[117] Barth, CD, IV/1, pp. 334–6.
[118] Ibid., p. 337.
[119] Barth, CD, II/1, pp. 53–4.

existence of the people of Israel . . . and forwards into the existence of . . . the Church'. By God's action 'the creature can be the temple, instrument and sign' of God. Barth's language and choice of words here is extremely guarded. He seems to strive to avoid tangling with history: we have 'existence', 'occurrence' and 'happening', but no mention of 'history'. It all takes place in the world, but not as part of the historical process.

So what is the empirical cash value of a 'sign' in this case? The saving action is ontological, for sure, but is it truly historical? Because, as Barth insists, the saving events are unique and definitive, they are not subject to historical constraints, nor are they mediated by history. History forms a detached backdrop; it is not part of the performance, the drama. Just as, for Barth, no natural theology could be allowed to condition or constrain the unique revelation of God in Jesus Christ (as he is attested in Holy Scripture), so no historical process can be allowed to condition or constrain God's acts in 'salvation history' (a misnomer, if ever there was one). Revelation and redemption are not mediated by history but by Scripture alone, taken at face value as far as the veracity of the narrative is concerned.[120] The biblical attestation to God's acts in revelation, redemption and so on, is protected from prying scholarly eyes because those acts constitute God's self-demonstration, and must remain uncontaminated by any human, historical, influence.[121] At the gateway to critical-historical enquiry into the 'events' of salvation history, Barth places an intimidating 'No Entry' sign.

The foundation of the church in Barth

Barth does speak from time to time about the founding or foundation of the church. Sometimes this is en passant, as when he says that, according to the Gospels, 'the Church came into being quite visibly with the calling of the twelve apostles', corresponding to the twelve tribes of Israel.[122] More substantially, he affirms that it was the resurrection of Jesus Christ that brought about the faith of the disciples in the living presence and action of Christ, and that in the creation of this Easter faith the foundation of the community was laid. However, the real foundation, the foundation of the church as such, as a basis for the apostolic proclamation, came about only with the outpouring of the Holy Spirit at Pentecost. Thus, we have a two-stage process: the forty days of resurrection appearances and teaching by the risen Christ concerning the kingdom of God, followed by the upsurge of the Spirit's power that would propel the apostles 'into all the world'. Through the Holy Spirit, the community was constituted as the church (though Barth continues to use the two terms interchangeably in the *Church Dogmatics*). It is as though (these are my words, not Barth's) the birth of Easter

---

[120] David F. Ford suggests that the concept of 'realistic narrative', derived from Hans Frei via Erich Auerbach, helps to elucidate Barth's approach. Thus literary, rather than historical, canons are what is appropriate for evaluating Barth's use of Scripture. Ford does not assume that Barth's method in this respect is adequate or cogent. David F. Ford, 'Barth's Interpretation of the Bible'; cf. Hans W. Frei, *The Eclipse of Biblical Narrative: A Study in Eighteenth and Nineteenth Century Hermeneutics* (New Haven, CT: Yale University Press, 1974); Erich Auerbach, *Mimesis: The Representation of Reality in Western Literature*, trans. Willard R. Trask; intro. Edward W. Said (Princeton, NJ: Princeton University Press, 2013 [1946]).

[121] Barth, CD, II/1, pp. 44–8.

[122] Barth, CD, IV/1, p. 653.

faith provided for the church *the foundation of the foundation*.[123] But how does Barth envisage or portray the church?

Schleiermacher and Troeltsch played down the institutional aspect of ecclesiology – the church as a visible, ordered or structured society – in Troeltsch's case even abandoning the notion of the church for today altogether and replacing it with a rather nebulous notion of a community of those who have been touched by the spiritual impulse that derives from the personality of Jesus. The trend to downplay the institutional nature of the church – the church embodied in time and place – was taken further by Barth, but for different, indeed completely opposed, reasons.[124] Von Balthasar noted that Barth 'always remains opposed to all institutional aspects of Christianity.' Von Balthasar continued perceptively: 'for this reason, the form given by him to dogmatics has never been able to take root undialectically in the visible reality of the Church. This form remains actualistic and energetic, and yet it was intended and presented as the *real form* of God's objective act of revelation.'[125] I think von Balthasar is saying that Barth's ecclesiology could not be put into practice in administering the church; it could not inform and guide church *policy* or be translated into an ecclesiastical *polity*. So we might ask what is intended by a *Church Dogmatics* that cannot serve the existing church: how is that a *church* dogmatics? It is hugely significant that, in his early commentary on Romans (Second edition), Barth described the church as merely 'the crater' or 'void' formed by the explosion of the gospel.[126] These images suggest a notion of the church as lacking in substance in its own right and as merely a space, a vacuum, or at best a theatre, for the performance of events that are not an expression of the nature of the church as such.[127] We may say that, for the early Barth, the reality of the church itself, as a visible, ordered society in the world, is definitely not an integral part of the church's proclamation and so does not belong to the gospel of Christ.

However, Barth's treatise on the church in his *Church Dogmatics* IV/1 §62 (pp. 642–725) is a landmark in Protestant ecclesiology and is theologically superior, in my opinion, to the other extensive tracts of the *Church Dogmatics* that are devoted to the church. Here Barth developed the impulse of his early theology (seen particularly in the second edition of the commentary on Romans) of divine revelation as intersecting the world vertically from above and as qualitatively different from all merely human

---

[123] Ibid., pp. 338–40.

[124] For a comprehensive study of Barth's ecclesiology see Kimlyn Bender, *Karl Barth's Christological Ecclesiology* (Aldershot: Ashgate, 2005; reprinted Eugene, OR: Cascade Books, 2013); id., 'Karl Barth', in Paul Avis (ed.), *The Oxford Handbook of Ecclesiology* (Oxford: Oxford University Press, 2018), chapter 17. A succinct introduction to Barth's ecclesiology and sacramental doctrine is James J. Buckley, 'Christian Community, Baptism, and Lord's Supper', in John Webster (ed.), *The Cambridge Companion to Karl Barth* (Cambridge: Cambridge University Press, 2000), chapter 12, pp. 195–211.

[125] Hans Urs von Balthasar, *The Glory of the Lord: A Theological Aesthetics, Volume I, Seeing the Form*, trans. Erasmo Leiva-Merikakis; ed. Joseph Fessio, S. J. and John Riches (Edinburgh: T&T Clark, 1982), p. 53.

[126] Barth, *Romans*, pp. 29, 36, 65, 110.

[127] A similar, but more positive image is provided by one of Barth's exponents, John Webster (1955–2016), when he affirms that '"Church" is the event of gathering around the magnetic centre of the good news of Jesus Christ': John Webster, 'What Is the Gospel?', in Timothy Bradshaw (ed.), *Grace and Truth in the Secular Age* (Grand Rapids, MI: Eerdmans, 1998), pp. 109–18, at p. 114.

spiritual aspirations, strivings and insights (which Barth included in the derogatory, catch-all phrase 'natural theology'). This early Barthian stance evolved into what we might call an 'ecclesiological actualism', whereby the church emerges into historical, worldly existence dynamically, but also sporadically and spasmodically, as it is called into being by God and the gospel. The reality of the church here and now is purely *kerygmatic*. 'The Church *is* when it takes place'.[128]

The positive substance of this approach is that the church is seen as the 'earthly-historical form of the existence' (*irdisch-geschichtliche Existenzform*) of Jesus Christ.[129] Barth here seems to be developing the theological insight that was expressed by Bonhoeffer in his youthful work of 1930 *Sanctorum Communio* in the slogan 'Christ exists as the Church'.[130] But (Barth insists), precisely because it is the mode of Christ's being in the world, the church in its true nature must remain transcendent. It exists only while a definite history takes place. This history is not the history of popes, bishops and councils, but the history of necessarily human, but ultimately God-given faith in the gospel. The church's act is its being, and its essence is its existence. The Christian church is not, in reality, a human, social and historical institution – a divine society on earth that spans the centuries – though that is how it appears to the unregenerate mind because it is what catches the eye. The church exists only as and when it occurs, so to speak; it is perceived by faith. The church is a happening, not a permanent state of affairs. Therefore no concrete, historical, empirical form of the community can be in itself the object of Christian faith. Barth was highly critical of the virtual identification, that he believed he could detect in the more triumphalist forms of Roman Catholic theology, between the mystery of the church as the body of Christ and the historical, empirical church with its law, organization and hierarchical structure. So he develops an alternative account of the history, law, organization and – not of course for him the hierarchical structure, but – the ordering of the church.

Within this ecclesiological framework Barth continues to resist any idea of the ecclesial mediation of grace, of salvation (a position that became explicit and extreme in the last volume of the *Church Dogmatics* [IV, 4], where Barth repudiated the concept of sacramentality and with it the understanding of the sacraments as means of grace).[131] The church can do no more – but no less – than to witness to Christ, to the saving acts of God in him. What it can never do is to point to or witness to the saving acts of God, the work of Christ, *within itself*. Like John the Baptist in the Eisenheim altarpiece at Colmar, by Matthias Grünewald, a reproduction of which Barth had constantly before him in his study, the church can only ever point away from itself to Christ.[132] Jesus Christ is the foundation of the church only in the action of God here and now. For Barth, any attempt to establish with certainty, by means of historical and biblical

---

[128] Barth, *CD*, IV/1, p. 652.
[129] Ibid., p. 643.
[130] Dietrich Bonhoeffer, *Sanctorum Communio* (London: Collins, 1963); also in *Dietrich Bonhoeffer, Works*, General Editor Wayne Whitson Floyd, Jr. (Minneapolis, MN: Fortress Press, 1996-2014), vol. 1. Barth pays tribute to this work by Bonhoeffer in Barth *CD*, IV/2, p. 641.
[131] See the critique in John Yocum, *Ecclesial Mediation in Karl Barth* (Aldershot: Ashgate, 2004).
[132] Here Barth can be contrasted with Roman Catholic, Orthodox and Anglican theology, where the worship, fellowship and mission of the church is regarded as an integral part of the gospel.

research, that Jesus of Nazareth founded it, or even intended its existence, in his earthly ministry would be a form of human striving to secure historical, empirical *guarantees* for the church's existence – and thus a blatant form of unbelief, devoid of faith.

Visible and/or invisible?

Paradoxically, having asserted the priority of the church of faith, Barth then goes on to insist on the imperative of visible Christian unity. There can be no theological justification for a plurality of churches that are genuinely separate and mutually exclusive. 'A plurality of churches in this sense means a plurality of lords, a plurality of spirits, a plurality of gods.'[133] Moreover, Barth blocks any escape route 'from the visibility of the divided Church to the unity of an invisible Church.'[134] This is a significant move for Barth because he believes that unity can be attained only when the Christian traditions take their historical identity and concrete existence seriously, not trading it in for the sake of ecumenical goodwill based on nebulous conceptions of an ideal church that is not grounded empirically. For him, there is no need to deceive ourselves about Christian disunity or to pretend that it is not an intolerable scandal and contradiction, because in every expression of the divided church, the real presence of Jesus Christ is to be found. He keeps his promise to be in the midst, even of a divided church. He does not disown the diversity of expression in traditions, doctrines and outward forms.[135] The catholicity of the church that is confessed in the creed refers to 'an identity, a continuity, a universality, which is maintained in all the differences'.[136] All this appears to take the empirical, historical existence of the church *as the church* seriously. But then Barth's argument swings back to its repeatedly established norm.

Barth develops an impressive exposition of the credal notes of the church in this same section of the *Church Dogmatics* (IV/1 §62). In so doing, he comes remarkably close to Schleiermacher by insisting that the catholicity of the church is the persistence of its true inner identity, centre and essence through all the many changes of its outward form (which are not theologically significant in themselves). *Credo catholicam ecclesiam* means 'I believe that the Christian community is one and the same in all places, in all ages, within all societies, and in relation to all its members' and that 'it can be the Christian community only in this identity' and therefore that its intentional task must be to continue and remain within this identity.[137] The church receives its identity from Jesus Christ, the 'source and norm' of ecclesial identity, the 'identical and continuing and universal essence' of the church.[138]

The centre of Christianity and of the church, for Barth, is Jesus Christ who is known – and known only – through his word within the community of faith. In an address

---

[133] Barth, *CD*, IV/1, p. 675.
[134] Ibid., p. 677. See also Barth's forthright address to the Second World Conference on Faith and Order, Edinburgh 1937, in id., *The Church and the Churches*, Foreword William G. Rusch (Grand Rapids, MI: Eerdmans, 2005), pp. 11–33.
[135] Barth, *CD*, IV/1, p. 683.
[136] Ibid., p. 701.
[137] Ibid., pp. 707–8.
[138] Ibid., p. 712.

of 1934, Barth first stated what the church is not. It is not (and here he is taking aim at the Roman Catholic Church) 'divine revelation institutionalized', 'an organization into whose possession, disposition and administration' God has handed over his truth and authority. But neither is the church a kind of cosy club for those who cherish heartfelt impressions of religious ideas and feelings. What then is the church? The church comes into existence where God speaks through the Scriptures and where humans hear and obey that word.[139] And that word subsists in a threefold form: Christ himself, the Scriptures as they testify to him, and the proclamation of the church on the basis of Scripture.[140] So, for Barth, it is true to say that the church is founded on the word of God (in its threefold form), not merely as an act within history at a particular time, but as ongoing act of God within salvation history here and now. But let us note for future reference (I mean exploration in a possible sequel to the present work) that Barth prefers the image of the centre to that of the foundation.[141] He is switching the semantic context from architecture and building (strongly biblical though that is) to geometry (or possibly cosmology). In doing so, he is changing the language and consequently the logic of the far-reaching ecclesiological question with which we are seeking to grapple in this current study – the question of foundations – and moving out of our present orbit.

   Christology is the key point at which Barth connects the church with the kingdom of God, that 'central New Testament concept'.[142] The kingdom of God is defined by Barth as 'the lordship of God established in the world in Jesus Christ'. Christ is himself the presence of the kingdom of God, the kingdom embodied. But Christ is also the church; the being of Jesus Christ is the being of the church. So we cannot divorce, as historical Protestantism has tended to do (Barth believes) the church and the kingdom, for 'the kingdom is the community'. The kingdom-filled community stems from the resurrection and traverses history towards the final consummation. In the interval between resurrection and consummation the community must pray for the fuller and final coming of the kingdom. 'But already on this side of the end, even in the form of the community which prays for its coming, the kingdom is really on earth and in time and history.' There is a dynamic identity or equivalence between kingdom and the community (though not, I think Barth would wish to add, between kingdom and a hierarchical, sacral ecclesiastical structure). Barth was excited by Origen's depiction of Jesus Christ as *autobasileia*, the self-kingdom, the kingdom in person. At the end of his life, when asked by an interviewer to sum up his theology in a word, Barth replied *'autobasileia'*. I regard this insight of Barth (albeit following Origen) as a priceless contribution to the understanding of the kingdom in its connection with the church.

---

[139] Barth, 'The Church', in id., *God in Action: Theological Addresses*, trans. E. G. Homrighausen and Karl J. Ernst, intro. Josias Friedli (Edinburgh: T&T Clark, 1936), pp. 20–38, at pp. 20–1, 29.
[140] Barth, *CD*, I/1 and I/2. For exposition see Thomas Christian Currie, *The Only Sacrament Left to Us: The Threefold Word of God in the Theology and Ecclesiology of Karl Barth* (Cambridge: James Clarke; Eugene, OR: Pickwick, 2016).
[141] Sykes, *The Identity of Christianity*, chapter 8; id. 'Barth on the Centre of Theology', in id. (ed.), *Karl Barth: Studies of His Theological Methods*.
[142] For what follows see Barth, *CD*, IV/2, pp. 655–8. There are several other mentions of *autobasileia* in the *CD*.

So we find a profound tension in Barth's understanding of the fundamental nature of the church. The kerygmatic and the empirical concepts strain against each other. The degree of paradox becomes acute, perhaps intolerable. However, this is not necessarily a weakness: to criticize a theology because it is full of paradox would be suicidal – nothing could more paradoxical than the gospel itself! Barth is actually an exemplar of the kind of dialectical ecclesiology that, in my view, is the only viable way of construing the church theologically. If, as Bonhoeffer said, Christ exists as the church, the church must be understood in an *incarnational* and *sacramental* way – though this is to go way beyond Barth who would have no truck with such language, regarding it as 'blasphemous'.[143] Vatican II described the church as the universal sacrament, so to speak, of salvation, and the principle of the sacramentality of the church has become widely accepted in modern ecclesiology. But both incarnation and sacrament are dialectical concepts: they reveal and conceal at the same time; they make present but the presence evades capture; they give and they take away. Similarly, the life of the church as a visible society truly mediates Christ, just as the human life of Jesus of Nazareth mediates the incarnate word while remaining a human life and just as the sacramental elements mediate the body and blood of Christ while remaining God's good creatures of bread and wine. The theology of incarnation, church and sacraments is nothing if not inherently dialectical. Barth's fears were exaggerated. The church is far more than a crater caused by the explosion of the gospel, a void waiting to be filled from above, as the early Barth put it. The incarnate Jesus Christ has substance in space and time; a sacrament has substance in space and time; the church has substance in space and time – in each case because, through the Holy Spirit, God gives them that substance in an act of grace-filled divine commitment, 'for the gifts and calling of God are irrevocable' (Rom. 11:29).

Where is eschatology in the dialectical dynamics of Barth's ecclesiology? There is clearly an acute tension there, but is the tension eschatological in nature? Barth clearly accepts the traditional language of a future 'second coming' or *parousia* of Christ in glory. He does not attempt to redefine conventional eschatological language or to explain it away. On the other hand, however, Barth has a form of realized eschatology in his key affirmation (echoing Origen) that Jesus Christ is *autobasileia*, the kingdom itself, and that there is an identity between Christ and the community and between the community and the kingdom. But, in terms of his approach to the task of theology, there is also what McCormack calls 'the eschatological reservation' that Barth understood to surround and underpin his life's work: that of invoking the coming of the Holy Spirit according to Christ's promise, 'the promise of the Father' (Lk. 24:49). The hope, longing and expectation of the Christian and of the theologian were expressed in the ancient hymn of the church *Veni creator spiritus*.[144]

Barth deplored ecclesiastical Docetism, which he identified with the doctrine of the invisible church.[145] Docetism was, of course, the early heresy that the ostensibly human experiences of Jesus Christ were illusory and unreal; his apparent humanity was a mere

---

[143] Barth, *CD*, IV/3.ii, p. 729.
[144] McCormack, *Karl Barth's Critically Realistic Dialectical Theology*, pp. 31–2.
[145] Barth, *CD*, IV/1, p. 653.

phantom concealing his divine nature. But Barth was somewhat half-hearted in his detestation of ecclesial Docetism. On the one hand, he insists on the visibility of the church. Lecturing in the post-war ruins of Berlin in 1946, he stated: 'In the Apostles' Creed it is not an invisible structure which is intended but a quite visible coming together, which originates with the twelve Apostles. . . . If the Church has not this visibility, then it is not the Church.'[146] But if we ask what he means by the visible church, the answer is highly circumscribed: 'What is visible to all is the event of the *congregatio* and *communio* of certain men.'[147] The suspicion lingers that, when Barth refers to the visible church, he means it in a merely sociological sense, as a phenomenon to be studied within the sociology of religion. To say, as Barth does, that the church is 'totally and properly both visible and invisible', just as Jesus Christ on earth was visible as man and invisible as God, is playing with words and dicing with dualism.[148]

In my view, however, to avoid ecclesiological Docetism, we must say that just as Jesus Christ on earth was a visible, tangible reality, so too the church is a visible, tangible reality – and with the church the sacraments of the church. When Barth affirms the visibility of the Church against any kind of 'ecclesiastical Docetism' – that is, contending against any suggestion that the church is really something other than what we see in our midst – he makes it clear that the Christian church is 'a phenomenon of world history which can be grasped in historical and psychological and sociological terms like any other'. But, Barth insists, it cannot be reduced to these terms. They do not tell us the secret of what the church is; that secret is revealed only to faith. *Credo ecclesiam* invokes what Barth calls a 'third dimension in which the church is what it is' – a christological reality. As Barth explains:

> [W]hat is this being of the community, this spiritual character, this secret, which is hidden in its earthly and historical form and [is] therefore invisible, or visible only to the special perception of faith? The answer – which does indeed point to the third dimension – can only be this: The community is the earthly-historical form of existence of Jesus Christ himself. . . . The Church is his body, created and continually renewed by the awakening power of the Holy Spirit.[149]

The church portrayed in the New Testament as the body and bride of Christ is primarily, according to Barth, a christological reality (it is also equally, for Barth, a pneumatological reality, and that will come into focus in a moment).[150] Consequently, he insists that whatever we say about the church must be capable of being validated christologically, through the word and the Spirit of Christ Jesus. Barth is not interested in the historical-critical question, whether Jesus of Nazareth founded the church as an

---

[146] Barth, *Dogmatics in Outline*, p. 142.

[147] Barth, *CD*, IV/1, p. 654.

[148] Barth, *CD*, IV/3.ii, p. 726.

[149] Barth, *CD*, IV/1, pp. 660–1. See also, among numerous uses of the phrase 'the earthly-historical form of existence' of Christ: *CD*, IV/2, pp. 653–4; IV/3.2, p. 681. Barth claimed that, in Schleiermacher's *Glaubenslehre*, this 'third dimension', which was of course, for Barth, the 'one thing needful', was 'completely absent': *CD*, IV/1, p. 656.

[150] Theodora Hawksley, 'The Freedom of the Spirit: The Pneumatological Point of Barth's Ecclesiological Minimalism', *SJT* 64 (2011), pp. 180–94.

intentional action, and he skates around it. He notes that the New Testament nowhere refers to the founding of the church by Christ and gives the reason as because 'this is the theme of the whole Gospel narrative', from the baptism of Jesus to the coming of the Holy Spirit at Pentecost.[151] But Barth is passionately committed to the truth that Jesus Christ is the one foundation – the reality and inner substance – of the church, even the church embedded in history. And Christ is that one foundation precisely through the power and presence of the Holy Spirit.

Pneumatology?

What is glaringly absent in those father figures of Liberal Protestantism, Harnack and Troeltsch, is any sense of the power and presence of the Holy Spirit, that is to say pneumatology. In Harnack's challenge to Barth and dialectical theology, mentioned above, there is no mention of the Holy Spirit. The Holy Spirit is also absent from Troeltsch's writings, as far as I am familiar with them. Both of these giants of Liberal Protestantism struggle to bridge the gap, the gulf, between the historical Jesus and the life of the church today (and through all the ages up to the present). Their struggle is laudable because they identified the problem that arises for ecclesiology from the historical-critical study of Christian origins. But the best that both Harnack and Troeltsch can offer to fill this lacuna is the continuing impact of the ethical personality of Jesus as it travels on its way through the generations. I do not entirely dismiss this gambit, because I think that the 'character of Christ', as portrayed in the Gospels, has compelling power (I think that 'character' is a theologically and ethically richer and more robust concept than 'personality' and that 'Christ' is a more theologically weighted concept than simply 'Jesus'). But then the question arises, 'How does the character of Christ live in the church today (and through all the ages up to the present)?' and that is where the doctrine of the Holy Spirit comes into the frame. And it is precisely why the church confesses in the Nicene–Constantinopolitan Creed, 'We believe in the Holy Spirit, the Lord and giver of life.' In relation to this ecclesiological crux, where the Liberal Protestants fall short, Barth does not fail. He sets out his case in two interconnected affirmations, concerned with Jesus Christ and with the Holy Spirit, respectively.

The church (or, in Barth's preferred terms, 'the Christian community') exists only as it is called into existence and upheld in existence by Jesus Christ. This must be so because it is the community of his witnesses, bound in covenant unity to him. So the church exists only as called by Christ into being. But how can this be? How does it happen? Christ calls it by his Word, through the preaching or proclamation of the biblical Word which testifies to Christ the incarnate Word (the *logos*). 'The power of His calling is the power of the living Word of God spoken in it.' But the power of the Word is nothing other than then power of the Holy Spirit of Christ. It is the Holy Spirit who empowers, energizes and vivifies the community in its threefold movement of gathering, upbuilding and sending out into the world. Through the Holy Spirit 'the

---

[151] Barth, *CD*, IV/3.ii, pp. 683–4.

existence of the community begins and endures'.[152] The Christian community comes into existence 'only as the Holy Spirit works in the quickening power of the living Lord Jesus Christ'.[153] The Holy Spirit is 'the authentic and effective self-attestation of the risen and living Lord Jesus' and as such the Spirit brings the *communio sanctorum* to realization.[154]

The great Liberal Protestant theologians may have paid lip service to the work of the Holy Spirit, but they psychologized the doctrine. For them, the spirit (the lower case is intentional) of Jesus was the inner emotional influence of the personality of Jesus, transmitted through history from one human psyche to another, especially through heroic individuals, like Martin Luther (so not even saints). In Barth, by contrast, the Holy Spirit is understood, not psychologically and reductively, but in an ontological and transcendent way, as the third 'Person' of the triune God, as God's presence and action in the world. As Barth demonstrates, ecclesiologically speaking, Jesus Christ and the Holy Spirit are practically interchangeable. To speak of the one is inevitably to speak of the other because 'the only content of the Holy Spirit is Jesus'.[155] I do not think that that fact points to a fundamental incoherence at all, but rather to harmony and integration. There is no room for divine dualism here. Barth helps us where Harnack and Troeltsch are found wanting. But Barth's mistake was to think that, once we have put our faith in the Holy Spirit of Christ, as far as the existence of the church is concerned, we can kick away the ladder of scholarly investigation into the historical origins of this Spirit-filled and Spirit-empowered (though deeply flawed and imperfect) community, as we see it in its trajectory through history. I do not believe (as Barth seems to have done) that *credo in spiritum sanctum* brings any theological – and specifically ecclesiological – guarantees. The historical questions have to be thrashed out on their merits and the church, along with everyone else, must take the consequences, even if they are, for the time, rather uncomfortable ones.

Emil Brunner

Like Karl Barth, Emil Brunner (1889–1966) was a Swiss, Reformed, systematic theologian and a major protagonist of the Dialectical Theology in the 1920s and early 1930s. Brunner is out of fashion now, but in his day he was a major global figure in Protestant theology, having many of his books translated into English. While the Barth industry continues unabated today, notwithstanding revelations of Barth's personal moral ambiguities, Brunner's theology has suffered eclipse. Whether their respective posthumous reputations are justified is a moot point. Brunner's approach ticks many boxes; it is biblical, critical, revelational, personalist, existential, apologetical, political and ethical. Brunner's is a dynamic theology of divine–human encounter in the context of human relations and society.

[152] Ibid., p. 752.
[153] Barth, *CD*, IV/2, p. 617.
[154] Ibid., pp. 651–2.
[155] Ibid., p. 654.

In their notorious argument over the role of natural theology and the 'point of contact' between human understanding and divine revelation as a kind of *praeparatio evangelica*, Barth mocked Brunner's *Natural Theology* in his hysterical riposte *Nein! Antwort an Emil Brunner* (both published in German in 1934). To the undiscerning reader, Barth made Brunner look weak and foolish; but Barth failed to respond to Brunner's arguments in a rational way (though Brunner continued to refer respectfully and appreciatively to Barth).[156] Brunner devoted the third and last volume of his systematic theology (*Dogmatics*; published in German in 1946, 1950 and 1960, respectively) mainly to ecclesiology.[157] There he faces head on the question of whether Jesus founded or intended the church and the related question of the connection of the church of today with the historical Christ event. Amid much that is striking and memorable, Brunner develops some entrenched idiosyncratic and tendentious positions – though in this respect too he is no different to Barth!

Brunner presents Jesus as the bearer of the 'new life of the people of God, the Ekklesia [*sic*]', which is 'the Messianic life in fellowship with God through the Holy Spirit' (p. 3). It is important to note that Brunner gives a special and rather elusive meaning to Ekklesia throughout this work. Brunner's Ekklesia is not identical with the Christian church and is actually its antithesis and nemesis, bringing the church into judgement for its failings. The Ekklesia is the form that the self-communication, the self-proclamation and the self-representation of God take in history.

Both revelation and redemption are defined by Brunner as forms of the self-proclamation of God. But how can we, 2,000 years after the Christ event, participate in them? Brunner's answer is that the self-communication of God in the biblical revelation and in Jesus Christ continues in the proclamation of the church, in its 'proclaiming existence', which is the very definition of the Ekklesia (p. 4). Brunner's key concept here is the self-representation (*Selbst-vergegenwärtigung*) of God in history and in the proclamation of the church. Alongside the objective historical transmission of God's revelatory and redemptive acts (enshrined in tradition), which leave us inwardly and spiritually unchanged, there is also a dynamic, spiritual transmission of the redemptive effect of the person and work of Jesus Christ through the presence and power of the Holy Spirit. Brunner invokes Calvin's phrase '*arcana operatio spiritus sancti*' the secret operation of the Holy Spirit (pp. 12–13). However, Brunner points out, our experience of the self-representation or self-communication of God through the Holy Spirit is merely the pledge (*arrabōn*) or foretaste of the future fulfilment and consummation, the two being held in a state of eschatological tension (pp. 17–18).

Brunner approaches his central question of what the Ekklesia is and of its connection, if any, to the existing Christian church by means of the question of the relation of personal faith to the church (pp. 19–23). He notes that Calvin revealingly placed his great treatise on the church as the fourth and last (though the longest) of

---

[156] Karl Barth and Emil Brunner, *Natural Theology*, trans. Peter Fraenkel (London: Bles, 1946). See further, John W. Hart, *Karl Barth Vs. Emil Brunner: The Formation and Dissolution of a Theological Alliance 1916-1936* (New York: Peter Lang, 2001).

[157] Emil Brunner, *The Christian Doctrine of the Church, Faith and the Consummation: Dogmatics Vol III*, trans. David Cairns with T. H. L. Parker (London: Lutterworth Press, 1962). Page references in my main text are to this volume.

the books that comprise his *Institutes of the Christian Religion*. Calvin could do this because he believed that personal, saving faith came first and that the church was there to support it, as it were externally (*externum subsidium fidei*).[158] This (as it were) hierarchy of truths – placing personal faith before the church's means of grace – which betrays a radical individualism, has been the downfall of his own Reformed tradition ever since, Brunner admits. Though he notes that such individualism has been resisted by the Roman Catholic, Anglican and Old Catholic traditions (he does not mention the Orthodox churches here). But the basic error of all the major traditions, according to Brunner, has been to regard the church as essentially an institution. In the New Testament, however (Brunner insists), the Ekklesia is never conceived of as an institution, but as 'the common life' (*koinonia*) of the brotherhood in fellowship with Jesus Christ in the Spirit. 'To be in Christ through faith and to be in this fellowship are one and the same thing' (p. 21). God's act of reconciliation in Christ brings personal isolation to an end. Because this fellowship is incompatible with institutional life, we cannot simply translate Ekklesia as 'church'. The churches do not equate to the Ekklesia, which is a spiritual fellowship, brotherhood and common life (*koinonia*), not an institution that is 'rationally regulated' (pp. 22, 68).

The truth of the Ekklesia is known, not through mystical intuitions (Brunner saw mystical experience as the enemy of the word of God), but solely through history. The 'historical fact' is that Christ came among the fishermen of Galilee and called them to follow him. His compelling call, 'Follow me!' was 'the beginning of their corporate existence over against the world', first as a band of disciples and later as a coherent witnessing community. The next step in the formation of the Ekklesia was the Last Supper when, by showing that he would be giving his body and blood for them, Jesus constituted them as the new Israel. Finally, the gift of the Holy Spirit at Pentecost created 'the body of Christ', thus drawing out the 'social character' of the Ekklesia (p. 24). Just as the self-communication of God in Jesus Christ through the Holy Spirit has created the Ekklesia, so too Christians give themselves to each other in self-communication (ironically, this sounds like Schleiermacher!). Faith is essentially 'communicating existence' and this makes the Ekklesia 'a spiritual brotherhood, free from law' (p. 24–5).

At this point in his exposition, Brunner's hostility to the institutional church in all its forms becomes blatant. For example, Brunner claims to find no support in the New Testament for the standard original meaning of *ekklēsia* as 'assembly' (which does sound rather institutional); instead he derives it from *klēsis*, the election or call of God (p. 32). Institutions, he believes, are structured by law, not by faith. Brunner endorses Rudolf Sohm's thesis that ecclesiastical law is incompatible with the true nature of the church (see above in this chapter in relation to Harnack). He also applauds Hans F. von Campenhausen's (tendentious) analysis of the emergence of institutional elements in the early church at the expense of its supposedly original, purely spiritual and informal

[158] John Calvin, *Institutes of the Christian Religion*, trans. H. Beveridge (London: James Clarke, 1962), vol. 2.

nature.[159] The teaching of the Pastoral Epistles (believed by Brunner to be pseudo-Pauline) is 'irreconcilable' with Pauline ecclesiology (p. 47). It was 'sacralization or sacramentalization' that caused the perversion of the Ekklesia into the church (p. 52). The church as an expression of 'monarchical institutionalism' began with Ignatius of Antioch who made the authority of the bishop essential to the gathering together of the church and to its celebration of the sacraments (pp. 67–72). Brunner claims (p. 74) that Martin Luther himself realized that the Christian fellowship was created not by sacraments, but by the word and the Spirit. (However, this claim is not quite correct; for Luther the church was indeed the creation of the word – *creatura verbi* – but Luther never opposed word and sacrament, but rather made them intrinsically inseparable). Brunner admits that even the churches of the Reformation remained tainted by the distortions of law and institutionalism (pp. 85ff). Nevertheless, the supreme paradigm of the distortion of the Ekklesia into the church for Brunner is the Roman Catholic Church (he is, of course, writing before – but only just before – the Second Vatican Council, which began in 1962). Brunner is appalled by the gradual metamorphosis of the New Testament Ekklesia into an institution governed by the 1917 Code of Canon Law, which supports a 'totalitarian authoritarian structure' (p. 58).

Brunner's anti-sacramentalism also emerges in his account of the New Testament Ekklesia: he depicts it as 'a thoroughly uncultic, unsacred spiritual brotherhood' (p. 33). Brunner attacks the idea that the sacraments have anything to do with conveying salvation. Baptism is simply 'an outward sign of repentance', so that 'any sacramental interpretation of it' is 'impossible' (p. 42). As a sign of repentance, baptism is not appropriately administered to infants; paedobaptism belongs with the concept of the national church, which is a far cry from the Ekklesia as a spiritual fellowship and brotherhood. Baptism is also one of the ways in which the Ekklesia becomes visible (rather surprisingly, the Ekklesia is ostensibly not assimilated to the 'invisible church'). Similarly, the Lord's Supper was originally 'an act of fellowship', in which believers built themselves up in their faith, and it remains 'a fellowship meal'. As such it contradicts any division between clergy and laity, those who bestow and those who receive (p. 64). Anything more, Brunner thinks, savours of 'a sacramental magic happening' and 'a miracle'. Paul's thought was completely 'unsacramental'(p. 63). Nevertheless, the Last Supper was the moment at which Jesus inaugurated the Ekklesia as 'the fellowship of those who were bound to God and to each other by the death of Jesus' (p. 61).

For Brunner, the self-communication of God, the key concept in his ecclesiology, stops short at the sacraments. It is confined to the word, the self-*proclamation* of God, which happened in Christ and continues through the church. Brunner is working against the background of the received Reformation antithesis of law and gospel, though this is a mainly Lutheran preoccupation; Calvin and other Reformed writers gave a privileged place to the law of God in the life of the church. But Brunner is obsessed with the notion that the Christian church, since Constantine the Great, has been taken over by law. He can hardly bring himself to admit that any body of people,

---

[159] Hans F. von Campenhausen, *Ecclesiastical Authority and Spiritual Power in the Church of the First Three Centuries* (London: A. and C. Black, 1969); cf. several relevant essays in id., *Tradition and Life in the Church: Essays and Lectures on Church History*, trans. A. V. Littledale (London: Collins, 1968).

gathered together for a common purpose, needs rules and that these rules cannot be optional. 'Institution' is a 'dirty word' for him. Although he is certainly concerned for mission and evangelism, he does not see that a 'church' that lacks a structure beyond the local will fail to project the Christian message to the wider society. Brunner's answer to the guiding question of our study in this book is, 'No, Jesus did not found the church as we see it in history; the church is a distortion of his intention.' Nevertheless, for Brunner, Jesus Christ remains the foundation of the church in the true sense of the Ekklesia, for 'Ecclesiology is Christology' (pp. 35, 84).

Paul Tillich

The language of 'foundations' was much favoured by the German-American, Lutheran, idealist–existentialist theologian Paul Tillich (1886–1965). He struck this note in a sermon shortly after the end of the Second World War. The sermon's title, 'The Shaking of the Foundations', was suggested both by one of his texts (Isa. 24:18, as quoted by Tillich: 'The foundations of the earth do shake. Earth breaks to pieces') and by the existential situation of his hearers in the chapel of Union Theological Seminary, New York City. These words of the prophet, Tillich said, 'describe with visionary power what the majority of human beings in our period have experienced, and what, perhaps in a not too distant future, all mankind will experience abundantly'. As we read such words, Tillich adds, 'we might easily imagine that we were reading the reports of eyewitnesses from Warsaw or Hiroshima or Berlin' (three cities razed to the ground in the recent world conflict).[160] Tillich was a theologian and preacher who sought for sure foundations for faith, for a human future and for the church. His proposals regarding the true foundation of the church deserve our attention.

I judge Tillich to be the equal of Barth in theological creativity and construction, but I also see him as Barth's polar opposite and indeed antidote! Of course, there is a glaring difference in their writing styles: while Barth is prolix, convoluted and repetitive, Tillich is aphoristic, cryptic and crisp. Tillich has been out of fashion in recent theology, but that has been our loss, I believe. I find his three-volume *Systematic Theology* more stimulating than Schleiermacher's *Glaubenslehre* (ET *The Christian Faith*) or even Barth's *Church Dogmatics*, while Pannenberg's own three-volume *Systematic Theology* is quite prosaic in comparison.[161] Tillich has aroused much suspicion among conservative students of his work and certainly there is some ambiguity in his system. Is it ultimately about the realization of human self-consciousness, dressed up in theological language? On balance, I think not. In assessing Tillich, we need to take the whole of his work into account: the German-language writings up to 1933, as well as the English-language writings for the next three decades. Tillich was a gifted popularizer of theology, one who engaged with the *angst* of the age in which he lived, overshadowed by two world wars (he served as an army chaplain in the First World War), the rise of Nazism, the Holocaust, the Atomic Bomb and the Cold War. Tillich did

---

[160] Paul Tillich, *The Shaking of the Foundations* (London: SCM Press, 1949), pp. 1–11.
[161] Paul Tillich, *Systematic Theology*, 3 vols in one (London: James Nisbet, 1968).

not flinch in the face of these terrors, but faced them with an intellectually convincing and faith-filled courage (as in his small book *The Courage to Be*) and brought hope to many.[162] Here we can merely note in passing the broad range of Tillich's interests and writing topics – philosophy, both idealist and existentialist; the philosophy of science; literature; music; psychoanalysis; the history of Christian thought; apologetics; social theory; and political philosophy – before focusing on Tillich's contribution to our enquiry regarding the connection between Jesus and the church.[163]

The church's one foundation, according to Tillich, is the *witness* given by the New Testament writers to Jesus as the Christ. 'The New Testament witness is unanimous in its witness to Jesus as the Christ. This witness is the foundation of the Christian Church.'[164] How does Tillich arrive at this position and is it valid? He sets out his approach in *Systematic Theology*, volume 2, pp. 112–38. I will now summarize the key points in his argument. (I will not be delving into Tillich's philosophy of history and its relation to the kingdom of God, which, in his case, do not seem to affect the key issue that concerns us here.)

1. Tillich repudiates Barth's method and system: his supernaturalism, his dualistic retreat from science, 'secular' knowledge and contemporary culture, when it comes to dogmatics/systematic theology. Tillich himself – though not particularly a biblical scholar – embraces the historical-critical method of biblical study that Barth tried to pretend had neither relevance nor authority in arriving at Christian doctrine derived from revelation. With all German Liberal Protestantism (and Roman Catholic Modernism), Tillich is searching for a way to avoid the historicist trap for faith – the trap that says, you need the permission of history in order to believe. Although Tillich takes the historical-critical method for granted, he nevertheless finds a way of unequivocally affirming that Jesus as the Christ is the final revelation of God and, on that basis, providing a christological foundation for the church.

2. Tillich's full acceptance of the historical-critical methodology means, of course, that he has to come to terms with what modern scholarship has to say concerning what we can reliably know about Jesus of Nazareth. Tillich regards the Liberal Protestant 'quest of the historical Jesus' as a complete failure. The real Jesus receded further and further from view as the quest was pursued, he claims. The reports that we have of him in the Gospels are not 'empirical' accounts because they are given by people who believed in him. They were motivated by their faith and were not interested in the biography of Jesus. Therefore, the

[162] Paul Tillich, *The Courage to Be* (London: Collins/Fontana, 1962 [1952]).
[163] A concise introduction to the scope and method of Tillich's theology is Avis, *The Methods of Modern Theology*, chapter VIII. Other secondary studies include J. Heywood Thomas, *Paul Tillich: An Appraisal* (London: SCM Press, 1963); Alexander J. McKelway, *The Systematic Theology of Paul Tillich: A Review and Analysis* (London: Lutterworth Press, 1964); Wilhelm and Marion Pauck, *Paul Tillich: His Life and Thought* (London: Collins, 1977); John Powell Clayton, *The Concept of Correlation: Paul Tillich and the Possibility of a Mediating Theology* (Berlin: de Gruyter, 1980); John P. Newport, *Paul Tillich*, ed. Bob E. Patterson (Waco, TX: Word Books, 1984); Andrew O' Neill, *Tillich: A Guide for the Perplexed* (London and New York: T&T Clark, 2008).
[164] Tillich, *Systematic Theology*, vol. 2, pp. 134–5.

historical Jesus himself cannot be the foundation of the church. (Tillich seems prepared to give up on critical enquiry into the history that lies behind the Gospels, taking a stance similar to Bultmann's assertion that it is enough to know 'that' there was a Jesus of Nazareth and not much more. Subsequent New Testament scholarship and theology generally has not followed Bultmann's and Tillich's historical scepticism to the same extent.)

3. Tillich is working in the wake of Martin Kähler's response to the historical problematic in German New Testament scholarship, in his *The So-Called Historical Jesus and the Historic Biblical Christ* (1892; 2nd edition 1896) which we have briefly discussed in Chapter 1.[165] Tillich had studied under Kähler and regarded Kähler's book as a 'prophetic' work that 'anticipates some of the most urgent problems in present day theology'. Bultmann's proposals for the demythogizing of the New Testament world view had now (Tillich is writing in 1964) pushed the question of the historical Jesus beyond the point where Kähler had left it, Tillich believed. But what was 'decisive' in Kähler's answer of the 1890s was the need 'to make the certainty of faith independent of the unavoidable incertitudes [*sic*] of historical research'.[166] That is precisely what Tillich himself is attempting.

4. It is an axiom of Tillich's approach that 'Christianity was born, not with the birth of the man who is called "Jesus", but in the moment in which one of his followers was driven to say to him, "Thou art the Christ". Jesus could not be the Christ without being received as such by his followers, even if he had openly claimed to be the Christ (Messiah). It is a strength of Tillich's approach to this question that he allows for the critical role of reception, of subjectivity, of the motivation of faith, on the part of the New Testament witnesses.

5. What the New Testament gives us, according to Tillich, is not a biography and not an 'objective' historical account (supposing that were possible), but a 'picture' of Jesus as the Christ, one created by faith in him, though not devoid of all historical substance. 'Jesus as the Christ is both an historical fact and a subject of believing reception.' There could be no 'foundation' of Christianity without a factual element. Faith cannot guarantee that the name of the historical person believed in as the Christ was 'Jesus', but it can 'guarantee the factual transformation of reality in that personal life which the New Testament expresses in its picture of Jesus as the Christ'.

6. This 'factual', 'historical' or 'empirical' 'transformation of reality' in one personal life is the appearance of the New Being under the conditions of existence in the world, 'conquering existential estrangement', making faith possible and thus effecting a 'new creation'. Faith cannot provide any 'guarantee' of the 'empirical factuality' of the biblical account, but it can guarantee the truth of the biblical picture of Jesus to the extent that the biblical picture has the power to impart a

---

[165] Martin Kähler, *The So-Called Historical Jesus and the Historic Biblical Christ*, trans., ed. and intro. Carl E. Braaten, from the 2nd German edition 1896 [1892]; Foreword Paul Tillich (Philadelphia, PA: Fortress Press, 1988 [1964]).

[166] Tillich, Foreword to Kähler, *The So-Called Historical Jesus and the Historic Biblical Christ*.

transformation of our own being (existence) through our 'personal participation in his being'. In Tillich's sermon 'The New Being' (preached in the early 1950s) he puts his point in Pauline terms (citing 2 Cor. 5:17: 'If anyone is in Christ, there is a new creation'). 'Christianity is the message of the New Creation, the New Being, the New Reality which has appeared with the appearance of Jesus who for this reason, and just for this reason, is called the Christ. For the Christ, the Messiah, the selected and anointed one is He who brings the new state of things.'[167]

7. Tillich is clear that history cannot provide a foundation for faith (though faith cannot exist without history); but in a sense faith can vouch for history. The ground of Christianity is the New Testament's witness to Jesus as the Christ and this witness takes the form of the presentation of the 'picture' of Jesus as the Christ. So, for Tillich, the existential reality of the New Being (new creation) in the life of a Christian (one who also accepts and receives Jesus as the Christ) is sufficient assurance for faith. Tillich could have quoted the First Epistle of Jn 5:10: 'Those who believe in the Son of God have the testimony in their hearts [NRSV; Greek: him/herself]'. Faith can guarantee only its own foundation, namely the appearance of the reality that has created that faith. Historical criticism cannot touch that certitude. '[H]istorical research can neither give not take away the foundation of the Christian faith.'

These are the main steps in the overall argument that leads Tillich to assert that the foundation of the Christian Church consists in the witness borne by the New Testament writings to Jesus who is received as the Christ. How should we evaluate his position? Tillich affirms that, in the New Testament, 'the picture of Jesus as the Christ' appears 'in its original and basic form', and that there is a sufficient consistency and consonance between the picture of Christ given by the Gospels and that given by Paul. So what is wrong with that robust affirmation? In my view Tillich does not go far enough; he needs to take a further step back. The New Testament witness is indeed the foundation of the church's *message*, but it is not the foundation of the church itself, as the community that continues to receive Jesus as the Christ, the ongoing institution embedded in history. To have integrity, the faith of the church requires that the church is founded upon an act of God in the incarnation, ministry, passion, death, resurrection, ascension and glorification of God's Son. The church's one foundation does not consist of words, ideas, statements or witness, however sublime and indeed however necessary they may be. The church is ultimately founded on the Christ event. Even though we cannot be sure of all its details and do not have direct access to it – even if it has to be postulated to some extent – the faith of the church is founded on an event in history. Words subsequently describe, explain and proclaim it – they witness to it – but they are no substitute for it. The Christ event alone makes it possible for us to believe that the church is now the body of Christ.

---

[167] Paul Tillich, *The New Being* (London: SCM Press, 1956), pp. 15–24, at p. 15.

Jürgen Moltmann

I want to note very briefly indeed the rather striking view of the foundation of the church held by the Lutheran theologian Jürgen Moltmann (b. 1926). Moltmann takes for granted the results of modern critical scholarship on the origins of Christianity, but that is not what interests him. He makes a theological critique of the terms 'founder' and 'foundation'. Moltmann objects to any talk of Jesus as the founder or the foundation of Christianity. To say that Jesus founded the church could suggest that the church merely looks back to Jesus who, as it were, laid the foundation stone for what came later, so that the church could go its own way without troubling to remember Jesus and his way. And to call Jesus the 'foundation' of the church suggests to Moltmann the idea of Jesus laying down a quasi-legal constitution for the church and continuing to dominate it by means of this 'last will and testament', and through his dead hand, not his living spirit. Both the ideas of 'founder' and 'foundation' imply that the church has emanated from a deceased historical person, rather than from a living contemporary.[168]

Moltmann provides a salutary corrective to any kind of static, juridical understanding of foundation imagery, as though Jesus had provided a kind of legal or constitutional blueprint for the church. Moltmann's radical, messianic, eschatological ecclesiology makes a salutary witness on this score. But I must confess that I find Moltmann's handling of the 'foundation' metaphor slightly perverse. When Paul declared, 'Other foundation can no man lay than that which is laid, which is Christ Jesus' (1 Cor. 3:11), was he inculcating a static, legalistic, merely historical view of the relation of Jesus to the Church? Hardly. Moltmann is dealing merely with an ideological perversion of the notion of 'foundation' and therefore limiting his discussion; in fact he was excluding an important biblical theme. Moltmann's treatment has not resolved the question of the foundation of the Christian church.

Wolfhart Pannenberg

Wolfhart Pannenberg (1928–2014) provides a sophisticated account of the connection between Jesus and the church, one that takes history seriously. In his early work – and he never reneged on this stance – Pannenberg puts into reverse the cavalier disregard of human, world, history on the part of the dialectical theologians, especially Barth and Gogarten. He repudiates such evasive concepts as 'supra-history' and 'pre-history'. He denounces the positivism of revelation, divorced from critical-historical criteria, that underlies Barth's standpoint from his early dialectical theology right through the *Church Dogmatics*. Equally, Pannenberg eschews Bultmann's distinctive method which entertains radical historical conclusions while not allowing them to affect the existentially transforming power of the preached word, with the result that each of the two axes of Bultmann's approach remain unconnected and unreconciled. Pannenberg's ambitious

---

[168] Jürgen Moltmann, *The Church in the Power of the Spirit*, trans. Margaret Kohl (London: SCM Press, 1977), pp. 70–1.

project, from the first, was to confront history, with all its relativity, and to be open also to all that the physical and social sciences can tell us about the world and ourselves – and to do all this while upholding Orthodox Christian and credal doctrine.[169]

So in his openness and receptivity to the universe of knowledge, Pannenberg stands with Troeltsch methodologically, but his conclusions are different because his standpoint of personal belief and church commitment is different. That is no doubt because the seismic theological event of Karl Barth took place in the interval between the work of Troeltsch and that of Pannenberg. In one sense, Pannenberg signals a violent reaction against Barth – against any positivism of divine revelation that is abstracted from other truth and other knowledge. But in another sense, Pannenberg carries on Barth's project by mounting a robust defence of divine revelation, mediated by Holy Scripture, and by setting the proclamation of the gospel (the apostolic *kerygma*) at the heart of his ambitious project.

Pannenberg does not give substantial consideration to the question whether Jesus intended to found the church as an institution: he presupposes, on the basis of modern historical and biblical research, that Jesus did no such thing; it is, he says, out of the question.[170] Jesus' mission was to Israel, to awaken and gather the people of God in response to the announcement, through his preaching, of the imminent arrival of the reign (kingdom) of God. We are not, Pannenberg insists, to regard Jesus' choosing of the Twelve as the symbolic founding of a church, of which they would be, as it were, twelve pillars. The calling of the Twelve was a symbolic eschatological action, signifying the restoration of Israel as the people of the twelve tribes within the future reign of God.[171] But the connection that Pannenberg does effect, between Jesus and the church, is strong and secure, enabling him ultimately to establish Jesus and his proclamation as the foundation of the church. Pannenberg establishes this connection through two main routes: (a) via the link between the Last Supper and the Lord's Supper, and (b) via the connection between the preaching of Jesus and the message of the apostles.

1. Whereas some other writers place the commencement of the church in the post-resurrection period, Pannenberg locates the Last Supper as the moment when Jesus inaugurated the new community by making the new covenant in his blood (sacrifice). Here Jesus not only initiated the Eucharist, but also, by so doing, launched the church, for the Eucharist is the covenant sacrament that brings the new community into being and holds it in existence. In the Last Supper, as in every celebration of the Eucharist, Jesus binds his people sacramentally to himself in fellowship or communion. Therefore, says Pannenberg, the Last Supper has

---

[169] Wolfhart Pannenberg (ed.), *Revelation as History*, trans. David Granskou (New York: Macmillan, 1968; London: Sheed and Ward, 1969), ET of *Offenbarung als Geschichte*, 3rd edn (Göttingen, 1965); id., *Basic Questions in Theology I*, trans. George H. Kehm (London: SCM Press, 1970 [1967]); id., *Theology and the Philosophy of Science*, trans. Francis McDonagh (London: Darton, Longman & Todd, 1976); id., *Anthropology in Theological Perspective*, trans. Matthew O'Connell (Philadelphia, PA: Westminster Press; Edinburgh: T&T Clark, 1985).

[170] Wolfhart Pannenberg, *Systematic Theology*, 3 vols, trans. Geoffrey W. Bromiley (Grand Rapids, MI: Eerdmans, 1991-97 [1988-93]), vol. 3, p. 29.

[171] Ibid., pp. 29, 290.

'decisive significance' for the connection between Jesus and the church.[172] In the ongoing life of the church, the 'vital fellowship of Christians as a people' is manifest in the Eucharistic liturgy (though not only there). In fact, it is only as the body of Christ, a reality that is seen most clearly at the celebration of the Eucharist, that the church can be 'a provisional sign of the eschatological fellowship of a renewed humanity in the kingdom of God'.[173] For Pannenberg, the link between the Eucharist and the Last Supper connects the church to the historical Jesus.

2. The second route, taken by Pannenberg to establish the connection between Jesus and the church, is to demonstrate the continuity – a continuity that is not without significant development – between Jesus' announcement of the immanent advent of the kingdom or reign of God, on the one hand, and the apostles' preaching. The content of the apostolic proclamation was the person and saving work of Jesus Christ and its purpose or goal was the reconciliation of the unconverted to God. There are four steps in Pannenberg's second main argument.

i. The first step is to show that, in neither Jesus nor Paul, did preaching the gospel consist merely in speaking a lot of words (so to speak). Rather, the proclamation itself was part of the work of redemption or reconciliation, powerful in itself to bring salvation to the hearer. Proclamation was an *event*. The words of preaching were put to work. God is at work in the message of the gospel.[174]

ii. The second step is to show how the preaching of Jesus evolved into the preaching of the early church, via the apostles. As Pannenberg puts it,

> Paul's concept of the gospel is the result of a development that derives from Jesus himself and then from the immediately ensuing usage of primitive Christianity. For the post-Easter community Jesus himself became the content of the gospel because in him the reign of God was already present and salvation was available through him. The gospel of Jesus Christ thus became the gospel concerning Jesus Christ.[175]

iii. The third step is to demonstrate the unity between the preaching of Jesus and that of the (early) church. The breaking in of the reign of God was the original content of the gospel in Jesus' preaching (what made it 'good news'). But then the person of Jesus himself, crucified and risen, became the content of the gospel for the apostles, because the salvation-bringing reign of God was present, was personified, in him. The development of the *kerygma* in the early church was smooth, logical and without distortion. The apostles correctly understood and interpreted the significance of Jesus. The continuity – with the crucial transition – is contained in the fact that 'gospel' is what both Jesus and the apostles preached.[176] (We recall immediately Bultmann's dictum, 'The proclaimer became the proclaimed.')

---

[172] Ibid., pp. 290, 465.
[173] Ibid., p. 478.
[174] Ibid., vol. 2, pp. 455–8.
[175] Ibid., p. 456.
[176] Ibid., pp. 457–8.

iv. The final step is to make the connection between the event of proclamation and the founding of churches. It was the proclamation of the church that called new churches into existence. '[T]he apostolic gospel includes the missionary activity that aims at the founding of congregations and the rise of the church.'[177] Paul reminded his churches that they were the product or fruit of his proclamation (1 Cor. 4:15; 1 Thess. 2).[178] Pannenberg expands this final step of his argument: 'Because the kingdom of God has the concrete form of fellowship with God and others, the gospel as the message of reconciliation to God must everywhere lead to the founding of congregations that have among themselves a fellowship that provisionally and symbolically represents the world-embracing fellowship of the kingdom of God that is the goal of reconciliation.'[179] The gospel contains the power of the reign of God in eschatological tension. 'The fellowship of the church that the gospel establishes is thus a sign and a provisional form of the humanity that is reconciled in the kingdom of God – the humanity that is the goal of the event of reconciliation in the expiatory death of Jesus Christ.'[180]

The argument is complete: the logic of Pannenberg's theology drives forward from the coming of Jesus and his proclamation of the breaking in of the reign of God to the fact of the church embedded in history. Is this argument persuasive? I must confess that I do find it the most convincing of all the accounts, by Protestant theologians, of the foundation of the church that we have reviewed. I am deeply impressed by Pannenberg's penetration to the heart of the meaning of the church in its identity with Jesus Christ. However, there is something more.

Pannenberg has not addressed head on the historico-critical question, 'Did Jesus of Nazareth intentionally found the church?' He believes, as we have seen, that it is out of the question that Jesus could have founded the church in an institutional sense. But, in a rather oblique and subtle way, he has given his answer. Jesus is the source or foundation of the church because he proclaimed the coming of a kingdom that was embodied in himself. But the coming of the reign of God necessitated the reconciliation of alienated, sinful humanity to God. So when the apostles preached Christ in order to reconcile their hearers to God and to gather them into churches, they were serving the same kingdom because they were serving Christ. Now when Pannenberg quotes St Paul's dictum that Jesus Christ is the foundation, laid by God's act, of the church (1 Cor. 3:11), he is not invoking history; he is thinking ecclesiologically and pneumatologically. On the basis of all that Paul says about believers being baptized by one Spirit into one body (1 Cor. 12:13) and being filled with and led by the Spirit, Pannenberg affirms, 'Only by the work of the Spirit . . . is Jesus Christ the church's foundation.'[181] So the foundation of the church, according to Pannenberg, is the person and work of Jesus Christ through the power of the Holy Spirit. The foundation is christological and pneumatological.

---

[177] Ibid., p. 462.
[178] Ibid.
[179] Ibid., pp. 462–3.
[180] Ibid.
[181] Ibid., vol. 3, pp. 15–16. The pneumatological dimension of Pannenberg's ecclesiology is brought out in Friederike Nüssel, 'Wolfhart Pannenberg', in Avis (ed.), *The Oxford Handbook of Ecclesiology*, chapter 22.

7

The foundation of the church in Roman Catholic theology

The present chapter is devoted to the response within modern Roman Catholic theology to our key question, 'Did Jesus of Nazareth found the church as an intentional act?'; and if that cannot be answered in the affirmative, the further question, 'What is the connection between Jesus Christ and the institutional, historical church?'; or to put it another way, 'How does the church of Christian history derive from the Christ event?' These are some of the ways of explicating what I regard as the most basic question of ecclesiology: 'What is the connection between Jesus and the church?'

I accept that the term 'Roman Catholic' is a blunt instrument for designating individuals and churches that stand in a relationship of sacramental, juridical and hierarchical communion with the pope. I realize that the term 'Roman' is not correctly applied to Greek Catholic and other non-Roman Churches that are in communion with the Holy See. But to say simply 'Catholics' or 'the Catholic Church' sounds to Anglicans as though 'Roman' Catholicism was claiming to be the only form or manifestation of Catholicism in the world. Any such implication is offensive to many Anglicans and Orthodox (also probably to High Church Methodists and Lutherans) who understand themselves and their churches as in no way less Catholic than the churches of the Roman obedience and therefore strongly object to the unqualified application of 'Catholic' to one particular church. A broader conception of Catholicism is intended and meant when Anglicans, for example, confess liturgically their faith in 'the One Holy Catholic and Apostolic Church' and pray for 'the good estate of the Catholic Church'. In any case, the debates that we are considering in this chapter took place among scholars who were definitely subject to Roman oversight and discipline, emanating from the Vatican, even from the pope himself, and nothing could be more 'Roman' than that. So, while acknowledging its inadequacies, I cannot find a better term for the writers whose views and conclusions are described in this chapter.

We begin this chapter with a French scholar and his epoch-making book, the publication of which – and the reaction to which by the Roman Catholic Church authorities – forms a watershed in the history of debates on our question. After Alfred Loisy and *L'Évangile et l'Église* (1902), the study of Christian origins – of the relation or connection between Jesus and the church – could never be the same again, not only in the Roman Catholic Church, but in Protestant and Anglican theology also. But first, it will be helpful to sketch in very lightly some features of the background to the theological developments that we will be considering in this chapter.

Before Loisy

Roman Catholic ecclesiology in the modern period was defined in the face of several external threats to the imperial, monopolistic conception of the church that had emerged from the Protestant Reformation to the confiscation of the papal states. The Conciliar Movement, which flourished in the first quarter of the fifteenth century, had failed to curb the power of the papacy, by subordinating the pope to councils, in order to reform the church. In fact, by unifying a fragmented papacy at the Council of Constance (1414–18) and then over-reaching itself, it had strengthened the papacy and undermined its own credibility. The Reformation can be seen as a consequence of that failure and as a distorted form of conciliarism, partially secularized by placing councils under the authority of princes and denying them the attribute of infallibility.[1] Although conciliar thinking had been suppressed, other threats provoked the Roman Catholic Church to harden its defensive posture. 'Gallicanism' was an assertion of French relative national autonomy, and Jansenism (also in France) was an attempt to assert Augustinian doctrines of grace (also crucial for the Reformers) within the Roman Catholic Church. The Enlightenment, particularly as represented by the French *philosophes*, signalled a resurgence of confidence in the power of unaided human reason to regulate human life and society and to critique received forms of belief and worship. The radical aspect of the Enlightenment was hostile to all forms of supernatural ecclesiastical authority that was based on tradition and privilege.[2] The revolutionary and Napoleonic decades, following the start of the French Revolution in 1789, reduced the Roman Catholic Church to its lowest ebb politically since the Reformation. The pope was exiled, religious orders were dissolved, seminaries were shut down and missions were suspended. The anticlerical war of attrition culminated in the progressive confiscation of the papal states between 1796 and 1870. So the Reformation, followed by the Enlightenment and the French Revolution, threw the Roman Catholic Church into a defensive posture until the mid-twentieth century and the convening of the Second Vatican Council by Pope John XXIII.

Rome's response to these multiple threats was largely defensive. The Council of Trent had repudiated the Reformation and reformed abuses, but without regenerating Roman Catholic theology. With its repeated anathemas, the Council of Trent set

---

[1]   Paul Avis, *Beyond the Reformation? Authority, Primacy and Unity in the Conciliar Tradition* (London and New York: T&T Clark, 2006), with extensive bibliography.

[2]   The Enlightenment was far from uniformly hostile to Christianity and the churches. In England and Germany Anglican and Lutheran writers, respectively, adopted Enlightenment tenets, especially the appeal to reason, without repudiating their faith or renouncing the church (e.g. in Samuel Johnson, William Law, Joseph Butler, John Wesley and Edmund Burke, to name but a few, in England). Paul Avis, *In Search of Authority: Anglican Theological Method from the Reformation to the Enlightenment* (London and New York: Bloomsbury T&T Clark, 2014), chapters 8 and 9. There was also an 'Enlightenment' among Roman Catholic thinkers: Ulrich Lehner and Michael Printy (eds), *A Companion to the Catholic Enlightenment in Europe* (Leiden: Brill, 2010).

the tone for a stringent, centralized Roman Catholic policy towards movements of incipient diversity of practice and theology (not only Protestantism, but Gallicanism and Jansenism being condemned by Rome). But the Roman Catholic Church emerged from this period of humiliation and weakness with its claims undiminished and soon to be enhanced.

In early nineteenth-century Tübingen, Johann Adam Möhler (1796–1838) and others provided a doctrine of the church as a Spirit-bearing body, living and dynamic, to counteract the standard backward-looking appeal to the church's historical foundation and unchanging tradition.[3] The French Ultramontanist thinkers, notable Joseph de Maistre (1753–1821), the author of *Du Pape* (1819) and other major works on the polity of the Roman Catholic Church and its relationship to the state and the constitution, linked an imperial concept of the Roman Church to a reassertion of the values of the *ancien régime*.[4] John Henry Newman's theory of the development of doctrine (1845) made it possible for him to reconcile the glaring discrepancies between the baroque, outwardly triumphalist pontificate of Pius IX and the simplicity of the apostolic church, with apparently a good conscience.[5] The First Vatican Council (1869–70), the culmination of decades of siege mentality in the Vatican under Pius IX, magnified the office of the pope in terms of universal, ordinary and immediate (unmediated) jurisdiction and magisterial infallibility. That infallible defining authority was exercised in the promulgation of the dogma of the bodily Assumption of the Blessed Virgin Mary in 1950. As we shall have cause to note again, Pius X moved, in 1907 and 1910, against the Roman Catholic Modernists, who were attempting to revitalize their church's theology by means of biblical criticism and the notion of development. The repression of theological dissent was repeated by Pius XII in *Humani Generis* in 1950. Pius X himself had promulgated the last official statement of high, exclusive Roman ecclesiology in *Mystici Corporis* (1943) which identified the mystical body of Christ unequivocally with the Roman Catholic Church.

The doctrine of the Catholic Church as a complete and self-sufficient society, endowed by Christ with plenary authority to legislate for its life *(a societas perfecta)* was dominant within Roman Catholic ecclesiology before Vatican II. Its ethos was juridical; its structure was pyramidal. Möhler held that, by creating the ecclesiastical hierarchy, God had provided everything that the church needed until the end of time. A draft 'Dogmatic Constitution on the Church' that was prepared for the First Vatican Council (1869–70) not only described the Roman Church as a perfect society, but also affirmed that its constitution had been conferred on it by Christ: 'The Church has all the marks of a true society. Christ did not leave this society undefined and without a set form. Rather, he himself gave it its existence . . . and gave it its constitution. . . . It is so

---

[3] Johann Adam Moöhler, *Unity in the Church or the Principle of Catholicism: Presented in the Spirit of the Church Fathers of the First Three Centuries*, ed., trans. and intro. Peter C. Erb (Washington, DC: The Catholic University of America Press, 1996).

[4] For an introduction to de Maistre, see Bernard Reardon, *Liberalism and Tradition: Aspects of Catholic Thought in Nineteenth-Century France* (Cambridge: Cambridge University Press, 1975), chapter 2.

[5] John Henry Newman, *An Essay on the Development of Christian Doctrine, The Edition of 1845*, ed. and intro. J. M. Cameron (Harmondsworth: Penguin, 1974 [1845]).

perfect in itself that it is distinct from all human societies and stands far above them.'[6] These sentiments had a long afterlife, notably in Pius XII's encyclical *Mystici Corporis* (1943) which defined the essential characteristics of the Church as baptism, Orthodox belief and juridical unity.

These themes appeared again in the draft schema for the *Constitution on the Church* at the Second Vatican Council, but this was thrown out by the Council, which set its face against a clerical, juridical and triumphalist understanding of the church. Vatican II began a rebalancing of Roman Catholic ecclesiology by upholding the integrity of the bishop's jurisdiction within the diocese and of the universal episcopal college, while retracting nothing from the papal claims of Vatican I. Other ecclesiological motifs of Vatican II – the positive engagement with the modern world (*aggiornamento*), the return to biblical and patristic sources (*ressourcement*), the church as the pilgrim people of God, the church as *communio*, the recognition of ecclesial elements in non-Roman churches, the commitment to ecumenical engagement – these together had the potential to revolutionize the policy and practice of the Roman Catholic Church. And Vatican II probably did more than anything else to stimulate a resurgence of ecclesiological research across the *oecumene*. The contrast between the promise of Vatican II and the reactionary reality under St John Paul II and Benedict XVI was a cause of grief and misery to many Roman Catholics and to ecumenically minded Christians of other traditions.

The Roman Catholic ecclesiology of the second half of the twentieth century, while it stagnated at the official level, tended to become radical and subversive (by Roman Catholic standards). Karl Rahner held that the pluralism of modern theology called into question the possibility of authoritative dogma.[7] Hans Küng embraced an ecclesiology close to Martin Luther's, with an emphasis on the universal priesthood of the baptized and an outright challenge to the infallibility of the church and the pope.[8] Küng's later ecumenical theology operated in the context of all the major world religions. Edward Schillebeeckx, though curbed by the Vatican under John Paul II, abandoned the traditional teaching *extra ecclesiam nulla salus* (no salvation outside the church) and developed a universal theology of salvation, taking as his slogan the truism 'No salvation outside the world'.[9] Johann Baptist Metz found his teacher Karl Rahner's theology to be innocent of ideological suspicion. Metz's political theology was subversive of all oppressive hierarchical systems, including that of his own church. Its starting point was the 'dangerous memory' of the crucified Messiah, which needs to be brought into bifocal vision with the communal narrative of an oppressed people.[10]

---

[6] Cited Avery Dulles, *Models of the Church*, expanded edn (New York: Doubleday/Image books, 1978), p. 29.

[7] Karl Rahner, 'Pluralism in Theology and the Unity of the Creed in the Church', in *TI* (London: Darton, Longman and Todd, 1965-), vol. VI, pp. 3–23.

[8] Hans Küng, *Structures of the Church*, trans. Salvator Attanasio (New York: Thomas Nelson, 1964 [1963]; id., *The Church*, trans. Ray and Rosaleen Ockenden (London: Search Press, 1968 [1967]); id., *Infallible?* trans. Erich Mosbacher (London: Collins, 1971 [1970]; Hans Küng et al., *Christianity and the World Religions*, trans. Peter Heinegg (London: Collins, 1986 [1985]).

[9] Edward Schillebeeckx, *Church: The Human Story of God* (London: SCM Press, 1990).

[10] J. B. Metz, *Faith in History and Society: Toward a Practical Fundamental Theology*, trans. David Smith (London: Burns & Oates, 1980 [1977]).

Metz looked to the marginalized grassroots Roman Catholic Christians to become conscientized and to undertake a second Reformation of the Church, from below.[11] Like Metz, the Latin American Liberation Theologians, especially Gustavo Gutierrez and Leonardo Boff, developed an ecclesiology orientated to egalitarian base communities.[12] However, Pope John Paul II and Cardinal Joseph Ratzinger – later of course Pope Benedict XVI – reinforced the traditional Roman ecclesiology of the *societas perfecta*, that of a hierarchical system mediating authoritative dogma, binding moral laws and salvific sacramental grace, from the top downwards. How did this massive edifice of official Roman Catholic ecclesiology, claiming dominical institution and built up over the centuries, stand up to the historical-critical movement in biblical and historical study that emerged in its full force in the late nineteenth and early twentieth centuries?

Alfred Loisy

Loisy, Duchesne, Renan and Harnack

Investigation on the part of modern Roman Catholic theologians of the question (in its compressed form), 'Did Jesus found the church?', inevitably takes its cue from Alfred Loisy's *L'Évangile et l'Église* (1902; E.T. *The Gospel and the Church*, 1903).[13] Alfred Firmin Loisy (1857–1940), a priest from a rural background, was inspired (as von Hügel would be later) by the great ecclesiastical historian Louis Duchesne (1843–1922), to devote himself to critical-historical research. But Loisy would travel much further into the realms of controversy than his mentor as a direct result of his research, beginning with a historical-critical-comparative study of ancient Near Eastern religion where Loisy specialized in Assyriology.[14] Duchesne himself sought to avoid controversy by sticking to documentary evidence and keeping his head down. In the Preface to the first volume (1909) of his three-volume *Early History of the Christian Church* (albeit the subtitle of the whole work was *From its Foundation* [*sic*] *to the End of the Fifth Century*) Duchesne expressed the hope that sensible people would understand 'why I have not lingered long over the very first beginnings, and why, without entirely ignoring theologians and

---

[11] J. B. Metz, *The Emergent Church: The Future of Christianity in a Postbourgeois World*, trans. Peter Mann (London: SCM Press, 1981 [1980]).

[12] Gustavo Gutierrez, *A Theology of Liberation: History, Politics, and Salvation* (London: SCM Press, 1988 [1974]) and many other works. Leonardo Boff, *Ecclesiogenesis: The Base Communities Reinvent the Church* (Maryknoll, NY: Orbis, 1986) and many other works.

[13] General: Alec R. Vidler, *The Modernist Movement in the Roman Church: Its Origins and Outcome* (Cambridge: Cambridge University Press, 1934); Bernard M. G. Reardon, ed. and intro., *Roman Catholic Modernism* (London: A. and C. Black, 1970), part I; Alec Vidler, *A Variety of Catholic Modernists* (Cambridge: Cambridge University Press, 1973), chapters 2 and 3; Bernard Reardon, *Liberalism and Tradition: Aspects of Catholic Thought in Nineteenth-Century France* (Cambridge: Cambridge University Press, 1975), pp. 255–81. For a concise, authoritative introduction see Bernard M. G. Reardon, 'Roman Catholic Modernism', in Ninian Smart, John Clayton, Steven Katz and Patrick Sherry (eds), *Nineteenth Century Religious Thought in the West, Volume 2* (Cambridge: Cambridge University Press, 1985), chapter 5.

[14] Jeffrey L. Morrow, Alfred *Loisy and Modern Biblical Studies* (Washington, DC: The Catholic University of America Press, 2019).

their work, I have not devoted overmuch attention to their quarrels.'[15] In spite of the subtitle, Duchesne does not refer to the founding of the church by Jesus, but simply speaks of the time 'when Christianity came into the world' or when 'Christianity first appeared'.[16] While Duchesne has been called 'the father of Modernism', the title is a serious misnomer. Although he was one of the founders and pioneers of historico-critical research within Roman Catholic institutions, he lacked the developmental philosophy of history and the theological accent on divine immanence to be a Modernist. As Phillips notes, 'He was essentially a savant, and had in him nothing of the stuff of a heresiarch. Profoundly sceptical in many ways, he at the same time shewed [sic] a consistent determination to avoid embroiling himself seriously with the ecclesiastical higher command, while allowing himself privately much latitude of satirical comment at its expense.'[17] Duchesne's caution did not prevent his *Early History of the Christian Church* being placed on the Index of forbidden books.

Loisy's introduction to historico-critical methods as applied to the Bible came with his attendance at Ernest Renan's lectures at the Collège de France from 1882. Although Loisy did not take Renan (1823–92) as a personal role model, the approach of a scholar who had depicted Christ in purely human (and political) terms in *La Vie de Jésus* (1863) may well have influenced him. Although Loisy's own faith in the traditional teaching and claims of the Roman Church was progressively undermined by his biblical and historical research, he continued his priestly and academic work within the ecclesiastical structures, hoping to bring theological enlightenment from within. Loisy later described the purpose of *L'Évangile et l'Église* as being 'tactfully to instruct the Catholic clergy about the real situation of the problem of Christian origins'.[18] After a series of publications of critical studies (including on the biblical canon, on ancient Near Eastern creation myths and on the inspiration of the Bible) and his consequent dismissal from his chair at the Institut Catholique, Loisy attempted to perform a supreme service for his church. It took the form of a revolutionary apologetic for the institutional church in principle and for Roman Catholicism – the only form of the church that Loisy knew or could imagine – in particular. This radical apologia was *L'Évangile et l'Église*.

The immediate trigger for Loisy's master-work was Adolf von Harnack's book, *Das Wesen des Christentums* (ET *What is Christianity?*, 1900) that we have looked at in the previous chapter. In his riposte to Harnack, Loisy chose to attack the German professor at his most dignified, most insistent and yet most vulnerable point: historical research. It was precisely Harnack's claim to occupy the academic high ground of 'historical science' that was the prime target of Loisy's attack. Harnack's method, Loisy insisted, was not 'historical': he had reinterpreted the history of Christianity by the

---

[15] Louis Duchesne, *The Early History of the Christian Church: From Its Foundation to the End of the Fifth Century*, trans. from the 4th edn, 3 vols (London: John Murray, 1909, 1912, 1914), vol. 1, p. ix.

[16] Ibid., pp. 1, 3.

[17] C. S. Philips, *The Church in France 1848-1907* (London: SPCK, 1936), p. 295. Duchesne privately described the French episcopate as 'imbeciles' and as fit only to be sacristans.

[18] Stephen Sykes, *The Identity of Christianity: Theologians and the Essence of Christianity from Schleiermacher to Barth* (London: SPCK, 1984), p. 127, citing the Preface to the fifth edition of *L'Évangile et l'Église* (Paris, 1929).

touchstone of his favoured 'essence'; and his account was not 'science' because his 'essence' did not encounter science at any point. By making the essence of Christianity a 'sentiment' (that of trust in the Fatherhood of God and an attitude of benevolence to humankind), Harnack had ensured that it was immune from any conclusions of biblical or philosophical criticism. He had not done justice to the biblical evidence, but had selected a very few congenial texts (especially Mt. 11:27 and Luke 17:21) on which to build a theological superstructure. It was also, Loisy protested, 'in the highest degree arbitrary' to exclude from authentic Christianity anything held in common with Judaism.[19]

The Gospel and the church

In *L'Évangile et l'Église* (translated as *The Gospel and the Church*), Loisy insisted on historical grounds that Jesus was not concerned with the institutional future of the church and that he devoted himself single-mindedly to the coming of the kingdom of God. An unpublished manuscript of Loisy ('Essais d'histoire et de critique religieuse'), that lies behind *L'Évangile et l'Église*, shows that Loisy had grasped the Jewish apocalyptic background to the Gospels even before the publication of the second (expanded) edition of Johannes Weiss' *Die Predigt Jesu vom Reiche Gottes* (1900) and Albert Schweitzer's *Von Reimarus zu Wrede* (1906). In *L'Évangile et l'Église* Loisy guardedly stated that the original institution of the church was 'not a tangible fact for the historian'. It was certain, he claimed, that Jesus himself did not provide systematically for the constitution of a church 'as that of a government established on earth and destined to endure' for many centuries.[20] But then Loisy turned the theological tables on Harnack.

Influenced by John Henry Newman's principle of development and convinced that change was pervasive, inevitable and to be welcomed, Loisy argued that the gospel of the kingdom did indeed have social and institutional implications. The gospel preached by Jesus contained the rudiments of social organization; the kingdom was conceived as a society. These were the seeds from which grew, over the centuries, the great tree of the (Roman) Catholic Church. The emerging ecclesiastical institution provided the framework within which the spirit of Christianity could evolve its changing expressions. The church was the product of the very same process of historical development that, centuries before, had produced the Gospels; the tradition generated by the life and teaching of Jesus was continuous through history. If we are to look for an 'essence' of Christianity (and Loisy was doubtful of the merits of this gambit and was here adopting the parameters of Harnack's thesis for the sake of argument), it is to the totality of Christian experience that we must look, including its institutions, creeds and liturgies.[21] 'We know Christ', Loisy insisted, not by a few selected texts, but 'only by the tradition . . . of the primitive Christians' as it has evolved through history to the

---

[19] Alfred Loisy, *The Gospel and the Church*, trans. Christopher Home (London: Isbister; New York: Scribner, 1903 [1902]), pp. 1–11.

[20] Ibid., p. 166.

[21] Ibid., p. 16.

church of today.[22] Loisy's opening salvo against Harnack is that Harnack has proposed 'a defence of Christianity which eliminates from its essence almost everything that is regarded ordinarily as Christian belief'.[23] Can such a rich and complex phenomenon as Christianity, Loisy asks, really be summed up in (we might say, boiled down to) one solitary thought?

'Jésus annonçait le Royaume et c'est l'Église qui est venue.' Although 'Jesus announced the kingdom', it was completely intentional and part of the divine purpose that 'it was the Church that came'. Loisy's famous dictum was not, as is sometimes supposed, ironical or sardonic. He was not saying, as it were, 'Jesus proclaimed the coming of a glorious kingdom, so much longed for, so long expected, but what we got instead was the institutional church that we know, with all its shortcomings – what a disappointment!' As far as Loisy was concerned, the coming of the church, as a result of the proclamation of the kingdom, was meant to happen; it was intentional and was in fact God's gift to the world.[24]

So Loisy takes away with one hand and gives back with the other. He makes you wait to discover authentic Christianity. He removes the imminently expected kingdom, but inserts the gradually evolving church in its place. This substitution mirrors the upheavals and retrievals of Loisy's own faith. In the years leading up to 1886 he experienced a spiritual crisis and loss of faith. His anguish was caused by two main factors: first, his study of the Bible (at this stage, the impossibility of reconciling his findings with the insistence of the Roman Catholic magisterium on a literal interpretation of the Old Testament, including Gen. 1–11); and secondly, by his cruel treatment at the hands of the ecclesiastical authorities (especially being prohibited from submitting his doctoral thesis on the inspiration of the Bible). But the multiple spiritual crises that Loisy experienced at this time did not destroy his commitment to the church or to the priestly ministry. In 1886 he confided to his journal,

> For several months past I have experienced no religious feeling. . . . I have practically nothing to look forward to. [But] I am determined to work and serve the Church which has been and is responsible for the education of humanity. Without disowning its tradition, and provided it holds to its spirit rather than its letter, it is still a necessary institution and the most divine thing on earth.[25]

Loisy's determination to continue to serve the church was reinforced in the following years by several circumstances, especially his teaching of the Scriptures at the Institut Catholique (until he was sacked in 1893), but also his chaplaincy at a convent school and his ministry of spiritual direction.

---

[22] Ibid., p. 13.

[23] Ibid., p. 1.

[24] On Loisy see Vidler, *A Variety of Catholic Modernists* (Vidler knew Loisy personally); id., *The Modernist Movement in the Roman Church: Its Origins and Outcome*; Reardon, *Roman Catholic Modernism*; id., *Liberalism and Tradition*, chapter 12; Gabriel Daly *Transcendence and Immanence: A Study in Catholic Modernism and Integralism* (Oxford: Clarendon Press, 1980).

[25] Vidler, *A Variety of Catholic Modernists*, p. 36.

Even as he shed the metaphysical elements of Christian belief, Loisy came to prize more highly the ethical aspects, centred on the moral imperative and sacrificial love exemplified by Jesus, though without ceasing to believe in a transcendent deity.[26] If there was, as Harnack assumed, an essence of the gospel, it was perpetuated in Catholic Christianity. Loisy was sustained in his writing and priestly ministry by this spiritual or mystical – that is, undogmatic – faith until 1904 when, appealing directly to the 'heart' of Pope Pius X, he received a crushing rebuke which, on top of previous rebukes and condemnations, accelerated his departure from Christian orthodoxy. In the latter part of his life, Loisy poured out a phenomenal quantity of biblical studies (mainly New Testament commentaries) and other works. But these were now marked by bold rationalist assumptions, over-emphatic assertions and frequent repetition of his conclusions without showing his working. In a stinging article in 1926 the British Methodist New Testament scholar Vincent Taylor attributed the neglect and distrust of Loisy's later work by British scholars to these dubious habits, so unpalatable to British academia. Where are his foundations and where is the evidence? Taylor asked.[27]

La Naissance du Christianisme (1933) is a case in point. In this work Loisy articulated a purely naturalistic account of Christian origins.[28] The church's faith with regard to Jesus Christ had a basis in fact, he admitted, but the whole dogmatic superstructure was mythical. By 'mythical' Loisy seems to mean that it conforms to universal archetypes of the dying and rising god, in parallel with the dying of the earth in Winter and its rising again in the Spring. The biblical sources, he asserts, are not robustly historical, but shaky. They are the product of faith and of the early Christian *cultus*: the memory of the disciples was transformed into adoration. Every event in early Christianity can be *explained* by the laws that govern human life, he argued. Religious faith represents the existential struggle to break out of the remorseless mechanical laws that govern our destinies.[29]

In *L'Évangile et l'Église*, Loisy argued his case in a potent combination of elegant prose, cloudy rhetoric and deceptive logic ('a dexterity that verges on sleight of hand', in Gabriel Daly's words). He diplomatically played down both his debt to Johannes Weiss' eschatological interpretation of the New Testament and his own common ground with Harnack (which is brought out by Sykes), for example, when he says, 'The Jewish exterior is the body of which the Gospel is the soul.'[30] He equally shrewdly – and disingenuously – sharpened the antithesis between progressive (later dubbed 'Modernist') Roman Catholic approaches and Liberal Protestant ideas. He also equivocated about what he meant by Catholicism; for him Catholicism now approximated to simply the ethical and social dimension of religion, though of course it was none the less vital for all that.[31] In *L'Évangile et l'Église*, Loisy's answer to our question, 'Did Jesus found the church and

---

[26] Ibid., pp. 37–8, 51–3.
[27] Vincent Taylor, 'The Alleged Neglect of M. Alfred Loisy', in id., *New Testament Essays* (London: Epworth Press, 1970), pp. 72–82, chapter V.
[28] Loisy, *The Birth of the Christian Religion*, trans. L. P. Jacks, Preface Gilbert Murray, O.M. (London: George Allen and Unwin, 1948).
[29] Ibid., pp. 11–14, 96–7, 358.
[30] Cited Reardon, *Liberalism and Tradition*, p. 268. Sykes, *The Identity of Christianity*, chapter 6, passim.
[31] Daly, *Transcendence and Immanence*, p. 56.

if not, how is the church founded on him?' was that although Jesus merely gathered his disciples and commissioned them to preach the gospel, the great edifice of the church, in its institutional, hierarchical Roman Catholic, form was divinely intended. Moreover, its continuity with the beginnings of Christianity in the New Testament was neither more nor less than the continuity of the full-grown human being with the new-born infant.[32]

Official response to Loisy

As a result of the great ongoing, international historical and biblical research project of the past century and more, which Loisy pioneered, represented and promoted, Roman Catholic academic theology has been undergoing profound revision and development at the hands of its theologians. This process of rethinking has served to moderate the Roman Catholic Church's traditional claim, classically formulated by Cardinal Robert Bellarmine in the sixteenth century, that Jesus Christ explicitly, objectively and (even) juridically (i.e. as a matter of divine law, *ius divinum*) instituted the (Roman Catholic) Church as a visible, hierarchical society with a sacramental system. This society's office holders, according to Bellarmine, were at first the apostles, with Peter at their head, and subsequently the bishops, with the pope at their head, standing in an unbroken personal succession and endowed with certain juridical powers. The role of Peter and of his presumed successors in the See of Rome, the popes, has been pre-eminent among these supposedly dominically instituted offices. In the pre-Vatican II official fundamental theology, set out in training manuals for the clergy, this institutional, juridical framework was taken to be a solidly attested historical fact, rather than a theological postulate that was open to exploration, or even an article of faith that could not be proved from history. Francis Fiorenza points to the key verbs of the manualist tradition: *instituere, fundare* and *aedificare*.[33]

Reflecting and reinforcing the prevailing orthodoxy on this question, the First Vatican Council (1869–70) laid down that Christ had explicitly instituted the papacy; and shortly afterwards Leo XIII decreed that Christ had established a permanent magisterium (authoritative teaching office). The Anti-Modernist Oath of 1910 required priests to swear: 'I will to affirm that Jesus historically founded the Church and papacy.' When, in the encyclical *Mystici Corporis Christi* (1943), Pius XII spoke of the church's 'Divine Founder', he was not making a point, but employing the received language of the institution, half a century after German and French biblical scholarship had undermined it. Vatican II (1962–5) stated, though without the same scholastic basis as the previous Vatican Council, that bishops are, by divine institution, successors of the apostles, endowed with the same powers. The whole edifice was basic to the understanding of the (Roman) Catholic Church as a *societas perfecta*, a complete and self-sufficient society and institution, beholden to no other. Although the language

---

[32] Loisy, *The Gospel and the Church*, pp. 170–1.
[33] Francis Schlüssler Fiorenza, *Fundamental Theology: Jesus and the Church* (New York: Crossroad, 1984), pp. 59, 73.

of *societas perfecta* was been quietly dropped in Vatican II and in subsequent official statements, Roman Catholic teaching still holds today that Jesus Christ historically founded an institutional church with all its present elements, including its structures of papacy, episcopacy, priesthood and seven sacraments.[34]

These traditional claims for the founding of the institutional structure and power of the (Roman Catholic) Church by Jesus Christ in person rested on a particular view of biblical inspiration and interpretation. Divine inspiration was understood to guarantee the historical and even scientific accuracy, correctness and inerrancy of the sacred text and its contents, which was then to be interpreted in the light of a scholastic theological system whose supreme exemplar was the *Summa Theologiae* of St Thomas Aquinas. The critical, historical method of biblical study, that had been developing for more than a century, was explicitly excluded and condemned.

In 1893, the year in which Loisy was removed from his chair at the Institut Catholique, Leo XIII issued the encyclical *Providentisimus Deus* ('*De studiis scripturae sacrae*'). It encouraged biblical scholarship in principle, but laid down criteria for it drawn from patristic spirituality, scholastic theology and church doctrine.[35] Scholars should be guided by deductive principles ('a scientific knowledge of dogma, by means of reasoning from the Articles of Faith to their consequences, according to the rules of approved and sound philosophy'), the study of St Thomas Aquinas being prescribed as the best preparation for biblical study. Given that foundation, there was also much value in also working inductively from the text of Scripture. The encyclical showed no awareness of the existence of an autonomous discipline of critical-historical research. For Roman Catholic scholars, their research remained under the guardianship of church doctrine, administered by the magisterium. Genuine scholars were lumped together with anticlerical rationalists in the encyclical. Although non-Catholic writers could be consulted with discretion, their use was described as 'perilous'; they could not be expected to arrive at any truth about the Bible since they were operating outside the Church. Loisy was condemned, though not by name. 'Higher criticism' was ruled out. Quoting Vatican I, Leo asserted that since God was the 'author' and 'composer' of Scripture and the Holy Spirit was speaking through it, the verbal inspiration and inerrancy of the Bible must be upheld; it was impossible that God should utter falsehood. Only subsequent scribal errors could be admitted in the sacred text. It was 'forbidden . . . to admit that the sacred writer has erred'. On the other hand, the purpose of the biblical revelation was not to teach science; while science and theology could be, and should be, 'reconciled', allowance should be made for the figurative nature of biblical language. The section headed 'What the Bible Owes to the Catholic Church' strikes a note antithetical to the ethos of the Reformation. Biblical research could

---

[34] Vatican I, *Pastor Aeternus*; Vatican II, *Lumen Gentium* 3; Fiorenza, *Fundamental Theology*, p. 69.
[35] For a highly readable, if rather idiosyncratic, narrative of the papal responses to Modernism, see Owen Chadwick, *A History of the Popes 1830-1914* (Oxford: Clarendon Press, 1998), pp. 246-59. Sidelights on 'Modernism' in the French Church under Leo XIII, particularly on *l'affaire Loisy*, which are not easily accessible elsewhere, are to be found in Phillips, *Church in France*, chapter XIII.

also serve an apologetic function in support of church structures: 'the institution of a hierarchical Church and the primacy of Peter and his successors'.[36]

In 1897 the Holy Office issued a decision, approved by Leo XIII, that 1 Jn 5:7 (the 'three witnesses in heaven') was authentic to the text of the epistle and must be regarded by the Catholic faithful as such. Not one of the cardinals who had decided this question was a biblical scholar; the decision had been taken on dogmatic, not exegetical grounds; the authority of tradition trumped scholarly investigation. Leo XIII's next step was the establishment of the Pontifical Biblical Commission in the period 1901–02. Von Hügel had high hopes in it at first, seeing it's establishment as a victory for the cause of scholarly enlightenment in the Roman Catholic Church; he was soon to be disillusioned.[37] It included some serious scholars, but their potentially salutary influence was swamped by scholastically trained, non-critical scholars, prelates and various non-entities or place-men. In 1906 the Commission issued a directive that Catholics must maintain the Mosaic authorship of the Pentateuch, though they were allowed to hold that Moses had secretarial help. Von Hügel, believing that the Commission had exceeded its brief and afraid that this directive, which he believed to have no more authority that that of the individual members of the Commission, would gain enhanced magisterial authority, wrote against it in *The Papal Commission and the Pentateuch*.[38] In 1907 the Commission laid down that the Fourth Gospel had been written by the Apostle John and was entirely historical, even to the extent of containing the *ipsissima verba* of Jesus. In the same year Pius X declared that all the faithful were bound in conscience to accept all the decrees of the Pontifical Biblical Commission, past and future.

In December 1903 the Holy Office placed five of Loisy's books, without explanation, on the Index of Forbidden Books – not only *L'Évangile et l'Église* and its defence (*Autour d'un petit livre*), but also his studies of ancient Israel and his most recent work, a study of the Fourth Gospel. The 1907 decree *Lamentabili* of the Holy Office condemned a number of theses – in caricature form – drawn from the writings of, among others, Loisy and Tyrrell, outlawing in principle the method of free, critical, historical study. *Lamentabili* was followed in the same year by the papal encylical *Pascendi dominici gregis*. It assumed throughout that the scholastic theological system could be equated to divine revelation. It created a fictitious anti-system that it termed 'modernism', 'the synthesis of all heresies'.[39] *Pascendi* concluded with a programme of action to wipe out 'modernism', including the enforcement of scholastic theology and a system of censorship of reading and of personal contact by Catholic clerics. Any challenge to the encyclical would meet with automatic excommunication. An anti-modernist oath was imposed on clergy, teachers and officials in 1910.[40]

[36] http://w2.vatican.va/content/leo-xiii/en/encyclicals/documents/hf_l-xiii_enc_18111893_prov
     identissimus-deus.html
[37] Michael de la Bedoyère, *The Life of Baron von Hügel* (London: Dent, 1951), pp. 136–9.
[38] Ibid., pp. 185–7.
[39] Lawrence F. Barmann, *Baron Friedrich von Hügel and the Modernist Crisis in England* (Cambridge:
     Cambridge University Press, 1972), p. 197.
[40] Texts in Reardon, *Roman Catholic Modernism*, pp. 237–48. The oath, which required adherence to
     Lamentabili and *Pascendi*, was not repealed until 1967 (by Paul VI).

In contrast to the official Roman position, as it stood at the end of the nineteenth century and the beginning of the twentieth, a succession of eminent Roman Catholic scholars has explored subtle and sophisticated ways of establishing the church firmly on the Christ event, without claiming that Jesus of Nazareth intentionally and explicitly 'founded' the institutional church with all its main constituent elements. I will now sketch out some of the most significant of these attempts at reinterpretation of the (Roman Catholic) Church's foundational constitution, following the Loisy cause célèbre and beginning with the deeply impressive figure of Baron Friedrich von Hügel.

Friedrich von Hügel

Baron Friedrich von Hügel (1852–1925) and John Henry Newman stand out as the two most profound and influential of nineteenth-century Roman Catholic religious thinkers in the English-speaking world (though, of course, Newman was a profound and influential religious thinker as an Anglican before that). It is true to say, however, that von Hügel was personally and intellectually admired, respected and revered in an almost unqualified way that was never true of Newman in either of his churches. Von Hügel's life's work – his supreme theological achievement – was the massive *The Mystical Element of Religion*, ostensibly a study of the mystical spirituality of St Catherine of Genoa, but almost an encyclopaedia of religion.[41] William Temple (writing in the *Guardian* after the Baron's death in 1925) described it as 'the most important theological work written in the English language during the last half-century'. It is a theological mountain that is often admired from afar, but seldom scaled to the summit.[42]

Austrian by birth, von Hügel resided in England for the whole of his adult life. He was in touch with an impressive range of British, French, German, Italian and other scholars, churchmen and statesmen. While he was fascinated by the physical sciences – his hobby was geology, in which he had been trained, and he was in close touch with several eminent scientists of the day – the domain where von Hügel was a master was that of the humanities. He worked with ease in several languages and the span of his endeavours stretched from erudite biblical, historical and philosophical researches to a kindly but searching ministry of spiritual guidance. To read his intimate letters of spiritual counsel is a humbling and shaping experience.[43] Von Hügel was an ardent seeker after truth and reality at any cost and believed that to establish the truth of Christian claims by critical and historical methods was imperative in order to defend

---

[41] Friedrich von Hügel, *The Mystical Element of Religion*, 2 vols, 2nd edn (London: Dent; New York: Dutton, 1923 [1908]).

[42] See Temple's tribute (and another, even more fulsome): de la Bedoyère, *The Life of Baron von Hügel*, pp. 223–4.

[43] Von Hügel, *Selected Letters of Baron Friedrich von Hügel*, ed. Bernard Holland (London: Dent; New York: Dutton, 1927); Friedrich von Hügel, *Letters from Baron Friedrich von Hügel to a Niece*, ed. and intro. Gwendolen Greene (London and Toronto: Dent, 1928).

the credibility of the faith in the modern world.[44] Bernard Holland, in his 'Memoir', justly said of him: 'The Baron's mind was laborious, many-side-regarding, fully weighing, slow-moving, deep ploughing.'[45] He was extremely devout in his religious observances: daily mass and/or adoration of the Blessed Sacrament; saying the rosary; daily reading from the Bible, the *Imitation of Christ* or the *Confessions* of St Augustine; weekly confession and so on.

Von Hügel's extraordinary combination of fearless critical investigation, even in the face of hostile ecclesiastical authority and the venerable traditions that it sought to uphold, on the one hand, and profound spiritual reflection and insight, formed and nurtured by prayer, sacrament and spiritual reading, on the other, is seen to advantage in his article on St John's Gospel in the Eleventh Edition of the *Encyclopædia Britannica* (1911). This article, written just at the time of the ferocious clamp-down on 'Modernist' writers, covers such matters as possible authorship and probable date, literary analysis, exegesis of the theological content of the Gospel and pointers to its significance. Von Hügel dismisses the notion that the Gospel was written by the Apostle John, Son of Zebedee and brother of James, but finds a role for John the Presbyter who appears in primitive tradition. He separates off the prologue and the appendix (chapter 21), brings out the major Johannine differences of structure, style and emphasis with the Synoptics and dwells on the allegorical (rather than parabolic, as in the Synoptics) character of the narrative. He daringly quotes Loisy as providing the best summary of the essence of the Gospel. Harmonization to appease authority is absent; undeflected attention to the particularities of the text guides von Hügel's method; but he never loses the wood for the trees, the text for the meaning. It is an impressive effort by a self-educated layman who was not a biblical specialist.[46]

Von Hügel and 'modernism'

Von Hügel was described by Vidler as 'the chief engineer of the modernist movement'; and that view was supported by the testimony of Maude Petre who dubbed him the 'arch-leader' of the modernists.[47] Von Hügel shared some of the methods and views of the so-called Catholic modernists, being wholly persuaded of the validity of scientific biblical criticism as a method and of its broad conclusions with regard to the historicity,

---

[44] See Bernard Holland, 'Memoir', in id. (ed.), *Selected Letters of Baron Friedrich von Hügel*; Barmann, *Baron Friedrich von Hügel and the Modernist Crisis*; Vidler, *A Variety of Catholic Modernists*, pp. 110–26; Maurice Neédoncelle, *La Penseée religieuse de Friedrich von Huügel, 1852-1925* (Paris, 1935); the English translation by Marjorie Vernon, is incomplete: Maurice Neédoncelle, *Baron Friedrich von Huügel: A Study of His Life and Thought* (London: Longmans & Co., 1937). The biography – de la Bedoyère, *The Life of Baron von Hügel* – is distorted by the author's blatant but unconvincing efforts to show that his subject was never a true Modernist, but was loyally Orthodox and, where he wavered in this, was led astray by George Tyrrell (on the lines of, 'How could a Jesuit, with his rigorous philosophical and theological training, be so influenced by a mere theologically uneducated layman?', and so on), rather than the dominant influence being the other way round, as I believe.

[45] Holland, 'Memoir', p. 13.

[46] 'John, Gospel of St', in *Encyclopædia Britannica*, 1911: https://en.wikisource.org/wiki/1911_Ency clop%C3%A6dia_Britannica/John,_Gospel_of_St

[47] Vidler, *Variety of Catholic Modernists*, p. 113.

or not, of the Gospel narratives. He was a personal friend and *confident* of Alfred Loisy (at one time they were exchanging letters several times a week), an avid though not uncritical reader of his biblical researches and a staunch defender of his right to pursue his investigations without fear of censure from the ecclesiastical authorities. He stood with Loisy and against the Liberal Protestants in repudiating their method of peeling away the layers of the onion or cracking the nut to get at the kernel.[48]

Von Hügel was more cautious – at least in writing; his privately expressed views were highly 'advanced'[49] – than George Tyrrell and, unlike Tyrrell, von Hügel never despaired of the Roman Church. Considering all that he, and even more, those he advised and supported, had to endure, he remained remarkably respectful towards the Roman authorities, tending to look for a silver lining in official actions that were intended to crush all that he represented and worked for. He was always trying to square the circle, wanting to affirm the authority of the church's oversight of Christian theology at the same time as fighting for scholarly freedom. He had an unbreakable emotional, mystical, attachment to Rome – the Roman Church of the ages and of history, not merely the dysfunctional Roman Church of his own day. Von Hügel was, to some extent, a mediating figure between moderate open-minded enquirers within his church and the more radical modernists, such as Loisy and Tyrrell. After Tyrrell's death, von Hügel back-tracked a bit, becoming less of a rebellious radical, and this perhaps suggests that he had come only temporarily under the sway of the excitable, rather fanatical Tyrrell. As a layman and an aristocrat, von Hügel was not vulnerable to ecclesiastical discipline in the way that lowly clergy such as Tyrrell were. But the casting of Tyrrell into outer darkness by the church might well have been enough to give the Baron cold feet and he feared the consequences for himself. Von Hügel was insistent that the questions raised by 'modernist' thinkers were by no means unique to the Roman Catholic Church. The problems that 'haunted' Tyrrell 'and helped to break his life' were 'besetting every form of traditional, institutional Christianity'; Anglican scholars such as William Sanday and Charles Gore were also wrestling with them.[50]

Von Hügel and historical science

Von Hügel described himself as an 'historical' Christian or Catholic, one who unequivocally accepted the methods and conclusions of modern, scientific historical study, including biblical criticism. He believed that such an approach belonged to the very nature of the faith (of all faiths in fact) and its integrity. In 1904 he wrote, for a French audience:

> Although the act of Christian faith necessarily goes beyond the historic facts – the object, each one for itself, of historico-critical proof – it nevertheless demands facts of that nature. It demands them because that is a condition of all human assent, since our souls are only awakened to the presence of spiritual realities

---

[48] Holland (ed.), *Selected Letters of Baron Friedrich von Hügel*, p. 111.
[49] Vidler, *Variety of Catholic Modernists*, pp. 112–21.
[50] Holland (ed.), *Selected Letters of Baron Friedrich von Hügel*, p. 167.

when a contingent and historical stimulus from without excites them. . . . The more complete and profound a religion is, the more it will present this paradox of the permanent seized through the transitory, the eternal manifested in time. This is so true that there would be no more Christianity, if the Christian faith did not rest on a basis of historic events.[51]

In 1908 von Hügel wrote to the Anglican philosopher of religion Clement C. J. Webb about Loisy's commentary on the Synoptic Gospels, hoping that Webb was not too shocked and adding, 'I feel as strongly as ever, that what claims to be history cannot escape being judged by historico-critical methods and tests.'[52] He agreed with Webb's view that there could no protected 'nucleus of hard fact, of undiscussible truth.'[53] What von Hügel was aiming for was 'a science of the Bible'. Only when the human element was given its due could the divine, revelatory element shine through. He regarded the historical revolution of the nineteenth century as a great watershed in human thought. Thus, he largely accepted the eschatological perspective of the New Testament, in which the imminent arrival of the kingdom of God was dominant, that had been pioneered by Weiss and Schweitzer (both of whom he had read, along with a deep, friendly engagement with Ernst Troeltsch), though he believed that they overstated their case a bit.[54] And, of course, he was steeped in Loisy. In the ministry of Jesus, von Hügel believed, the kingdom is presented to the world 'directly and emphatically, as, not present but future; not distant but imminent; not gradual but sudden; not as at all achieved by man, but as simply given by God'.[55] Nothing, von Hügel insisted, could be more certain than this interpretation, though it did not exclude a complementary element of realized (not his word), present, ethical eschatology, the stewardship of the kingdom, so to speak, that we find in some of the parables.[56]

But von Hügel remained a (Roman) Catholic in heart and mind, rejecting out of hand, in contrast to Tyrrell, any suggestion that he might find a new home in the more tolerant Church of England – though he had cordial relations with several Anglican biblical scholars, including S. R. Driver, T. K. Cheyne, William Sanday and Charles Gore (as well as close friendships with the Anglican lay philosopher Clement C. J. Webb and with Bishop Edward Talbot). He had deeply imbibed the writings of Samuel Johnson and Edmund Burke, two seminal Anglican minds of the eighteenth century.

---

[51] Cited de la Bedoyère, *The Life of Baron von Hügel*, pp. 165–66. Von Hügel says 'historic' when we would normally say 'historical'.
[52] Holland (ed.), *Selected Letters of Baron Friedrich von Hügel*, p. 146.
[53] Ibid., p. 156.
[54] Friedrich von Hügel, 'On the Specific Genius and Capacities of Christianity, Studied in Connection with the Works of Professor Ernst Troeltsch', in *Essays and Addresses on the Philosophy of Religion* [First Series] (London and Toronto: Dent; New York: Dutton, 1921), chapter 6, at pp. 145–6: 'For now over twenty years, I have learnt quite massively from Troeltsch. . . . Possibly no Englishman, probably no American, knows his mind and works as intimately as I know them myself.' In his discussion of selected parts of Troeltsch's vast *oeuvre*, von Hügel mixes praise and criticism in roughly equal measure.
[55] Friedrich von Hügel, *Eternal Life: A Study of Its Implications and Applications*, 2nd edn, rev. (Edinburgh: T&T Clark, 1913), p. 56. This huge book (493 pages) was originally intended to fulfil a commission for the Eleventh Edition of the *Encyclopædia Britannica* (1911)!
[56] Von Hügel, *Eternal Life*, pp. 58–9.

Von Hügel was aware that the Lambeth Conference 1897 had stated that it was the right and duty of Christian scholars to apply critical methods of study, with moderation and reverence, to every part of the Bible.[57] Von Hügel was also in touch with non-Anglican British scholars, such as the Scottish Presbyterians William Robertson Smith and Alexander Whyte, and with German Lutheran scholars, such as Rudolf Euken, Heinrich Holtzmann, Friedrich Heiler and, above all, Ernst Troeltsch. He consulted all of these and sought their moral support in his battle for the toleration of critical biblical study in his own church. Von Hügel never abandoned the Catholic conception of the church as a divine yet visible society, embedded in history. Notwithstanding the imminent arrival of the kingdom, Jesus conceived his community as 'a social organism'. Since the kingdom is present wherever God's will is done (as the Lord's Prayer teaches), it 'evidently coincides with the totality of those through whom God's will is accomplished'. It is, moreover, he insists, 'an organized community'.[58]

The influence of Newman

This theological ferment was taking place in the wake of John Henry Newman's *Essay on the Development of Christian Doctrine*, published more than half a century before (1845).[59] Although they were on friendly terms, von Hügel tended to speak slightly patronisingly of Newman as a convert and thought that he lacked the inner joy of the cradle Catholic, being unable to escape the gravitational pull of the Evangelical Calvinism of his youth. Although von Hügel's biographer notes that '[t]here are surprisingly few references to Newman in the baron's writings, and these few usually sound a critical note',[60] Newman's writings exerted a profound influence on his personal development.[61] Von Hügel was an avid reader even of Newman's Anglican works, especially the novel *Loss and Gain*, which the young von Hügel found revelatory of the nature of Catholicism, and the volumes of the *Parochial and Plain Sermons*.[62] Newman's 1884 essay 'On the Inspiration of Scripture' was also a stimulus and encouragement to von Hügel's critical biblical studies; ten years' later von Hügel was speaking of the development of doctrine as though it were a natural, uncontroversial, fact.[63] Paul Misner states that 'the role of Newman's writings and thought in von Hügel's development was cardinal' (no pun intended, presumably). Misner adds that von Hügel 'would never have come to Duchesne and Wellhausen and Holtzmann and Loisy with

---

[57] Resolution 13 received the report of the Lambeth Conference Committee on the Critical Study of Holy Scripture and commended it to all Christian people. Roger Coleman (ed.), *Resolutions of the Twelve Lambeth Conferences 1867-1988* (Toronto: Anglican Book Centre, 1992), p. 18; Alan M. G. Stephenson, *Anglicanism and the Lambeth Conferences* (London: SPCK, 1978), pp. 105–6.

[58] Von Hügel, *Eternal Life*, p. 62.

[59] Newman, *An Essay on the Development of Christian Doctrine, The Edition of 1845*.

[60] de la Bedoyère, *The Life of Baron von Hügel*, p. 32.

[61] Von Hügel, *Essays and Addresses on the Philosophy of Religion* (Second Series) (London and Toronto: Dent; New York: Dutton, 1926), p. 242; de la Bedoyère, *The Life of Baron von Hügel*, p. 43.

[62] Barmann, *Baron Friedrich von Hügel and the Modernist Crisis*, pp. 3–4. John Henry Newman, *Loss and Gain* (Oxford: Oxford University Press, 1986 [1848]).

[63] Barmann, *Baron Friedrich von Hügel and the Modernist Crisis*, pp. 6–7, 51. John Henry Newman, *On the Inspiration of Scripture*, ed. and intro. J. Derek Holmes and Robert Murray, S. J. (London: Geoffrey Chapman, 1967).

the same openness had it not been for the large doses of Newman he took in at critical junctures along the way'.[64]

Newman was wrestling with the phenomenon of massive change through time in how the church was constituted (which he baptized with the beneficent word 'development'), from the church of the apostles, martyrs and fathers in the first centuries to the Roman Catholic Church of the mid-nineteenth century. Setting those two manifestations of the church side by side was enough to induce an attack of ecclesiological vertigo. But, ironically, it was Newman's embrace of the fact of change in the church that made it possible for him to convert from Anglicanism to Roman Catholicism, even though (a second irony) his interpretation of Roman Catholicism was unacceptable to the Roman Catholic authorities and was in fact condemned by his new church. It was widely believed that Newman's views had been assimilated by Rome to those of the 'Modernists', so that they also fell under the condemnations of *Pascendi*, though Newman was not named (Wilfred Ward, Newman's biographer and himself certainly no Modernist, believed that Newman had been condemned by the pope, though unintentionally!).[65] Similarly, von Hügel himself was not explicitly condemned in *Pascendi*, though he believed that the encyclical had ignorantly and ineptly consigned to the bonfire whole swathes of the central theological tradition of the Western Church that had previously been acceptable, including much of St Augustine, St Thomas Aquinas' doctrine of analogy, and aspects of the writings of St John of the Cross and of St Theresa of Avila.[66]

Von Hügel's view of the church deriving only 'germinally' from the historical Jesus – which resonates with Loisy's recently published *L'Évangile et l'Église* – seems a remarkable admission by a Roman Catholic theologian at the time. But von Hügel goes further when he acknowledges that historical criticism shows that Jesus shared the thought world and the level of knowledge of his time; that he was not infallible in the sphere of human knowledge; and that this lack of infallibility included his expectation of an imminent coming of God's kingdom. In other words, Jesus was mistaken, though von Hügel does not put it as bluntly as that. It did not trouble him unduly that Jesus accepted the world view of his time and place, including its demonology and its belief in eternal punishment, or the fact that he did not know when the *parousia* would happen. All this he regarded as 'a supreme exemplification of the law obtaining in all religions, of the condition indeed of all characteristically human life and dignity', namely that truth – even religious truth – is compelled 'to express and clothe itself in certain contingencies of space and time'. By doing so it gains strength for a while, but at the cost of weakness when new times and new questions come along.[67]

---

[64] Paul Misner, 'The "Liberal" Legacy of Newman', in Mary Jo Weaver (ed.), *Newman and the Modernists* (College Theological Society, Resources in Religion I; Lanham, NY: University Press of America, 1985), chapter 1, at p. 20. For Duchesne's influence on von Hügel see de la Bedoyère, *The Life of Baron von Hügel*, pp. 47–50. Von Hügel found it difficult to understand why Duchesne would not commit himself publicly on questions of biblical criticism; he kept his powder dry.

[65] Mary Jo Weaver, 'Wilfred Ward's Interpretation and Application of Newman', in id. (ed.), *Newman and the Modernists*, chapter 2.

[66] Barmann, *Baron Friedrich von Hügel and the Modernist Crisis*, pp. 205–6.

[67] Holland (ed.), *Selected Letters of Baron Friedrich von Hügel*, pp. 158–60.

The church grounded in the mission of Jesus

Von Hügel accepts that 'historical criticism' has established that 'church organization', as we know it, 'is not the direct and deliberate creation of Our Blessed Lord Himself', except in the rudimentary form that we see in the Synoptic Gospels, which is akin in its simplicity to the Franciscan Brotherhood during the lifetime of St Francis.[68] Any more elaborate organization in the apostolic church was precluded by the expectation of Christ's 'Proximate Second Coming', so that all subsequent forms of ecclesiastical structure 'beyond that humble brotherhood . . . can go back germinally and not formally and materially' to Jesus.[69] The form in which we now have the (Roman Catholic) church is 'mostly of divine institution [only] in the sense in which the family and human society are' – that is to say they are 'God's work', built up by human effort, but actually by God's grace working through human instruments.[70] We can accept, von Hügel believes, that the thought-forms of Jesus, and the disciples were apocalyptic and eschatological through and through, and yet we can still hold that he gathered, trained and commissioned his followers to go out on his behalf. With the fading away of the imminent expectation of the kingdom, 'the Preaching Band automatically becomes the Church. For already . . . there is mission, subordination, unitary headship.'[71] It seems not unfair to von Hügel to sum up his position like this: the origins of the Christian church as a fully developed institution lie in the ministry of Jesus (though Jesus could not be expected to know this), as a seed or embryo, that would mature and flourish according to the divine purpose. Von Hügel did not waver in his conviction that the Roman Catholic Church was the principal expression of that purpose.

In 1918, well after the official condemnation and suppression of Roman Catholic Modernism, von Hügel elaborated a defence of the necessarily institutional character of Christianity, from which, he admits, there was widespread alienation. The main steps in his argument are as follows.[72] (a) He begins by attacking the radical individualism of Harnack and Troeltsch (though he does not name those two, he does name Kant and Luther) that would make religion the most entirely private and therefore incommunicable experience. (b) He points out that all significant dimensions of human life, such as art, science, philosophy and ethics, depend on institutional structures, such as academies, schools, traditions and collective disciplines. (c) Similarly, all religion, even that taught by the great prophets who stood head and shoulders above their fellows, has an institutional basis, especially in the Old Testament and the work of St Paul. The fact that Jesus did not leave much, if any, teaching about the social, political and economic conduct of the Christian life can be attributed to the 'expectation of His Proximate Second Coming' as held by Jesus and the first witnesses and writers. Even

[68] Von Hügel, 'Official Authority and Living Religion', in id., *Essays and Addresses on the Philosophy of Religion* (Second Series), chapter 1, pp. 3–23, at p. 18.
[69] Ibid., p. 19.
[70] Ibid., p. 20.
[71] Friedrich von Hügel, 'The Apocalyptic Element in the Teaching of Jesus', in id., *Essays and Addresses on the Philosophy of Religion* [First Series], (London and Toronto: Dent; New York: Dutton, 1921), chapter 5, pp. 119–43, at p. 129.
[72] Friedrich von Hügel, 'Institutional Christianity or the Church, Its Nature and Necessity', in id., *Essays and Addresses on the Philosophy of Religion* [First Series], chapter 10.

if Jesus never uttered the word 'Church', the essence of the thing itself is present in all he said and did. (d) Thus Jesus formed his twelve apostles into a 'visible College' and placed Peter, 'the Rock', at its head. The institutional nature of Christianity is contained in St Paul's image of the Body and in what he teaches about 'the two great central Sacraments, Baptism and the Holy Eucharist'. (e) Citing the Congregational preacher and writer P. T. Forsyth, Ernst Troeltsch and the agnostic historian F. W. Maitland, von Hügel insists that Christianity needs a defined identity, one that is discernible by the senses, not merely by spiritual intuition: 'a certain nucleus of historical happenednesses', though these happenings should be exposed to 'sober and reverent historical criticism'. (f) Such criticism has already brought to light the fact of pseudonymity in the New Testament writings, but (von Hügel points out) this was a widespread practice or convention in the ancient world and is nothing to worry about. (g) The Pauline epistles and the Four Gospels 'picture Jesus as solemnly founding this One Church for all ages and races'. Although he next endorses Loisy's famous dictum when he concedes that 'The Church is doubtless, historically speaking, rather the substitute for, than the expansion of, the Kingdom of God', it seems that, in his passionate enthusiasm, von Hügel is forgetting much of what he supported the Modernists for holding (or rather, denying). (h) In the same fervent vein, the argument culminates in an apologia for the Roman Catholic Church, the 'one great international, supernatural Church'. This is the church that had caused von Hügel and his friends enormous grief, pain and frustration. He was absolutely wedded to the Roman Church in a way that George Tyrrell, S. J. in the end was not, but the tension between his impregnable loyalty to his church and his passionate commitment to unfettered scholarly enquiry caused him deep inward suffering (on top of the suffering caused by his deafness and the weak health of his wife and eldest daughter, Gertrud).

George Tyrrell, S. J.

George Tyrrell (1861–1909) was, as Bernard Reardon puts it, 'Modernism's prophet, apostle and most conspicuous martyr'.[73] Brought up in as a nominal Anglican, it was (he recalled) a 'very crude study' of Bishop Joseph Butler's *Analogy of Religion* (1736) that awakened him to the religious and theological quest.[74] Tyrrell attributed the genesis of his distinctive ideas to a later study of the *Spiritual Exercises* of St Ignatius Loyola and the works of St Thomas Aquinas, the latter taken not as a dogmatic system but as an exemplar of the method and spirit of theology.[75] At eighteen, Tyrrell converted

---

[73] Reardon, *Roman Catholic Modernism*, p. 37.
[74] George Tyrrell, *Medievalism: A Reply to Cardinal Mercier* (London: Longmans, Green, and Co., 1908), p. 99. M. D. Petre (ed.), *Autobiography and Life of George Tyrrell*, 2 vols, vol. 1: *Autobiography of George Tyrrell 1861-1884* (London: Edward Arnold, 1912), pp. 95–6. See also the perceptive discussion in Hastings Rashdall, 'George Tyrrell', in id., *Ideas and Ideals*, ed. H. D. A. Major and F. L. Cross (Oxford: Basil Blackwell, 1928), pp. 132–41.
[75] Tyrrell, *Medievalism*, p. 112. Petre (ed.), *Autobiography and Life of George Tyrrell*, vol. 1, pp. 242–52; Nicholas Sagovsky, *Between Two Worlds: George Tyrrell's Relationship to the Thought of Matthew Arnold* (Cambridge: Cambridge University Press, 1983), p. 6.

to Roman Catholicism and at nineteen he entered the Society of Jesus. Tyrrell was a man who rushed straight to the logical conclusion of things; he would always 'go the whole hog'. He was not a measured scholar and was barely a theologian by the standards of that tribe; he was a poetic and intuitive thinker and a visionary. It matched his impetuous temperament to hold that Jesus' transcendent visions were imaginative glimpses into the divine, which were then not conceptualized, but lived out in sacrificial love. But Tyrrell was also a formidable controversialist; his reply in *Medievalism* to Cardinal Mercier's calumnies is devastating. Tyrrell's onslaughts on official teaching and practice, in the first decade of the twentieth century, were not answered by any arguments from officialdom, but were first caricatured, then condemned, and finally crushed by naked ecclesiastical authority.

Tyrrell and von Hügel

It was Tyrrell's spiritual–mystical leanings that initially commended him to von Hügel and he became a friend of his family. Probably, von Hügel had pushed Tyrrell, who was ill-equipped by his education and temperament to handle it, too rapidly into the heady world of German biblical criticism and its radical consequences. Von Hügel himself came to believe this, as did Maud Petre, Tyrrell's supporter, advocate, literary executor and biographer.[76] (Von Hügel did exactly the same with his gifted and delicate daughter Gertrud, loading her with too much theological and spiritual responsibility at a tender age. Tyrrell had to correct him and von Hügel was later remorseful for his behaviour.)[77] It was not at all a case of Tyrrell hustling von Hügel into extreme views. On the other hand, Von Hügel sought to restrain Tyrrell from going too far in an immanentist direction, which was the Modernist tendency and for which the 'Modernists' were – in part justly – castigated by the Vatican.[78] Von Hügel was responsible for Tyrrell's critical awakening, opening his eyes to the seismic questions raised by the work of Weiss, Loisy and Schweitzer on the New Testament, especially the eschatological world view of the Gospels. But Tyrrell and von Hügel were in fact deeply indebted to one another, intellectually and spiritually. Tyrrell found in von Hügel a profundity of learning and sound judgement and a coherence and rigour of thought that he himself lacked. In turn, von Hügel experienced Tyrrell as a catalyst and agent provocateur to his own more steady and solid, approach to questions of theology, philosophy and ecclesiastical politics. In contrast to the caution, sense of propriety and diplomatic approach of von Hügel, the cosmopolitan aristocrat, Tyrrell was passionate, reckless and incendiary.

The eschatological horizon and Loisy's thesis

Both von Hügel and Tyrrell embraced Loisy's central thesis that while Jesus announced the imminent, cataclysmic arrival of God's kingdom, it was in full accord with God's providential purposes that it was the church that appeared on the earthly stage. Tyrrell

---

[76] M. D. Petre, *Von Huügel and Tyrrell: The Story of a Friendship* (London: Dent, 1937), pp. 5, 8.
[77] Holland (ed.), *Selected Letters of Baron Friedrich von Hügel*, pp. 113, 222, 251.
[78] Ibid., p. 139.

accepted that Jesus believed in the imminence of the *parousia* and that this belief was the stimulus for the urgency of his mission. But, Tyrrell comments:

> [I]t is vain to pretend that belief in a near cataclysm is a permanent and essential part of Christianity. The Kingdom of God *for us* is the result of a slow and continuous process. The psychological force of such an ideal is totally different from that of a near cataclysm. It is neither possible nor desirable that the world should live permanently in a state of hysterical apprehension, and be always expecting a violent revolution . . . society cannot live in a chronic state of disturbance. The state of the earliest Church was, after all, fanatical and unhealthy. . . . I dislike the view which makes the feverish apocalyptic spirit *essential* to Christianity. I regard the illusion of Christ and His Apostles . . . as irrelevant to the essence of the Gospel.[79]

Tyrrell's work is a commentary on, and an elaboration of, Loisy's famous dictum to the effect that the church arrived on the scene instead of the expected violent in-breaking of the kingdom. For Tyrrell, this church, even in its earliest institutional form (the first expressions of 'Catholicism'), was connected by gossamer-thin, but immensely strong, threads of continuity with the mission and destiny of Jesus. Tyrrell's mission was an apologetic one: to secure and to establish the 'transition from Christ to Catholicism'. His ambitious and all-consuming project was 'to find in the earliest [form of] Catholicism a true development of the "idea" of Christ'.[80]

Tyrrell and Liberal Protestantism

Having absorbed the electrifying thought of Weiss, Loisy and Schweitzer into their thinking, neither von Hügel nor Tyrrell was in the least attracted by Liberal Protestantism in its German, French or British forms, finding it basically anodyne and insipid – both historically implausible and spiritually arid. Harnack and company, Tyrrell sneered, 'wanted to bring Jesus into the nineteenth century as the Incarnation of its ideal of Divine Righteousness', but their ideal of divine righteousness was little more than the sum of 'all the highest principles and aspirations that ensure the healthy progress of civilization', in other words 'modern morality'. The God that was left – if any (Tyrrell's reservation) – was 'only the God of moralism and rationalism', not the biblical God of the patriarchs and prophets. The Liberal Protestants were 'smoothing away the friction between Christianity and the present age'. Their religion of 'sweet reasonableness' was barely Christian. Tyrrell's verdict is as famous as it is damning: 'The Christ that Harnack sees, looking back through nineteen centuries of Catholic darkness, is only the reflection of a Liberal Protestant face, seen at the bottom of a deep well.'[81] As Maud Petre wrote in introducing his last book and testament, *Christianity at the Crossroads* (1909), what Tyrrell was seeking was 'not the Christ of humanitarianism

[79] M. D. Petre (ed.), *George Tyrrell's Letters* (London: T. Fisher Unwin, 1920), pp. 115–16.
[80] George Tyrrell, *Christianity at the Crossroads*, ed. Maud Petre, Foreword A. R. Vidler (London: George Allen and Unwin, 1963 [1909]), pp. 44–5.
[81] Ibid., pp. 47–9, 123, 179.

and philanthropy, but the Christ of a transcendent kingdom'.[82] And Tyrrell himself says in his Preface to that book, 'Whatever Jesus was, He was in no sense a Liberal Protestant.'[83] Between Liberal Protestantism and Jesus there was, for Tyrrell, an unbridgeable gulf. The Liberal Protestant Christ was as mythical as the supernatural Christ.

The question that arises, as we read Tyrrell's scornful comments on Liberal Protestantism, is whether he 'doth protest too much' when he presents his ideas as its antithesis and antidote. 'Liberal Catholicism', according to Tyrrell, was something completely other than Liberal Protestantism.[84] The truth is, however, that Tyrrell and Harnack (like Loisy and Harnack) have much in common. Tyrrell thought Loisy unfair to Harnack at some key points.[85] Von Hügel corrected Tyrrell's tendency to downplay the externals of religion and to privilege pure interiority, the experiential, the inward spiritual disposition, just like a Liberal Protestant.[86] Like Harnack, Tyrrell rejects the supernaturalistic, miraculous and apocalyptic world view of the Gospels, as then portrayed in avant garde New Testament scholarship. He translates the biblical imagery, not into an ethic of benevolence and goodwill, as Harnack does, but into new symbols of transcendence, vaguely specified. With Harnack, he uses the image of the kernel and the husk.[87] Like Harnack, he finds the driving force of Christianity in the power of Jesus' personality to inspire. He has the same belief in the moral and religious progress of humankind (of 'man'), the upward ascent of the spirit. Tyrrell's theology makes much of transcendence, but in fact it is not dialectical enough. While holding on to transcendence, he abandons the theme of judgement. He comes close to Albert Schweitzer's Christ-mysticism ('Christ in you . . .').[88] The religion that Jesus taught represented 'a return to inwardness'.[89] For all his scathing attacks on the authoritarianism and obscurantism of Rome, what he mainly condemns is ignorance, superstition and self-seeking, not flagrant sin in the church. For Tyrrell, Christ reigns in the sphere of individual spiritual subjectivity, not in the clash of nations.

Undialectical transcendence

Tyrrell died in 1909, five years before the outbreak of the Great War, but preparations for it were intensifying, for example, in the naval arms race, the 'battle of the Dreadnoughts'. Tyrrell's theology lacks the dialectical thrust, the biblical theme of judgement, that was beginning to shape the thinking of Karl Barth in Switzerland, and Peter Taylor Forsyth and John Neville Figgis in England. Dean Inge pointed out that the Roman Catholic Modernists were tainted with rationalism: they had no place for divine action in the world and Tyrrell despised 'supernatural mechanism' and 'supernaturalistic

---

[82] Ibid., p. 16.
[83] Ibid., p. 22.
[84] George Tyrrell, S. J., *Through Scylla and Charybdis; or, The Old Theology and the New* (London: Longman, Green, and Co., 1907), pp. 78–9.
[85] Holland (ed.), *Selected Letters of Baron Friedrich von Hügel*, pp. 117–21.
[86] Ibid., p. 119.
[87] Tyrrell, *Medievalism*, p. 50.
[88] Tyrrell, *Christianity at the Crossroads*, pp. 171–7.
[89] Tyrrell, *Essays on Faith and Immortality*, ed. M. D. Petre (London: Edward Arnold, 1914), p, 65.

dualism', which were fundamental and pervasive in the Roman Catholic doctrine and cultus. Amateurs in philosophy (in contrast to Inge himself, of course!), the Roman Catholic Modernists were in thrall to 'metaphysical pragmatism', and some of Tyrrell's statements were 'ultra-pragmatist', evading the truth question. Inge had a point: in *Through Scylla and Charybdis* Tyrrell discusses pragmatism and in a letter of 1901, Tyrrell admits to being drawn to William James' pragmatist philosophy, especially his lecture *The Will To Believe* (1896).[90] For Inge himself, however, there must eventually be a reconciliation of faith and knowledge, *fides* and *gnosis*.[91]

Tyrrell held in common with Liberal Protestantism that the supernaturalistic, miraculous and apocalyptic framework of the Gospels was untenable. Miracle was a temporary historical vehicle of higher truths. Thus Tyrrell says, 'The conception of miraculous revelation and miraculous religions was necessary to safeguard those instinctive religious intuitions which explicit reason, during its minority, could not justify, and to lend them that divine authority and stability that is their due.'[92] But in place of the Liberal Protestant translation of the supernatural into an ethic of benevolence, he transposed it into something approaching a universal concept of mystical transcendence, which he somewhat implausibly attached to the Roman Catholic Church and saw as mediated by its sacramental system. He believed that this evolution remained faithful to the original idea of Christianity. Thus, Tyrrell's project was an imaginative and sophisticated apologia for Catholic Christianity, but one that required the Church to be willing to evolve out of all recognition, to become something else in order (as Newman said in the essay on development) to remain the same – and that was not going to happen.

Tyrrell held that it was impossible merely to discard the apocalyptic framework of the New Testament, as something superficial or trivial, in order to reveal beneath it an essence or a kernel of timeless truths, as Harnack proposed. Instead, Tyrrell believed, apocalyptic needed to be taken seriously; it stood for the experiential theme of transcendence, which was the unique *caché* of Jesus' proclamation. However, he claimed that the 'immediacy' element in apocalyptic was 'no part of the idea of Jesus', but was purely circumstantial. It was the kingdom itself, not the immediacy of its coming that mattered. The kingdom itself was the sole reason, in Jesus' preaching, for repentance and right living; immediacy or urgency was simply the stimulus.[93] Subsequent generations would need to find new and living symbols of a transcendent spiritual reality that could not be expressed literally, in order to reinterpret the original religious 'idea' or 'spirit', found in the Gospels. But how would we know that these symbols were authentic expressions of the original 'idea'? Tyrrell's answer is pragmatic, but has good precedent: we will know them by their fruits. 'We have to compare life with life; feeling with feeling; action with action.'[94] He quotes at length

[90] Petre (ed.), *George Tyrrell's Letters*, p. 22. Reardon underlines the pragmatism point: 'Roman Catholic Modernism', pp. 162–3 (Tyrrell) and 168 (Edouard Le Roy).
[91] William Ralph Inge, 'Roman Catholic Modernism', in his *Outspoken Essays* [First Series] (London: Longmans, Green, and Co., 1919), chapter VI.
[92] Petre (ed.), *George Tyrrell's Letters*, p. 28.
[93] Tyrrell, *Christianity at the Crossroads*, p. 63.
[94] Ibid., p. 82.

from Samuel Taylor Coleridge's *Confessions of an Inquiring Spirit* (1840) to support the argument that it is the intrinsic spiritual vitality of the Scriptures that gives them their authority for us – and then Tyrrell applies this equally and by analogy to the church's theological tradition and – here's the leap – to a putative future repertoire of symbols of transcendence.[95] Given the demanding process of the translation or transformation of inherited vital symbols, Tyrrell believes that the church could survive the critical-historical revolution. It could continue to be seen as 'a mystery and sacrament; like the humanity of Christ of which it is an extension', and this would prove to be 'the true Catholicism'.[96] The church would be 'an art-school of Divine majesty'.[97] However, with the Tyrrell scholar Nicholas Sagovsky, I am not convinced that Tyrrell 'solved the question of the cognitive significance of the symbols'.[98] What he projects on to the screen of the Christian future remains aspirational, dreamy and frankly nebulous. The question of the revitalization, rebirth or recreation of Christian symbols remains as a major challenge on the theological agenda – one not unrelated to the question of the essence of Christianity which lies beyond the scope of this present work.

Unending development

Tyrrell had no doubt that change and development were all-pervasive in Christianity, as elsewhere, and that they were unambiguously brought to light by critical-historical research. Tyrrell had freely translated, with considerable improvisation and what he regarded as improvement, a riposte to the encyclical *Pascendi* by Ernesto Buonaiuti, an apologia for what the encyclical dubbed 'Modernism'. In *The Programme of Modernism* Buonaiuti/Tyrrell claimed that 'modernism' was not the fruit of the influence of immanentist philosophy on Christian theology, as the Roman authorities tended to claim, but the result of prolonged wrestling with the findings of biblical and historical research. By careful exposition of the historical-critical method – of which both Vatican officials and almost all bishops of the Roman Church were culpably ignorant – Buonaiuti/Tyrrell showed that 'everything in the history of Christianity has changed – doctrine, hierarchy, worship'.[99] This claim was the antithesis of the traditional, official position. As Tyrrell puts it in his last book: 'According to the orthodox theory, as defended by [Bishop] Bossuet [1627-1704], as assumed by the Councils and the Fathers, the doctrines and essential institutions of the Catholic Church have been always and identically the same.' The rationale for this ecclesiological uniformitarianism was this:

> The whole dogmatic, sacramental and hierarchical system, as it now stands, was delivered in detail by Christ to His Apostles and by them to their successors. He proclaimed, not the very words, but the very substance in all detail of the doctrines

[95] Tyrrell, *Through Scylla and Charybdis*, pp. 66–71.
[96] Tyrrell to von Hügel, 9 April 1909, cited Nicholas Sagovsky, *On God's Side: A Life of George Tyrrell* (Oxford: Oxford University Press, 1990), pp. 255–7.
[97] Tyrrell, *The Church and the Future* (edition of 1910), cited Reardon, *Roman Catholic Modernism*, p. 44.
[98] Sagovsky, *Between Two Worlds*, p. 147.
[99] Sagovsky, *On God's Side*, pp. 230–1.

of [the Council of] Trent and the [First] Vatican [Council]. He instituted the papacy, the episcopate, the seven sacraments. The Immaculate Conception of Mary was familiar . . . to the Apostles.[100]

Tyrrell's indictment was no exaggeration: in 1904 – and to the acute embarrassment of the educated Roman Catholic world – Pius X had taught in that 'the Hebrew patriarchs were familiar with the doctrine of the Immaculate Conception, and found consolation in the thought of Mary in the solemn moments of their life.'[101] Tyrrell himself commented to Wilfred Ward that the belief of some of their contemporaries that Christ 'said the first "Mass"' at the Last Supper and that St Paul 'paid triennial visits *ad limina*' to the Holy See were merely survivals of 'what was once universally held'.[102]

As the idea of ecclesiastical immutability became increasingly untenable in the light of historical research, it was modified to state that the developed doctrine and practice of the church was *logically implied* in earlier stages, even though it had not been either said or done at that time. So Newman proposes, in *The Development of Christian Doctrine*, that even though the apostles or Fathers might not have articulated certain dogmas themselves, they would have recognized and embraced them if they had been put to them. 'Thus, the holy Apostles would know without words all the truths concerning the high doctrines of theology, which controversialists after them have piously and charitably reduced to formulae, and developed through argument.' And Justin Martyr, Irenaeus, Athanasius and so on would have 'an intense feeling' about matters that would later be articulated in doctrine.[103] As Tyrrell puts it: 'Thus St Augustine, St Anselm, St Bernard, St Thomas, while, explicitly denying, implicitly believed the Immaculate Conception of Mary.'[104] He is scathing about this tactic: 'If a man is said to believe and admit, in spite of his explicit denial, all that is objectively implied by his data, then every avowed atheist is a theist, and every heretic orthodox.'[105] No, a theory of development that is designed to maximize continuity and minimize discontinuity involves 'a torturing of texts and documents incompatible with any sort of historical sincerity'.[106] It was merely 'architectural' development, building dogma on top of dogma, while true development was 'organic', the outworking of the inner dynamism of the tradition.[107]

---

[100] Tyrrell, *Christianity at the Crossroads*, p. 32.
[101] Cited in 'What We Want: An Open Letter to Pius X from a Group of Priests', trans. A. L. Lilley (1907): wikisource.org/wiki/What_We_Want:_An_Open_Letter_to_Pius_X_from_a_Group_of_ Priests. However, no encyclical, of Pius X is listed anywhere for 27 October 1904.
[102] Petre (ed.), *George Tyrrell's Letters*, p. 73.
[103] John Henry Newman, *An Essay on the Development of Christian Doctrine, The Edition of 1845*, pp. 138–9.
[104] Tyrrell, *Christianity at the Crossroads*, p. 36.
[105] Ibid., p. 36.
[106] Ibid., p. 40.
[107] Tyrrell, *Through Scylla and Charybdis*, chapter V: 'Semper Eadem II'.

Tyrrell and Newman

John Henry Newman was Tyrrell's foil in several respects; we find him continually engaging in mental dialogue with Newman (who had died in 1890). Tyrrell asserts that Newman preferred to ignore what was happening in German scholarship in his lifetime. He points out that (unlike Tyrrell himself) Newman did not read German. He notes that there had been less scholarly traffic between England and Germany than there is 'now'. Then German critics could be disregarded as rationalists and infidels who disagreed with each other anyway and would probably self-destruct, while the faithful in both countries were unlikely to be affected. But, as a matter of fact, Tyrrell asserts, the results of New Testament criticism were more 'assured' than conservatives like Newman had persuaded themselves, and had now reached even railway bookstalls.[108] (If any theologian was going to see his books on station bookstalls, it was Tyrrell.)

Although Tyrrell chose to play down his debt to Newman, he had read and re-read key texts of Newman's several times, particularly the essay on the development of doctrine and the later *Essay in Aid of a Grammar of Assent*.[109] Putting these two influences together fuelled Tyrrell's quest for the elusive, intuitively grasped 'idea', 'spirit', 'essence' or 'life' of Christianity, embodied or incarnated in Jesus Christ,[110] the creative impulse that was continually manifesting itself in fresh forms in relation to a changing intellectual environment.[111] He seized on Newman's concept of 'complex inductive inference' in the *Grammar of Assent*. He believed that the Roman guardians of orthodoxy had been misled by the fact that Newman spoke of Christianity as the development of an 'idea', since for them ideas meant 'intellectual concepts, universals, definitions, from which a doctrinal system could be deduced syllogistically'.[112] Tyrrell could also have pointed out that Newman's use of 'idea' was located in the tradition of Samuel Taylor Coleridge, especially in his book *On the Constitution of the Church and State, According to the Idea of Each* (1829).[113] Tyrrell insisted that Newman's notion of development was biological and organic, not logical and deductive ('dialectical'), and that this is what makes Newman 'modern'. Here I think he was giving Newman some benefit of the doubt, because 'Logical sequence' is one of Newman's seven 'tests' (i.e. in the first edition, 1845; in the second edition, 1878, the 'tests' become 'notes') of true development, even though Newman insists that the sequence is not deductive but probative.[114]

---

[108] Tyrrell, *Christianity at the Crossroads*, p. 44.
[109] See Nicholas Sagovsky, "'Frustration, Disillusion and Enduring Filial Respect': George Tyrrell's Debt to John Henry Newman', in Weaver (ed.), *Newman and the Modernists*, chapter 5. See also Tyrrell's assessment of Newman in his 'Introduction' to Henri Bremond, *The Mystery of Newman*, trans. H. C. Corrance (London: Williams and Norgate, 1907), pp. 1–16.
[110] Expounded at length in George Tyrrell, *Lex Credendi* (London: Longmans, Green, and Co., 1906), part I, 'The Spirit of Christ'.
[111] Reardon, *Roman Catholic Modernism*, pp. 45–6.
[112] Tyrrell, *Christianity at the Crossroads*, p. 41.
[113] Samuel Taylor Coleridge, *On the Constitution of the Church and State, According to the Idea of Each*, ed. John Colmer, *The Collected Works of Samuel Taylor Coleridge*, General Editor Kathleen Coburn (Princeton, NJ: Princeton University Press; London: Routledge and Kegan Paul, 1976), vol. 10. See John Coulson, *Newman and the Common Tradition: A Study in the Language of Church and Society* (Oxford: Clarendon Press, 1970).
[114] Newman, *An Essay on the Development of Christian Doctrine, The Edition of 1845*, pp. 136–41.

Tyrrell claims that Newman shows that theology and revelation must be distinguished: theology evolves, revelation is unchanging; theology is a human work, revelation is a divine gift. We respond to revelation experientially; it is poetic or prophetic in character and evokes devotion, and devotion is prior to theology. To claim that the church's theology has never changed is 'preposterous', Tyrrell insists. The content of revelation 'is not a statement, but an "idea" – embodied, perhaps, in certain statements and institutions, but not exhausted by them'. It is this embodiment that is susceptible to development, 'but the animating "idea" is the same under all the variety of its manifestations and embodiments'. The idea is a teleological force, 'a concrete end whose realization is the term of a process of action and endeavour'. Thus, it is the institutions and formulas that develop, but not the revealed idea, not 'the Faith'.[115] As Tyrrell explained in a letter to von Hügel, 'I am driven to a revolutionary view of dogma. . . . I distinguish sharply between the Christian revelation and the theology that rationalizes and explains it.' He continued:

> The former [revelation] was the work of the inspired era of origins. It is prophetic in form and sense; it involves an idealised reading of history past and to come. It is, so to say, an inspired construction of things in the interests of religion; a work of inspired imagination, not of reflection and reasoning. It does not develop or change like theology; but is the subject matter of theology.[116]

Where is divine revelation?

The magisterium of his church, Tyrrell believed, had an inveterate tendency to identify its official theological statements with divine revelation itself. It prioritized the human formula over the divine experience that gave rise to it, thus sidelining the living power of the truth. He parodied this position as 'the intellectualist notion of Faith as an assent to mental puzzles on the strength of divine testimony'.[117] Authoritative formulations have been consistently substituted for the revelatory experiences that they symbolize.[118] Tyrrell insists that God is not known through propositions, but only in immediate experience.[119]

Revelation, for Tyrrell, was not a set of supernaturally imparted propositions, held within the custody of an ecclesiastical hierarchy, but a living experience that had the power to generate vital responses in every generation.[120] Revelation itself is not susceptible to development, any more than poetry or art is, so it should not be identified with the official theology or doctrine.[121] The 'deposit of faith' of which official Roman theology made much, was not revealed, because revelation was inaccessible to

---

[115] Tyrrell, *Christianity at the Crossroads*, pp. 42–3, 59, 77. See also Oliver P. Rafferty (ed.), *George Tyrrell and Catholic Modernism* (Dublin: Four Courts Press, 2010), esp. chapters 1 (Rafferty) and 3 (Andrew Pierce).
[116] Petre (ed.), *George Tyrrell's Letters*, p. 57.
[117] Tyrrell, *Essays on Faith and Immortality*, p. 3.
[118] Ibid., p. 25.
[119] Ibid.
[120] Tyrrell, *Through Scylla and Charybdis*, pp. 204ff.
[121] Ibid., pp. 295–6.

all except its original recipients, and must change through time and circumstance.[122] This creative restructuring of religious experience, and its effect on life, was the motive power of development in religion. 'Duly controlled by the critical conscience [,] it is the chief instrument of theological progress, of those epoch-making, harmonizing hypotheses, which are hardly distinguishable from revelations except as the laboured products of talent are from the sudden inspirations of genius.' The basic landscape of Christian doctrine remained, but its provenance was evacuated of infallible divine authority. 'The leading ideas of Catholic dogma, the ground-plan of its construction of the supernatural world, have been more or less consciously divined by the inventive faculty, inspired by the Spirit of Christian Love.'[123]

Embracing 'modernity'

Tyrrell went well beyond both Newman's and von Hügel's ideas of development, embracing an evolutionary concept of change without limit and without end. Whatever came along as the historical process unfolded was to be engaged with, even embraced. Faith was a great adventure, without security and without guarantees. Thus, Tyrrell accepted the validity of 'modernity' and the designation 'modernist', which he defined as 'a churchman, of any sort, who believes in the possibility of a synthesis between the essential truth of his religion and the essential truth of modernity'.[124] In practice, this meant for Roman Catholics (Tyrrell's consistent term) the reconciliation of their Catholicism with the accepted facts of historical criticism. Indeed, he is specific that the hoped for synthesis would be 'between the essentials of Christianity and the assured results of criticism'.[125] Criticism showed that Jesus was not infallible or omniscient.[126] While the 'personality' of Jesus remained the inspiration, he was no longer looking for the foundation of the church in the explicit words and deeds of Jesus of Nazareth. He was not looking to the past at all. His faith was ultimately grounded in the (divinely bestowed) creative capacity of the spiritual imagination.

George Tyrrell's quest had been to effect a reconciliation between Christian belief and modern thought (which he expressed in very similar words to those of Charles Gore in introducing the symposium *Lux Mundi* in 1889). The cutting edge of modern thought was historical – and above all, biblical – criticism. But at the end of his life, Tyrrell wrote, 'My own work — which I regard as done — has been to raise a question which I have failed to answer.' Intriguingly, Tyrrell continued: 'I am not so conceited as to conclude that it is therefore unanswerable. And I think it may be the destiny of the Church of England to answer it.'[127]

---

122 Ibid., chapter IV on 'the deposit of faith'.
123 Tyrrell, *Essays on Faith and Immortality*, pp. 119–20, cited Reardon, *Roman Catholic Modernism*, p. 146. See also Tyrrell, *Through Scylla and Charybdis*, chapter VII, esp. p. 285: 'Revelation consists in the total religious experience and not simply in the mental [i.e. cognitive] element of the experience.'
124 Tyrrell, *Christianity at the Crossroads*, p. 26.
125 Ibid., p. 19.
126 Tyrrell, *Essays on Faith and Immortality*, chapter III.
127 Petre (ed.), *George Tyrrell's Letters*, p. 119. Cf. in the same letter (p. 118): 'Possibly the Church of England may be able to accept the results of history, and yet retain the substance of her Catholicism, i.e. she may have room for Modernism.'

I will conclude this section on Tyrrell – and make a link with the following chapter, on the foundation of the church in Anglican theology – by quoting from Michael Ramsey. 'The crushing of this movement [Roman Catholic Modernism] by Papal authority did not rob it of its significance for theology or of its influence upon Anglican thought.'[128] Ramsey singles out von Hügel as the favourite Roman Catholic theologian of Anglicans before the Second World War. Von Hügel, said Ramsey, 'influenced Anglicans so greatly because his teaching was congruous with that unity of theology and worship [that is] always latent in our tradition.'[129]

Karl Rahner, S. J.

For Karl Rahner, S. J. (1904–84), as he expressed the matter in the last decade of his life, the central problem of ecclesiology is the question of 'the provenance of the Church'. To quote Rahner more fully, it is the question of 'the provenance of the Church from Jesus of Nazareth, the crucified and risen Christ, and the question of the foundation of the Church by the same Jesus Christ'.[130] Rahner's way of posing the issue here in 1980, towards the end of his life, shows that, as far as he is concerned, this 'great, difficult and complex subject', which was neglected (as Rahner notes: p. 19) in traditional Roman Catholic scholastic fundamental theology, almost equates to ecclesiology tout court. It is the presupposition of all further ecclesiological investigations; it dominates our ecclesiological discourse; it is inconceivable that we should not start with this question. For the reasons that I have outlined in Chapter 1, I share Rahner's sense of the priority, the overriding importance of the question of the 'provenance' of the church because it takes us to the heart of the question of the connection between the church and Jesus Christ – the relationship between the two greatest empirical 'givens' of theology. There can be no more crucial question for ecclesiology to wrestle with. Ecclesiology first and foremost concerns the provenance, the 'whence?', of the church. Only when we have asked and begun to answer the question of the provenance, source or origin of the church as it exists empirically in history can we go on to ask the question that inevitably follows: What is the connection between the church and Jesus Christ *today*?

Rahner breaks down the historical question – namely whether the church has its provenance in specific actions of 'the historically tangible Jesus' – into two parts: the possible founding of the church by Jesus before the Easter event, or the possible founding of the church by Jesus after Easter. In other words, we have to consider (according to Rahner) whether the church was founded by Jesus of Nazareth in his ministry up to (shall we say) Good Friday, or whether it was perhaps founded by the

---

[128] Arthur Michael Ramsey, *From Gore to Temple: The Development of Anglican Theology between Lux Mundi and the Second World War 1889-1939; The Hale Memorial Lectures of Seabury-Western Theological Seminary, 1959* (London: Longmans, 1960), p. 63.

[129] Ibid., p. 59.

[130] Karl Rahner and Wilhelm Thüsing, *A New Christology*, trans. David Smith and Verdant Green (London: Search Press, 1980 [1972]); new material by Rahner in this edition, p. 18. Further page references are embedded in my main text. The phrase 'provenance from' is not normal or good English.

risen Christ at some moment or series of moments from Easter Day onwards (p. 19)? Of course, one could point out that to have recourse to the post-Easter Jesus for the 'historical' foundation of the church is actually to move beyond the normally accepted parameters of historical enquiry based on measurable criteria of causality, continuity and uniformity, and to impinge on the specifically theological approach to the question of provenance.

Rahner sets down two presuppositions of the constructive argument that he will develop, which are derived from critical biblical research. Such research has unequivocally established, he believes, (a) Jesus' imminent expectation of the kingdom of God (which was not fulfilled in the way that he expected), but which would have made the founding of the institutional church pointless and irrelevant; and (b) the fluidity and diversity of the New Testament picture of the church, which strongly suggests that the early Christians did not believe that Jesus had mandated a specific form of the church (and, as we have noted before, Jesus could not have founded the church as an historical act without specifying a particular form or shape of the church – that is, he could not have founded a church merely in principle (pp. 21–3). These two aspects of the New Testament evidence make the conclusion that Jesus 'did not found a church' (as Rahner baldly puts it) difficult to avoid.

In response to this unavoidable conclusion, Rahner proposes to see the church as the historical–social embodiment of the effectual work of salvation that had been wrought by Jesus. Here he appeals to the Pauline concept of the 'body of Christ', which he interprets as postulating the church as 'the fundamental sacrament of salvation or the continuing presence of the eschatological act of salvation brought about by Jesus Christ' (p. 19). To put it another way, 'the church comes from the death and resurrection of Jesus' as an expression of 'the lasting eschatological value of the crucified and risen Christ', because in those acts God's 'definitive self-communication finally appeared' (p. 24). In the purposes of God, the church is the historical–social vehicle for the ongoing proclamation and communication of Christ's saving victory (pp. 26–7). In that sense, God's salvific purpose requires the church; God needs the church. As Francis Schüssler Fiorenza starkly puts it in a helpful explication of Rahner's argument, the church must be the church if Christ is to be Christ.[131]

In *Foundations of Christian Faith* (ET 1978), a slightly more discursive and less programmatic statement of his position, Rahner typically poses our question in a subtle – one might even say, ambiguous – way. The question becomes: '[W]hy and to what extent the church was founded by the historical and risen Jesus.'[132] Rahner insists that it is vital to hold that the church originated with Jesus. The alternative would be to say that the church is a human construction, the autonomous product of merely human action – actually self-originating and self-validating – which is unthinkable. Such a position would destroy the integrity of the church as the body of Christ. The church must – *a priori* – result from the action of Jesus Christ.[133] In the light of the

[131] Francis Schüssler Fiorenza, *Foundational Theology: Jesus and the Church* (New York: Crossroad, 1984), pp. 93–5.
[132] Karl Rahner, *Foundations of Christian Faith* (London: Darton, Longman & Todd, 1978), p. 326.
[133] Ibid., p. 329.

imminent eschatological horizon of the New Testament, which Rahner fully accepts, claims for the divine origin of the church are constrained. He finds himself unable to affirm that the essential structures and polity of the Roman Catholic Church – the episcopate and the papacy – can be traced back directly to the words or deeds of the historical Jesus. Papacy and episcopacy need a different rationale.

On the other hand – and now we come to Rahner's constructive or re-constructive argument – the fact of the kingdom's presence in history entails 'a people of God and a people of salvation who form the kingdom, for this kingdom is an event which God's salvific will brings about precisely by the fact that he gathers a people of believers'.[134] Rahner also thinks that Jesus expected a period of time to elapse between his death and the coming of the kingdom in its fullness – an interval in which the community could begin to be gathered.[135] He accepts without overt investigation the authenticity of Mt. 16:18 and one of his less subtle arguments is that Jesus must have intended the church because he commissioned Simon Peter to be the 'rock' on which he would build his church and gave him the keys of the kingdom.[136] Having characteristically paid lip service to official Roman Catholic dogma (that the popes are the successors of Peter as head of the church and are endowed with what is presumed to have been Christ's authority), Rahner's tactics then take a twofold course.

First, Rahner argues that there is a genetic connection between the historical polity or structures of later Roman Catholicism, particularly the papacy and the historic episcopate, on the one hand, and the developments of the formative period of the early church, on the other. In the apostolic and post-apostolic era, the Christian community took certain critical, formative and irreversible decisions – for example, concerning the canon of Scripture. Other decisions of this kind concerned the structures of pastoral authority of the church. Such decisions became constitutive of the church, in the sense that they came to form part of its permanent identity, an identity that originated with the death and resurrection of Jesus; the empirical church rests on these structures. The history of the early church (to look no further) is a history of decisions.[137] So it can truly be said that these structures originated with Jesus of Nazareth, though he did not formally and intentionally institute them.[138] However, Rahner does not really explain why some decisions should be permanent and irreversible and others not.

Secondly, Rahner sets out the sort of *a priori* argument at which he excelled, drawing out what is logically entailed in uncontroversial theological axioms – theological truisms, in fact – to show that the salvation announced by Jesus entailed a corporate dimension: 'the full and historically actualized Christianity of God's self-communication is an ecclesial Christianity'. The social or ecclesial character of Christianity corresponds to an essential characteristic of human nature, namely that it is grounded in interpersonal communication. Religion therefore cannot be based on individual subjectivity, mere interiority, but must (Rahner proposes) confront us

[134] Ibid., p. 327.
[135] Ibid., p. 328.
[136] Ibid., pp. 333–5.
[137] Ibid., p. 330.
[138] Karl Rahner, 'The Church's Redemptive Historical Provenance from the Death and Resurrection of Jesus', in *TI* (London: Darton, Longman & Todd, 1984), vol. XIX, pp. 24–38.

with objective authority vested in an ordered community that endures in history. Thus, Rahner is able to claim with assurance that the hierarchical church, with an authoritative (and under certain conditions, infallible) teaching office (magisterium), 'springs from the very essence of Christianity'.[139] Has Rahner answered the question he set himself, regarding the provenance or founding of the church by Jesus Christ, or has he in fact moved the goalposts? As often with Rahner, it is the theological journey, not the arrival that is most rewarding.

Edward Schillebeeckx

Edward Schillebeeckx (1914–2009), on the other hand, abandoned even Rahner's subtle and sophisticated reinterpretation of the traditional doctrine of the institution of the church by divine law or divine right (*ius divinum*). Schillebeeckx points out that it is clear, historically speaking, that Jesus of Nazareth did not intend to found a new religion or even a new community. He addressed Israel, the whole of Israel (symbolized by the twelve apostles), and the earliest Christians were conscious of being simply a special community within the fold of the Jewish church. It is, he says, 'historically untenable' and 'a sign of ideological fundamentalism' to claim, as many Christians still do, that the historical forms of the church can be derived from Jesus' own institution, and that the shape that the historical growth of the church took represents a necessary development willed by God.[140] To say even that much was to pose a direct challenge to the traditional and official position of the Roman Catholic Church. But, according to Schillebeeckx, there is more to be said. Jesus most certainly did intend that faith in his message should lead to a life of discipleship, a discipleship lived in community. So Schillebeeckx rather cryptically asserts that 'the historical phenomenon which calls itself the Church of Christ is a divine foundation by Jesus for humankind.' In other words, he seems to be saying: 'Although we cannot claim that the church was founded *by* Jesus, we can at least insist that the church is founded *on* Jesus.'[141]

In his earlier work *Jesus: An Experiment in Christology* (1974), Schillebeeckx develops another, complementary and subtle line of reflection about Jesus of Nazareth's connection to the later church. Against the background of his consistent, compassionate table fellowship and solidarity with 'sinners', outcasts and others who found themselves alienated from general Jewish society, that is, the community of faith, Jesus at the Last Supper gives the cup to his disciples as a pledge of continued fellowship with him in the kingdom or reign of God in a future beyond death. Their fellowship and discipleship with him will be resumed, not in heaven, as we might assume, but in the coming kingdom on this earth. The promise of Jesus is that death may – and actually

---

[139] Rahner, *Foundations of Christian Faith*, pp. 322–44.
[140] Schillebeeckx, *Church: The Human Story of God*, pp. 155–7.
[141] Louis Bouyer discusses this question in the chapter 'From the Jewish Qahal to the Christian Ecclesia', in *Liturgical Piety* (Notre Dame, IN: Notre Dame University Press, 1955). Even at that date, a Roman Catholic scholar, loyal to the magisterium, prefers to avoid the historical question ('Did Jesus found the church?') in favour of the theological approach that sees the church as the assembly of those called together by God's word in the present time.

will – interrupt their fellowship with him, but it will not bring that fellowship to an end. '[T]he coming of God's rule remains linked to fellowship with Jesus of Nazareth . . . fellowship with Jesus is stronger than death.'[142] We may extrapolate a little from what Schillebeeckx himself says in this way: the essence of that fellowship or communion with Jesus, that he promises his disciples and pledges to them in the cup at the Last Supper, is precisely discipleship. And this means following him in life, being taught by him day and night, in order that they might witness to him, proclaiming him in word and deed. Since the church understands itself as the community of his disciples, continuing through history, in that sense and to that extent Jesus foresaw and intended the church – though not of course the church as we know it. I think that Schillebeeckx would accept that, for that complex, diverse, chaotic and contradictory historical process, that we call church history, to be reconciled with Jesus' minimal intentions, other theological constructs are needed, particularly those concerned with providence, development, the essence of Christianity and the work of the Holy Spirit through word and sacrament.

George Tavard and Richard McBrien

George Tavard (1922–2007), the prolific Roman Catholic historical theologian and ecumenist, seemed to side with Schillebeeckx in adopting a radically minimalist interpretation of Jesus' intentions for the community. 'In no way', asserts Tavard, 'can the institution of the Church as a social and spiritual entity be traced directly to the recorded words of Jesus.' Tavard concedes that 'the formation of a distinct community by his followers did correspond to Jesus' intent. But that such an intent was explicitly formulated in his teaching is a much more hazardous proposition.' So, for Tavard, the idea that Jesus actually 'instituted' the church has to be taken 'with a grain of salt.'[143] However, Tavard points out that the fact of the church is now a 'given' of the Christian life; we accept that it is 'there'; we work with it and within it, so we can set to one side the question that was so urgent and unavoidable for Rahner, concerning the 'provenance' of the church. But is Tavard's pragmatic position really adequate?

Richard McBrien's impressive synthesis *Catholicism* deals rather tersely or cryptically, but without apparent equivocation, with our question. If we are looking for an explicit, deliberate act whereby Jesus 'established a new religious organization', McBrien asserts, we will search in vain. Any direct 'founding' would have meant setting up a rival synagogue and would have undermined his call and proclamation to all Israel. But if we accept (McBrien suggests) that 'founding' the church may mean laying the foundations for the future church in various rather indirect ways, we can see that the church indeed has its *origin* in Jesus. McBrien seems to be saying that Jesus laid the foundations for the future church in three ways: (a) by gathering his disciples around

---

[142] Edward Schillebeeckx, *Jesus: An Experiment in Christology*, trans. Hubert Hoskins (New York: Seabury Press; London: Collins, 1979 [1974]), pp. 306–12, at p. 308.

[143] George Tavard, *The Church, Community of Salvation: An Ecumenical Ecclesiology* (Collegeville, MN: Liturgical Press, 1992), pp. 31, 50.

him; (b) by anticipating an interim period between his death and the *parousia*, a space in which something could develop; and (c) by preparing and instructing his disciples to stay together after the crucifixion and resurrection in the expectation that a new thing would come about – which turned out to be the descent of the Holy Spirit. These three factors enable us, McBrien affirms, to conclude that 'there never was a churchless period in the New Testament following the resurrection.' The church emerges into history in continuity with the mission and destiny of Jesus. How tenuous that historical continuity actually might turn out to be, is not a question that McBrien goes into.[144]

Hans Küng

Hans Küng (1928–), in his great work of ecclesiology *The Church* (ET 1968) takes his starting point, like others, from an exegesis of Jesus' proclamation of the imminent approach of the kingdom within an exchatological framework. But, in my opinion, Küng offers a more satisfying synthesis than the other modern Roman Catholic scholars whom we have mentioned. He sets out his case in four terse propositions.[145]

1. During his earthly ministry Jesus did not found a church. He addressed his message to Israel as a totality, seeking to gather the whole people. He did not call individuals out of the community; even the Twelve were simply representative of the twelve tribes of Israel. He did not form his followers into a society separate from the Jewish temple and synagogues. Before the crucifixion and resurrection, there could not have been any thought of a church. Talk of a church coming into being is a post-Easter phenomenon, lacking any explicit basis in the preaching of Jesus.
2. Jesus' preaching and ministry did, however, lay the foundations for the emergence of a post-resurrection church. He expected his followers to gather together around the common meal and to suffer similar persecution to his own from the Jewish religious leaders.
3. The church has been in existence from the time that faith in the resurrection was born. As soon as his followers 'gathered together in faith in the resurrection of the crucified Jesus of Nazareth and in expectation of the coming consummation of the reign of God and the return of the risen Christ in glory, the Church came into existence.'[146]
4. The origin of the church lies in the whole history of Jesus' life and ministry, in the entire action of God in Jesus' birth, ministry, calling of the disciples, crucifixion, resurrection and the sending of the Holy Spirit upon the community. The total Christ event gives birth, by a natural and inevitable process, to the church.

---

[144] Richard McBrien, *Catholicism*, 3rd edn (London: Geoffrey Chapman, 1994), pp. 577–9.
[145] Hans Küng, *The Church* (London: Search Press, 1968 [1967]), pp. 72–9. In *On Being a Christian* (London: Collins, 1977), Küng places more emphasis on the crucifixion, seeing it as the defining event of Christ's destiny and identity, but without playing down the resurrection.
[146] Küng, *The Church*, p. 75.

In Küng's holistic way of looking at our question, the total Christ event that takes place within history must necessarily generate a corresponding social and communal outcome, also within history. But that New Testament community was not recognizably what the church became in the historical process. So it fits with Küng's approach to the question of the founding of the church that he should have been one of the most radical reforming voices, campaigning consistently for his church to return to the comparative simplicity of the primitive church in terms of ministry, dogma and authority.

Francis Schüssler Fiorenza

A former student of Karl Rahner and J. B. Metz, Francis Schüssler Fiorenza (b. 1941) is another Roman Catholic theologian who faces head on our two (related) central questions, 'Did Jesus of Nazareth found the church as an historical act?' and 'Did Jesus want and intend the church?' Fiorenza places these questions (as does this present book) firmly within the business of fundamental theology or, as he aptly calls it, 'Foundational Theology'. The title of the main work in which Fiorenza addresses these issues is *Foundational Theology*; the subtitle is *Jesus and the Church*.[147] So, in this present book, I am pursuing a similar agenda to Fiorenza. We will need to see quite shortly whether Fiorenza is able to answer satisfactorily the questions that he has set himself (and by the same token, whether I am able, by the end of this book, to answer the same questions myself!).

At one point Fiorenza poses the issue like this: Is ecclesial Christianity a legitimate continuation of Jesus' vision and praxis? (p. 59). I find that a rather intriguing, if not teasing, formulation for several reasons. (a) 'Ecclesial Christianity' is really a tautology because Christianity has not existed in the world, in history, except in 'ecclesial' form, namely as the church or the churches. But the phrase underlines the point that we are talking about the church, not merely about ideas floating in the ether. This is an *ecclesiastical* question. (b) The 'legitimacy' of ecclesial Christianity (taking 'legitimacy' in its metaphorical rather than literal juridical sense) can be decided only by theological enquiry and argument (and that is exactly what Fiorenza does very well). But then it becomes more clearly the question of the *theological validity* of ecclesial Christianity. (c) 'Continuity' is good framework for addressing the question of Jesus and the church, but what kind of continuity are we looking for? Clearly, there is some historical continuity between Jesus and the apostles, on the one hand, and the beginnings of the church in a recognizable form at the end of the first century, on the other. But that raises the question of the *development* of doctrine and practice and therefore the possibility within such a trajectory of radical development, that is to say *discontinuity*. (d) The question whether we actually know enough about the 'vision' of Jesus is at the heart of this whole enquiry (hence the connection with the 'quest' or 'quests' of the historical Jesus) and cannot be addressed by theologians (specifically, ecclesiologists) without turning to specialized historico-critical research by New Testament scholars (which is

---

[147] Fiorenza, *Foundational Theology*; page references to this work are embedded in my main text.

why, in my first chapter 'Jesus and the Church', I have summarized the main findings of research on this matter that have emerged during the past century and more, before going on, in this second half of the book, to look at the *theological* responses that have been put forward within the major Christian traditions). But we probably know more about the practice of Jesus than of his mind or consciousness so – to the extent that his practice reflected his vision, his intentions – I agree with Fiorenza that the *praxis* of Jesus is our main source of evidence.

Fiorenza is appropriately cautious about any appeal to the intentions of Jesus. He points out that it accords with the hermeneutics of the Romantic and Idealist traditions to ask, What did Jesus intend by gathering disciples, giving the Last Supper and so on? What was his meaning in this? Fiorenza recalls the insistence of such modern hermeneutical theorists as H.-G. Gadamer and Paul Ricoeur that meaning resides in the interaction of the text and the reader or interpreter. Since the words and deeds of Jesus are mediated to us (to the church) by the Gospels and so by the four Evangelists who wrote or compiled the Gospels that bear their names, we do not have direct access to them (pp. 108–09). Fiorenza is also aware that 'institution' is a modern concept, a construction, stemming from the fantasies of Romanticism about the deeds of great men (*sic*), the superhuman heroes of history. But the fact is that institutions develop a life of their own which evolves over time and may move away from whatever their founders envisaged for them. So the notion of the 'founder' of any institution is inherently problematical. The effect of an action (which may actually be a speech) – and therefore its 'meaning' – always goes well beyond the original intention of the actor or agent (pp. 110–11) and this applies to the church too.

What are Fiorenza's constructive proposals? Indebted to Rahner's theological method generally and to his argument in *A New Christology* (1980) in particular, Fiorenza deploys transcendental or *a priori* principles to establish the connection between the church and Jesus. Basically, the church must be the church if Jesus is to be Christ (p. 95). In a manner reminiscent of Paul Tillich, Fiorenza seems to be arguing (soundly enough) that Jesus can only be the Christ as he is believed in to be such by his people. His mission will fail unless he is *received* as the Christ. But the church is the 'place' where Christ is 'received', where he is acknowledged to be the Christ, the Messiah, the promised Saviour. And the church necessarily has historical and social dimensions (as Rahner typically insisted). So it follows that it belongs within the purposes of God, the divine economy, that the church should exist, that there should indeed be a church on earth. As a society within history, the church continues the self-communication of God in Jesus Christ, so becoming, like Jesus himself in his humanity, the symbolization of God's salvific will for humankind. Thus, there is a functional continuity, in the service of God's salvific work, between Jesus and the church, though a leap of faith is still needed to bridge the gap between them. While we cannot claim that Jesus founded the church, let alone the ministry and the sacraments, by any specific historical actions, we can affirm that the church is 'grounded' on Jesus and has its 'provenance' in him. The ministry and the sacraments, though not specifically ordained by Jesus, are proper expressions of the nature and essence of the church that depends on him. Thus, the church is connected to Jesus, not by 'external' means, but 'intrinsically' through the experience of salvation that was present in him and is now received precisely through the church with its ministry and sacraments. Just as Jesus in his person and work is the sacrament of God's salvation, so the church, as the channel of his self-communication today, is a sacrament of salvation in the midst of the world (p. 96).

Fiorenza admits that his argument does not resolve the historical questions that surround the relationship of the historical Jesus to the emergence of the church; to do that was not his intention or approach. So the central question remains unanswered: Did Jesus 'want' the church? (pp. 97–8). What Fiorenza has – very suggestively – given us is an approach that centres on *the hermeneutics of reception*. What typically happens within the community of the church is that we receive, interpret, internalize and put into practice what the church mediates to us, especially through word and sacrament, of the salvific significance of Jesus, so that we may become his disciples today. This approach postulates a living, dynamic tradition of interpretation that can be held only within an historical community, that is to say within an institution. It is the dynamic, existential hermeneutics of the reception and the embrace, through faith, of Jesus as the Christ that enables us to acknowledge the church as the sacrament of salvation.

Joseph Ratzinger

Joseph Ratzinger (b. 1927) held, at least from 1968 when he was rather abruptly converted to strongly conservative views, that it was vital to believe that Jesus both intended and founded the church, complete with its ministerial, legal and sacramental structures, with the universal primacy of the pope at its apex. Both as Prefect of the Congregation of the Faith (CDF; 1981–2005) and then as Pope Benedict XVI (2005–13), Ratzinger taught, upheld and enforced this doctrine. He was convinced that the integrity of the church – as a divine society and the authority of the episcopal–papal hierarchy, the magisterium – would be jeopardized if the belief that Jesus intentionally, deliberately and by concrete acts founded the church as a structured, juridical institution were to be called into question. 'If they [the structures of the church] are not willed by Christ', he writes, 'then it is no longer possible to conceive of the existence of the hierarchy as a service to the baptized established by the Lord himself.'[148]

In 1991 Ratzinger reviewed the exegetical history of the problem.[149] He observes that the critical question regarding Jesus' founding of the church arose within 'liberal' (he means Liberal Protestant) exegesis, which 'regards Jesus according to the liberal world picture as the great individualist who liberates religion from cultic institutions and reduces it to ethics, which for its part is founded entirely upon the individual responsibility of conscience' (here he is in effect summarizing Harnack). A Jesus so conceived, Ratzinger continues, who 'repudiates cultic worship' and 'translates religion

---

[148] Joseph Ratzinger, *The Essential Pope Benedict XVI: His Central Writings and Speeches*, ed. John F. Thornton and Susan B. Varenne (New York: Harper Collins, 2007), p. 66.

[149] Joseph Cardinal Ratzinger, *Called to Communion: Understanding the Church Today*, trans. Adrian Walker (San Francisco, CA: Ignatius Press, 1996 [1991]); page references are embedded in my main text.

into morality and then defines it as the business of the individual', obviously could not have founded the church (p. 1). As the enemy of all institutions, according to the liberal–individualistic perspective, Jesus could hardly have wished to found one himself. Ratzinger does not consider the counterargument, which we find most clearly articulated in the theology, teaching and personal life of Karl Rahner, S. J., that one could love liturgical worship, be devoted to the sacramental life, uphold the social and historical pillars of Catholic ecclesiology, yet still insist, on historical-critical grounds, that Jesus did not, as a matter of historical fact, found the church.

After the Second World War, Ratzinger believes that 'the yearning for communion in the sacred was reawakened', even in Protestantism (I think it would be more correct to say 'after World War One'). But the impulse to communion (*communio*) was stifled (Ratzinger claims) by such Protestant scholars as Rudolf Bultmann who, in embracing the eschatological world view of the New Testament, set in opposition the prophetic and the priestly elements in the Bible and depicted Jesus as opposed to cult and ritual and as individualistic in his theology and ethics (p. 17). The same anti-hierarchical, anti-hieratic bias, this time in the form of the economic class struggle, infected Liberation Theology (which had been condemned by Ratzinger and the Congregation for the Doctrine of the Faith in the 1984 'Instruction on Certain Aspects of the "Theology of Liberation"').[150] Divine truth needs to be sifted from such ideological distortion in every age and the key criterion, the touchstone, for Ratzinger, is the deep memory of the church (p. 20). Ratzinger does not consider the possibility that his own stance here may be equally ideologically distorted.

Ratzinger notes that the expression 'the kingdom of God' ('the kingdom of heaven' in Matthew's Gospel) occurs 122 times in the New Testament, of which 99 occurrences are in the Synoptic Gospels, almost all instances there being attributed to Jesus himself. But he opposes the Protestant tendency to play off kingdom against church, and vice versa, for the sound reason that, in Jewish thought, the gathering and cleansing of God's people for the kingdom is part of what the kingdom stands for (pp. 21–2). He refers to Joachim Jeremias' *New Testament Theology* (volume 1) to support the argument that Jesus' very belief that the end was near would have impelled him to gather together the eschatological people of God. In Jesus the 'soon' of John the Baptist and the Qumran Community passes over into the 'now' of New Testament Christology (p. 22). Jesus is in his person the action, the presence and the reign of God. 'Wherever he is, is the Kingdom' (p. 23). But to take this line, Ratzinger continues, is not to marginalize the church because Jesus can never be alone; he cannot be without his people. 'His entire work is thus to gather a new people.' There is a 'dynamic of unification' at work (p. 23). Jesus' favourite image for the community that he gathered around him (Ratzinger rather unusually suggests) was 'the family of God' (p. 23). The request by one disciple that Jesus teach them how to pray 'as John [the Baptist] taught his disciples' (Lk. 11:1) shows, Ratzinger claims (p. 24), that they saw themselves as a new community. (But, as far as we know, John the Baptist's disciples did not see themselves as a new community). However, Ratzinger goes on, it was the Last Supper that decisively signalled the transition from temple worship

---

[150] http://www.vatican.va/roman_curia/congregations/cfaith/documents/rc_con_cfaith_doc_19 840806_theology-liberation_en.html (accessed 28 June 2018).

to worship in communion with Jesus. Thus, Jn 2:21 speaks of 'the temple of his body' (p. 26). The image 'people of God' should not be allowed to become the controlling image of ecclesiology, Ratzinger warns. It needs to be placed under the rubric of *ecclesia*, which forms the spiritual and eschatological centre of the concept of 'people', a people gathered in unity (pp. 31–2). We cannot help noticing that, in Ratzinger's ecclesiology, 'the dynamic of unification' resonates strongly with what we might call 'the dynamic of centralisation', a centralization and concentration of doctrinal authority that, in the pontificates of John Paul II and himself, as Benedict XVI, was underpinned and enforced by juridical sanctions.

For Ratzinger the position of Peter is integral to the original founding of the church. While he disarmingly admits that it would be 'misguided to pounce immediately' on the classic proof text for the Petrine primacy (Mt. 16:13-20), he points out that all the various strata of the New Testament agree on Peter's leading role. This unanimity can be explained, Ratzinger believes, only if Jesus' commission to Peter in Matthew 16 goes back to Jesus himself (pp. 48, 58). But (and here I find Ratzinger's method of argument alarming) the truth of the Matthean text does not depend on the vagaries of historical scholarship, with its short-lived hypotheses, but on the faith of the church that Scripture is God's word, 'the trustworthy ground of our existence' (pp. 58–9). Having forsaken the historical-critical ground that he has mainly traversed until now, Ratzinger's argument suddenly shifts, without explanation or justification, to an apologia for the papacy on the grounds of the (Roman) church's traditional faith. Although he admits that individual popes have given rise to scandal, he nevertheless affirms that the papacy as an institution 'remains the foundation of the Church' (p. 61). I confess that Ratzinger's claim here clashes with the text that has guided my investigation in the present book: 1 Cor. 3:11: 'Other foundation can no one lay than that which God has laid, which is Jesus Christ.'

It can come as no surprise that the Congregation for the Doctrine of the Faith under Cardinal Ratzinger was far from happy with the proposals of the Anglican–Roman Catholic International Commission (ARCIC) with regard to papal primacy. ARCIC's *Final Report* of 1982 reflected an abatement of traditional Roman Catholic claims. ARCIC abandoned the standard Roman Catholic appeal to divine right (*ius divinum*), based on the Petrine texts in Matthew, for the role of a universal primate (the pope), acknowledging that this could not be supported from the New Testament or the very early church. Such claims could not have been accepted by Anglicans anyway. In its place ARCIC proposed an appeal to the providential government of the church which had allowed the office and ministry of the Bishop of Rome to develop over the centuries into that of a universal pastor (as asserted by the First Vatican Council).[151] The 1981 response of the CDF under Cardinal Ratzinger poured liberal doses of cold water on several aspects of the ARCIC report.[152] The claim of the divine institution of the papacy and of the popes as the successors of Peter, with full Petrine powers, is still uncompromisingly maintained in official Roman Catholic teaching. The revolution in

---

[151] Anglican–Roman Catholic International Commission, *The Final Report* (London: CTS/SPCK, 1982), p. 84.
[152] Congregation for the Doctrine of the Faith, 'Observations on the ARCIC Final Report', *Origins* 11 (1982), pp. 752–6.

biblical scholarship that has been gathering speed for more than a century, since the work of Johannes Weiss, Albert Schweitzer and Alfred Loisy (while he was still in the Roman Catholic Church) has not been allowed to impinge on traditional doctrinal positions with regard to the dominical founding of the institutional church with its dominically mandated hierarchical, juridical and sacramental structures.

Leonardo Boff

Leonardo Boff (b. 1938), at the time a priest, a professor and a Franciscan, working in Brazil, a champion of Liberation Theology and of the base communities of Latin America, was a casualty of Joseph Ratzinger's regime of censorship in the CDF, being silenced for a year and banned from teaching as a punishment for expressing critical views of the ecclesiastical establishment.[153] In his explosive and fearless book *Church, Charism and Power: Liberation Theology and the Institutional Church*, published in Portuguese in 1981 and in English in 1985, Boff drew out the consequences of modern historical research and ideological critique for the Roman Catholic Church's structures of authority, focusing particularly on the ambiguous, double-sided nature of the institution.[154] I will attempt to summarize some key aspects of his not entirely logical argument.

The institution of the church is the Christian community in its organizational aspect; its characteristics are hierarchy, sacral powers, dogmas, rites, canon law and hallowed traditions. The institution is theologically and morally ambiguous, so our attitude towards it should be ambivalent. On the one hand, the institutional structure provides vital stability and a sense of identity; it makes for ordered administration and enables the propagation of its message. But the institution serves a higher function; it is not an end in itself. So it must continually be converted to its true, original purpose, which is to serve the Christian community and its mission in the world. If it forgets this original purpose, it becomes 'a ghetto'. The centralization of ecclesial power causes its life to stagnate, fostering passivity, monotony, mechanical responses and a deep sense of alienation among its members. The institutional church can then begin to understand itself ideologically, 'as the epiphany of the promises it safeguards'. What ideology does is to present as natural what is historical, what is necessary what is contingent and as divine what is actually human (p. 72). Institutional 'sclerosis' sets in (pp. 48–9). The key category for interpreting the-church-as-institution is power (*potestas*). The distribution of power in the church is such that the hierarchy is invested with power, while the laity is deprived of it. We are impelled to seek the true power of the church, which derives from its origin, its provenance – and to that it must continually return (pp. 51–8). Boff has learnt from modern, critical Bible study that 'Jesus did not preach the Church but rather the Kingdom of God'. His proclamation of the message included

---

153 Harvey Cox, *The Silencing of Leonardo Boff: The Vatican and the Future of World Christianity* (Oak Park, IL: Meyer-Stone Books, 1988; London: Collins, 1989).

154 Leonardo Boff, *Church, Charism and Power: Liberation Theology and the Institutional Church*, trans. John W. Diercksmeier (New York: Crossroad; London: SCM Press, 1985); page references are in my main text.

liberation for the poor, the advent of comfort, justice, peace, forgiveness and love for those who longed for it (p. 59). The mission of Jesus remains of decisive authority for the church. 'The actions of the humanity of Jesus Christ must remain as the critical norm for the Church built upon them' (p. 61). The church exists for the sake of that kingdom and is therefore provisional and orientated to the future (p. 64). Where does that argument leave the (Roman) Catholic Church?

Boff has learnt from his reading in history and social philosophy that 'Catholicism is the concrete and historical form of Christianity' and of the gospel (pp. 69, 77). To put it another way, the form of Christianity and of the gospel that exists concretely in the world is Catholicism. The New Testament too is an expression of Catholicism, a 'book of the Church'. But there is no hint in the New Testament of the official doctrine that Jesus Christ formally founded the church, commissioning and validating its structures and their powers for all time. For Boff, Catholicism is never monochrome, but internally diverse and continually developing. Just as there are four Gospels, so the Catholicity of the church is multiform, incarnated in the changing circumstances of history, beginning with the New Testament itself (pp. 69–70). 'Catholicism is the *sacramentum* of what is Christian' (p. 78), for it belongs to the nature of a sacrament that there is both identity and non-identity, presence and absence. The institution both represents Christ and obscures him. But when the institution's mediation role is absolutized, pathology sets in, Boff argues. The current concretization of the gospel in the church is merely one particular and contingent mediation of the gospel, and as such it obscures the gospel as well as revealing it. There is identity but also non-identity. Boff insists that critique and reform, such as that represented by the base communities that he was close to, can help to bring the institution back to its true identity.

Walter Kasper

As a senior Vatican official – former president of the Pontifical Council for Promoting Christian Unity – and therefore a pillar of the institution and close to the papacy, as well as a distinguished theologian and ecclesiologist in his own right, Walter Kasper (1933–) is a particularly interesting example of a Roman Catholic scholar grappling with the question of whether Jesus founded (historically) or intended in some sense (theologically) the church.[155] Like almost all other scholars addressing this question, Kasper starts from the proclamation of the kingdom or reign of God by Jesus, who is, in his person, his words and deeds, the embodiment of the kingdom. The kingdom is 'close at hand' precisely because it comes by being proclaimed; Christ's word is a performative proclamation that effects and manifests what it announces (pp. 84–6). There is nothing in the public ministry of Jesus that 'speaks explicitly' of the founding of a church (p. 86), but it may be helpful, Kasper suggests, to look for an implicit ecclesiology. He fully takes on board the eschatological horizon of the Synoptic Gospels that was brought to

---

[155] Walter Kasper, *The Catholic Church: Nature, Reality and Mission*, trans. Thomas Hoebel, ed. R. David Nelson (London and New York: Bloomsbury T&T Clark, 2015); page references in are my main text.

light in the work of Weiss, Schweitzer and Loisy. He recognizes that it is precisely the eschatological framework that generates the question of Jesus and the church. So Kasper poses the challenge in this way: 'How could the apocalyptic charismatic preaching of Jesus become a sacramental-institutionally constituted church?' (p. 87).

The reason why there is no word from Jesus about founding a church is simply and decisively that his mission was to 'the lost sheep of the house of Israel' (Mt. 10:6; cf. 9:36). The calling of the Twelve does not point, at that stage, to a universal mission, but simply reinforces the mission focus on Israel (p. 87). Kasper is unwilling to appeal to Matthew 16:18 ('on this rock I will build my church'), because in its present version, he says (very boldly for someone in his position), the statement cannot be regarded as authentic; it is not reliably attributed to Jesus. As it stands, it points to 'a one-sidedly institutional view of the Church' (p. 372 n. 120). Kasper regards the Last Supper and Jesus' words over the cup, which are (he believes) undoubtedly authentic (Mk 14:25 and parallels) as 'the decisive step that led to the constitution of the Church'. In this moment, Jesus looks forward, beyond his death, to drinking the fruit of the vine anew in the kingdom of God. Kasper comments: 'He does not consider his death a failure of the eschatological message, but rather [as] the final dawn of the coming of God's eschatological kingdom. The Last Supper of Jesus is thus [the] anticipation of the eschatological feast in the kingdom of God' (88). So the Last Supper, while 'not a Church establishing act in the juridical sense . . . lays the foundation for . . . the centre of the Church', which is the celebration of the Paschal Mystery in the Eucharist. 'In this comprehensive sense it is the founding event of the Church' (p. 89). The Eucharist links Jesus' proclamation of the kingdom, which he sealed with his death, with its eschatological fulfilment, which it anticipates and celebrates. The church is (we may say) the sign, instrument and foretaste of the eschatological gathering of God's people out of all the peoples, the fulfilment of the eschatological hope and promise of the prophets (p. 89). In the church, the *eschaton* has begun. So it is mistake to get hung up, as many exegetes since Weiss have done, on the supposed delay to the *parousia*. There is no delay to the *parousia*; the eschatological moment is ongoing; it is always now. 'The actual foundation of the Church is Jesus himself resurrected and present in the Spirit' (p. 90). The origin of the church should not be attributed to any particular word or act of Jesus. Rather, it 'emerged out of the overall dynamics of the coming of God's kingdom and appeared publicly for the first time at Pentecost' (p. 90). The church is the kingdom 'present in mystery' (p. 90).[156] In the above brief exposition of Kasper's argument, I have joined up some of the dots of his rather compressed, somewhat cryptic, presentation. But, all in all, I find his case probably the most persuasive and theologically cogent of all those that we have examined from within the Roman Catholic Church.

---

[156] See also the brief discussion in Roger Haight, *Christian Community in History*, vol. 3, *Ecclesial Existence* (London and New York: Continuum, 2008), pp. 75–7, 84. Haight proposes that the question of whether Jesus founded the Church may be approached in two ways: doctrinally or historically and these are not mutually exclusive; both point to the truth that Jesus was and is the founder of the Church. 'Being its foundation means that Jesus is the central and centering mediator of the church's understanding of God. Specifically Christian faith in response to specifically Christian revelation caused the church to come into being' (pp. 75–6).

8

The foundation of the church in Anglican theology

The pre-critical institution

At the Reformation the English church received Martin Luther's gospel of justification by grace through faith. This gospel was embodied in the preaching of the scriptural word and the administration of the dominical sacraments as signs and seals of grace. Luther's was essentially a dynamic or *kerygmatic* ecclesiology, and the early English Reformers sat lightly to the question of the visible continuity of the church, especially through the 'Middle Ages'. However, the English church retained the major institutional structures of medieval Catholicism (the parochial system, the historic sees and the episcopate, cathedral foundations, the Convocations of the clergy, infant baptism, liturgical worship, canon law), though it abolished a number of medieval developments that, it was believed, could not be justified from Scripture or the primitive church (compulsory clerical celibacy, communion in one kind, the propitiatory sacrifice of the mass for the living and the dead, prayer to the saints). The reformed Church of England gave the literate laity an institutional voice by providing the Bible and the Prayer Book in the vernacular, retaining lay patronage, reaffirming the office of churchwarden, giving the laity in Parliament authority in doctrine and worship (in conjunction with the role of the Convocations) and, above all, by replacing the jurisdiction of the pope with the Royal Supremacy. Richard Hooker (1554–1600) had moved beyond the first Reformers' doctrine of a church defined by word and sacrament to a concept of a continuous visible divine society, identified by its outward profession of faith, divided into several branches and enjoying a mystical participation in the life of God through the sacraments. Hooker played down the aspect of divine right in connection with both the episcopate and the monarchy. The assumption that Jesus Christ had founded this divine society, with its ministry and sacraments, went unquestioned.

The Jacobean English Church of the early seventeenth century was regarded as a sister church by the Reformed churches on the Continent.[1] The English (or rather British) Civil War of the mid-seventeenth century resulted in the abolition of the episcopate and the liturgy and the execution of the Archbishop of Canterbury (William

---

[1]　See Anthony Milton (ed.), *The Oxford History of Anglicanism, Volume I: Reformation and Identity, c.1520 – 1662* (Oxford: Oxford University Press, 2017).

Laud) and then of King Charles I. Monarchy, episcopate and liturgy represented for Anglicans three divinely ordained institutions. The doctrine of the 'divine right of kings' held sway in England as it did in Roman Catholic countries such as Louis XIV's France. At the Restoration in 1660 the episcopal hierarchy and the liturgy were re-established along with the monarchy, and a more emphatically episcopalian form of Anglicanism held the field *de iure divino*. As successive sovereigns failed in their duty as 'nursing fathers' of the church (sometimes because they were Roman Catholic, Calvinist or Lutheran), the role of the bishop became accentuated.

The Methodist movement generated a spiritual fervour and seriousness from the 1740s that expressed itself in open-air preaching of the gospel and the formation of small communities, held together by a shared conversion experience and strong leadership. In the Oxford Movement, launched in 1833 with the *Tracts for the Times*, this emotional religiosity, now tinged with Romanticism, joined forces temporarily with the old High Church tradition emphasized the church as a visible divine society with salvation-imparting sacramental and hierarchical structures. The Tractarian alliance between High Anglican ecclesiology and Romantic subjective intensity was broken by the hostility of the Church of England episcopate and the University of Oxford to John Henry Newman's radicalizing of this platform, with the result that Newman and his closest disciples went over to Rome.

Evangelical High Churchmen, who held together justification by faith with apostolic succession and sacramental worship, came to seem anomalous (though they were not extinct). The most impressive work of ecclesiology of this period is William Palmer's *A Treatise on the Church of Christ* (1838), which combined a positive verdict on the Reformation with an insistence on the doctrine of apostolic succession.[2] The standard High Church position was put with characteristic authority and intended finality by William Ewart Gladstone (whose High Church convictions had been shaped by his early reading of Palmer's *A Treatise on the Church of Christ*): '[O]ur Lord founded the Church as a visible and organised society, by a commission from Himself . . . he did this in the most definite and pointed way by a charge . . . to the Apostles.'[3] Christ's promise to be with them always, even to the end of the world (Mt. 28:20), signified to Gladstone that the apostolic mission would continue, through history, in the form of the episcopate. Although in later life Gladstone was certainly open to the critical-historical study of the Bible and church history, even finding an affinity to the (Anglican) 'Liberal Catholic' views of the early Charles Gore and the *Lux Mundi* school,[4] this openness seems not to have affected his belief in the historical founding of the church in institutional form by Christ. Late nineteenth-century Anglican ecclesiology, notably in Gore and R. C. Moberly, redressed the antipathy of the Tractarians to lay church privileges and, while not compromising the doctrine of 'apostolic succession', emphasized the priesthood of all the baptized and advocated a notion of ordained ministerial priesthood, understood as a difference of calling or function in the body of Christ.

2   William Palmer, *A Treatise on the Church of Christ*, 2 vols, 3rd edn (London: Rivington, 1842 [1838]). See further on Palmer's ecclesiology, Paul Avis, *Anglicanism and the Christian Church: Theological Resources in Historical Perspective*, 2nd edn (London: T&T Clark, 2002), pp. 188–95.
3   W. E. Gladstone, 'The Place of Heresy and Schism in the Modern Christian Church [1894]', in id., *Later Gleanings (Gleanings of Past Years, 1885-96*, vol. VIII) (London: John Murray, 1898), p. 280.
4   David Bebbington, *The Mind of Gladstone* (Oxford: Oxford University Press, 2004).

In the twentieth century Anglican ecclesiology suffered academic neglect in favour of a dominantly historico-critical emphasis on the biblical text and patristic theology. But two works by Catholic Anglicans held out the promise of a rebirth of a ecclesiology that was both biblical and Catholic: Lionel Thornton, C. R.'s ecclesiology of communion *(koinonia)* in *The Common Life in the Body of Christ* and A. M. Ramsey's *The Gospel and the Catholic Church* which attempted a synthesis between Tractarian and Reformation principles, between an episcopate within 'apostolic succession', regarded as indispensable, and Martin Luther's watchword from his Ninety-five Theses, 'The true treasure of the Church is the holy gospel of the glory and the grace of God.'[5]

Anglo-Catholics still generally hold that Christ founded the church in an institutional sense and at the same time instituted the episcopate. Anglo-Catholics therefore insist that the transmission of apostolic authority through the historic episcopate is an indispensable condition for valid ordinations and for achieving the interchangeability of ministries and Eucharistic communion with other churches. Other Catholic Anglicans (including the present writer), perhaps more aware of the limitations of an appeal to New Testament precedents, also hold to the ecumenical consensus that the historic episcopate is a condition of visible unity and historical continuity in a church, but is not an indispensable prerequisite for churches to recognize one another as churches of Christ with authentic ministries and sacraments.

A familiar example of the assumption that Jesus Christ laid down a blueprint for the church and in particular instituted the pattern of its ministry, is the claim (following official Roman Catholic precedents) made by some Anglo-Catholics who are opposed to the admission of women to the priesthood and the episcopate, that if Jesus had intended women to be ordained, he would not have chosen only male apostles. Those who hold that view are unlikely to be persuaded by the argument that not only did Jesus not institute an all-male ministry, he also did not institute an ordained ministry at all. There were no priests and no bishops in the New Testament church (which is not to say that a case cannot be made from Scripture, reason and tradition for such ministries). Anglicans are equipped by their theological tradition, stemming from Richard Hooker, to recognize that in matters of outward order the church is not bound to the letter of Scripture or to precedents within tradition, but has been entrusted with the freedom to make rules for its life, in the light of reason, provided that they are not 'repugnant to Scripture'.[6]

F. J. A. Hort

Modern, critical Anglican theology began in the mid-nineteenth century with the collection *Essays and Reviews*.[7] But that explosive symposium had nothing to say about

---

[5]   L. S. Thornton, C.R., *The Common Life in the Body of Christ*, 3rd edn (London: Dacre Press, 1950 [1942]); A. M. Ramsey, *The Gospel and the Catholic Church* (London: Longmans, Green & Co., 1936).

[6]   For the theologians discussed in the body of this chapter, see also *ODNB*.

[7]   *Essays and Reviews*, 9th edn (London: Longman, Green, Longman, and Roberts, 1861 [1860]).

the origins of the church. *Essays and Reviews* represented the liberal – and in one or two cases somewhat sceptical – end of the Broad Church spectrum. But F. J. A. Hort, who also stands within the Broad Church tradition, an admirer of Samuel Taylor Coleridge and the academic colleague of Joseph Barber Lightfoot and Brooke Foss Westcott in Cambridge (the only one of the three not to become a bishop and, to be precise, not to become Bishop of Durham), stood for a critical-historical method applied to the origins of Christianity within the parameters of credal orthodoxy. Here Hort, Lightfoot and Westcott are fairly typical of Anglican theology and biblical scholarship; as Robert Morgan comments, 'the most persistent thread in English reactions to German theology [from the 1870s to the 1970s] has been hostility and resistance to sceptical results in gospel criticism.'[8]

Fenton John Anthony Hort (1828–92) was deeply influenced by the so-called Broad Church tradition stemming from Coleridge, Thomas Arnold and F. D. Maurice, rather than, as Charles Gore was, by the Oxford Movement. We may note his views on our question here as a foil to Gore's, to be taken next. More or less coinciding with the publication of *Lux Mundi* (1889), Hort gave a series of Cambridge lectures on 'The Early History and the Early Conceptions of the Christian Ecclesia' which, after Hort's death, were revised for publication and appeared in 1897 as *The Christian Ecclesia*.[9] Hort was a polymath, working over many years with B. F. Westcott on the text and translation of what became the Revised Version of the Bible, engaging with new discoveries in natural science and producing a remarkable personal *credo* – biblical exposition, philosophical reflection and spiritual meditation all at once – in his Hulsean Lectures of 1871 *The Way, The Truth, The Life*.[10] Hort does not directly tackle the question, 'Did Jesus found the Church?'; that would have been too crude a way of putting it for him: his thought was nuanced and sophisticated. Neither does Hort engage explicitly with other scholars, such as Gore or Edwin Hatch, author of *The Organization of the Early Christian Churches* (1881) who had – to Gore's disgust – reduced the origins of episcopacy to the need for competent administrators of church funds, on secular models.[11] But Hort is clear that Jesus did not institute any particular structures of governance for the church. He believed that the first offices – the Seven of Acts 6, and then deacons and presbyters – emerged as the need arose to adapt to circumstances; they were functions, not titles. Even the authority of the apostles accrued by the action of divine providence, rather than by any formal divine command (pp. 231–2). Hort points up the 'futility' of treating the history of the apostolic age as 'a set of authoritative precedents, to be rigorously copied without regard to time and place', like a new Levitical Code. With Richard Hooker (d. 1600), Hort insists that the responsibility for ordering its life rests with the church, 'guided by ancient precedent on the one hand and adaptation to present and future needs on the other' (pp. 232–3).

---

8 Robert Morgan, 'Non Angli sed Angeli: Some Anglican Reactions to German Gospel Criticism', in Stephen Sykes and Derek Holmes (eds), *New Studies in Theology* (London: Duckworth, 1980), pp. 1–30, at p. 1.
9 F. J. A. Hort, *The Christian Ecclesia* (London: Macmillan, 1914 [1897]).
10 F. J. A. Hort, *The Way, The Truth, The Life*, 2nd edn (London: Macmillan, 1894).
11 Edwin Hatch, *The Organization of the Early Christian Churches* (London: Rivingtons, 1881).

However, Hort certainly holds that Jesus laid the foundations for 'the future Ecclesia'. Unlike most modern scholars, Hort accepts the historicity and authenticity of Mt. 16:18: 'You are Peter (*petros*) and on this rock (*petra*) I will build my church', and to this extent his assumptions and methods are dated (though not necessarily mistaken). But he understands Christ's stated intention here as a 'rebuilding' and 'completion' of Israel (pp. 10–7), the fulfilment of the old as well as the beginning of something new. Since he was writing before the work of Weiss and Schweitzer, the eschatological note is muted in Hort, but he rejects the identification of the kingdom of God with the church; rather the church is 'the visible representative' of the kingdom and 'the primary instrument of its sway' (p. 19). Hort's emphasis falls much more on discipleship than on apostleship. The teaching and shaping of the disciples by Jesus, calling them to be with him and then sending them out in mission (Mk 3:13-16), was 'a direct preparation for the founding of the Ecclesia'; the apostles were those who were 'most completely disciples' (pp. 20–3). At the Last Supper in the Synoptics Jesus is secluded with his chosen disciples; in the Farewell discourses of Jn 13–17 he prays for 'his own'. They are now very near him and will soon receive their commission to go forth to preach and heal. Here, for Hort, we have the beginning of the 'future' church. It seems that, for him, Jesus did intend the church to come about and prepared for it to emerge after his death and resurrection, but that he certainly did not lay upon it any blueprint for its ministry and organization.

Charles Gore

Charles Gore (1853–1932) was the most theologically powerful priest and bishop within Anglicanism in the last decade of the nineteenth century and the first two decades of the twentieth. Gore was bishop successively of Worcester, Birmingham and Oxford. As a young priest, Gore led the so-called Holy Party, a vacational residential seminar of mainly Oxford clerics that combined fervent Anglo-Catholic religion in the Tractarian tradition with progressive views about Darwinian natural science, Hegelian idealist philosophy and critical-historical research. They published their collective findings in *Lux Mundi* (1889), a watershed moment in Anglican theology.[12] Gore's first major work *The Church and the Ministry* (1886; 2nd edition 1889), to which we will come in a moment, is a model of scholarly classical Anglo-Catholic ecclesiology.[13] It predates the impact of Johannes Weiss and Albert Schweitzer on New Testament eschatology, but not, of course, the critical, historical study of the Bible. This method had been embraced by Gore in his (at the time) notorious essay 'The Holy Spirit and Inspiration' in *Lux Mundi*. In the Church of England Gore could – just about – get away with saying such

---

[12]   Charles Gore (ed.), *Lux Mundi: A Series of Studies in the Religion of the Incarnation* (London: John Murray, 1889).

[13]   Charles Gore, *The Church and the Ministry*, 2nd edn (London: Rivington's/Longmans, 1889; further revised in 1919 by C. H. Turner; republished by SPCK as late as 1936); see also Paul Avis, *Gore: Construction and Conflict* (Worthing: Churchman Publishing, 1988), pp. 97–100. Further on Gore: G. L. Prestige, *Charles Gore, A Great Englishman* (London: William Heinemann, 1935); James Carpenter, *Gore: A Study in Liberal Catholic Thought* (London: Faith Press, 1960).

things, but that was not the case in the Roman Catholic Church and Gore – a dyed in the wool Anglican Catholic – deplored that fact. Writing in the *Guardian*, Gore attacked the decree of the Holy Office in January 1897 that the text in the First Epistle of John (5:7), referring to the 'three witnesses in heaven', was to be held to be authentic – when all New Testament scholars knew it to be a late interpolation.[14]

Gore devotes the first main section of *The Church and the Ministry* to a defence of the view that Christ intentionally founded a church 'in the sense of a visible society' (p. 9). He acknowledges that Christianity would never have become the force in the world and in history if it had been promoted merely as a set of ideas, like a philosophy, or as a body of teaching in a book. But the question for Gore is, Did Christ leave his followers to organize themselves, as they thought best, without any foundation provided by him – in which case presumably later generations would be free to organize their own Christian communities on any model they chose (p. 10)? Or did 'the divine Founder of the Christian religion Himself institute *a* society, *a* brotherhood, to be the home of the grace and truth which He came to bring . . . so that becoming His disciple meant from the first this – in a real sense this only – incorporation into His society?' (p. 10). This society was, according to Gore, shaped, structured or patterned in some detail by Christ for implementation by his apostles, with sacraments ('social ceremonies': p. 40), teaching and oversight provided for. It would have been simple enough to be Catholic, that is to be inclusive of diverse cultures and peoples in the future, but it would also need to be organized sufficiently to enable it to stand as a visible institution among the other great institutions of the world, with a recognizable and permanent character (p. 12). Gore assumes that the Acts of the Apostles is a reliable historical record of the earliest Christian communities; he accepts the Pauline authorship of the Pastoral Epistles; and he also stakes quite a lot on the authenticity of Mt. 16:18-19 ('... on this Rock . . .', etc.). He quotes Cyprian, Irenaeus and Augustine in his support, but of course that only proves that those Fathers *believed* that Christ founded a church that was designed in that way, not that he actually did so. Gore also quotes an array of other Fathers in support of such a portrait of the church, but that in itself sheds little light on the intentions that Christ might have had several centuries before.

Gore's core argument is conducted in two stages. First he contends, on the basis of Scripture, history and theology, that the church should be understood as a continuous visible society, bound together by sacraments which are visible, social ceremonies, bestowing grace (p. 57). Secondly, he argues on the same triple basis, that Christ instituted a ministry to serve such a church, as 'an organised body, with a differentiation of functions impressed upon it from the beginning' (p. 63). The visible, tangible succession of this ministry was instituted by Christ and remains absolutely vital to the integrity of the Church. This is what is meant by 'the apostolic succession'.

In Gore's view, Jesus consciously planned a church that would perpetuate his work through the centuries, entrusting the continuation of his mission to the apostles who

---

[14] Lawrence F. Barmann, *Baron Friedrich von Hügel and the Modernist Crisis in England* (Cambridge: Cambridge University Press, 1972), pp. 66–8. Gore also fiercely attacked the Roman Catholic Church's hostility to scholarly enquiry, its obscurantism, in his *Roman Catholic Claims* (London: Rivington, 1889).

were, in a sense, the first bishops. Gore describes the apostolic church as a spiritual hierarchy of graduated orders. For Gore, episcopacy was a divinely ordained paradigm for the church of all time. A violation of apostolic succession was the equivalent in the matter of the ministry to heresy in the matter of doctrine. Therefore, he concluded, various Protestant 'organizations' had 'violated a fundamental law of the Church's life' in doing away with episcopal ordination in visible succession (p. 344). Gore drew the conclusion (which was thoroughly in line with the teaching of John Keble and the Oxford Movement generally) that only a ministry that has been received by episcopal ordination within the historic succession could be regarded as legitimate or valid.[15]

In his later works – particularly *Belief in Christ* and *The Holy Spirit and the Church*, parts two and three of his great trilogy *The Reconstruction of Belief*, and in *Christ and Society* – Gore tackles the issues raised by the discovery in the Synoptic Gospels of an eschatology that was both future and catastrophic: Did this scenario preclude Jesus founding the church? In one sense Gore by-passes the difficulty by stating that it was a mistake to ask whether Christ founded the church, because it was already in existence. 'We understand nothing if we do not understand this.'[16] Agreed, Jesus did not found the church in the sense of a *new* Church, but what he did was to *refound* the old, the existing, Jewish church on the new basis of faith in his Messiahship, equipping it with teaching, sacraments and 'authoritative officers' in the person of the Twelve Apostles.[17] In the light of the evidence that he brings forward, Gore believes that 'it is mere wilfulness to deny that Christ did thus found, or rather refound, the Church as the new Israel and did supply it with a rudimentary organization.'[18] There is a touch of exasperation in Gore's tone here, towards the end of his life, because many scholars did in fact deny what Gore held to be self-evident.[19] In the Preface (dated Epiphany 1924) to *The Holy Spirit and the Church*, Gore notes significant hostility to his thesis: 'It is widely denied that the Church represented the deliberate intention of Jesus Christ. He founded no Church, we are told, and instituted no sacraments.'[20] Against this challenge, Gore proposes to undertake a 'purely critical' enquiry. His contemporary interlocutors and their successors were not persuaded that he had achieved his avowed objectivity.

R. P. C. and A. T. Hanson's critique of Gore

I am briefly going to break into this roughly chronological sequence of theologians to glance at two Anglican scholars – brothers actually – writing in the late twentieth century, who chose Charles Gore as the most effective spokesman of the high Anglo-

[15] See also Gore, *Orders and Unity* (London: John Murray, 1909).
[16] Gore, *The Reconstruction of Belief* [3 vols in one] (London: John Murray, 1926), p. 662.
[17] Ibid., p. 671.
[18] Gore, *Church and Society* (London: George Allen and Unwin, 1928), p. 41; cf. pp. 47, 61, 63. See also Gore, 'The Church's Common Confession of Faith', in H. N. Bate (ed.), *Faith and Order: Proceedings of the World Conference, Lausanne, August 3-21, 1927* (London: SCM Press, 1927), pp. 160–6, where Gore succinctly reiterates his position. Thus 'the Gospel of the Kingdom' includes the Church from the beginning 'as a visible, organic society, representative of the kingdom [*sic*] in the world' (p. 161).
[19] See further Mark D. Chapman, *The Coming Crisis: The Impact of Eschatology on Theology in Edwardian England* (Sheffield: Sheffield Academic Press, 2001).
[20] Gore, *The Reconstruction of Belief*, p. xv.

Catholic view of the divine institution of the church and the ministry. The Hanson
brothers – R. P. C. (Richard, 1916–88), patristic scholar and one-time bishop in the
Church of Ireland and A. T. (Anthony, 1916–91), New Testament scholar – take issue
with Gore's teaching that Jesus of Nazareth consciously intended to found the church as
a structured, hierarchical society in order to continue his mission. They criticize Gore's
view on six counts. First, the evidence for that assumption is 'flimsy in the extreme,
and is mostly drawn from those parts of the Fourth Gospel which are least likely to
be historical' (presumably chapters 20 and 21 of John). Secondly, the Pastoral Epistles,
on which Gore has to rely considerably, probably belong at the end of the first century
and portray a situation that emerged after a prolonged period of development. Thirdly,
the New Testament offers not a single example of any one of the original apostles
transmitting his authority to someone else. Fourthly, those who had pastoral oversight
in the Pauline churches did not comprise a distinct order of church officers who had
been commissioned in a regular way. Fifthly, the episcopate seems to have developed
locally, mainly from below, rather than stemming from a central commissioning body
such as the apostles. Finally, the ordained ministry, when it becomes recognizable in
the early centuries, is not explicitly associated with the Eucharist and is not regarded
as sacerdotal; so no direct implications can be drawn from the early evidence for the
sacramental efficacy or validity of any form of ministry. In the light of this evidence,
Richard and Anthony Hanson stand by three conclusions. (1) Jesus did not formally
institute a ministry for the church. (2) The apostles did not transmit authority to any
successors. (3) The ordained ministry, in a form that is recognizable to us, first appears
– and on a local scale – at the end of the first century, so it cannot go back to Jesus and
the apostles.[21]

A. J. Mason

Arthur James Mason (1851–1928) was a near contemporary of Charles Gore and,
like Gore, might be described as a 'Prayer-Book Catholic Anglican'. Mason had a
distinguished career in the church and university. He held the Lady Margaret Chair
of Divinity at Cambridge and was Master of Pembroke College and Vice-Chancellor
of the University. Mason's most famous works are *The Relation of Confirmation to
Baptism as Taught by the Western Fathers: A Study in the History of Doctrine* (1893)
and *The Church of England and Episcopacy* (1914). In an essay of 1918 he wrestled with
the problem of 'the historical relation between the Church and Christ'. Put sharply, this
was the question, 'Did Christ in His earthly career contemplate the foundation of a
religious system, to continue till [*sic*] the end of the world?' And what weight should be
given to the saying attributed to Jesus in Mt. 16:18: 'I will build my church'?[22]

---

[21] R. P. C. Hanson and A. T. Hanson, *The Identity of the Church* (London: SCM Press, 1987), p. 18.
[22] A. J. Mason 'Conceptions of the Church in Early Times', in H. B. Swete (ed.), *Essays on the Early
      History of the Church and the Ministry* (London: Macmillan, 1918), reproduced in Everett Ferguson,
      et al. (eds), *Church, Ministry and Organization in the Early Church* (New York: Garland, 1993),
      chapter 1, pp. 1–56.

Like Gore again, Mason is significant as a High Churchman who is coming to terms with the recent revolution in the understanding of New Testament eschatology, launched by Weiss and prosecuted by Schweitzer.[23] Mason points to texts in Matthew, in the Farewell Discourses in John and in Ephesians ('Christ loved the church and gave himself for her', 5:15) which strongly suggest that significant first-century canonical authors believed that Christ, 'before His death, had set His heart upon establishing the society' of the church (pp. 4–5). Mason points out that, because of their intimate experience of the Holy Spirit, the Spirit of Christ, first-century Christians would not have understood our modern question. He underlines the audacity of the early Christians' claim to be the *ekklēsia* of God and believes that it cannot be disregarded. He demolishes the views of Rudolph Sohm (1841–1917) and Adolf von Harnack (1851–1930) who had postulated a original purely spiritual, non-institutional church, which had been obscured by medieval priest-craft, legalism and politicization until Martin Luther arose to revive the primitive ideal. For Mason, however, whatever the questions about the intentions of the historical Jesus, 'The Church was Catholic from the outset' (p. 56). In other words, the Christian community was an ordered, structured society with its own rites, officers and rules. In fact, however, this affirmation does not dispose of the question of Jesus' intention: such a society might have arisen on other grounds, quite apart from what Jesus intended, if it was anything so concrete. Our question stands unanswered so far.

A. C. Headlam

Arthur Cayley Headlam (1862–1947) was a formidable and often wrong-headed scholar, administrator and bishop. Principal of King's College, London (1903–13), Regius Professor of Divinity in the University of Oxford (1918–23) and Bishop of Gloucester (1923–45), Headlam was the author of many books on the New Testament and on Christian belief, as well as being the joint author, with the eminent New Testament scholar William Sanday, of the *International Critical Commentary* on Romans.[24] A passionate ecumenist, Headlam gave the Bampton Lectures at Oxford in 1920 on *The Doctrine of the Church and Reunion*, which were published in the same year.[25] We are not directly concerned with Headlam's ecumenical theology, which was in fact out of sympathy with official Anglican policy then and since: his ecclesiology was more 'broad' than 'high' and the publication of his book clashed with the approach

---

[23] See Arthur Michael Ramsey, *From Gore to Temple: The Development of Anglican Theology between Lux Mundi and the Second World War 1889-1939; The Hale Memorial Lectures of Seabury-Western Theological Seminary, 1959* (London: Longmans, 1960), Appendix A: 'The Influence of Albert Schweitzer', pp. 171–4.

[24] William Sanday and Arthur C. Headlam, *A Critical and Exegetical Commentary on the Epistle to the Romans*, 5th edn (Edinburgh: T&T Clark, 1902). See also R. C. D. Jasper, *Arthur Cayley Headlam: Life and Letters of a Bishop* (London: Faith Press, 1960).

[25] Arthur C. Headlam, *The Doctrine of the Church and Reunion: Being the Bampton Lectures for the Year 1920* (London: John Murray, 1920). Page references to this volume are given in my main text.

of the Lambeth Conference 1920 and its 'Appeal to All Christian People'. Our interest is in Headlam's contribution to the central issue that we are tackling in this book.

In *The Doctrine of the Church and Reunion* Headlam accepts that you cannot have a coherent doctrine of the church without squarely facing the question, 'Did Jesus found the church?' His own answer to the question is that Jesus did not directly found the church – incontrovertibly this was the work of the apostles – but Jesus anticipated the church and prepared for it (pp. 27, 31). The disciples (later apostles) were bound together by their common attachment to Jesus; they had all heard the call to follow him and they remained close to his person and teaching (p. 25). Headlam identified several building blocks of the emerging church: the calling of the disciples; the forming of an apostolic community in fellowship with Jesus and with each other; the institution (or rather, the adaptation) of baptism; the Last Supper and the inauguration of the new covenant. Through a natural process of development, these merged into the early church (p. 42). Without these actions on the part of the Jesus of history, Headlam insists, the subsequent growth of the Christian church would be completely inexplicable (p. 42).

Headlam accepts with Loisy and the consensus of post-Loisy scholarship that Jesus preached the kingdom, not the church as such (p. 45). But, like Loisy, he sees that kingdom and church are not opposed to one another, but are linked together by a process of historical and theological development. He anticipates the Second Vatican Council's affirmation in *Lumen Gentium* that Jesus founded the church by proclaiming the gospel of the kingdom of God (p. 46). In summary, Headlam accepts that there was no specific dominical act that inaugurated the church, but he also believes that Jesus foresaw, intended and prepared for the church. To that extent, he stands with Gore and Mason.

Hastings Rashdall

Hastings Rashdall (1858–1924), a much under-rated and currently neglected Anglican divine of great intellectual stature, made an arresting cross-bench contribution to our topic as someone who was an historian, a theologian, an apologist, an ethicist and a philosopher.[26] As an historian, Rashdall made his reputation with *The Universities of Europe in the Middle Ages* (1895). His reputation as a theologian rests mainly on his Bampton Lectures for 1915, *The Idea of Atonement in Christian Theology*. As a philosopher and ethicist, Rashdall produced a number of books on the philosophy of religion and on current ethical issues.[27] Rashdall was Fellow and Tutor at New College,

---

[26] Introductory: Percy Ewing Matheson, *The Life of Hastings Rashdall* (London: Oxford University Press [Humphrey Milford], 1928); includes an appendix, pp. 240–9 on 'Rashdall as Philosopher and Theologian' by C. C. J. Webb. Margaret Marsh (ed.), *Hastings Rashdall: Bibliography of the Published Writings*, intro. Antony Dyson (Leysters : Modern Churchpeople's Union, 1993).

[27] Hastings Rashdall, *The Universities of Europe in the Middle Ages* (Oxford: Clarendon Press, 1895; reprinted Cambridge: Cambridge University Press, 2010); *The Idea of Atonement in Christian Theology* (London: Macmillan, 1919); *The Theory of Good and Evil* (Oxford: Clarendon Press, 1907); *Philosophy and Religion* (London: Duckworth, 1909; New York: Scribners, 1910).

Oxford, and became Dean of Carlisle in 1917. He achieved undeserved notoriety (stirred up on the basis of insufficient evidence by Bishop Charles Gore, now retired) for his contribution to the conference on Christology and the creeds of the Modern Churchman's Union at Girton College, Cambridge, in 1921. Though Rashdall was in effect an Anglican Modernist, he was not heterodox; he affirmed the divinity of Christ and believed in the incarnation, albeit his Christology was one of degree.[28] Nevertheless, Rashdall was not one to shirk daring conclusions if facts and thought pointed to them. For example, his radical views on the limitations of knowledge in Christ predated Charles Gore's more restrained views on this subject in *Lux Mundi* and subsequent works.[29]

Rashdall openly avowed a 'Liberal' theological stance. In his essay on 'Modernism' (1918), he pointed out that there had been a 'Liberal' wing of the church in every age. It consisted of those Christian teachers who 'attempted to interpret Christian doctrine in accordance with the best science of the day, to welcome and adopt newly discovered truth, to give up disproved errors, honestly to face intellectual difficulties'.[30] In the Preface to his collection of university sermons *Doctrine and Development* (1898) he described his aim as 'a modest attempt to translate into the language of modern thought some of the leading doctrines or ideas of traditional Christianity', as others in England and Germany had attempted to do in recent years – though he adds that his work involves 'a franker admission of the necessity for theological reconstruction'.[31]

Rashdall was unashamedly combative in denouncing illiberal and obscurantist actions by church authorities, especially the Vatican of his day. Leo XIII's encyclical of 1893 *Providentissimus Deus*, 'On the Study of Holy Scripture', which asserted the infallibility of Scripture, 'defied all modern learning', said Rashdall.[32] The suppression of Roman Catholic 'Modernism' by Leo's successor Pius X (a 'pious but ignorant Venetian peasant') in fact imposed 'a reign of terror' on all honest theological students.[33] This punitive regime, coupled with the disestablishment of the Catholic Church in France under the same pope, had brought that church to a point of unprecedented political weakness and intellectual irrelevance.[34]

Massively learned, incisive in intellect, fearless in reaching his conclusions and formidable in debate, Rashdall excelled at showing, by a superior acquaintance with the sources to that of his critics, that the great teachers of the church in history had not always held the views so conveniently attributed to them by partisans in controversy. What a liberal method in theology was opposed to, Rashdall told a gathering of North-

---

[28] Alan M. G. Stephenson, *The Rise and Decline of English Modernism: The Hulsean Lectures 1979-80* (London: SPCK, 1984), pp. 117–19, 123–4, 128–9; Ramsey, *From Gore to Temple*, Chapter 5: 'Modernism', esp. pp. 69–71; G. K. A. Bell, *Randall Davidson: Archbishop of Canterbury*, 3rd edn (London: Oxford University Press, 1952), pp. 1134–43; Avis, *Gore: Construction and Conflict*, pp. 76–96.

[29] Rashdall, 'Limitations of Knowledge in Christ' (1889), in id., *Doctrine and Development* (London: Methuen, 1898), pp. 33–57, at p. 33 n.

[30] Rashdall, 'Modernism', in id., *Ideas and Ideals*, ed. H. D. A. Major and F. L. Cross (Oxford: Basil Blackwell, 1928), pp. 94–116, at p. 94.

[31] Rashdall, *Doctrine and Development*, Preface, p. vii.

[32] Rashdall, 'Modernism', p. 97.

[33] Ibid., p. 97.

[34] Ibid., pp. 98, 110.

of-England clergy, was the assumption, which (he said) reared its head at every clerical meeting, every debate of Convocation (before the Church Assembly and the General Synod, but the same applies) and in the (partisan) religious newspapers, namely, that

> everything has been settled once for all – that there is a certain body of Christian truth which has been always taught from the first and taught universally, and that we can dispose of a doubt as to some matter of historical fact, of doctrine, or of ethics by saying that there is a *consensus patrum* against it or even by quoting the words of an individual Father.[35]

That prevailing assumption, 'of an unvarying and universally accepted body of truth', Rashdall insisted, 'cannot outlive serious study'. What we now regard as orthodox Christian doctrine has evolved slowly over time, and there are no grounds for assuming that the process of development has come to an end.[36] We Anglican scholars are all 'Modernists' now in the eyes of the Roman Catholic Church, Rashdall points out. The most conservative evangelical dean or bishop in the Church of England, who uses to any extent the tools of historical-critical scholarship, would be condemned by Rome. Even the eminent Bishop of Oxford (Charles Gore, until 1919, and now regarded as a rather reactionary conservative) would receive short shrift from the Vatican. Against this background, Rashdall's perspective on the question of the foundation of the church can be summarized as follows.

History and revelation

Rashdall was an historian of renown, thanks to the years of toil that he had spent on the medieval history of the European universities. Basic to his 'Liberal' standpoint was the conviction that every age is compelled to interpret the faith that is has received and to do so in the light of 'its own ruling ideas'; and without question the ruling idea of 'our own age', he says, is 'the historical way of looking at things'.[37] So what Rashdall has to say about the historical reliability of the Gospels (and the Acts of the Apostles), in the light of historical-critical research, carries weight. In short, Rashdall is convinced of the substantial historicity of the Gospel account, including the healing miracles of Jesus and the resurrection understood as visions of his existence beyond death (though not the Virginal Conception of Jesus or the empty tomb, it seems).

     More importantly, Rashdall advocates what he regards as a vital methodological principle, namely that our judgement of the substantial historicity of the Gospel narrative will depend on how we view Jesus – whether we are persuaded that the character and teaching of Jesus constitute 'a phenomenon unique in human history and unique in its present spiritual significance'.[38] It is 'the originality of the character of

---

[35] Ibid., pp. 108–9.
[36] Ibid., p. 109.
[37] Rashdall, 'The Historic Christ' (1896), in *Doctrine and Development*, pp. 89–109, at p. 95.
[38] Rashdall, 'The Historical Value of the Gospels' (1895), in *Doctrine and Development*, pp. 58–76, at p. 72.

Christ which constitutes the greatest of all guarantees of its historical existence'.[39] But the character of Christ is not merely *evidence* of divine revelation; it *is* the revelation.[40] In the sermon 'Revelation by Character' (1894), Rashdall argues that divine revelation has a twofold aspect: moral and theological. We do not (or perhaps should not) accept theological propositions, derived by some church authority from revelation, unless those propositions approve themselves at the bar of our moral judgement. Moral discernment is essential in the interpretation of any claimed revelation. Revelation speaks not only of God and God's nature, but also of 'man and his duty'. Theological truths and moral imperatives go hand in hand in the content of divine revelation and not least in the revelation given in Jesus Christ.[41] In the character of Jesus, disclosed in his words and deeds, and in his exceptional consciousness of a filial relationship to God and of God's fatherly relationship to him, we see mirrored the character of God, as love.[42] It is in this light that we read the Gospels and form a view as to the degree of their historicity.

Eschatology

Rashdall follows the typical Liberal Protestant line, and particularly Harnack, to this extent, when he states that, from among the various conflicting ideas about the kingdom of God that were current in first-century Judaism, Jesus selected the most ethical and spiritual of them and then further spiritualized them. Jesus' idea of the kingdom of God was emphatically ethical and spiritual. For him, the coming of the kingdom was not '*primarily* [italics original] a cosmic catastrophe which should bring an end to the social and political world-order. It was essentially a state of society in which God's will should be perfectly done . . . as it is in heaven'. The essence of the kingdom in the teaching of Jesus, Rashdall the ethicist affirmed, was the Fatherhood of God and the brotherhood of man. Much of the lurid eschatological language attributed to Jesus in the Gospels, Rashdall believed, was of 'very doubtful authenticity'. It was not present in the sayings source 'Q' on which Matthew and Luke drew. Rashdall accepted that there was 'a residuum of truth' in these eschatological ideas, but he was not sure that they were ever meant to be interpreted with the 'deadly literalness' with which the extreme eschatologists took them, making of them 'a tawdry apocalyptic romance'.[43] His verdict was that 'The details of this eschatological language cannot be trusted.' Nevertheless, it was probable that Jesus did expect some kind of catastrophic judgement of the world

---

[39] Ibid., pp. 72–3.
[40] Ibid., p. 75.
[41] Rashdall, 'Revelation by Character', in *Doctrine and Development*, pp. 110–27, at p. 110. See also Rashdall's comments on divine revelation and on the inspiration of the Bible in *Christus in Ecclesia: Sermons on the Church and Its Institutions* (Edinburgh: T&T Clark, 1904). His summary: 'Revelation is gradual. Revelation is progressive. Revelation admits of degrees', p. 247.
[42] Rashdall, 'The Historic Christ', pp. 97, 102.
[43] Rashdall, *Conscience and Christ: Six Lectures on Christian Ethics* (London: Duckworth, 1916), pp. 49, 55; see also his comments on Tyrrell's eccentric eschatology in Rashdall, 'George Tyrrell', in id., *Ideas and Ideals*, pp. 132–41, at p. 139.

and the setting up of a visible kingdom on earth, in which he would be recognized as Messiah or king.[44]

While Rashdall affirmed that Jesus believed himself to be the Messiah, he denied that Jesus thought of himself as divine. Of course that did not necessarily mean that Rashdall believed that Jesus was not divine. And there is nothing untoward, from the point of view of orthodox Christology, about making a distinction between Messiahship and divinity; indeed, it is a vital distinction. Rashdall recognized that, alongside the 'futuristic' eschatological sayings, there were others that pointed to the presence and action of the kingdom in the midst here and now. But (and here Rashdall is in tune with early twentieth-century theological liberalism, both Protestant and Roman Catholic) 'all this eschatological language must be treated as the accidental historical dress in which the ethical and religious ideas of Jesus would appear to have clothed themselves.'[45] Whatever might be the correct understanding of the eschatology of the Gospels, the kingdom proclaimed by Jesus was 'at bottom ethical and spiritual'; and this interpretation was supported by the fact that, in his preaching, the first step to entering the kingdom was repentance.[46]

Although Rashdall agrees with the members of the eschatological school up to a point about the 'cosmology' of the Gospels, he parts company with them over their downgrading of the ethical teaching of Jesus. With Albert Schweitzer particularly in mind, Rashdall deplores the fact that '[t]he supposed discovery that the teaching of Jesus consisted mainly in "Eschatology" has led to the adoption of an almost contemptuous attitude towards His ethical teaching on the part of writers who describe that teaching as a mere "Interimsethik" of little present value or significance.'[47] Because Christianity is 'a Religion rooted and grounded in Ethics', any Christology that is not based primarily on the appeal that the teaching of Jesus makes to our conscience rests on 'an extremely precarious foundation'. In the conscience of humanity there is to be found 'a progressive and evolving revelation of God'.[48]

Rashdall is unconvinced by George Tyrrell's reinterpretation of biblical eschatology. Tyrrell's 'attempt to combine a pessimistic contempt for the present life with optimistic hopes for the future' is 'profoundly illogical and self-contradictory'.[49] The self-same reasons that give us hope for the future of the individual soul after death should prevent us from completely despairing of the present life. Our hope for this life and the next rests on the moral character of God.[50] The fact that we no longer expect the present world order to be brought to an end by a catastrophic judgement of the world and replaced all at once with a perfect realization of the kingdom of God is 'ethically speaking an unimportant detail'.[51] The possibility that Jesus may have thought that 'the

---

[44] Rashdall, *Idea of Atonement*, pp. 7–13 and see Footnote 2, pp. 7–8 where Rashdall deprecates the exaggerated place given to eschatology in the teaching of Jesus by Schweitzer and others.
[45] Rashdall, *Idea of Atonement*, pp. 7–13.
[46] Rashdall, *Conscience and Christ*, p. 56.
[47] Ibid., p. viii.
[48] Ibid., p. ix.
[49] Ibid., p. 68.
[50] Ibid., pp. 68–9.
[51] Ibid., p. 70.

physical universe was on the eve of a vast catastrophe' is not a reason why the ethic of Jesus should not be 'an Ethic of universal, paramount, and eternal value'.[52]

Development

Rashdall believed in facing facts head on with courage and resourcefulness. One unavoidable fact was that Christian beliefs had evolved over time. For him, the principle of development in theology and belief was not something to be defensive about, or to seek to justify with elaborate casuistry as Newman had done in his famous *Essay on the Development of Doctrine* of 1845. It was 'inherent in the very plan of Christianity' because Christianity is an historical religion, institutionally embodied in the historical process.[53] In a nutshell, his view of development was that all theology is the result of development and that development is ongoing. Development of thought reflects change in the world and in our understanding of the world through philosophy, science and history; it is a law of life. Christian theology is none the worse for being the result of a process of development and Christian doctrine is not of less value because it is not explicitly contained in the actual teaching of Jesus Christ or of the New Testament writers. Some things that have been believed by Christians of the past, or even by the whole church at some point, are no longer believable by us. Our knowledge of the facts changes as science moves on; and our interpretation also changes as our thought-forms evolve. '[I]t is impossible that a critical age should think exactly like an uncritical one.'[54] As Rashdall puts it in his direct way, in discussing Loisy's *L'Évangile et l'Église*: development is a proper function of the church; it is the church's business.[55]

William Temple

William Temple (b. 1881) was the most considerable, most influential and most representative churchman of his age, dominating the thought and action of the Church of England from the 1920s until his untimely death in 1944 after a mere two and a half years as Archbishop of Canterbury.[56] Intellectually, Temple was many things – philosopher, apologist, evangelist, ecumenist, social reformer, educationalist and theologian – but we would not normally think of him as an ecclesiologist. However, in 1912, as a young headmaster, Temple contributed a remarkable essay on 'The Church'

---

[52] Ibid., p. 72.
[53] Rashdall, 'The Historic Christ', p. 92. Therefore, '[t]here can be no Christianity without the Church', p. 93.
[54] Rashdall, *Doctrine and Development*, pp. vii–x, at p. ix.
[55] Rashdall, 'Harnack and Loisy', in id., *Principles and Precepts* (Oxford: Blackwell, 1927), pp. 228–36, at p. 231.
[56] F. A. Iremonger, *William Temple, Archbishop of Canterbury: His Life and Letters* (Oxford: Oxford University Press, 1948); John Kent, *William Temple* (Cambridge: Cambridge University Press, 1992); Stephen Spencer, *William Temple: A Calling to Prophecy* (London: SPCK, 2001); id. (ed.), *Christ in All Things: William Temple and His Writings* (Norwich: Canterbury Press, 2015).

to the progressive theological symposium *Foundations*.[57] Temple later returned to the doctrine of the church in two major works of philosophical theology and apologetics *Mens Creatrix* (1917) and *Christus Veritas* (1924). In these works he affirms that the 'task' of the church is to be 'the herald and foretaste of the Kingdom of God'.[58] The kingdom is a realm of values and is destined to permeate first Christendom and eventually the whole world with righteousness, love and unity. Temple's is a progressive understanding of the kingdom and therefore of the church – an immanent eschatology.[59]

In the 1912 article on 'The Church', Temple not only articulates a fully sacramental and eucharistic understanding of the church (in this respect he was far from unique in Anglican theology, though this is not our concern here), but also addresses the question of Jesus and the foundation of the church. Temple is clear that Jesus Christ 'founded' a 'society' 'to proclaim and carry on' his redeeming work. The church is a divine act; its character is given to it by Christ alone, not by any human action. Having stated that 'The Church was founded by the Life, the Teaching, the Death and Resurrection of Christ, and by the consequent outpouring of the Holy Spirit', Temple immediately qualifies this by adding (p. 341, fn 3) that the early church saw itself as the true Israel, the 'remnant' of which the prophets had spoken. In St Paul's view (which is clearly Temple's too), he states, 'Christ did not found the Church but redeemed a Church which was already there.' Temple's is a soundly christocentric doctrine of the founding of the church, and his recognition that Jesus could not have founded a new church because the church of Israel already existed is also sound; but what is missing in Temple at this stage and for long afterwards is the eschatological dimension.

Albert Schweitzer's *Vom Reimarus zu Wrede* had been published in English as *The Quest of the Historical Jesus* two years' before *Foundations* appeared. And the editor of the symposium, B. H. Streeter, in his own chapter, expounds positively the eschatological revolution in German biblical scholarship.[60] But I suspect that the eschatological turbulence and violence, postulated by Weiss and Schweitzer, was unpalatable to Temple the ardent Platonist and consummate reconciler. It would take until the late 1930s for Temple, influenced by Karl Barth and Reinhold Niebuhr and faced with the possible extinction of Christian civilization at the hands of the totalitarian, barbarian threat of Nazi Germany, to recognize the shortcomings of the theology to which he had devoted his life – namely, how to explain the world in the light of the love, beauty and wisdom of God – and in its place to embrace, all too briefly, the theology of judgement and redemption that he now saw to be the authentic voice of the New Testament. But that is another story.[61]

---

[57] William Temple, 'The Church', in B. H. Streeter (ed.), *Foundations: A Statement of Christian Belief in Terms of Modern Thought; By Seven Oxford Men* (London: Macmillan, 1912), pp. 337–59.

[58] William Temple, *Christus Veritas* (London: Macmillan, 1924), p. 158.

[59] William Temple, *Mens Creatrix* (London: Macmillan, 1917), pp. 324–50.

[60] B. H. [Burnett Hillman] Streeter, 'The Historic Christ', in *Foundations*, pp. 73–145.

[61] See Temple's 'Chairman's Introduction', in *Doctrine in the Church of England (1938): The Report of the Commission on Christian Doctrine appointed by the Archbishops of Canterbury and York*, with a new Introduction by G. W. H. Lampe (London: SPCK, 1982 [1938]); Archbishop of York [William Temple], 'Theology Today', *Theology* XXXIX, no. 233 (November 1939), pp. 326–33.

R. Newton Flew

At this point I am going to slip in a brief discussion of a New Testament scholar, theologian and ecumenist who bucks the trend. R. Newton Flew (1886–1962) was not an Anglican, but as a British Wesleyan Methodist, he was not far removed. He is a rare example of a twentieth-century scholar who, in spite of embracing the historical-critical method, argued that Jesus of Nazareth intended and planned the Christian church and took concrete steps to found or inaugurate it. In his forcefully argued book *Jesus and His Church* (1938), Flew began, like so many other accounts of the mission of Jesus, from the nature of the kingdom of God.[62] Accepting the conclusions of modern New Testament scholarship that the *basileia* refers primarily to the sovereignty, rule or reign of God, Flew nevertheless sees a secondary meaning in the New Testament usage of this term, which is crucial for his argument: the kingdom is not only the *reign* of God, but also the *domain* within which God's reign is accepted and obeyed. *Basileia* therefore comes to mean a company or community of people who accept God's reign and live by it. Flew chooses the word 'domain' to stand for the sphere of God's reign in order not to imply, as Liberal Protestantism tended to do, that the reign can be identified with those who, individually, inhabit the domain, as though the reality of God's rule depended on human response. The critical step in the argument now is from *domain* to *church*, since the church is the company or community of those who intentionally embrace the reign of God : 'The Ecclesia is indeed the necessary correlative to the *Basileia*, or Kingly Rule' (p. 13). The church is 'correlative' to the kingdom, not identical with it, as medieval Catholic theology and some modern Roman Catholic apologists tended to assume.[63]

But what of the eschatological perspective, the foreshortening of history, of the Gospels – does that not preclude Jesus actually 'founding' the church? Flew accepts the arguments of Weiss and Schweitzer that point to the eschatological framework and foreshortened time span of the New Testament and he believes that Jesus himself shared it. But Flew argues that Jesus' teaching and actions suggest that he expected an interval to occur between his first announcement of the presence of the kingdom and the final consummation, though Jesus did not know how long that interval would be. (We have noted that Kümmel also interpreted the evidence to suggest a gap before the end.) This space, this interim, gave scope (Flew believes) for 'a series of events in time', during which the church would be established and undertake its mission (p. 14). Flew suggests that instead of the question, 'Did Jesus found the Church?', we should ask whether Jesus directed his teaching to a particular community, drawn from the masses,

---

[62]   R. Newton Flew, *Jesus and His Church*, 2nd edn (London: Epworth Press, 1943 [1938]); page references are embedded in my main text. See especially chapter 1: 'The *Basileia* and the *Ecclesia*'.

[63]   Flew refers (*Jesus and His Church*, p. 20, n. 1) to Karl Adam (1876-1966), *The Spirit of Catholicism* (ET, London: Sheed & Ward, 1938). p. 16; 'The Church is the realization on earth of the Kingdom of God.' Adam quotes Augustine, *De Civitate Dei* [*City of God*], XX, ix, 1, where Augustine equates the church in this world with the kingdom of heaven: Augustine, *City of God*, trans. Henry Bettenson; intro. David Knowles, O.S.B. (Harmondsworth: Penguin, 1972), pp. 914–15. The language of ecumenical theology today is more nuanced; while not identifying the church and the kingdom, it speaks of the church as the 'sign, instrument and foretaste' of the kingdom.

and whether his ministry had as one of its aims the formation and consolidation of such a community.

Flew admits – and this is a major concession – that 'Jesus nowhere speaks of the disciples . . . as the nucleus for a new Israel', but he claims that Jesus' 'actions speak more clearly than any words', actions that show that 'the old Israel was to be purged and reconstituted in view of the nearness of the Kingdom of God' (p. 36). Flew then puts forward a five-fold argument, based on the evidence of the Gospels with regard to the actions of Jesus, to support his claim that Jesus intentionally founded the church (summary, p. 14; details, chapter 3):

- Jesus' proclamation is directed to the 'reconstitution' of Israel in view of the coming of God's reign. Jesus regarded the 'little flock' (Lk. 12:32), whom he gathered around him, as 'the Remnant', equivalent to 'the true Israel'.
- The radical ethical teaching of Jesus was directed towards this nucleus of disciples, 'the New Israel'. The gift of the Spirit, promised for the last days, would empower the disciples to live out his teaching.
- The idea of Messiahship, especially as understood by Jesus, 'inevitably implies the gathering of a new community' in the last days. The choice of the Twelve implies 'the beginning of an organization' and the teaching of the Lord's Prayer is 'the beginning of a distinctive worship' (p. 19).
- The 'word' or 'gospel' or 'mystery', proclaimed by Jesus, is 'constitutive of the new community'. The new covenant is made with 'the newly constituted People of God'. At the Last Supper, Jesus instituted the new covenant with his disciples 'as representing the new people of God'.
- The mission of the new community is declared when Jesus sends out his disciples, the Twelve and the Seventy. This is the new community in action.

There is much stimulating material in *Jesus and His Church* and one cannot help being impressed with Flew's passionate commitment to the church as a good Wesleyan Methodist. His argument is congenial in several respects, but I find his overall case unconvincing, in fact rather worrying, for two main reasons.

1. There seems to be an unargued supersessionist assumption lurking behind Flew's argument, namely that the church replaced the nation of Israel as God's chosen people. While Flew concedes that Jesus 'did not deliberately plan for a community which should be immediately separated from Judaism' and even that this separation might not have occurred to Jesus (pp. 18–19), he also points out that the early Christians were universally convinced that the church was the 'true Israel' (p. 15). This assumption weakens the force of the argument that Jesus could not have intended to start a new church, because there was already a church of God in existence.

2. There is considerable theological slippage from Jesus' appeal for a renewed and reconstituted Israel to the founding of the church as a separate community, and from 'true Israel' to 'new Israel'. The sending out of the Twelve does not form

the basis of an ecclesial organization by any stretch of the imagination; nor does the teaching of a prayer point to a new kind of worship: there is nothing in the Lord's Prayer that could not be prayed by a faithful Jew of that time or of today. The mission of Jesus of Nazareth was to the nation and people of Israel: it had nothing to do with gathering a new, alternative and replacement community. The Remnant, in the prophetic literature, represented Israel as a whole; it was not a substitute for it. And, crucially, a new covenant does not entail a new people – the prophets spoke of a new covenant without any such implication: it was with the old people, 'the house of Israel and the house of Judah' (Jer. 31:31–5).

Altogether, Flew's case is overstated at best and tendentious at worst, showing signs of sleight of hand, which I am sure was unintentional. This rare modern attempt, by a distinguished scholar, churchman and ecumenist, to claim that Jesus intended and actually inaugurated the church, as an historical event, must be judged to have failed.

Alan Richardson

I turn next to the respected Anglican churchman, scholar and biblical theologian who flourished a couple of generations after Gore, Mason and Rashdall, Alan Richardson (1905–75). Professor of Theology at the University of Nottingham and then Dean of York, Richardson was the author of many books on theology, biblical interpretation and apologetics. He is the exponent of a basically biblical theology that is enriched by philosophical and systematic theology. His most substantial work, *An Introduction to the Theology of the New Testament* (1958), was widely used and, though generally regarded as out of date now, it is in my view still worth consulting by non-specialists.[64] Richardson roundly declares that 'Jesus intended to "found" the church'. How does he arrive at this conclusion and what does he mean by putting 'found' in inverted commas?

Richardson accepts the perspective of Weiss and Schweitzer with regard to the eschatological framework of the New Testament, particularly the Synoptic Gospels, and the expectation of an imminent *parousia*. But he disagrees with their conclusion that the eschatological context made it impossible for Jesus to envisage a church to continue, in a sense, his mission. Eschatology and the concept of the church are not incompatible. '[B]iblical eschatology always involved a doctrine of the Church as the Messianic community of the last times, the gathering together by the Shepherd-Messiah of the scattered, elect people of God, the corporate Son of Man which constitutes the

---

[64] Alan Richardson, *An Introduction to the Theology of the New Testament* (London: SCM Press, 1958); the quotations are from pp. 307–11. Richardson's methods of interpretation were criticized, basically as tendentious in a conservative direction, by Robert Morgan in *The Nature of New Testament Theology: The Contribution of William Wrede and Adolf Schlatter* (London: SCM Press, 1973). An even-handed and partial vindication of Richardson's handling of the New Testament is provided in Anthony Hanson, 'Alan Richardson and his Critics in the Area of Hermeneutics', in Ronald H. Preston (ed.), *Theology and Change: Essays in Memory of Alan Richardson* (London: SCM Press, 1975), pp. 25–52.

persona of the Christ.' Moreover, 'Jesus conceived of his divinely appointed mission as that of creating the Church, the new people of God, and that from the beginning he intended that there should be a definite ministry within it.'

Richardson lays considerable store by Matthew 16:17-19 ('On this rock I will build my church'). Following Cullmann, he defends the authenticity of this text on the grounds that there is no evidence of it being a late interpolation into the Gospel, that it is thoroughly Semitic in character and must, therefore, have originated in the Palestinian community. Moreover, the special designated role of Peter is supported by several other Gospel texts whose authenticity is uncontested. Richardson dismisses the familiar fudge that, when Jesus spoke of building his church on 'this rock', he meant the faith and confession of Peter, rather than his person. Of course, confession and faith cannot be divorced from person, but it is the entirely human and fallible Peter who has the leadership role among the disciples and apostles in the New Testament. Richardson, the Anglican, believes that Jesus intended his community of disciples to gather around Peter after his own departure, but he does not see any connection with the papacy.

Richardson points out that when we say that Jesus 'founded' the church, it sounds to modern ears as though he was perhaps gathering together a group of like-minded people in a good cause, like setting up a charitable foundation. But the Matthaean text speaks of 'building' the church: there is a dynamic, constructive purpose in this statement. So, for Richardson, 'Christ is not so much the "Founder" of the Church as he *is* himself the Church . . . the body of those who have been incorporated into the *persona* of Christ.' Richardson sees the clue to the relation of Jesus to the origin of the church in the Semitic notion, which has its roots in the theological anthropology of the Hebrew Bible, of a corporate person (*persona*). The corporate person was at first merely a remnant, but would grow and spread into the church we know.

In a late article (1971), Richardson shows that he has moved away somewhat from the approach typical of the biblical theology movement in order to do better justice to the existential dimension of theology. Writing on the resurrection, he comments, in a rather Bultmannian way: 'The resurrection of Jesus . . . created the Church by calling faith into being.'[65] But whether the resurrection, rather than Pentecost, is correctly to be identified as the birth of the Christian church, is a moot point, though of course the latter could not have happened without the former. Richardson agrees, however, with those scholars who posit the emergence of a distinctive Christian community as a post-crucifixion and post-resurrection phenomenon.

Michael Ramsey

Finally, in this account of Anglican views of the connection between Jesus and the church, we would do well to note that Gore's approach, purportedly based on historical research (Gore was deeply versed in the patristic writings, both of the East and the

---

[65]   Alan Richardson, 'The Resurrection of Jesus Christ', *Theology* LXXIV (1971), pp. 146–54.

West), is not the only major contender. A much more subtle approach was taken by Arthur Michael Ramsey (1904–88), later Archbishop of Canterbury, in his first and greatest work *The Gospel and the Catholic Church* (1936).[66] Ramsey's method was not purely historical, but was shaped by the movement of twentieth-century scholarship known as biblical theology, an approach to theological research which exaggerated the theological unity of the Bible and treated it – in a quite sophisticated way; not by proof-texting – as a source of doctrine, without paying sufficient regard to its cultural context and the world views that it presupposes. Following this method, Ramsey found the source of the episcopate in the Passion of Jesus Christ as interpreted particularly by St Paul and in the Pauline image of the church as Christ's body, in which all have died and been raised. Ramsey affirms: 'From the deeds of Jesus in the flesh there springs a society which is one in its continuous life' (p. 44). That is not the same as saying that Jesus of Nazareth intentionally and explicitly founded the church, but it is to bind the church to the earthly ministry of Jesus and to say that his ministry – his words and actions – generated the church, calling it into existence.

Ramsey shows how Christ died as a corporate figure, representing Israel, the church of the Old Covenant. Christ's mission fulfilled the Jewish Scriptures. 'The Old Testament has both its Church and its Passion, and Christ is the fulfilment of both' (p. 10). God's purpose was to unite humankind in worship, in love and service to himself, and to do this through the instrumentality of a particular people. Amid various Old Testament sources, the Servant Songs of Deutero-Isaiah are key. According to Ramsey, the Jews did not interpret the Servant Songs as speaking of the Messiah, but only as referring to the destiny of the nation, with the result that 'the prophecy stands in the Book of Isaiah mysterious, baffling, uninterpreted by the race for whom it was written' (p. 16). But Jesus certainly identified his mission with that of the Suffering Servant and when the New Testament writers proclaimed Jesus as the Servant of God whom Isaiah had foretold, they were being true to the teaching of Jesus himself (p. 17). Despised and rejected, Jesus stands alone; in his solitary obedience to the will of God he *is* the church. Through his death and resurrection he brings a new Israel, a new church into being.

Ramsey now needs to tackle the question of continuity and discontinuity between Jesus and the post-apostolic church. In particular, this is the question whether the development of episcopacy in the second century can be said to 'speak of the Gospel and the one Body' in the same way that the other ecclesial structures that emerged at this time – the sacraments, the canon and the creeds – do (p. 69). To answer this question, Ramsey surveys the evidence of the New Testament and the post-apostolic church. In Luke, we find Christ training and commissioning the Twelve for 'a unique office, to order and unite the Christians in one fellowship, in union with the historic events of which the Apostles are witnesses' (p. 71). And in Matthew, we learn that the apostolic office is shared equally by all the apostles, for the command to 'bind and loose' is given to them all. Moreover, Eph. 2:20 speaks of the apostles (plural) as the foundation of the church. Although the apostolate became considerably broader than the Twelve – Paul being the prime example – we can be 'certain', Ramsey says, of this

---

[66] Ramsey, *The Gospel and the Catholic Church*.

much: that there was an apostolic body whose functions were, first, to be a living link between contemporary Christians and the founding events of their faith, and secondly, to represent the unity and continuity of the church, both to itself and to the world, in bearing witness to the gospel. There are threads of continuity, binding the later church to the mission of Jesus Christ.

The organic conception of the church, identified with Christ's presence and action in its midst, meant for Ramsey that its bonds of communion, particularly the episcopate, were integral to the gospel, part of the *kerygma*. He had learnt from Luther, Barth and Hoskyns that the church is created by the gospel, but it was axiomatic for Ramsey, as a Catholic theologian, that in speaking of Christ the gospel also speaks of the church. When he wrote *The Gospel and the Catholic Church* in the mid-1930s, Ramsey believed that there could be no true church that did not have bishops in historical succession. Although Ramsey revered Gore and largely shared Gore's ecclesiology, he later came to regard Gore's stance as too extreme and softened his own view of apostolic succession. As we see in his advocacy of Anglican-Methodist unity in the 1960s and early 1970s, Ramsey would not unchurch ecclesial bodies that lacked the historic episcopate; he refused to make it the sine qua non of a church. Although I personally identify with Ramsey's later, softer ecumenical stance, I still regard *The Gospel and the Catholic Church*, taken as a whole, as a paradigm of an ecclesiology that is both Catholic and reformed.[67]

---

[67] Here I would refer to my *Reshaping Ecumenical Theology* (London and New York: T&T Clark, 2010).

9

The Paschal Mystery the foundation of the church

The journey so far

The Paschal Mystery of the death and resurrection of Jesus Christ is the climax of salvation history. As such it is also the matrix – the source, basis and criterion – of the church. In the first main part of this book we proposed as our topic of enquiry the foundation of the church and of its faith, of which Paul speaks in 1 Cor. 3:11 ('no other foundation than Jesus Christ'), a text that is paraphrased in the well-known hymn 'The Church's one foundation is Jesus Christ her Lord'. We then established beyond any serious doubt, on the basis of the consensus of modern biblical study, that Jesus of Nazareth neither founded by any explicit act, nor intended as part of his purpose, the church that soon emerged in history bearing his name and claiming his authority. Clearly, Jesus could not have conceived of a new, different and separate church, because there was already in existence a church of God, 'the congregation of the people of Israel' (Exod. 17:1; 35:1; Lev. 19:2; etc.). He belonged to it, knew and loved its Scriptures; participated in its worship and festivals; and addressed his message to it – as did his disciples and apostles. That fact is decisive in itself and to appreciate it does not require historical-critical methods of biblical research, only an intelligent reading of the Old and New Testaments. But, in addition, the eschatological horizon of the New Testament, the imminent expectation of the manifestation of the reign of God, and thereby the transformation of the world order into one of justice, peace and plenty, precluded any kind of design or blueprint for the long-term future of his mission. Against that background, our study of the ecclesial language of the Gospels and Epistles, including the images or metaphors (body, people, temple, spouse, household, priesthood, etc.) that are used to describe the early Christian communities, revealed the intimate connection and unbreakable bond between the church and Jesus that was experienced with such vibrancy by the first generation or two of Christians.

In the second main part of the book we examined the arguments, regarding the relationship of the church to Jesus, of a representative selection of Protestant, Roman Catholic and Anglican theologians (plus one Methodist), all of whom accepted the historical-critical method of research into the Bible and church history. Almost all of them recognized that Jesus' mission was to the existing church, 'the lost sheep of the house of Israel' (Mt. 10:6; 15:24); they also reckoned with the foreshortened time-scale of New Testament expectation. Some rather impatiently dismissed the suggestion that Jesus could have explicitly founded the Christian church, but, even for them, that was not the end of the story. They went on to elaborate subtle and sophisticated theological models of the connection between Jesus and the church, between the church and Jesus. Some placed the 'launch' point of the church at the calling of the disciples or the commissioning of the apostles, others at the Last Supper, the Ascension or Pentecost. All were agreed that Jesus' mission to proclaim the nearness or actual presence of the reign of God was not extinguished with his death on the cross – rather the death brought his work to completion – and that his mission revived through the resurrection appearances to the apostles and their being filled with his Spirit, and that his mission was invested in a small body of inspired followers, a faithful remnant. This tiny group formed the core or nucleus of the *ekklēsia* which then followed the trajectory, so familiar to us, of development and change, decline and expansion, corruption and reformation, through the centuries until the present time.

The Liberal Protestants, especially Harnack, Schweitzer and Troeltsch, tended to see the enduring power of Jesus in the impact of his personality then and now. His personal influence was like a great river, carving its way through the centuries and gathering individuals (I mean individuals) to itself as it moved. It is too easy to dismiss this notion as a crude psychologizing of Christology, excessively influenced by the fascination with personality that was current at the start of the twentieth century in the West. But if we replace 'personality' with 'character' – namely 'the character of Christ' – I think we are on firmer ground, partly because the ethical element is to the fore. To explore this idea further here, would take us into a fascinating theological exploration of the essence of Christianity which is an area that I wish to reserve for future treatment. But the image of the river for the impact of Jesus on the future church is suggestive in itself. We recall from Chapter 1 Wordsworth's phrase 'a rock with torrents roaring'. It is not enough to hold on to the rock, 'impregnable' though it may be thought; we must have movement, dynamism, refreshment and irrigation! Psalm 46:4, in the King James Bible, springs to mind: 'There is a river, the streams whereof shall make glad the city of God, the holy place of the tabernacles of the most high.' John Buchan chose this verse as the epigraph for his most explicitly Christian (and posthumously published) novel, *Sick Heart River*.[1] For the deeper understanding of that great unfolding, flowing ecclesial narrative, the two key interpretative ideas, for me, are *development* and *reform* – they belong together and should never be separated. They are equally imperative. Development is a function of the church; it is part of its business; we need not apologize for it. But reform acts as a check on undisciplined, ill-considered development. Therefore, *ecclesia reformata semper reformanda!* In the interplay and interaction of development and reform the integrity of the church, as the people of God and the body of Christ, is to be discovered.

However, we still need to ask, 'Why is there a river at all?' and 'What happened at the source of the river for it to have such a powerful effect?' So, having prepared the ground through these biblical, historical and theological enquiries, we will now examine, in this concluding chapter, some of the ways in which the prophetic themes of

---

[1]   John Buchan, *Sick Heart River* (London: Hodder and Stoughton, 1941).

the Old Testament and the ecclesial and metaphorical language of the New Testament come together in 'the Christ event' in a way that sheds light on the connection between Jesus Christ and the church that bears his name. And at this turn of the argument, I will be looking for more help from Rahner, Ramsey, Pannenberg and Kasper than from the Liberal Protestants. What *event* launched the church? According to the New Testament, in the event of Jesus Christ, in his words and deeds, the key eschatological motifs of the Old Testament prophetic writings were being fulfilled.[2] A passage in the Book of Tobit in the Apocrypha recapitulates these prophetic themes: the return of the Jewish people to their homeland from exile and their being gathered together; the rebuilding of Jerusalem and of the temple within it; the conversion of the Gentiles and the restoration of the fortunes of Israel:

> But God will have mercy on them, and God will bring them back into the land of Israel; and they . . . will rebuild Jerusalem in splendour; and in it the temple of God will be rebuilt . . . then the nations in the whole world will all be converted and worship God in truth. . . . All the Israelites who are saved in those days and are truly mindful of God will be gathered together; they will go to Jerusalem and live in safety forever in the land of Abraham. (Tob. 14:5-7)

The restoration of Israel and of the Temple

The restoration of Israel is a dominant theme in Old Testament prophecy. Isa. 52:7-9 holds together three of these motifs: the herald of salvation who proclaims good tidings; the reign of God that brings salvation; and the restoration of Israel, invoked here as Zion or Jerusalem. In this thematic constellation of prophetic hope, God's act of salvation and the fortunes of the people of Israel were inseparable. The good tidings of the reign of God were addressed to the covenant people, the *ekklēsia*. In other words, God's coming salvation was understood in ecclesial terms.[3]

The preaching of John the Baptist seems to have been primarily denunciatory (Mt. 3:7-12). But by becoming a voice crying precisely in the wilderness, his mission also evoked the hope of Israel's eschatological restoration. It was in the wilderness that Yahweh had betrothed Israel to himself in covenant and (by the eschatological logic of 'as in the beginning, so in the end'), it was in the wilderness that Yahweh would, as he had promised, woo her back again (Hos. 2:14-15). John the Baptist's message contains an implicit 'scenario of fulfilment' for, as well as the chaff that would be consumed by unquenchable fire, there would remain the wheat that the Lord would gather into his barn (Mt. 3:12). Although John's message was addressed to the nation collectively, it would have the effect of dividing Israel: through repentance and purification, a remnant would be gathered for the promised restoration.[4] It seems that the public

---

[2]   Dunn provides a succinct summary of those expectations: James D. G. Dunn, *Jesus Remembered, Christianity in the Making, Volume 1* (Grand Rapids, MI: Eerdmans, 2003), pp. 393–6.
[3]   Ben Meyer, *The Aims of Jesus* (London: SCM Press, 1979), pp. 133–4.
[4]   Ibid., pp. 118, 128, 139.

call to national repentance, issued by John, formed the presupposition, as well as the preparation, of Jesus' own mission. But after the failure of his public proclamation, Jesus concentrated instead on private preparation of the disciples – perhaps seeing them already as the 'elect remnant' – for the coming restoration. The remnant concept brings together the biblical themes of election, judgement, promise and restoration and is linked to the figure (both individual and corporate) of the Servant of Deutero-Isaiah.[5] In the Servant Song of Isa. 49:1-7, for example, we find the themes of 'bringing back' from exile, being gathered together, the restoration of Israel, the giving of the Servant/Israel as 'a light to the nations', so that God's 'salvation may reach to the ends of the earth'. The remnant that Jesus cherished became the nucleus of the community that would bear his name (Rom. 11:5-7).[6]

Like Moses viewing the Promised Land from Mount Pisgah, John the Baptist announces an event – the arrival of the kingdom of God – that he does not live to enjoy. 'The least in the kingdom of heaven is greater than he' (Mt. 1:11; Lk. 7:28). Christopher Rowland writes: 'John stands at the fulcrum of the ages; he is the hinge upon which the aeons move. He stands on the brink of the age of fulfilment, but is not himself part of it.'[7] But Jesus himself comes both announcing and fulfilling the promise of the kingdom at the same time: both heralding the kingdom and ushering it in. In Jesus the kingdom not only is imminent or at hand, but already impinges on the world in the sense that in him it is personified, embodied and enacted. Jesus' own proclamation and action are concerned with the kingdom and as such are filled with images of a restored and renewed Israel. The restoration is signalled by several intentional actions of Jesus: the healing of the afflicted; the gathering of the outcasts; the deliverance of those who are in captivity to evil powers; the sending out of twelve apostles to the twelve tribes; the promulgation of the new Torah by the new Moses ('You have heard . . . but I say unto you') from the mountain; the table fellowship pointing to the messianic banquet with Abraham, Isaac and Jacob; the promised rebuilding of the temple, and so on. Jesus not only announces a restoration that is to come (conditional on repentance, faith and obedience though this promise must be), but also effects it there and then. As sinners are restored, sick persons are healed and the possessed are set free, God's restoration of his covenant people is effected in anticipation and in sign. Jesus is the sign of the times that must be discerned. He embodies proleptically the presence of the restored Israel of the kingdom. The kingdom is encapsulated in one person, one human (and divine) life.

Perhaps the most revealing of the symbolic enactments that pointed to a restored and renewed Israel is the 'cleansing' of the Temple and with it the sayings that speak of a spiritual temple (and in John, of 'the temple of his body'). The cleansing was not merely the purifying of the cultus so that it could continue in a better state, but an enacted parable of judgement and restoration. Sanders insists that the 'cleansing'

[5]   G. A. Danell, 'The Idea of God's People in the Bible', in Anton Fridrichsen (ed.), *The Root of the Vine: Essays in Biblical Theology* (London: Dacre Press/ A. and C. Black, 1953), pp. 23–36.

[6]   E. P. Sanders, *Jesus and Judaism* (London, SCM Press, 1985), p. 227; T. W. Manson, *The Teaching of Jesus* (Cambridge: Cambridge University Press, 1935 [1931]), pp. 175-7 (for the notion of the remnant).

[7]   Christopher Rowland, *Christian Origins: An Account of the Setting and Character of the most Important Messianic Sect of Judaism* (London: SPCK, 1985), p. 133.

represented first, the impending destruction of the temple and second, its corollary, the arrival from heaven of the eschatological temple 'not made with hands' that was the received symbol of the restored Jerusalem/Israel. The traditional designation of Jesus' action as one of 'cleansing' is inadequate.[8] Sanders' point that Jesus was concerned with restoration, not simply the reform of the status quo, is well taken, but once this is understood, 'cleansing' in the sense of Malachi's refiner's fire and fuller's soap (Mal. 3:2-3), remains an appropriate metaphor. What Jesus did in the temple seems to have been an intentional messianic act, in fulfilment of Mal. 3:1-4, combining judgement of Israel's sins and her restoration to the purity and faithfulness of her first love. In prophesying the destruction of the Temple, Jesus appeared to threaten the supposedly inviolate symbol of national sacred identity. But in speaking of the raising up of a new temple after three days he was evoking eschatological visions of a restored and triumphant Israel. As Meyer puts it, 'Epitomized in the radiant image of the temple, the goal of Jesus' career was the messianic restoration of Israel.'[9]

The Johannine gloss ('He spoke of the temple of his body': Jn 2:21) encapsulates the crucial transition from Jewish apocalyptic to Christian ecclesiology. The logic of this transition, crystallized in the Johannine verse, is telescoped through a sequence of theological paradigms (which are also historical stages) of temple, people, remnant, crucified and risen body of Christ, Holy Spirit, Eucharist and church. This logic points to the central Pauline image of the church as the body of Christ. Paul would have built on what he had received in the tradition (1 Cor. 11:23; 15:3). John does not pretend that the temple/body concept is anything other than a retrospective interpretation in the light of the cross and resurrection: 'After he was raised from the dead, his disciples remembered that he had said this; and they believed the scripture ["Zeal for your house will consume me": Ps. 69.9] and the word that Jesus had spoken' (Jn 2:17, 22). In other words, they understood that it had been foretold that Jesus would suffer death for the sake of what God would create: the people-temple-building-garden-body-church in which it was God's good pleasure to dwell in glory.

The fulfilment of Jesus' prophetic act in the new spiritual temple is underlined in Jn 4:20-24: 'The hour is coming when you will worship the Father neither on this mountain [Gerizim, where the Samaritans looked for the restoration of their own temple, which had been destroyed in 129 BC] nor [on the other mountain: Zion] in Jerusalem . . . but in spirit and in truth.' The oracular utterance of Jesus, 'The hour is coming and now is [here]' (Jn 4:23), is a striking example of the construction of realized eschatology: it is coming and it is already here! This saying probably points forward (within the narrative) to the destruction of the Jerusalem temple – for the Fourth Gospel is not completely lacking in futurist eschatology – but, more importantly, it points to the presence of the one in and through whom that spiritual worship of the Father has become a possibility and a reality. With this saying we should compare Jn 5:25: 'The hour is coming, and now is [here], when the dead will hear the voice of the Son of God, and those who hear will live.' In this saying spiritual resurrection to eternal life is given already through the words and deeds of Christ, but without prejudice to the

[8]   Sanders, *Jesus and Judaism*, pp. 61–3, 77–9.
[9]   Meyer, *The Aims of Jesus*, p. 202.

general resurrection in the last day (cf. 5:28-29; 11:24-25). In the Fourth Gospel, the 'hour' signifies the eschatological destiny of Jesus Christ (Jn 2:4; 12:23, 27; 13:1; 17:1). In John, Christ's 'words', 'works' or 'signs' are virtually synonymous. His words and his deeds are equally the vehicles of revelation, the bearers of salvation.[10]

The harvest of the nations

'The gospel' (*euaggelion*, 'good news', 'glad tidings') is the banner under which the proclamation of and about Jesus Christ first went forth. 'Jesus came to Galilee, proclaiming the good news (*euaggelion*) of God, and saying, "The time is fulfilled and the kingdom of God is at hand; repent and believe in the good news (*euaggelion*)' (Mk 1:14-15). But the term *euaggelion* has a secular sense too and is used outside of the canonical literature. In the Roman Empire 'gospel' referred to the proclamation of the birthday, the majority or the accession of the emperor. An inscription dated to c. 9 BC says of Octavian (Augustus), 'the birthday of the god [*sic*] was for the world the beginning of joyful tidings (*euaggelion*), which have been proclaimed on his account.' The first words of Mark's Gospel, though dating from around half a century later than the inscription, 'the beginning of the gospel', and so on, are an uncanny echo of this. Gospel was not of merely local relevance; it meant joy to the world. The meaning of 'gospel' in the Roman Empire was 'an historical event which introduces a new situation for the world'.[11] This seems to me to provide a suitable cue to discuss the call of the Gentiles through the gospel into the fellowship of the church of Christ.

The abrogation of temple worship in Jerusalem (which was a fait accompli in the destruction of the Temple by the Romans in AD 70) and the vision of the worship that is in spirit and truth that supersedes the temple cultus both point to the calling of the Gentiles and their gathering into the people of God. The Gentiles were held to include the Samaritans. Although the Samaritans were descended from the ten northern tribes of Israel, their ethnic identity had been diluted by the admixture of pagan peoples whom the Assyrians had imported, together with their gods, from other parts of their empire. Jewish tradition had it that the original tribes of Samaria had suffered mass deportation and had been replaced by pagans (2 Kgs 17; 18:9-12). The five previous husbands of 'the woman of Samaria' with whom Jesus conversed at Jacob's well in Jn 4:1-42 almost certainly refers to the five nations that colonized Samaria at this time (2 Kgs 17:24, 28-30). The Jews of Jesus' day regarded Samaritans not so much as apostate Jews but as Gentiles, or worse than Gentiles. Both Luke and John see a special significance in Jesus' contact with the Samaritans. Luke, unlike his main source Mark, has Jesus pass through Samaria (Lk. 9:52; 17:11). The Samaritans are explicitly designated by Luke as 'foreigners' (Lk. 17:18). While some Samaritans oppose Jesus' ministry, others are held up in his Luke's Gospel as examples of saving faith and good works (Lk. 9:53ff; 10:30-7; 17:16). Luke sees these Samaritan episodes as anticipating and perhaps also

[10] Andrew T. Lincoln, *The Gospel According to St John*, Black's New Testament Commentaries (London and New York: Continuum, 2005), pp. 505–6.
[11] W. L. Lane, *The Gospel of Mark*, NICNT (Grand Rapids, MI: Eerdmans, 1974), pp. 42–3.

justifying the later mission of the apostles, especially of Peter and John, together with Philip the Evangelist, in Samaria (Acts 8:1-25), and he regards Samaria as a stepping stone to 'the ends of the earth' (Acts 1:8). The third and fourth Gospels corroborate each other in indicating the significance of Jesus' ministry to Samaritans as a foretaste of the Gentile mission of the church. The faith of these Samaritans, that Jesus is not only the Jewish Messiah (the Messiah was expected also by the Samaritans: Jn 4:25-26), but also 'the Saviour of the world' (Jn 4:42), represents the first fruits of the harvest of the Gentiles (Jn 4:35-42).

The 'first-fruits' motif becomes explicit in John when some 'Greeks' ask to see Jesus (Jn 12:20-28). These were not Hellenistic Jews but Gentile 'Godfearers', attracted to the faith of Israel, as is indicated by the fact that the two apostles with Greek names and who come from 'Galilee of the Gentiles', Philip and Andrew, mediate with Jesus for them. Jesus is moved by this request to speak once more of a harvest to be reaped and of the prior condition that a grain of wheat must fall into the earth and die in order to bring forth much fruit. 'And I, when I am lifted up from the earth, will draw all people to myself' (Jn 12:32). In John's narrative, the longing of the Gentiles for their Saviour brings home to Jesus that 'the hour' – the fulfilment of his destiny of suffering (which is also and as such, according to John, precisely his glorification) – has arrived (Jn 12:27-28). When we set these two Johannine passages (the Samaritan woman and the enquiring Greeks) side by side, we can say with Hoskyns and Davey, 'In the perspective of the Fourth Gospel . . . the advancing Samaritans anticipate the movement of the Gentiles to Jesus which was the consequence of his death.'[12]

Through the death and resurrection ('seed . . . die . . . lifted up') of Jesus, the Gentiles also will be incorporated into the spiritual temple, that is Christ's body, in fulfilment of the prophetic promise that one day the Gentiles would flock to the temple (Isa. 2:2-3; Mic. 4:1-5) which would be a 'house of prayer for all nations' (Isa. 56:7; Mk 11:17; Mt. 21:13; Luke has 'My house shall be a house of prayer' (though he omits 'for all nations': Lk. 19:45)). The Epistle to the Ephesians uses the imagery of body and temple for the church, just as John does and as Paul does in 1 Corinthians. As foretold by the prophets, the Gentiles would be gathered for worship in the temple. Through the cross, Jesus Christ has reconciled both Jews and Gentiles to God 'in one body', making the Gentiles 'no longer strangers and aliens, but citizens with the saints and members of the household of God, built upon the foundation of the apostles and prophets, with Christ Jesus himself as the cornerstone'. The passage continues: 'In him the whole structure is joined together and grows into a holy temple in the Lord; in whom you [Gentiles] also are built together in the Spirit into a dwelling place for God' (Eph. 2:19-22).

The late Jewish concept of the eschatological temple, built without hands and descending from heaven to earth, is explicitly invoked – and decisively reinterpreted in the light of the death and resurrection of Jesus – in the Revelation of St John. John sees 'the holy city Jerusalem coming down out of heaven from God.' Its gates bear the names of the twelve tribes of Israel and are always open to welcome the pilgrim Gentiles (cf. Isa. 60:11). Its foundations are inscribed with the names of the twelve apostles of the

[12]   Edwyn Clement Hoskyns, *The Fourth Gospel*, ed. Francis Noel Davey, 2nd edn (London: Faber and Faber, 1947), p. 246.

Lamb. But the presence of God and of the crucified and risen one replaces the temple: 'I saw no temple in the city, its temple is the Lord God the Almighty and the Lamb'. As foretold (in Isa. 60:19ff), the city needs no natural light, for 'the glory of God is its light, and its lamp is the Lamb'. Ancient prophecies are fulfilled that the Gentiles would be drawn to the shining light of Israel and would offer their wealth in sacrifice on the altar of the Lord (Isa. 60.3, 7, 11: 'Nations shall come to your light . . . nations shall bring you their wealth'). 'The nations will walk by its light, and the kings of the earth will bring their glory into it . . . People will bring into it the glory and honour of the nations' (Rev. 21:10-14, 22-26). The imagery in the First Epistle of Peter of Christians as 'living stones built into a spiritual house' of which Jesus Christ is the cornerstone, and where spiritual sacrifices are offered by the holy priesthood of the people of God (1 Peter 2:4-10) completes the picture that has been forming of a consensus among the early Christians that Jesus' words and deeds with regard to the temple in Jerusalem were fulfilled in the creation of the Christian community. The expectation of the restoration of Israel and the Jerusalem temple, symbolized by the 'cleansing' of the temple, but disappointed in the event, was reinterpreted to refer to the creation of the Christian church. This reinterpretation was a legitimate one, for all along the expectation of restoration had been an ecclesiological matter.

If it had known it, the early church would have endorsed Loisy's dictum that Jesus announced the kingdom, and it was the church that came. In the light of the above exposition, we can say with some assurance that the historical Jesus is the source of this reinterpretation. In late Jewish thought, one of the tasks of the Messiah was to build the eschatological temple or to herald its descent from heaven. Jesus interpreted the temple symbolically to represent the community (church) when he said to Peter, 'On this rock I will build [not 'my temple', note, but] my *ekklēsia*' (Mt. 16:18). At the Last Supper Jesus himself introduces the final layer of interpretation, the metaphor of the body, when in the context of the covenant, he breaks bread and gives it to them saying, 'This is my body'. The implied meaning is, 'You all who receive this bread from me on the eve of my sacrificial death are now my body'. There is an implied extrapolation from eating to being and from receiving to becoming. As we saw in an earlier chapter, Paul's central image is of the church as the body of Christ, but he also speaks of both the individual believer and the local church as the temple of Christ and the Holy Spirit. Both images are an elaboration of the founding dominical metaphor of temple-body.

Good news for the oppressed

In the preaching and ministry of Jesus it is above all the poor, the oppressed and the excluded who are the beneficiaries of the good news or gospel (*euaggellion*). John the Baptist had also come proclaiming good news or gospel, according to Luke only (3:18), while according to Matthew (only) John also proclaimed that the reign of God was at hand (Mt. 3:2), which on Jesus' lips was the good news. John's message was one of judgement preceding restoration, hence the emphasis on repentance. Jesus' message was pure good news, though Jesus also pronounced 'woes' against hypocrites and oppressors. The contrast between John and Jesus is apparent, and it is made explicit in the Gospels (Mt. 11:7-19; Lk. 7:24-34). But it should not be overdrawn; there is commonality and continuity, though a difference of emphasis. However, Jesus' reply to the question that came from John the Baptist, 'Are you the one who is to come, or should we look for another?' is decisive in marking a boundary and a new departure: 'The blind receive their sight, the lame walk, the lepers are cleansed, the deaf hear, the dead are raised and the poor have the good news (gospel) brought to them' (Mt. 11:2-5; Lk. 7:22). It is pure good news. John must accept the prophetic signs of the imminence of the reign of God in their midst (Mt. 11:6; Lk. 7:23). The poor and oppressed have at last found favour with God.

In the Beatitudes, it is to the poor that the promise of the kingdom of God, which is the content of the good news, is given (Lk. 5:20). According to Luke's account of Jesus' reading from the scroll of Isaiah in the Nazareth synagogue, the Spirit of the Lord has anointed him precisely 'to bring good news to the poor' (Lk. 4:18). He proclaims the year of the Lord's favour, but significantly not 'the day of vengeance of our God' (Lk. 4:19; cf. Isa. 61:2). The poor, the hungry and the sorrowful know good news when they see it. As for the rich, the replete, those who make merry, it passes them by (Lk. 6:20-25). When Matthew alters his and Luke's common source ('Q') from 'poor' to 'poor in spirit' (Mt. 5:3), is he distorting the intended meaning or elucidating it? Matthew knows that the Aramaic term underlying the Greek has connotations that are not brought out by simply saying 'poor'. 'It denotes those who are oppressed by the tyrannical power of evil and who long for the intervention of God. The poor are primarily the faithful men and women whose spirits are oppressed by the present order.'[13] So while Matthew loses something of the social and political radicalism of Luke, he extends the promise of blessedness to the greater number of those who are burdened with poverty in another sense.

Gospel and kingdom

The content of the gospel is at first the kingdom, the sovereign rule or reign of God. 'Now after John was arrested, Jesus came to Galilee, proclaiming the gospel of God and saying, "The time is fulfilled and the kingdom of God has come near; repent and believe in the gospel"' (Mk 1:14-15). As Loisy said, '"the kingdom of God is at hand" . . . without doubt is the essence of the gospel, the "good news" announced by Jesus.' Loisy went on: 'No other idea holds so prominent and so large a place in the teaching of Jesus. . . . Everywhere the gospel is subordinated to the kingdom.'[14] Gospel scholarship, during the more than a century since Loisy wrote, would not demur. God's sovereign rule has drawn near; it has in fact come upon the world. The metaphors used of the coming of the kingdom are not only temporal ('the time is fulfilled') but

---

[13] Sir Edwyn Hoskyns, Bart and Noel Davey, *The Riddle of the New Testament* (London: Faber and Faber, 1936), pp. 117–18.
[14] Alfred Loisy, *The Gospel and the Church*, trans. Christopher Home (London: Isbister; New York: Scribner, 1903), pp. 57, 59, 67.

also spatial ('drawn near'; cf. 'You are not far from the kingdom') and local ('in your midst/among you').[15] Manifested in exorcisms, healings, table fellowship with 'sinners', and in parables and pithy sayings, the announcement of the kingdom demands the response of repentance and faith. The good news in the preaching of Jesus is that the reign of God brings not – at least at first – the terrors of judgement, as John the Baptist had threatened, but the free offer of salvation. In the first half of Mark, as in the whole of Matthew and in Luke to some extent, the gospel tells of the kingdom. But in the second half of Mark and in Paul, the gospel becomes identified with the person and destiny of Jesus Christ. As Bultmann put it, 'He who formerly had been the *bearer* of the message was drawn into it and became its essential *content. The proclaimer became the proclaimed.*'[16] Parables such as the mustard seed, the leaven, and the sower show that the kingdom of God is present in obscurity, contingency and failure – just like Jesus and his fate. What is greatest of all is hidden from proud human eyes, but is active in what is most humble and despised.[17] The trajectory of Jesus' ministry, as he draws near to Jerusalem, raises the question of his own relation to the kingdom that he has announced. As Walter Kasper puts it: 'An unknown rabbi from a remote corner of Palestine with a handful of uneducated disciples and surrounded by a disreputable rabble – tax collectors, prostitutes, sinners – was this the new age, the kingdom of God?'[18] It was the presence of the reign of God not in spite of but because of those facts.

What these perplexities are leading us to see is that Jesus himself, in his person, his words and his deeds, *is* the kingdom. The reign of God is manifest in him. As he moves among men and women – teaching in riddles, performing exorcisms, touching the unclean, making many whole, gathering the faithful – the kingdom is revealed in their midst. The person of Christ, poured out in ministry, was (as Schillebeeckx puts it) 'a concrete tender of salvation then and there. . . . Where he appears he brings salvation and becomes God's rule already realised.'[19] The kingdom is perfectly realized in him because he is totally open to God's will and utterly at the service of God's purpose. As he proclaims the promised salvation, Jesus at the same time constitutes in his person the availability, the offer, the presence of that salvation. As Cranfield comments, it is because Jesus is in their midst that the kingdom is in their midst.[20] The life of Jesus embodies the kingdom and fully articulates it. He is the concrete manifestation in one human life of God's loving and gracious purpose for all humankind. He is fully transparent to God and the love of God. In him God is stretching out a loving hand – indeed, a loving Son – to the world. With an insight that reverberates down the centuries, Origen first suggested that Jesus is *autobasileia* – the kingdom itself. When in old age Karl Barth was asked whether there was one word that summed up his theology, he replied '*Autobasileia*'. This term – this explosive concept in one

---

[15] C. E. B. Cranfield, *The Gospel according to St Mark* (Cambridge: Cambridge University Press, 1966), p. 68.

[16] Rudolf Bultmann, *Theology of the New Testament*, trans. Kendrick Grobel, 2 vols (London, SCM Press, 1952), vol. 1, p. 33; italics original.

[17] Walter Kasper, *Jesus the Christ* (London: Burns & Oates; New York: Paulist Press, 1976), p. 75.

[18] Ibid., p. 75.

[19] Edward Schillebeeckx, *Jesus: An Experiment in Christology*, trans. Hubert Hoskins (London: Collins, 1979), p. 306.

[20] Cranfield, *The Gospel according to St Mark*, p. 66.

word – suggests the identity of Jesus with God in the divine action. Jesus is more than the prophetic representative of God, which in an unqualified form would be a low functionalist Christology, though one that can find some scriptural support. He becomes, perhaps unwittingly, the channel or vehicle of the self-communication of God in the midst of the world. The words and deeds of Jesus are the words and deeds of God performed in the world by human means; divine action mediated through human agency. Thus, God's faithfulness to all God's promises through the prophets is revealed and sealed in the person and destiny of Jesus believed in as the Christ. 'For all the promises of God are "Yes" in him' (2 Cor. 1:20). Karl Barth wrote in the second edition of his commentary on Romans: 'In Christ the consistency of God with himself – so grievously questioned throughout the whole world, among both Jews and Greeks – is brought to light and honoured.'[21]

The Paschal Mystery

'The Paschal mystery of Christ's cross and resurrection stands at the centre of the good news (gospel) that the apostles, and the church following them, are to proclaim to the world.'[22] As I conclude this rather protracted journey through the New Testament and modern theology, I want to put the Paschal Mystery of Christ's death and resurrection at the centre. I have used the expression 'the Christ event' occasionally in this book. 'The Christ event' is a convenient theological shorthand for the unfolding narrative of all that is contained in Jesus and his mission. It embraces the coming, life, ministry, character, passion, death, resurrection and ascension of Jesus Christ, which cannot be spelt out in full every time. Similarly, the phrase 'the Paschal Mystery' on the face of it refers only to Easter, to the crucifixion and resurrection of Jesus, not to the whole of his words and deeds. But this too is shorthand. The expression 'the Paschal Mystery' presupposes the incarnation, life, ministry, character, proclamation, teaching, passion, resurrection and whole destiny of Jesus Christ. The time from Good Friday to Easter Day is the final earthly drama of his story, but it would not mean much, theologically and personally, without all that led up to it. So the Paschal Mystery speaks not only of all that Jesus was and did, but also of his connection to the church. The nub of my argument throughout this book has been that the content of the Paschal Mystery is not only about the death and resurrection of Jesus Christ, but also about the connection between that event and the church. I will go slightly further and say that the Paschal Mystery is also about the church as such, the church that is his body, his people, his bride. Jesus enters upon his passion and sacrifice with his community, his Israel, on his heart.

It is the church's celebration of the Eucharist, above all, that makes the connection between the church and the Paschal Mystery – that shows in fact that the church belongs within the Paschal Mystery and is integral to it. The logic of our exploration

---

[21] Karl Barth, *The Epistle to the Romans*, trans. from the 6th German edition by Edwyn C. Hoskyns (Oxford: Oxford University Press, 1933), p. 40.
[22] *The Catechism of the Catholic Church* (London: Geoffrey Chapman, 1994), p. 128 (§571).

of 'Jesus and the church' has been moving from the proclamation of the gospel of the reign of God *by* Jesus to the proclamation of the person and work *of* Jesus, who is confessed to be the Christ, by the apostles and New Testament writers. Now a further and decisive shift takes place in our thinking from the person of Jesus, confessed as the Christ, to his destiny as it is specifically focused in the Paschal Mystery of his death and resurrection, as it is represented, commemorated, participated in and celebrated, in the Eucharist of the Christian church.

The kingdom is concentrated in his person. He commits himself without reservation to God's saving purpose. But that purpose is not heeded by the people. He came to his own and his own received him not (Jn 1:11). Although his summons is addressed to all Israel, its effect is to divide the covenant people. The 'sons of the kingdom' – those for whom the kingdom is really their birthright – will be cast into outer darkness, while the Gentiles will flock in, as had been foretold, to sit down at the messianic banquet with the patriarchs and the true Israelites (Mt. 8:11). The tender (through him) of God's salvation (through him) is generally refused by the people (his people). The momentum of his mission and ministry leads inexorably to his passion and death. It is a single continuous action of self-giving and self-communication in which we can discern two distinct moments which traditional theology has called the active and the passive obedience of Jesus Christ. His sacrifice in life (active) leads to his sacrifice in death (passive). But these two aspects of his obedience belong together in a continuum. The self-oblation of the eternal Word to the Father is continuous and uninterrupted through the incarnation itself, the ministry of preaching, teaching and healing, the passion, the crucifixion and entombment. His active and passive obedience are of a piece; it is simply a matter of emphasis. In fact, in the Fourth Gospel, Jesus' whole trajectory, his fulfilment of his destiny, is one of active obedience: he is in control all the way to his last breath.

So the world does not bow, in repentance and faith, to God's sovereign rule. The Jews will not have this man to rule over them (cf. Lk. 19:14, 28). Rejection of Jesus is rejection of the kingdom, and rejection of the kingdom is rejection of God. 'At first Jesus goes about as one who offers the eschatological rule of God; then after the offer is rejected by Israel he does so as the one who, with the rejection of the offer, is himself rejected.'[23] As the fulfilment of the prophetic type of the Suffering Servant of Isa. 52–53, he was, according to the libretto of G. F. Handel's 'Messiah', 'despisèd, despisèd and rejected, rejected of men, despisèd'.

However, before his death Jesus does something of momentous significance for the future of the mission that he has inaugurated. He gathers his disciples around him at the Passover season when sacrifice was offered to commemorate sacramentally the act of divine deliverance that had brought Israel into being as the people of God. By means of the symbols of the broken bread and the shared cup of wine, Jesus shows his disciples that his impending death will be, not the failure of his mission, but its intended completion. His sacrifice will serve the purpose of God's sovereign rule. He vows not to drink of the fruit of the vine until he drinks the new wine that belongs to the kingdom of God on the far side of his death (Mk 14:25; Lk. 22:18). That death will make possible

---

[23]   F. Muszner, cited Schillebeeckx, *Jesus: An Experiment in Christology*, p. 298.

a new relationship or covenant of God with God's people. By ensuring that they eat and drink his death as a sacrifice – an oblatory, dedicatory sacrifice, acceptable to God – Jesus incorporates the disciples into a purpose that stretches beyond the darkness of Good Friday.[24] He has proclaimed in word and deed the good news of the imminent and already present reign of God. The hopes thereby evoked have (as it were) collapsed inwards upon his own person in a christological concentration of the kingdom. When the disciples run away, Jesus stands alone and alone represents the kingdom of God in the midst of the world and with it his own mission received from God. He is now the remnant personified. But he has not failed to provide – in an utterly unexpected and unimaginable way – for the promised restoration of Israel, the renewed life of the covenant people, even though this hope must be carried forward by a tiny community: the faithful remnant in the person of Jesus will overflow into the fellowship of his disciples. The last testament of Jesus in his earthly life, as he confronts the cross, is of an *ecclesial* nature.

Soon after the events of Easter, the disciples are found gathered together in fellowship and solidarity, proclaiming the Messiahship of Jesus, baptizing the new converts into Christ's death and resurrection, breaking the bread of his body and celebrating his victory in a common cup. The Paschal Mystery is being – and would continue to be – carried forward *in* the church and *as* the church. It is in truth the Paschal Mystery of Christ and his church together. Sacramentally, Christians would continue to be drawn into the movement of his self-offering and the church would be caught up eucharistically in the continual momentum of his sacrifice. The centre of gravity in the dynamic narrative of Jesus Christ has now moved through several stages: from the gospel of the reign of God that is 'at hand'; from the reign of God to the one person in whom that reign is embodied; from that one person standing for the kingdom that has been rejected, to the Paschal Mystery in which he becomes the representative corporate person, holding his people in his heart as he passes through death, burial and resurrection; and then from the Paschal Mystery, via his self-communication in the word and the sacraments, in the power of the Holy Spirit, to the church.

The sacraments of baptism and the Eucharist, that derive from the mission of Jesus and the apostles, unite believers intimately with Christ and his redemptive destiny that culminated in the Paschal Mystery. In the waters of baptism we die with Christ on the cross (Good Friday); our old sinful life is buried with him in the grave (Holy Saturday); and just as he was raised from the dead by the glory of the Father (Easter Day), so we also walk in newness of life (Rom. 6:3-4). In the church's celebration of the Eucharist we are taken into the heart of the Paschal Mystery and drawn into the movement of his self-sacrifice for the world and his self-communication to the world. For the bread that we break is our participation in the body of Christ, crucified and risen; and the cup of blessing that we bless is our participation in the blood of Christ, signifying his redeeming sacrifice (1 Cor. 10:16-17). I see word and sacrament (the subjects of a sequel to this book) as twin pillars of the church, rising up from the foundation, but also grounded in the Paschal Mystery deep within it. The community to which Jesus came

---

[24]   Cf. Schillebeeckx, *Jesus: An Experiment in Christology*, p. 311.

(even the faithful remnant) abandoned him and he went to the cross and the grave alone; but when he rose again from the dead he brought the community into existence. Bultmann said that he rose into the *kerygma* of the early church. Since the *kerygma* is the proclamation of the Paschal Mystery by word and sacrament, Bultmann's assertion is not as far-fetched as it sounds. If Jesus Christ is *autobasileia*, the kingdom itself, he is also *autoekklēsia*, the church itself.

Bibliography

Abbott, Walter M. (ed.), *The Documents of Vatican II*. London and Dublin: Geoffrey Chapman, 1966.

Adam, Karl, *The Spirit of Catholicism*. London: Sheed & Ward, 1938.

Allison, Dale C., *The End of the Ages Has Come: An Early Interpretation of the Passion and Resurrection of Jesus*. Edinburgh: T&T Clark.

Anglican–Roman Catholic International Commission [ARCIC], *The Final Report*. London: SPCK & CTS, 1982.

Anglican–Roman Catholic International Commission [ARCIC], *Church as Communion* London: CTS/SPCK, 1990.

Ashton, John, *Understanding the Fourth Gospel*. Oxford: Clarendon Press, 1991.

Auerbach, Erich, *Mimesis: The Representation of Reality in Western Literature*, trans. Willard R. Trask; intro. Edward W. Said. Princeton, NJ: Princeton University Press, 2013 [1946].

Augustine, *City of God*, trans. Henry Bettenson; ed. David Knowles, O.S.B. Harmondsworth: Penguin, 1972.

Avis, Paul [P. D. L.], *The Church in the Theology of the Reformers*. London: Marshall, Morgan and Scott; Atlanta, GA: John Knox Press, 1981; reprinted Eugene, OR: Wipf and Stock, 2002.

Avis, Paul [P. D. L.], 'The Church's One Foundation', *Theology* LXXXIX, no. 730 (July 1986): pp. 257–63.

Avis, Paul [P. D. L.], *The Methods of Modern Theology*. Basingstoke: Marshall Pickering, 1986.

Avis, Paul [P. D. L.], *Gore: Construction and Conflict*. Worthing: Churchman Publishing, 1988.

Avis, Paul [P. D. L.], *Anglicanism and the Christian Church: Theological Resources in Historical Perspective*, 2nd edn. London and New York: T&T Clark, 2002 [1989].

Avis, Paul [P. D. L.], *Christians in Communion*. London: Geoffrey Chapman Mowbray; Collegeville, MN: Liturgical Press, 1990.

Avis, Paul [P. D. L.], *God and the Creative Imagination: Metaphor, Symbol and Myth in Religion and Theology*. London and New York: Routledge, 1999.

Avis, Paul [P. D. L.], *Beyond the Reformation? Authority, Primacy and Unity in the Conciliar Tradition*. London and New York: T&T Clark, 2006.

Avis, Paul [P. D. L.], *Reshaping Ecumenical Theology*. London and New York: T&T Clark, 2010.

Avis, Paul [P. D. L.], 'The Church and Ministry', in David M. Whitford (ed.), *T&T Clark Companion to Reformation Theology*, chapter 9. London and New York: T&T Clark, 2012.

Avis, Paul [P. D. L.], *In Search of Authority: Anglican Theological Method from the Reformation to the Enlightenment*. London and New York: T&T Clark, 2014.

Avis, Paul [P. D. L.], *The Vocation of Anglicanism*. London and New York: T&T Clark, 2016.

Avis, Paul [P. D. L.] (ed.), *The Oxford Handbook of Ecclesiology*. Oxford: Oxford University Press, 2018.

Avis, Paul [P. D. L.], 'Revelation, Epistemology and Authority', in Balázs M. Mezei, Francesca Murphy and Kenneth R. Oakes (eds), *The Oxford Handbook of Divine Revelation*. Oxford: Oxford University Press, forthcoming.

Balabanski, Vicki, *Eschatology in the Making: Mark, Matthew and the Didache*. Cambridge: Cambridge University Press, 1997.

Balthasar, Hans Urs von, *The Glory of the Lord: A Theological Aesthetics, Volume I, Seeing the Form*, trans. Erasmo Leiva-Merikakis; ed. Joseph Fessio, S.J. and John Riches. Edinburgh: T&T Clark, 1982.

Banks, Robert, *Paul's Idea of Community*, revised edn. Peabody, MA: Hendrikson, 1994.

Baptism, Eucharist and Ministry [BEM]. Geneva: World Council of Churches, 1982.

Barker, Margaret, *Temple Theology: An Introduction*. London: SPCK, 2004.

Barmann, Lawrence F., *Baron Friedrich von Hügel and the Modernist Crisis in England*. Cambridge: Cambridge University Press, 1972.

Barr, James, *The Semantics of Biblical Language*. Oxford: Oxford University Press, 1961.

Barrett, C. K., *The Epistle to the Romans*. London: A. & C. Black, 1962.

Barrett, C. K., *The First Epistle to the Corinthians*, 2nd edn. London: A. & C. Black 1971.

Barrett, C. K., *Church, Ministry and Sacraments in the New Testament*. Exeter: Paternoster Press, 1985.

Barth, Karl, *The Epistle to the Romans*, trans. from the 6th German edition by Edwyn C. Hoskyns. London: Oxford University Press, 1933.

Barth, Karl, *God in Action: Theological Addresses*, trans. E. G. Homrighausen and Karl J. Ernst; intro. Josias Friedli. Edinburgh: T&T Clark, 1936.

Barth, Karl and Emil Brunner, *Natural Theology*, trans. Peter Fraenkel. London: Bles, 1946.

Barth, Karl, *Dogmatics in Outline*, trans. G. T. Thomson. London: SCM Press, 1949.

Barth, Karl, *Christ and Adam: Man and Humanity in Romans 5*, trans. T. A. Smail from *Christus und Adam nach Römer 5* in *Theologische Studien*, 35. Evangelische Verlag A. G. Zollikon--Zurich, 1952 (published for the *SJT*), Edinburgh: Oliver and Boyd, 1956.

Barth, Karl, *Theology and Church*, intro. T. F. Torrance. London: SCM Press, 1962.

Barth, Karl, *Schleiermacher-Auswahl*, ed. H. Bolli. Siebenstern Taschenbuch: Munich and Hamburg, 1968.

Barth, Karl, *Church Dogmatics*, ed. G. W. Bromiley and T. F. Torrance. Edinburgh and London: T&T Clark, 1975-.

Barth, Karl, *The Theology of Schleiermacher*, ed. Dietrich Ritschl. Edinburgh: T&T Clark, 1982.

Barth, Karl, *The Göttingen Dogmatics: Instruction in the Christian Religion*, ed. Hannelotte Reiffen, vol. 1. Grand Rapids, MI: Eerdmans, 1991; Edinburgh: T&T Clark, 1993.

Barth, Karl, *Protestant Theology in the Nineteenth Century: Its Background and History*, trans. Brian Cozens and John Bowden, new edn. London: SCM Press, 2001.

Barth, Karl, *The Church and the Churches*, Foreword William G. Rusch. Grand Rapids, MI: Eerdmans, 2005.

Barton, John, *The Nature of Biblical Criticism*. Louisville, KY: Westminster John Knox Press, 2007.

Beale, Gregory K., *The Temple and the Church's Mission: A Biblical Theology of the Dwelling Place of God*. Downers Grove, IL: IVP, 2004.

Bebbington, David, *The Mind of Gladstone*. Oxford: Oxford University Press, 2004.

Bell, George [G. K. A.], *Randall Davidson: Archbishop of Canterbury*, 3rd edn. London: Oxford University Press, 1952.

Bender, Kimlyn, *Karl Barth's Christological Ecclesiology*. Aldershot: Ashgate, 2005; reprinted Eugene, OR: Cascade Books, 2013.

Bender, Kimlyn, 'Karl Barth', in Paul Avis (ed.), *The Oxford Handbook of Ecclesiology*, chapter 17. Oxford: Oxford University Press, 2018.

Benedict XVI (Pope); see Ratzinger, Joseph.

Benko, Stephen, *The Meaning of Sanctorum Communio*. London: SCM Press, 1964.

Berlin, Isaiah, *Four Essays on Liberty*. Oxford: Oxford University Press, 1969.

Best, Ernest, *One Body in Christ: A Study in the Relationship of the Church to Christ in the Epistles of the Apostle Paul*. London: SPCK, 1955.

Blackwell, Albert L., *Schleiermacher's Early Philosophy of Life: Determinism, Freedom and Phantasy*, Harvard Theological Studies 33. Chico, CA: Scholars Press, 1982.

Bockmuehl, Marcus and M. B. Thompson (eds), *A Vision for the Church: Studies in Early Christian Ecclesiology in Honour of J. P. M. Sweet*. Edinburgh: T&T Clark, 1997.

Boff, Leonardo, *Church, Charism and Power: Liberation Theology and the Institutional Church*, trans. John W. Diercksmeier. New York: Crossroad; London: SCM Press, 1985.

Boff, Leonardo, *Ecclesiogenesis: The Base Communities Reinvent the Church*. Maryknoll, NY: Orbis, 1986.

Bonhoeffer, Dietrich, *Sanctorum Communio*, trans. from the 3rd German edition by Ronald Gregor Smith. London: Collins, 1963.

Bonhoeffer, Dietrich, *Act and Being: Transcendental Philosophy and Ontology in Systematic Theology*, trans. H. Martin Rumscheidt, *Dietrich Bonhoeffer's Works*, vol. 2. Minneapolis, MN: Fortress Press, 1996.

Bonhoeffer, Dietrich, *Dietrich Bonhoeffer, Works*, General Editor Wayne Whitson Floyd, Jr. Minneapolis, MN: Fortress Press, 1996–2014.

Bouyer, Louis, 'From the Jewish Qahal to the Christian Ecclesia', in Louis Bouyer, *Liturgical Piety*. Notre Dame, IN: Notre Dame University Press, 1955.

Bowie, Andrew (trans.), *Schleiermacher: Hermeneutics and Criticism and Other Writings*. Cambridge: Cambridge University Press, 1998.

Brandt, R. B., *The Philosophy of Schleiermacher*. Westport, CT: Greenwood Press, 1968 [New York: Harper Bros., 1941].

Brown, Raymond E., Karl P. Donfried and John Reumann (eds), *Peter in the New Testament: A Collaborative Assessment by Protestant and Roman Catholic Scholars*. Minneapolis, MN: Augsburg Publishing House; Paramus NJ: Paulist Press, 1973; London and Dublin: Geoffrey Chapman, 1974.

Brunner, Emil, *The Christian Doctrine of the Church, Faith and the Consummation: Dogmatics Vol III*, trans. David Cairns with T. H. L. Parker. London: Lutterworth Press, 1962.

Buber, Martin, *Kingship of God*, trans. Richard Scheimann from 3rd German edition. London: George Allen and Unwin, 1967 [1956].

Buchan, John, *Sick Heart River*. London: Hodder and Stoughton, 1941.

Buckley, James J., 'Christian Community, Baptism, and Lord's Supper', in John Webster (ed.), *The Cambridge Companion to Karl Barth*, chapter 12. Cambridge: Cambridge University Press, 2000.

Bultmann, Rudolf, *Theology of the New Testament*, trans. Kendrick Grobel, 2 vols. London: SCM Press, 1952.

Bultmann, Rudolf, 'The Primitive Christian Kerygma and the Historical Jesus', trans. from 3rd German edition, 1962, in Carl E. Braaten and Roy A. Harrisville (eds), *The Historical Jesus and the Kerygmatic Christ: Essays on the New Quest of the Historical Jesus*, pp. 15–42. New York and Nashville: Abingdon Press, 1964.

Burkitt, F. C., 'The Eschatological Idea in the Gospel', in H. B. Swete (ed.), *Essays on Some Biblical Questions of the Day*, pp. 193–213. London: Macmillan, 1909.

Burridge, Richard A., *Imitating Jesus: An Inclusivist Approach to New Testament Ethics*. Grand Rapids, MI: Eerdmans, 2007.

Busch, Eberhard, *Karl Barth: His Life from Letters and Autobiographical Texts*, trans. John Bowden from 2nd German edition. London: SCM Press, 1976.

Caird, George B., *New Testament Theology*, ed. L. D. Hurst. Oxford: Clarendon Press, 1994.

Calvin, John, *The First Epistle of Paul The Apostle to the Corinthians*, trans. J. W. Fraser, Calvin's Commentaries; ed. D. W. and T. F. Torrance. Edinburgh: Saint Andrew Press, 1960.

Calvin, John, *Institutes of the Christian Religion*, trans. H. Beveridge, 2 vols. London: James Clarke, 1962.

Campbell, J. Y., *Three New Testament Studies*. Leiden: Brill, 1965.

Campenhausen, Hans F. Von, *Tradition and Life in the Church: Essays and Lectures on Church History*, trans. A. V. Littledale. London: Collins, 1968.

Campenhausen, Hans F. Von, *Ecclesiastical Authority and Spiritual Power in the Church of the First Three Centuries*, trans. John Austin Baker. London: A. & C. Black, 1969.

Carlston, Charles E. and Craig A. Evans, *From Synagogue to Ecclesia: Matthew's Community at the Crossroads*. Tübingen: Mohr Siebeck, 2014.

Carpenter, James, *Gore: A Study in Liberal Catholic Thought*. London: Faith Press, 1960.

Catechism of the Catholic Church. London: Geoffrey Chapman, 1994.

Chadwick, Owen, *A History of the Popes 1830–1914*. Oxford: Clarendon Press, 1998.

Chalamet, Christophe, *Dialectical Theologians: Wilhelm Herrmann, Karl Barth and Rudolf Bultmann*. Zurich: TVZ, 2005.

Chapman, Mark D., *The Coming Crisis: The Impact of Eschatology on Theology in Edwardian England*. Sheffield: Sheffield Academic Press, 2001.

Chapman, Mark D., *Ernst Troeltsch and Liberal Theology: Religion and Cultural Synthesis in Wilhelmine Germany*. Oxford: Oxford University Press, 2001.

Chilton, Bruce (ed.), *The Kingdom of God*. London: SPCK; Philadelphia, PA: Fortress Press, 1984.

Clayton, John Powell (ed.), *Ernst Troeltsch and the Future of Theology*. Cambridge: Cambridge University Press, 1976.

Clayton, John Powell, *The Concept of Correlation: Paul Tillich and the Possibility of a Mediating Theology*. Berlin: de Gruyter, 1980.

Clements, Ronald E., *Old Testament Theology: A Fresh Approach*. London: Marshall, Morgan & Scott, 1978.

Coakley, Sarah, *Christ Without Absolutes: A Study of the Christology of Ernst Troeltsch*. Oxford: Clarendon Press, 1988.

Coleman, Roger (ed.), *Resolutions of the Twelve Lambeth Conferences 1867–1988*. Toronto: Anglican Book Centre, 1992.

Coleridge, Samuel Taylor, *On the Constitution of the Church and State, According to the Idea of Each*, ed. John Colmer, *The Collected Works of Samuel Taylor Coleridge*, General Editor Kathleen Coburn, vol. 10. Princeton, NJ: Princeton University Press; London: Routledge and Kegan Paul, 1976.

Congar, Yves M.-J., *The Mystery of the Temple: Or God's Presence to His Creatures from Genesis to the Apocalypse*. London: Burns & Oates, 1962 [1958].

Congregation for the Doctrine of the Faith, 'Observations on the ARCIC Final Report', *Origins* 11 (1982): pp. 752–6.

Coulson, John, *Newman and the Common Tradition: A Study in the Language of Church and Society*. Oxford: Clarendon Press, 1970.

Cox, Harvey, *The Silencing of Leonardo Boff: The Vatican and the Future of World Christianity*. Oak Park, IL: Meyer-Stone Books, 1988; London: Collins, 1989.

Cranfield, C. E. B., *The Gospel according to St Mark*. Cambridge: Cambridge University Press, 1966.

Crouter, Richard, *Friedrich Schleiermacher: Between Enlightenment and Romanticism*. Cambridge: Cambridge University Press, 2005.

Cullmann, Oscar, *The Earliest Christian Confessions*. London: Lutterworth Press, 1949.

Cullmann, Oscar, *Baptism in the New Testament*, trans. J. K. S. Reid. London: SCM Press, 1950.

Cullmann, Oscar, *Peter: Disciple, Apostle, Martyr*, trans. Floyd V. Filson, 2nd edn. London: SCM Press, 1962.

Cullmann, Oscar, *The Christology of the New Testament*, trans. Shirley C. Guthrie and Charles A. M. Hall, 2nd edn. London: SCM Press, 1963.

Curran, Thomas H., *Doctrine and Speculation in Schleiermacher's* Glaubenslehre. Berlin: Walter de Gruyter, 1994.

Currie, Thomas Christian, *The Only Sacrament Left to Us: The Threefold Word of God in the Theology and Ecclesiology of Karl Barth*. Cambridge: James Clarke; Eugene, OR: Pickwick, 2016.

Daly, Gabriel, O.S.A, *Transcendence and Immanence: A Study in Catholic Modernism and Integralism*. Oxford: Clarendon Press, 1980.

Danell, G. A., 'The Idea of God's People in the Bible', in Anton Fridrichsen (ed.), *The Root of the Vine: Essays in Biblical Theology*, pp. 23–36. London: Dacre Press and A. & C. Black, 1953.

Davies, W. D., *Paul and Rabbinic Judaism: Some Rabbinic Elements in Pauline Theology*, 2nd edn. London: SPCK, 1955 [1948].

Davies, W. D., *The Gospel and the Land: Early Christian and Jewish Territorial Doctrine*. Berkeley, CA: University of California Press, 1974.

Davies, W. D. and D. C. Allison, *Matthew 8-18, ICC*. London and New York: T&T Clark, 1991.

Davison, James E., 'Can God Speak a Word to Man? Barth's Critique of Schleiermacher's Theology', *SJT* 37 (1984): pp. 189–211.

de Lubac, Henri, *Catholicism: A Study of Dogma in Relation to the Corporate Destiny of Mankind*, trans. Lancelot C. Sheppard. London: Burns, Oates & Washbourne, 1950.

Dearmer, Percy, *Songs of Praise Discussed: A Handbook to the Best-Known Hymns and to others Recently Introduced with Notes on the Music by Archibald Jacob*. London: Oxford University Press, 1933.

Denzinger, H. and A. Schönmetzer, S.J. (eds), *Enchiridion Symbolorum: Definitionum et Declarationum de Rebus Fidei et Morum*, 22nd edn. Freiburg im Breisgau: Herder, 1963.

Dieter, Theodor, 'Joseph Ratzinger', in Paul Avis (ed.), *The Oxford Handbook of Ecclesiology*, chapter 20. Oxford: Oxford University Press, 2018.

Dix, Gregory, *Jurisdiction in the Early Church, Episcopal and Papal*, intro. T. M. Parker. London: Church Literature Association, 1975 [1938].

Doctrine in the Church of England (1938): The Report of the Commission on Christian Doctrine appointed by the Archbishops of Canterbury and York, with a new Introduction by G. W. H. Lampe. London: SPCK, 1982 [1938].

Dodd, C. H., *The Interpretation of the Fourth Gospel*. Cambridge: Cambridge University Press, 1953.

Dodd, C. H., *The Parables of the Kingdom*. London: Nisbet, 1961.

Dodd, C. H., *The Founder of Christianity*. New York: Macmillan, 1970; London: Collins, 1971; Fontana edition 1973.

Dodd, C. H., 'Ernst Troeltsch's Intellectual Development', trans. Michael Pye, in Clayton (ed.), *Ernst Troeltsch and the Future of Theology*, chapter 1. Cambridge: Cambridge University Press, 1976.

Drescher, Hans-Georg, *Ernst Troeltsch: His Life and Work*, trans. John Bowden. London: SCM Press, 1992 [1991].

Duchesne, Louis, *The Early History of the Christian Church: From Its Foundation to the End of the Fifth Century*, trans. from the 4th edn, 3 vols. London: John Murray, 1909, 1912, 1914.

Duke, James O. and Robert F. Streetman (eds), *Barth and Schleiermacher: Beyond the Impasse*. Philadelphia, PA: Fortress Press, 1988.

Dulles, Avery, *Models of the Church*. New York: Doubleday, 1974; 2nd edn, 1987; Dublin: Gill and Macmillan, 1988.

Dunn, James D. G., *Romans 1-8*, Word Biblical Commentary. Waco, TX: Word, 1988.

Dunn, James D. G., *Christology in the Making*, 2nd edn. London: SCM Press, 1989.

Dunn, James D. G., *The Theology of Paul the Apostle*. London and New York: T&T Clark, 1998.

Dunn, James D. G., *Jesus Remembered, Christianity in the Making, Volume 1*. Grand Rapids, MI: Eerdmans, 2003.

Dunn, James D. G., *Beginning from Jerusalem, Christianity in the Making, Volume 2*. Grand Rapids, MI: Eerdmans, 2009.

Dyson, Anthony O., *The Immortality of the Past*, Hensley Henson Lectures, 1972–1973. London: SCM Press, 1974.

Eichrodt, Walther, *Theology of the Old Testament*, trans. John Baker, 2 vols. London: SCM Press, 1967.

Elliott, John H., *The Elect and the Holy: An Exegetical Examination of I Peter 2: 4–10 and the phrase Βασίλειον ἱεράτευμα*. Leiden: Brill, 1966.

Elliott, John H., *1 Peter: A New Translation with Introduction and Commentary*, Anchor Bible. New York: Doubleday, 2000.

Essays and Reviews, 9th edn. London: Longman, Green, Longman, and Roberts, 1861 [1860].

Fee, Gordon, *The First Epistle to the Corinthians*, NICNT. Grand Rapids, MI: Eerdmans, 1987.

Feldmeier, Reinhard, *The First Letter of Peter: A Commentary on the Greek Text*, trans. Peter H. Davids. Waco, TX: Baylor University Press, 2008.

Ferguson, Everett (ed.), *Church, Ministry and Organization in the Early Church Era*. New York: Garland, 1993.

Fiorenza, Francis Schlüssler, *Fundamental Theology: Jesus and the Church*. New York: Crossroad, 1984.

Fitzmyer, Joseph A., *Romans*, Anchor Bible. New York: Doubleday, 1992; London: Geoffrey Chapman, 1993.

Flew, R. Newton, *Jesus and His Church*, 2nd edn. London: Epworth Press, 1943 [1938].

Ford, David F., 'Barth's Interpretation of the Bible', in Sykes (ed.), *Karl Barth: Studies of His Theological Methods*. Cambridge: Cambridge University Press, 1979.

Fornberg, Tord, 'The People of God', in Sven-Olav Back and Erkki Koskenniemi (eds), *Institutions of the Emerging Church*, Library of New Testament Studies 305, pp. 129–44. London and New York: Bloomsbury T&T Clark, 2016.

Forstman, Jack, *A Romantic Triangle: Schleiermacher and Early German Romanticism*. Missoula, MT: Scholars Press for the American Academy of Religion, 1977.

Forsyth, Peter Taylor, *The Church and the Sacraments*. London: Longmans, Green & Co., 1917.

Frei, Hans W., *The Eclipse of Biblical Narrative: A Study in Eighteenth and Nineteenth Century Hermeneutics*. New Haven, CT: Yale University Press, 1974.

Fridrichsen, Anton (ed.), *The Root of the Vine: Essays in Biblical Theology*. London: Dacre Press and A. & C. Black, 1953.

Gärtner, Bertil, *The Temple and the Community in Qumran and the New Testament*. Cambridge: Cambridge University Press, 1965.

Gerrish, Brian A., 'Ernst Troeltsch and the Possibility of a Historical Theology', in John Powell Clayton (ed.), *Ernst Troeltsch and the Future of Theology*, chapter 4. Cambridge: Cambridge University Press, 1976.

Gerrish, Brian A., 'Friedrich Schleiermacher', in Ninian Smart, John Clayton, Steven Katz and Patrick Sherry (eds), *Nineteenth Century Religious Thought in the West, Volume 1*, chapter 4. Cambridge: Cambridge University Press, 1985.

Gladstone, William Ewart, 'The Place of Heresy and Schism in the Modern Christian Church [1894]', in *Later Gleanings* (*Gleanings of Past Years, 1885-96*, vol. VIII), pp. 280–311. London: John Murray, 1898.

Glasson, T. F., *The Second Advent: The Origin of the New Testament Doctrine*. London: Epworth Press, 1963 [1945].

Glick, G. Wayne, *The Reality of Christianity: A Study of Adolf von Harnack as Historian and Theologian*. New York: Harper and Row, 1967.

Gooder, Paula, 'In Search of the Early Church', in Gerard Mannion and Lewis S. Mudge (eds), *The Routledge Companion to the Christian Church*, chapter 1. New York and London: Routledge, 2008.

Gore, Charles, *The Church and the Ministry*, 2nd edn. London: Rivington/Longmans, 1889; further revised in 1919 by C. H. Turner; republished by SPCK, 1936.

Gore, Charles (ed.), *Lux Mundi: A Series of Studies in the Religion of the Incarnation*. London: John Murray, 1889.

Gore, Charles, *Roman Catholic Claims*. London: Rivington, 1889.

Gore, Charles, *Orders and Unity*. London: John Murray, 1909.

Gore, Charles, *The Reconstruction of Belief*, 3 vols in one. London: John Murray, 1926.

Gore, Charles, 'The Church's Common Confession of Faith', in H. N. Bate (ed.), *Faith and Order: Proceedings of the World Conference, Lausanne, August 3-21, 1927*, pp. 160–6. London: SCM Press, 1927.

Gore, Charles, *Church and Society*. London: George Allen and Unwin, 1928.

Gray John, *Isaiah Berlin: An Interpretation of His Thought*. Princeton, NJ: Princeton University Press, 2013.

Greenslade, S. L., trans. and ed., *Early Latin Theology*, *The Library of Christian Classics*, vol. V. Philadelphia, PA: Westminster Press; London: SCM Press, 1956.

Grenz, Stanley J., 'Articulating the Christian Belief Mosaic: Theological Method after the Demise of Foundationalism', in John G. Stackhouse, Jr. (ed.), *Evangelical Futures: A Conversation on Theological Method*, chapter 4. Grand Rapids, MI: Baker Books, 2000.

Grenz, Stanley J. and John R. Franke, *Beyond Foundationalism: Shaping Theology in a Postmodern Context*. Louisville, KY: Westminster John Knox Press, 2001.

Groll, Wilfried, *Ernst Troeltsch und Karl Barth – Kontinuität im Widerspruch*. Munich: Kaiser Verlag, 1976.

Gundry, E. H., *SŌMA in Biblical Theology*. Cambridge: Cambridge University Press, 1976.

Gundry, Robert H., *Matthew: A Commentary on His Handbook for a Mixed Church under Persecution*, 2nd edn. Grand Rapids, MI: Eerdmans, 1994 [1982].

Gutierrez, Gustavo, *A Theology of Liberation: History, Politics, and Salvation*. London: SCM Press, 1988 [1974].

Hafemann, Scott J., 'The Covenant Relationship', in Scott J. Hafemann and Paul R. House (eds), *Central Themes in Biblical Theology: Mapping Unity in Diversity*, chapter 1. Nottingham: Apollos, 2007.

Haight, Roger, *Christian Community in History*, 3 vols; vol. 1: *Historical Ecclesiology*; vol. 3: *Ecclesial Existence*. New York and London: Continuum, 2004, 2008.

Hansen, Bruce, *All of You Are One: The Social Vision of Galatians 3.28, 1 Corinthians 12.13 and Colossians 3.11*. London and New York: T&T Clark, 2010.

Hanson, Anthony T., 'Alan Richardson and His Critics in the Area of Hermeneutics', in Ronald H. Preston (ed.), *Theology and Change: Essays in Memory of Alan Richardson*, pp. 25–52. London: SCM Press, 1975.

Hanson, Paul D., *The People Called: The Growth of Community in the Bible*, with new intro. Louisville, KY, and London: Westminster John Knox Press, 2001 [1986].

Hanson, Richard P. C. and A. T. Hanson, *The Identity of the Church*. London: SCM Press, 1987.

Harnack, Adolf von, *Christianity and History*, 2nd edn, trans. Thomas Bailey Saunders. London: A. & C. Black, 1900 [1896].

Harnack, Adolf von, *The Constitution and Law of the Church in the First Two Centuries*, trans. F. L. Pogson; ed. H. D. A. Major. London: Williams & Norgate, 1910.

Harnack, Adolf von, *What Is Christianity? Sixteen Lectures Delivered in the University of Berlin during the Winter Term, 1899–1900*, trans. Thomas Bailey Saunders, 3rd edn. London: Williams and Norgate, 1912.

Harnack, Adolf von, *Outlines of the History of Dogma*, trans. E. K. Mitchell. Boston, MA: Starr King Press, 1957.

Hart, John W., *Karl Barth Vs. Emil Brunner: The Formation and Dissolution of a Theological Alliance 1916–1936*. New York: Peter Lang, 2001.

Harvey, Van A., *The Historian and the Believer: The Morality of Historical Knowledge and Christian Belief*. London: SCM Press, 1967.

Hatch, Edwin, *The Organization of the Early Christian Churches*. London: Rivingtons, 1881.

Hawksley, Theodora, 'The Freedom of the Spirit: The Pneumatological Point of Barth's Ecclesiological Minimalism', *SJT* 64 (2011): pp. 180–94.

Headlam, Arthur C., *The Doctrine of the Church and Reunion: Being the Bampton Lectures for the Year 1920*. London: John Murray, 1920.

Hefner, Philip (ed.), *Albrecht Ritschl: Three Essays*. Philadelphia, PA: Fortress Press, 1972.

Helmer, Christine, 'Schleiermacher's Exegetical Theology and the New Testament', in Jacqueline Mariña (ed.), *The Cambridge Companion to Friedrich Schleiermacher*, chapter 12. Cambridge: Cambridge University Press, 2005.

Holland, Bernard (ed.), *Selected Letters of Baron Friedrich von Hügel*. London: Dent; New York: Dutton, 1927.

Hooker, Morna, *From Adam to Christ: Essays on Paul*. Cambridge: Cambridge University Press, 1990.

Hooker, Morna, *The Gospel According to St Mark*. London: A. & C. Black, 1990.

Horrell, David G., *Solidarity and Difference: A Contemporary Reading of Paul's Ethics.*
London: T&T Clark, 2005.

Horrell, David G., *Becoming Christian: Essays on 1 Peter and the Making of Christian Identity.* London and New York: Bloomsbury T&T Clark, 2015.

Hort, F. J. A., *The Way, The Truth, The Life*, 2nd edn. London: Macmillan, 1894.

Hort, F. J. A., *The Christian Ecclesia.* London: Macmillan, 1914 [1897].

Hoskyns, Sir Edwyn [Clement], *The Fourth Gospel*, ed. Francis Noel Davey, 2nd edn.
London: Faber and Faber, 1947 [1945].

Hoskyns, Sir Edwyn [Clement], Bart, and Noel Davey, *The Riddle of the New Testament.*
London: Faber and Faber, 1936.

Hügel, Friedrich von, 'John, Gospel of St', *Encyclopædia Britannica*, 1911. https://en.wiki
source.org/wiki/1911_Encyclop

Hügel, Friedrich von, *Eternal Life: A Study of Its Implications and Applications*, 2nd edn,
revised. Edinburgh: T&T Clark, 1913.

Hügel, Friedrich von, 'The Apocalyptic Element in the Teaching of Jesus: Its Ultimate Significance and Its Abiding Function', in *Essays and Addresses on the Philosophy of Religion (First Series)*, chapter 5, London and Toronto: Dent; New York: Dutton, 1921.

Hügel, Friedrich von, 'On the Specific Genius and Capacities of Christianity, Studied in Connection with the Works of Professor Ernst Troeltsch', in Friedrich von Hügel, *Essays and Addresses on the Philosophy of Religion (First Series)*, chapter 6. London and Toronto: Dent; New York: Dutton, 1921.

Hügel, Friedrich von, *The Mystical Element of Religion*, 2 vols, 2nd edn. London: Dent;
New York: Dutton, 1923 [1908].

Hügel, Friedrich von, *Essays and Addresses on the Philosophy of Religion (Second Series).*
London and Toronto: Dent; New York: Dutton, 1926.

Hügel, Friedrich von, 'Official Authority and Living Religion', in Friedrich von Hügel, *Essays and Addresses on the Philosophy of Religion (Second Series)*, chapter 1. London and Toronto: Dent; New York: Dutton, 1926.

Hügel, Friedrich von, *Letters from Baron Friedrich von Hügel to a Niece*, ed. and intro.
Gwendolen Greene. London and Toronto: Dent, 1928.

Hugenberger, G. P., *Marriage as Covenant: A Study of the Biblical Law and Ethics Governing Marriage, Developed from the Perspective of Malachi*, Supplement to *VT*, vol. 52. Leiden: Brill, 1994.

Ignatieff, Michael, *Isaiah Berlin: A Life.* London: Chatto & Windus, 1998.

Inge, William Ralph, 'Roman Catholic Modernism', in His *Outspoken Essays (First Series)*, chapter VI. London: Longmans, Green, and Co., 1919.

Iremonger, F. A., *William Temple, Archbishop of Canterbury: His Life and Letters.* London:
Oxford University Press, 1948.

Jacob, Edmond, *Theology of the Old Testament*, trans. A. W. Heathcote and P. J. Allcock.
London: Hodder and Stoughton, 1958 [1955].

Jasper, David (ed.), *The Interpretation of Belief: Coleridge, Schleiermacher and Romanticism.* London: Macmillan, 1986.

Jasper, Ronald C. D., *Arthur Cayley Headlam: Life and Letters of a Bishop.* London: Faith
Press, 1960.

Jeremias, Joachim, *The Parables of Jesus*, trans. S. H. Hooke, revised edn. London: SCM
Press, 1963.

Jeremias, Joachim, *New Testament Theology*, 2 vols, *Volume 1: The Proclamation of Jesus*,
trans. John Bowden. London: SCM Press, 1971.

Jewett, Robert, *Paul's Anthropological Terms: A Study of their Use in Conflict Settings*. Leiden: Brill, 1971.

Johnson, Luke Timothy, 'Paul's Ecclesiology', in J. D. G. Dunn (ed.), *The Cambridge Companion to St Paul*, chapter 14. Cambridge: Cambridge University Press, 2003.

Kähler, Martin, *The So-Called Historical Jesus and the Historic Biblical Christ*, trans., ed. and intro. Carl E. Braaten, from the 2nd German edition 1896 [1892]; Foreword Paul Tillich. Philadelphia, PA: Fortress Press, 1988 [1964].

Käsemann, Ernst, 'An Apologia for Primitive Christian Eschatology', in Ernst Käsemann, *Essays on New Testament Themes*, trans. W. J. Montague, pp. 169–95, chapter VIII. London: SCM Press, 1964 [1960].

Käsemann, Ernst, *Commentary on Romans*, trans. and ed. from 4th German edition [1980] Geoffrey W. Bromiley. Grand Rapids, MI: Eerdmans, 1980.

Kasper, Walter, *Jesus the Christ*. London: Burns & Oates; New York: Paulist Press, 1976.

Kasper, Walter, *Theology and Church*. London: SCM Press, 1989.

Kasper, Walter, *Harvesting the Fruits: Aspects of Christian Faith in Ecumenical Dialogue*. London and New York: Continuum, 2009.

Kasper, Walter, *The Catholic Church: Nature, Reality and Mission*, trans. Thomas Hoebel; ed. R. David Nelson. London and New York: Bloomsbury T&T Clark, 2015.

Kee, Howard Clark, *Community of the New Age: Studies in Mark's Gospel*. London: SCM Press, 1977.

Kelly, J. N. D., *Early Christian Doctrines*, 3rd edn. London: A. & C. Black, 1965.

Kelly, J. N. D., *The Epistles of Peter and Jude*, Black's New Testament Commentaries. London: A. & C. Black, 1969.

Kelsey, David, *The Uses of Scripture in Recent Theology*. Philadelphia, PA: Fortress Press, 1975.

Kent, John, *William Temple*. Cambridge: Cambridge University Press, 1992.

Kimmerle, Heinz (ed.), trans. James Duke and Jack Forstman, *F. D. E. Schleiermacher, Hermeneutics: The Handwritten Manuscripts*. Missoula, MT: Scholars Press for the American Academy of Religion, 1977.

King, Karen L., 'Which Early Christianity?', in Susan Ashbrook Harvey and David G. Hunter (eds), *The Oxford Handbook of Early Christian Studies*. Oxford: Oxford University Press, 2008.

Kittel, Gerhard (ed.), *Theological Dictionary of the New Testament (TDNT)*, trans. G. W. Bromiley, 8 vols. Grand Rapids, MI: Eerdmans, 1965.

Knox, John, *The Church and the Reality of Christ*. London: Collins, 1963.

Koehler, Ludwig, *Old Testament Theology*, trans. A. S. Todd. London: Lutterworth Press, 1957.

Kooten, George H. van, Ἐκκλησία τοῦ θεοῦ: The "Church of God" and the Civic Assemblies (ἐκκλησίαι) of the Greek Cities in the Roman Empire: A Response to Paul Trebilco and Richard A. Horsley', *NTS* 58, no. 4 (2012): pp. 522–48.

Korner, Ralph J., *The Origin and Meaning of Ekklēsia in the Early Jesus Movement*. Leiden: Brill, 2017.

Kümmel, Werner G., *Promise and Fulfilment: The Eschatological Message of Jesus*, 2nd edn. London: S.C.M. Press, 1961.

Kümmel, Werner G., 'Eschatological Expectation in the Proclamation of Jesus', in James M. Robinson (ed.), *The Future of our Religious Past: Essays in Honour of Rudolf Bultmann*, chapter 2. London: SCM Press, 1971 [1964].

Kümmel, Werner G., *The Theology of the New Testament*, trans. John E. Steely. London: SCM Press, 1974.

Küng, Hans, *Structures of the Church*, trans. Salvator Attanasio. New York: Thomas Nelson, 1964 [1963]; London: Burns & Oates, 1965.

Küng, Hans, *The Church*, trans. Ray and Rosaleen Ockenden. London: Search Press, 1971 [1968].

Küng, Hans, *Infallible?*, trans. Erich Mossbacher. London: Collins/Fontana, 1972.

Küng, Hans, *On Being a Christian*, trans. Edward Quinn. London: Collins, 1977.

Küng, Hans, Josef van Ess, Heinrich von Stietencron and Heinz Bechert, *Christianity and the World Religions*, trans. Peter Heinegg. London: Collins, 1986 [1985].

Ladd, George Eldon, *Jesus and the Kingdom: The Eschatology of Biblical Realism*. London: SPCK, 1966 [1964].

Ladd, George Eldon, *The Presence of the Future*. London: SPCK, 1974.

Lane, William L., *The Gospel of Mark*, NICNT, Grand Rapids, MI: Eerdmans, 1974.

Lang, Bernhard (ed.), *Anthropological Approaches to the Old Testament*. Philadelphia, PA: Fortress Press; London: SPCK, 1985.

Lee, Michelle V., *Paul, the Stoics and the Body of Christ*, SNTS. Cambridge: Cambridge University Press, 2006.

Lehner, Ulrich and Michael Printy (eds), *A Companion to the Catholic Enlightenment in Europe*. Leiden: Brill, 2010.

Lessing, Gotthold Ephraim, *Lessing's Theological Writings: Selections in Translation with an Introductory Essay*, ed. Henry Chadwick. London: A. & C. Black, 1956.

Levi, Primo, *If This Is a Man and The Truce*, trans. Stuart Woolf; intro. Paul Bailey. London: Abacus/Sphere Books, 1987.

Lincoln, Andrew T., *The Gospel According to St John*, Black's New Testament Commentaries. London and New York: Continuum, 2005.

Lincoln, Andrew T., 'Communion: Some Pauline Foundations', *Ecclesiology* 5, no. 2 (2009): pp. 135–60.

Lindars, Barnabas, *New Testament Apologetic: The Doctrinal Significance of Old Testament Quotations*. London: SCM Press, 1961.

Loisy, Alfred, *The Gospel and the Church*, trans. Christopher Home. London: Isbister; New York: Scribner, 1903 [1902].

Loisy, Alfred, *The Birth of the Christian Religion*, trans. L. P. Jacks, Preface Gilbert Murray, O.M. London: George Allen and Unwin, 1948.

Lonergan, Bernard, S.J., *Doctrinal Pluralism*. Milwaukee, WI: Marquette University Press, 1971.

Longnecker, Richard N. (ed.), *Community Formation in the Early Church and Today*. Grand Rapids, MI: Baker Academic, 2002.

Luther, Martin, *Luther's Works*, General Editor Helmut T. Lehmann. Philadelphia, PA: Fortress Press, 1958-.

Luz, Ulrich, 'The Primacy Saying of Matthew 16.17–19 from the Perspective of Its Effective History', in Ulrich Luz, *Studies in Matthew*, trans. Rosemary Selle, chapter 9. Grand Rapids, MI: Eerdmans, 1991.

Manson, T. W., *The Teaching of Jesus*. Cambridge: Cambridge University Press, 1935 [1931].

Mariña, Jacqueline (ed.), *The Cambridge Companion to Friedrich Schleiermacher*. Cambridge: Cambridge University Press, 2005.

Markus, Robert A., *Saeculum: History and Society in the Theology of St Augustine*. Cambridge: Cambridge University Press, 1988 [1970].

Marsh, Margaret (ed.), *Hastings Rashdall: Bibliography of the Published Writings*. Leysters : Modern Churchpeople's Union, 1993.

Martin, Dale, *The Corinthian Body*. New Haven, CT: Yale University Press, 1995.

Mascall, Eric L., *Christ, the Christian and the Church: A Study of the Incarnation and Its Consequences*. London: Longman, Green & Co., 1946.

Mason, A. J., 'Conceptions of the Church in Early Times', in H. B. Swete (ed.), *Essays on the Early History of the Church and the Ministry*. London: Macmillan, 1918, reproduced in Everett Ferguson, et al. (eds), *Church, Ministry and Organization in the Early Church*, pp. 1–56, chapter 1. New York: Garland, 1993.

Matera, Frank, 'Theologies of the Church in the New Testament', in Peter C. Phan (ed.), *The Gift of the Church: A Textbook on Ecclesiology in Honor of Patrick Granfield, O.S.B.*, chapter 1. Collegeville, MN: Liturgical Press, 2000.

Matheson, Percy Ewing, *The Life of Hastings Rashdall*. London: Oxford University Press [Humphrey Milford], 1928.

Matthew, H. C. G. [Colin] and Brian Harrison (ed.), *Oxford Dictionary of National Biography (ODNB)*, 61 vols. Oxford: Oxford University Press, 2004.

Maurice, Frederick [son], *The Life of Frederick Denison Maurice*, 2 vols. London: Macmillan, 1884.

Maurice, Frederick Denison, *The Kingdom of Christ*, ed. Alec R. Vidler. London: SCM Press, 1958 [1838].

McBrien, Richard, *Catholicism*, 3rd edn. London: Geoffrey Chapman, 1994.

McCormack, Bruce L., 'Historical Criticism and Dogmatic Interest in Karl Barth's Theological Exegesis of the New Testament', in Mark S. Burrows and Paul Rorem (eds), *Biblical Hermeneutics in Historical Perspective*, pp. 322–38, chapter 19. Grand Rapids, MI: Eerdmans, 1991.

McCormack, Bruce L., *Karl Barth's Critically Realistic Dialectical Theology: Its Genesis and Development 1909–1936*. Oxford: Clarendon Press, 1995.

McKelvey, R. J., *The New Temple: The Church in the New Testament*. Oxford: Oxford University Press, 1969.

McKelway, Alexander J., *The Systematic Theology of Paul Tillich: A Review and Analysis*. London: Lutterworth Press, 1964.

Mersch, Emile, *The Whole Christ: The Historical Development of the Doctrine of the Mystical Body in Scripture and Tradition*, trans. J. R. Kelly. London: Dobson, 1938.

Metz, Johannes Baptist, *Faith in History and Society: Toward a Practical Fundamental Theology*, trans. David Smith. London: Burns & Oates, 1980 [1977].

Metz, Johannes Baptist, *The Emergent Church: The Future of Christianity in a Postbourgeois World*, trans. Peter Mann. London: SCM Press, 1981 [1980].

Meyer, Ben, *The Aims of Jesus*. London: SCM Press, 1979.

Migne, J.-P., *Patrologia Graeca*. Paris: J.-P. Migne, 1862.

Milton, Anthony (ed.), *The Oxford History of Anglicanism, Volume I: Reformation and Identity, c.1520 – 1662*. Oxford: Oxford University Press, 2017.

Minear, Paul S., *Images of the Church in the New Testament*. London: Lutterworth Press, 1960.

Misner, Paul, 'The "Liberal" Legacy of Newman', in Mary Jo Weaver (ed.), *Newman and the Modernists*, chapter 1, College Theological Society, Resources in Religion I. Lanham, NY: University Press of America, 1985.

Möhler, Johann Adam, *Unity in the Church or the Principle of Catholicism: Presented in the Spirit of the Church Fathers of the First Three Centuries*, ed., trans. and intro. Peter C. Erb. Washington, DC: The Catholic University of America Press, 1996.

Moltmann, Jürgen, *The Church in the Power of the Spirit*, trans. Margaret Kohl. London: SCM Press, 1977.

Morgan, Robert, ed., trans. and intro., *The Nature of New Testament Theology: The Contribution of William Wrede and Adolf Schlatter*. London: SCM Press, 1973.

Morgan, Robert, 'Ernst Troeltsch and the Dialectical Theology', in John Powell Clayton (ed.), *Ernst Troeltsch and the Future of Theology*, chapter 2. Cambridge: Cambridge University Press, 1976.

Morgan, Robert, 'Introduction: Ernst Troeltsch on Theology and Religion', in Robert Morgan and Michael Pye (eds), *Ernst Troeltsch: Writings on Theology and Religion*, pp. 1-51. London: Duckworth; Atlanta, GA: John Knox Press, 1977.

Morgan, Robert, 'Non Angli sed Angeli: Some Anglican Reactions to German Gospel Criticism', in Stephen Sykes and Derek Holmes (eds), *New Studies in Theology*, pp. 1-30. London: Duckworth, 1980.

Morgan, Robert and Michael Pye (eds), *Ernst Troeltsch: Writings on Theology and Religion*. London: Duckworth; Atlanta, GA: John Knox Press, 1977.

Morrow, Jeffrey L., *Alfred Loisy and Modern Biblical Studies*. Washington, DC: The Catholic University of America Press, 2019.

Nédoncelle, Maurice, *La Pensée religieuse de Friedrich von Hügel, 1852-1925*. Paris, 1935.

Neill, Stephen, *The Interpretation of the New Testament, 1861-1986*. Oxford : Oxford University Press, 1988.

Neuner, J., S.J., and J. Dupuis, S.J. (eds), *The Christian Faith in the Doctrinal Documents of the Catholic Church*, revised edn. London: Collins, 1983.

Newbigin, Lesslie, *The Household of God*. London: SCM Press, 1957.

Newman, John Henry, *On the Inspiration of Scripture*, ed. and intro. J. Derek Holmes and Robert Murray, S.J. London: Geoffrey Chapman, 1967.

Newman, John Henry, *An Essay on the Development of Christian Doctrine, The Edition of 1845*, ed. and intro. J. M. Cameron. Harmondsworth: Penguin, 1974 [1845].

Newman, John Henry, *Loss and Gain*. Oxford: Oxford University Press, 1986 [1848].

Newport, John P., *Paul Tillich*, ed. Bob E. Patterson. Waco, TX: Word Books, 1984.

Niebuhr, Richard R., *Schleiermacher on Christ and Religion*. London: SCM Press, 1965.

Niles, D. T., *The Message and Its Messengers*. Nashville, TS: Abingdon, 1966.

Nüssel, Friederike, 'Wolfhart Pannenberg', in Paul Avis (ed.), *The Oxford Handbook of Ecclesiology*. Oxford: Oxford University Press, 2018.

Ogletree, T. W., *Christian Faith and History: A Critical Comparison of Ernst Troeltsch and Karl Barth*. New York: Abingdon Press, 1965.

O' Neill, Andrew, *Tillich: A Guide for the Perplexed*. London and New York: T&T Clark, 2008.

Palmer, William, *A Treatise on the Church of Christ*, 2 vols, 3rd edn. London: Rivington, 1842 [1838].

Pannenberg, Wolfhart, *Basic Questions in Theology I*, trans. George H. Kehm. London: SCM Press, 1970 [1967].

Pannenberg, Wolfhart, *Theology and the Philosophy of Science*, trans. Francis McDonagh. London: Darton, Longman & Todd, 1976.

Pannenberg, Wolfhart, *Anthropology in Theological Perspective*, trans. Matthew O'Connell. Philadelphia, PA: Westminster Press; Edinburgh: T&T Clark, 1985.

Pannenberg, Wolfhart, *Systematic Theology*, 3 vols, trans. Geoffrey W. Bromiley. Grand Rapids, MI: Eerdmans, 1991-97 [1988-93].

Pannenberg, Wolfhart (ed.), *Revelation as History*, trans. from 3rd edition David Granskou. New York: Macmillan, 1968; London: Sheed and Ward, 1969 [1965].

Park, Young-Ho, *Paul's Ekklesia as a Civic Assembly*. Tübingen: Mohr Siebeck, 2015.

Pauck, Wilhelm, *Harnack and Troeltsch: Two Historical Theologians*. New York: Oxford University Press, 1968.

Pauck, Wilhelm and Marion Pauck, *Paul Tillich: His Life and Thought*. London: Collins, 1977.

Pedersen, Daniel J., *The Eternal Covenant: Schleiermacher on God and Natural Science*. Berlin: De Gruyter, 2017.

Perrin, Nicholas, *Jesus the Temple*. London: SPCK, 2000.

Perrin, Norman, *The Kingdom of God in the Teaching of Jesus*. London: SCM Press, 1963.

Peter, Maud D. (ed.), *Autobiography and Life of George Tyrrell*, 2 vols, vol. 1: *Autobiography of George Tyrrell 1861–1884*. London: Edward Arnold, 1912.

Peter, Maud D. (ed.), *George Tyrrell's Letters*. London: T. Fisher Unwin, 1920.

Peter, Maud D., *Von Hügel and Tyrrell: The Story of a Friendship*. London: Dent, 1937.

Peterson, Paul Silas, *The Early Karl Barth: Historical Contexts and Intellectual Formation 1905–1935*. Tübingen: Mohr Siebeck, 2018.

Philips, C. S., *The Church in France 1848–1907*. London: SPCK, 1936.

Porter, J. R., 'The Legal Aspects of the Concept of "Corporate Personality" in the Old Testament', *VT* XV (1965): pp. 361–80.

Prestige, G. L., *Charles Gore, A Great Englishman*. London: William Heinemann, 1935.

Preston, Geoffrey, O.P., *Faces of the Church*, ed. Aidan Nichols, O.P.; Foreword Walter Kasper. Edinburgh: T&T Clark, 1997.

Preston, Ronald H. (ed.), *Theology and Change: Essays in Memory of Alan Richardson*, pp. 25–52. London: SCM Press, 1975.

Rafferty, Oliver P. (ed.), *George Tyrrell and Catholic Modernism*. Dublin: Four Courts Press, 2010.

Rahner, Karl, 'Pluralism in Theology and the Unity of the Creed in the Church', in *Theological Investigations*, vol. VI, pp. 3–23. London: Darton, Longman and Todd, 1965-.

Rahner, Karl, *Theological Investigations (TI)*, 23 vols. London: Darton, Longman & Todd, 1965-.

Rahner, Karl, *Foundations of Christian Faith*. London: Darton, Longman & Todd, 1978.

Rahner, Karl, 'The Church's Redemptive Historical Provenance from the Death and Resurrection of Jesus', in *Theological Investigations*, vol. XIX, pp. 24–38. London: Darton, Longman & Todd, 1984.

Rahner, Karl and Wilhelm Thüsing, *A New Christology*, trans. David Smith and Verdant Green. London: Search Press, 1980 [1972].

Ramsey, Arthur Michael, *The Gospel and the Catholic Church*. London: Longmans, Green and Co, 1936.

Ramsey, Arthur Michael, *F. D. Maurice and the Conflicts of Modern Theology*. Cambridge: Cambridge University Press, 1951.

Ramsey, Arthur Michael, *From Gore to Temple: The Development of Anglican Theology between Lux Mundi and the Second World War 1889–1939; The Hale Memorial Lectures of Seabury-Western Theological Seminary, 1959*. London: Longmans, 1960.

Rashdall, Hastings, *The Universities of Europe in the Middle Ages*. Oxford: Clarendon Press, 1895; reprinted Cambridge: Cambridge University Press, 2010.

Rashdall, Hastings, *Doctrine and Development: University Sermons*. London: Methuen, 1898.

Rashdall, Hastings, 'The Historic Christ' (1896), in *Doctrine and Development: University Sermons*, pp. 89–109. London: Methuen, 1898.

Rashdall, Hastings, 'The Historical Value of the Gospels' (1895), in *Doctrine and Development: University Sermons*, pp. 58–76. London: Methuen, 1898.

Rashdall, Hastings, 'Revelation by Character', in *Doctrine and Development: University Sermons*, pp. 110–27. London: Methuen, 1898.

Rashdall, Hastings, *Christus in Ecclesia: Sermons on the Church and Its Institutions*. Edinburgh: T&T Clark, 1904.

Rashdall, Hastings, *The Theory of Good and Evil*. Oxford: Clarendon Press, 1907.

Rashdall, Hastings, *Philosophy and Religion*. London: Duckworth, 1909; New York: Scribners, 1910.

Rashdall, Hastings, *Conscience and Christ: Six Lectures on Christian Ethics*. London: Duckworth, 1916.

Rashdall, Hastings, *The Idea of Atonement in Christian Theology*. London: Macmillan, 1919.

Rashdall, Hastings, 'Harnack and Loisy', in Hastings Rashdall, *Principles and Precepts*, pp. 228–36. Oxford: Blackwell, 1927.

Rashdall, Hastings, 'George Tyrrell', in Hastings Rashdall, *Ideas and Ideals*, ed. H. D. A. Major and F. L. Cross, pp. 132–41. Oxford: Basil Blackwell, 1928.

Rashdall, Hastings, *Ideas and Ideals*, ed. H. D. A. Major and F. L. Cross. Oxford: Basil Blackwell, 1928.

Rashdall, Hastings, 'Modernism', in Hastings Rashdall, *Ideas and Ideals*, ed. H. D. A. Major and F. L. Cross, pp. 94–116. Oxford: Basil Blackwell, 1928.

Ratzinger, Joseph (Pope Benedict XVI), *Called to Communion: Understanding the Church Today*, trans. Adrian Walker. San Francisco, CA: Ignatius Press, 1996 [1991].

Ratzinger, Joseph (Pope Benedict XVI), *The Essential Pope Benedict XVI: His Central Writings and Speeches*, ed. John F. Thornton and Susan B. Varenne. New York: Harper Collins, 2007.

Reardon, Bernard M. G., ed. and intro., *Roman Catholic Modernism*. London: A. & C. Black, 1970.

Reardon, Bernard M. G., *Liberalism and Tradition: Aspects of Catholic Thought in Nineteenth-Century France*. Cambridge: Cambridge University Press, 1975.

Reardon, Bernard M. G., 'Roman Catholic Modernism', in Ninian Smart, John Clayton, Steven Katz and Patrick Sherry (eds), *Nineteenth Century Religious Thought in the West, Volume 2*, chapter 5. Cambridge: Cambridge University Press, 1985.

Redeker, Martin, *Schleiermacher: Life and Thought*, trans. John Wallhausser. Philadelphia, PA: Fortress Press, 1973 [1968].

Reimarus, Hermann Samuel, 'Concerning the Intention of Jesus ...', in *Reimarus Fragments*, ed. Charles H. Talbert; trans. Ralph S. Fraser. Philadelphia, PA: Fortress Press, 1970; London: SCM Press, 1971.

Reimarus, Hermann Samuel, *The Goal of Jesus and His Disciples*, intro. and trans. George Wesley Buchanan. Leiden: Brill, 1970.

Rendtorff, Rolf, *The Covenant Formula*, trans. Margaret Kohl. Edinburgh: T&T Clark, 1998.

Rendtorff, Trutz and Friedrich Wilhelm Graf (trans. Sarah Coakley), 'Ernst Troeltsch', in Ninian Smart, John P. Clayton, Steven Katz and Patrick Sherry (eds), *Nineteenth Century Religious Thought in the West, Volume III*, chapter 9. Cambridge: Cambridge University Press, 1985.

Reumann, John, 'Koinonia [sic] in Scripture: Survey of Biblical Texts', in Thomas F. Best and Günther Gassmann (eds), *On the Way to Fuller Koinonia*: Official Report of the fifth World Conference on Faith and Order (Faith and Order Paper no. 166), pp. 37–69. Geneva: World Council of Churches Publications, 1994.

Reventlow, Henning Graf, *The Authority of the Bible and the Rise of the Modern World*, trans. John Bowden. London: SCM Press, 1984 [1980].

Richardson, Alan, *An Introduction to the Theology of the New Testament*. London: SCM Press, 1958.

Richardson, Alan, *History Sacred and Profane: Bampton Lectures for 1962*. London: SCM Press, 1964.

Richardson, Alan, 'The Resurrection of Jesus Christ', *Theology* LXXIV (1971): pp. 146–54.

Ritschl, Albrecht, *The Christian Doctrine of Justification and Reconciliation*, trans. H. R. Mackintosh and A. B. Macaulay. Edinburgh: T&T Clark, 1900.

Robinson, H. Wheeler, *The Christian Doctrine of Man*, 3rd edn. Edinburgh: T&T Clark, 1926 [1911].

Robinson, H. Wheeler, *Corporate Personality in Ancient Israel*, introductions by John Reumann and Cyril S. Rodd, 'Revised Edition'. Edinburgh: T&T Clark, 1981 [previous edition, without Rodd's Introduction, Fortress Press, 1964].

Robinson, John A. T., *The Body*. London: SCM Press, 1952.

Robinson, John A. T., *Jesus and His Coming*, 2nd edn. London: SCM Press, 1979.

Rogerson, John, 'The Hebrew Conception of Corporate Personality: A Re-Examination', *JTS* 21 (1970): pp. 1–16.

Rogerson, John, *Anthropology and the Old Testament*. Oxford: Blackwell, 1978.

Rogerson, John, *Old Testament Criticism in the Nineteenth Century: England and Germany*. London: SPCK, 1984.

Rowland, Christopher, *The Open Heaven: A Study of Apocalyptic in Judaism and Early Christianity*. London: SPCK, 1982.

Rowland, Christopher, *Christian Origins: An Account of the Setting and Character of the Most Important Messianic Sect of Judaism*. London: SPCK, 1985.

Rowley, H. H. [Harold Henry], *The Faith of Israel*. London: SCM Press, 1956.

Rumscheidt H. M. (ed.), *Revelation and Theology: An Analysis of the Barth-Harnack Correspondence of 1923*. Cambridge: Cambridge University Press, 1972.

Sagovsky, Nicholas, *Between Two Worlds: George Tyrrell's Relationship to the Thought of Matthew Arnold*. Cambridge: Cambridge University Press, 1983.

Sagovsky, Nicholas, '"Frustration, disillusion and enduring filial respect": George Tyrrell's Debt to John Henry Newman', in Mary Jo Weaver (ed.), *Newman and the Modernists*, chapter 5. College Theological Society, Resources in Religion I; Lanham, NY: University Press of America, 1985.

Sagovsky, Nicholas, *On God's Side: A Life of George Tyrrell*. Oxford: Oxford University Press, 1990.

Sanday, William, *The Life of Christ in Recent Research*. Oxford: Clarendon Press, 1907.

Sanday, William and Arthur C. Headlam, *A Critical and Exegetical Commentary on the Epistle to the Romans*, 5th edn. Edinburgh: T&T Clark, 1902.

Sanders, Edward P., *Jesus and Judaism*. London: SCM Press, 1985.

Schillebeeckx, Edward, *The Understanding of Faith*. London: Sheed and Ward, 1974.

Schillebeeckx, Edward, *Jesus: An Experiment in Christology*, trans. Hubert Hoskins. London: Collins; New York: Seabury Press, 1979 [1974].

Schillebeeckx, Edward, *Church: The Human Story of God*, trans. John Bowden. London: SCM Press, 1990 [1989].

Schleiermacher, Friedrich D. E., *Schleiermacher's Soliloquies: An English Translation of the Monologen, with a Critical Introduction and Appendix*, trans. H. L. Friess. Chicago: Open Court Publishing Co., 1926.

Schleiermacher, Friedrich D. E., *The Christian Faith*, trans. H. R. Macintosh and J. S. Stewart. Edinburgh: T&T Clark, 1928.

Schleiermacher, Friedrich D. E., *On Religion: Speeches to Its Cultured Despisers*, trans. John Oman; intro. Rudolf Otto. New York: Harper and Row, Harper Torchbooks, 1958.

Schleiermacher, Friedrich D. E., *On Religion: Addresses in Response to Its Cultured Critics*, trans. and ed. Terrence N. Tice. Richmond, VA: John Knox Press, 1969.

Schleiermacher, Friedrich D. E., *Brief Outline on the Study of Theology*, trans. Terence N. Tice. Richmond, VA: John Knox Press, 1966.

Schleiermacher, Friedrich D. E., *The Life of Jesus*, trans. S. Machean Gilmore; ed. and intro. Jack C. Verhyden. Philadelphia, PA: Fortress Press, 1975.

Schleiermacher, Friedrich D. E., *On Religion: Speeches to Is Cultured Despisers*, intro., trans. (of original 1799 edition) and notes Richard Crouter. Cambridge: Cambridge University Press, 1988.

Schleiermacher, Friedrich D. E., trans. and intro. Connop Thirlwall; ed. Terrence N. Tice, *Luke: A Critical Study*. Lewiston, etc.: Edwin Mellen Press, 1993 [1825].

Schleiermacher, Friedrich D. E., *Christian Faith: A New Translation and Critical Edition*, trans. Terrence N. Tice, Catherine L. Kelsey and Edwina Lawler; ed. Catherine L. Kelsey and Terrence N. Tice, 2 vols. Louisville, KY: Westminster John Knox Press, 2016.

Schnackenburg, Rudolf, *God's Rule and Kingdom*, trans. John Murray, 2nd edn. New York: Herder and Herder; London: Burns & Oates, 1968.

Scholder, Klaus, *The Birth of Modern Critical Theology: Origins and Problems of Biblical Criticism in the Seventeenth Century*, trans. John Bowden. London: SCM Press, 1990 [1966].

Schweitzer, Albert, *The Quest of the Historical Jesus: A Critical Study of Its Progress from Reimarus to Wrede*, trans. William Montgomery; Preface by F. C. Burkitt. London: Adam and Charles Black, 1910.

Schweitzer, Albert, *The Mystery of the Kingdom of God: The Secret of Jesus' Messiahship and Passion*, trans. and intro. Walter Lowrie. London: A. & C. Black, 1914.

Schweitzer, Albert, *My Life and Thought: An Autobiography*. London: George Allen and Unwin, 1933.

Schweitzer, Albert, *The Mysticism of Paul the Apostle*, trans. William Montgomery, Prefatory Note by F. C. Burkitt, 3rd edn. London: A. & C. Black, 1933.

Schweitzer, Albert, *The Kingdom of God and Primitive Christianity* by L. A. Garrard. London: A. & C. Black, 1968.

Schweitzer, Albert, *The Quest of the Historical Jesus: First Complete Edition*, ed. John Bowden; Foreword Dennis Nineham; trans. W. Montgomery, J. R. Coates, Susan Cupitt and John Bowden. London: SCM Press, 2000.

Schweizer, Eduard, *A Theological Introduction to the New Testament*, trans. O. C. Dean, Jr. London: SPCK, 1992.

Selwyn, E. G., *The First Epistle of St. Peter: The Greek Text with Introduction, Notes and Essays*, 2nd edn. London: Macmillan, 1947.

Skydsgaard, K. E., 'Kingdom of God and Church', *SJT* 4, no. 4 (1951): pp. 383–97.

Smart, James D., trans., *Revolutionary Theology in the Making: Barth-Thurneysen Correspondence, 1914–1925*. Richmond: John Knox Press, 1964.

Smart, Ninian, John P. Clayton, Steven Katz and Patrick Sherry (eds), *Nineteenth Century Religious Thought in the West*, 3 vols. Cambridge: Cambridge University Press, 1985.

Spencer, Stephen, *William Temple: A Calling to Prophecy*. London: SPCK, 2001.

Spencer, Stephen (ed.), *Christ in All Things: William Temple and His Writings*. Norwich: Canterbury Press, 2015.

Spiegler, Gerhard, *The Eternal Covenant: Schleiermacher's Experiment in Cultural Theology*. New York: Harper and Row, 1967.

Stephenson, Alan M. G., *Anglicanism and the Lambeth Conferences*. London: SPCK, 1978.

Stephenson, Alan M. G., *The Rise and Decline of English Modernism: The Hulsean Lectures 1979-80*. London: SPCK, 1984.

Strauss, David Friedrich, *The Christ of Faith and the Jesus of History: A Critique of Schleiermacher's Life of Jesus*, trans., ed. and intro. Leander K. Keck. Philadelphia, PA: Fortress Press, 1977 [1865].

Streeter, B. H. (ed.), *Foundations: A Statement of Christian Belief in Terms of Modern Thought; By Seven Oxford Men*. London: Macmillan, 1912.

Streeter, B. H., 'The Historic Christ', in *Foundations: A Statement of Christian Belief in Terms of Modern Thought; By Seven Oxford Men*, pp. 73–145. London: Macmillan, 1912.

Summers, Steve, *Friendship: Exploring Its Implications for the Church in Postmodernity*. London and New York: T&T Clark, 2009.

Swete, H. B. (ed.), *Essays on the Early History of the Church and the Ministry*, pp. 1–56, chapter 1. London: Macmillan, 1918.

Sykes, Stephen W. (ed.), *Karl Barth: Studies of His Theological Methods*. Oxford: Oxford University Press, 1979.

Sykes, Stephen W., *The Identity of Christianity: Theologians and the Essence of Christianity from Schleiermacher to Barth*. London: SPCK, 1984.

Sykes, Stephen W. and J. P. Clayton (eds), *Christ, Faith and History: Cambridge Studies in Christology*. Cambridge: Cambridge University Press, 1972.

Tavard, George H., *The Church: Community of Salvation: An Ecumenical Ecclesiology*. Collegeville: Liturgical Press, 1992.

Taylor, Nicholas, *Paul on Baptism*. London: SCM Press, 2016.

Taylor, Vincent, 'The Alleged Neglect of M. Alfred Loisy', in id., *New Testament Essays*, pp. 72–82, chapter V. London: Epworth Press, 1970.

Temple, William, 'The Church', in B. H. Streeter (ed.), *Foundations: A Statement of Christian Belief in Terms of Modern Thought; By Seven Oxford Men*, pp. 337–59. London: Macmillan, 1912.

Temple, William, *Mens Creatrix*. London: Macmillan, 1917.

Temple, William, *Christus Veritas*. London: Macmillan, 1924.

Temple, William, 'Chairman's Introduction', in *Doctrine in the Church of England (1938): The Report of the Commission on Christian Doctrine appointed by the Archbishops of Canterbury and York*, with a new Introduction by G. W. H. Lampe. London: SPCK, 1982 [1938].

Temple, William, Archbishop of York [William Temple], 'Theology Today', *Theology* XXXIX, no. 233 (November 1939): pp. 326–33.

Thate, Michael J., Kevin J. Vanhoozer and Constantine R. Campbell (eds), *'In Christ' in Paul: Explorations in Paul's Theology of Union and Participation*. Grand Rapids, MI: Eerdmans, 2018 [2014].

The Cloud of Unknowing, trans. Clifton Wolters. Harmondsworth: Penguin, 1961.

Thiel, John E., *God and World in Schleiermacher's Dialektik and Glaubenslehre*. Bern: Peter Lang, 1981.

Thiel, John E., *Nonfoundationalism*. Minneapolis, MN: Fortress Press, 1994.

Thiselton, Anthony C., *The First Epistle to the Corinthians*, NIGTC. Grand Rapids, MI: Eerdmans; Carlisle: Paternoster, 2000.

Thomas, J. Heywood, *Paul Tillich: An Appraisal*. London: SCM Press, 1963.

Thornton, Lionel, C.R., *The Common Life in the Body of Christ*, 3rd edn. London: Dacre Press, 1950 [1942].

Thrall, Margaret E., *The Second Epistle to the Corinthians*, 2 vols, Vol. 1, *ICC*. London and New York: T&T Clark, 1994.

Tillich, Paul, *The Shaking of the Foundations*. London: SCM Press, 1949.

Tillich, Paul, *The New Being*. London: SCM Press, 1956.

Tillich, Paul, *The Courage To Be*. London: Collins/Fontana, 1962 [1952].

Tillich, Paul, *Systematic Theology*, 3 vols in one. London: James Nisbet, 1968.

Tindal, Matthew. *Christianity as Old as the Creation*, facsimile of 1730 edition, ed. G. Gawlick. Stuttgart-Bad Cannstatt: Freidrich Frommann Verlag, 1967.

Torrance, Thomas F., *Karl Barth: An Introduction to His Early Theology, 1910–1931*. London: SCM Press, 1962.

Tracy, David, *Blessed Rage for Order*. New York: Seabury Press, 1975.

Tracy, David, *The Analogical Imagination: Christian Theology and the Culture of Pluralism*. London: SCM Press, 1981.

Tracy, David, *Plurality and Ambiguity*. London: SCM Press, 1987.

Trebilco, Paul, 'Why did the Early Christians Call Themselves ἡ ἐκκλησία?', *NTS* 57, no. 3 (2011): pp. 440–60.

Troeltsch, Ernst, *The Social Teaching of the Christian Churches*, 2 vols, trans. Olive Wyon. London: George Allen & Unwin, 1931 [1911].

Troeltsch, Ernst, *The Absoluteness of Christianity and the History of Religions*, trans. David Reid from the 3rd German edition, 1929, intro. James Luther Adams. London: SCM Press, 1972 [1902].

Troeltsch, Ernst, 'Half a Century of Theology: A Review' (1908), in Robert Morgan and Michael Pye (eds), *Ernst Troeltsch: Writings on Theology and Religion*, chapter 1. London: Duckworth; Atlanta, GA: John Knox Press, 1977.

Troeltsch, Ernst, 'The Significance of the Historical Jesus for Faith' (1911), in Robert Morgan and Michael Pye (eds), *Ernst Troeltsch: Writings on Theology and Religion*, chapter 4. London: Duckworth; Atlanta, GA: John Knox Press, 1977.

Troeltsch, Ernst, 'What Does "Essence of Christianity" Mean?' (1903, 1913), in Robert Morgan and Michael Pye (eds), *Ernst Troeltsch: Writings on Theology and Religion*, chapter 3. London: Duckworth; Atlanta, GA: John Knox Press, 1977.

Troeltsch, Ernst, *The Christian Faith*, Foreword Marta Troeltsch; ed. Gertrud von le Fort; trans. Garrett E. Paul. Minneapolis: Fortress Press, 1991.

Troeltsch, Ernst, *Religion in History*, ed. James Luther Adams; trans. James Luther Adams and Walter F. Bense. Edinburgh: T&T Clark, 1991.

Tyrrell, George, *Lex Credendi*. London: Longmans, Green, and Co., 1906.

Tyrrell, George, *Through Scylla and Charybdis: Or the Old Theology and the New*. London: Longmans, Green, and Co., 1907.

Tyrrell, George, 'Introduction', in Henri Bremond (ed.), *The Mystery of Newman*, trans. H. C. Corrance, pp. 1–16. London: Williams and Norgate, 1907.

Tyrrell, George, *Medievalism: A Reply to Cardinal Mercier*. London: Longmans, Green, and Co., 1908.

Tyrrell, George, *Essays on Faith and Immortality*, ed. M. D. Petre. London: Edward Arnold, 1914.

Tyrrell, George, *Christianity at the Crossroads*, ed. Maud Petre; Foreword A. R. Vidler. London: George Allen and Unwin, 1963 [1909].

Vidler, Alec R., *The Modernist Movement in the Roman Church: Its Origins and Outcome*. Cambridge: Cambridge University Press, 1934.

Vidler, Alec R., *A Variety of Catholic Modernists*. Cambridge: Cambridge University Press, 1973.

Walls, Jerry L. (ed.), *The Oxford Handbook of Eschatology*. Oxford: Oxford University Press, 2007.

Weaver, Mary Jo (ed.), *Newman and the Modernists*. College Theological Society, Resources in Religion I. Lanham, NY: University Press of America, 1985.

Weaver, Mary Jo, 'Wilfred Ward's Interpretation and Application of Newman', in Mary Jo Weaver (ed.), *Newman and the Modernists*, chapter 2. College Theological Society, Resources in Religion I. Lanham, NY: University Press of America, 1985.

Webster, John, 'What Is the Gospel?', in Timothy Bradshaw (ed.), *Grace and Truth in the Secular Age*, pp. 109–18. Grand Rapids, MI: Eerdmans, 1998.

Weiss, Johannes, *Jesus' Proclamation of the Kingdom of God*, trans., ed. and intro. Richard H. Hiers and David L. Holland from the 1st edition of *Die Predigt Jesu vom Reiche Gottes*, 1892. London: SCM Press; Philadelphia, PA: Fortress Press, 1971.

Welch, Claude, *Protestant Theology in the Nineteenth Century, Volume I, 1799–1870*. New Haven and London: Yale University Press, 1972.

Williams, Robert R., *Schleiermacher the Theologian: The Construction of the Doctrine of God*. Philadelphia, PA: Fortress Press, 1978.

Willis, Wendell, 'The Koinonia [sic] of Christians – and Others: I Corinthians 10: pp. 14–22', in Wendell Willis (ed.), *Eucharist and Ecclesiology: Essays in Honor of Dr. Everett Ferguson*, chapter 12. Eugene, OR: Pickwick Publications, 2017.

Wordsworth, William, *The Prelude: A Parallel Text*, ed. J. C. Maxwell. Harmondsworth: Penguin, 1972.

Wright, N. T., *The New Testament and the People of God*. London: SPCK, 1992.

Wright, N. T., *Jesus and the Victory of God*. London: SPCK, 1996.

Yocum, John, *Ecclesial Mediation in Karl Barth*. Aldershot: Ashgate, 2004.

Index of Names

Note: This Index contains the names mentioned in the main text. There is no subject index because the same constellation of themes is explored throughout the book, though from various perspectives, of course. The analytical Contents indicates what those perspectives are. The name 'Jesus' or 'Jesus Christ' also pervades the whole book, so is not indexed.